Central America

Central America

The Crisis and the Challenge

by

JOHN D. MARTZ

Chapel Hill

THE UNIVERSITY OF NORTH CAROLINA PRESS

COPYRIGHT, 1959, BY

THE UNIVERSITY OF NORTH CAROLINA PRESS

Manufactured in the United States of America

The Library of Congress has cataloged this publication as follows:

Martz, John D
    Central America, the crisis and the challenge.   Chapel
Hill, University of North Carolina Press ₍1959₎

    356 p. 23 cm.

    Includes bibliography.

    1. Central America—Politics.

F1436.M36   972.805   59–8105 ‡

Library of Congress

Dedicado con cariño
y abrazos fuertes a
ANITA Y HUMBERTO

Preface

FOR SOME TIME I have been puzzled by the lack of attention in the United States to that vast territory and conglomeration of peoples loosely referred to as Latin America. It is perhaps understandable that Latin America is not well known. Less apparent, however, is the reason for semi-active resistance to knowledge of and interest in the area, particularly in scholarly circles. A few years ago one of my university professors—an erudite, rational interpreter of political affairs and international relations—speaking of a general university examination on international government, offered the following question: "What would happen if Latin America suddenly sank into the seas, engulfed by the surrounding oceans? Discuss in 20 words or less!" While this remark was made lightly, it was in part serious. Such an attitude is too common in the United States today.

I have no personal desire to "beat the drum" for Latin America in a frenetic claim that no area is more important to the U. S. today. That is clearly contrary to fact. At the same time, there is a definite need for aroused attention to Latin American affairs. Today's attitude is too similar to that of a few years ago toward other regions. Nowadays, knowledge of the entire region is altogether perfunctory; persons searching for a basic understanding of the area must weed their way through an underbrush of false generalizations and unsubstantiated opinions. In recent years Latin America has made headlines in but a few instances—the overthrow of the Peron dictatorship in Argentina, the communist threat in Guatemala, and the anti-Nixon riots in Peru and Venezuela. The melodrama of such moments is soon forgotten, news turns cold, public notice is even more frigid. Readers of the *New York Times* find relatively little in its pages except in moments of civil crisis or communist obstruction. Many other journals fail to cover even these elements of Latin American current affairs.

Central America itself is even more slighted. General surveys of Latin American politics devote perhaps fifty of five hundred pages to the six republics—the "banana states," a misnomer in itself. Even Latin Americans often commit the same errors of omission. To my knowledge there is no recent book dealing exclusively with Central American politics; I have been frustrated in my search for one during the past few years. What follows is an attempt to fill that gap.

For the novice this book will provide an initial encounter with some of the facts, persons, and characteristics of Central American political affairs. Should he propose to pursue the subject further, the bibliography, while not exhaustive, should serve as a guide. Several of the opinions expressed—for example, what one friend has already called my "cavalier treatment" of Nicaraguan dictator Anastasio Somoza—are admittedly debatable. I have no wish to impose my opinions; I feel at the same time the need for their expression. They have been formed on the basis of all the facts I have been able to assemble. For the person who questions my opinions, let him read further to verify or refute them. I should like to think this book might encourage further reading and, perhaps, even further research.

This is primarily a treatment of Central American politics in the post-World War II period. At times I have had to go back much farther; individual circumstances in the six republics have dictated that. In these cases I have tried to summarize without great detail. Only the last ten or twelve years—years of transition and disappointment—are carefully detailed and analyzed.

Research on this subject began some five years ago; since 1954, my academic work has been centered on the subject, and I have spent much of that time in Central America. I have traveled the length of the region twice by car and made countless individual trips by other means of transportation. I also spent ninety days as member of a delegation touring the South American nations. Political figures throughout the Americas are uncommonly easy to interview. Few men are inaccessible. Of perhaps greater value is the opportunity to talk and discuss affairs with the people themselves, especially the rural elements, so often overlooked by journalists and political analysts. Their testimony has always been interesting and, at times, highly provocative.

I am indebted to the staffs of the Widener Memorial Library at Harvard, the Library of Congress, and the national libraries of Guatemala, Honduras, Costa Rica, and Nicaragua. All were eager to help—at times in the face of what must have seemed perculiar requests from the visiting "yanqui." My personal debt to friends and associates is too large to specify. I urge them to include their names on the unwritten list of those to whom I give thanks. Of all these I can mention but the two to whom the book is dedicated, Anita and Humberto, whose help was non-academic but certainly essential.

I wish to acknowledge my indebtedness to the Ford Foundation for generous aid in the publication of this book by a grant under its program for assisting American university presses in the publication of works in the humanities and the social sciences.

Absolving others of errors of authorship is an unwritten tradition, one that has always irritated me greatly. However, I cannot but follow the same course. Errors in the pages that follow are necessarily mine.

John D. Martz

Contents

Central America

Chapter One

SUB-CONTINENT IN CRISIS

THE MOST TRAGIC BLOODBATH in the history of that human folly called war came to a close over twelve years ago. Once and for all the enemies of democracy, enlightened progress, and so-called Western civilization had been annihilated. At last the world was prepared to launch its most determined drive toward that millenium of perfection augured by the advent of atomic energy. For the more advanced, civilization would provide the ultimate in scientific and mechanical achievement. For less fortunate peoples, standards of living would be raised. Disease, illiteracy, and ignorance were to be banished. After centuries of hardship, these elements of the world population would receive the inheritance that twentieth-century industry and intelligence could bestow.

Among the different areas attracting attention was Latin America, including that part of the Western hemisphere known as Central America —the six republics bridging North and South America. In the first blush of postwar optimism, no geographic region seemed unpromising. For material, economic, and political reasons—elaborated below—it was reasonable to assume that with the passing of time the region might lift itself from its antiquated existence and take a position alongside older members of the global community. What has happened, instead, is a gradual series of events culminating in the little recognized crisis of today.

For better than a decade the nations of Central America have followed the course of least resistance. Possible sources of aid, notably the United States, have failed dismally to capitalize upon the potentialities of the immediate postwar period. This same span of time has seen the growth of the very specters which were to be dissipated: communism, rampant nationalism, illiteracy, abject poverty, rigid social class stratification, political unrest, economic infirmity, and dictatorship. It is the growth of these factors that makes tragic the story of the past ten or twelve years in Central America; even more critical is the present situation which threatens further deterioration. No true progress can come to Central America without first a modicum of stable, relatively mature political government. Yet an individual examination of the six republics shows extraordinary lack of maturity. Guatemala has experienced a repressive communist government, a full-scale revolution, and more recently a presidential assassination. Costa Rica, after the bloodiest civil war in its history, followed four years of tranquility with an administration which opened old wounds and divided the populace. Panama has witnessed a series of revolutions, a presidential assassination, and the complicity of a vice-president in the same incident. Honduras barely survived a nationwide communist-manipulated strike and completed almost three years of government by decree before returning to constitutionality. Nicaraguan dictatorship was ended only by an assassination that left the murdered president's family in power. And El Salvador, finally, has recently elected a new "official" president who was virtually unopposed in the electoral contest.

The causes of this decade of failure are complex and varied. Many will become obvious after examination of the six individual Central American countries. Reserved for the concluding chapter will be suggestions and speculations as to future policies and potentialities. There also the role of the United States and the Department of State will be analyzed. For the present, concern will be directed toward environmental circumstances and characteristics by which these nations must be viewed.

THE REALITY OF GEOGRAPHY

Six sovereign nations lie between Mexico and the United States, to the north, and the continent of South America. Comprising what is known as Central America, these nations form a geographic bridge between the two halves of the hemisphere. At times diminishing to a width of barely sixty miles, the Central American sub-continent withstands oceans on two sides to link the continents. Geographic reality simultaneously has converted this connective into a land barrier which has contributed to the marked contrasts between the Anglo and Latin races in the New World. Some of the world's most varied geography is found on this sub-continent. Running northwest and southeast throughout Central America is the central cordillera, a plateau from three to six thousand feet above sea level. On this plateau lives the great bulk of the population, and nearly all capital cities and commercial centers—excluding seaports—are located here. But above the plateau itself is projected a series of mountains jutting as high as eleven thousand feet. These are uniformly rugged, often craggy. In other places they are heavily forested and the vegetation is thick. This is but one barrier to land communication. Although high altitude itself is not exceptional, the impassable nature of the mountains is. After twenty years of construction there is only a dirt road leading over the mountains of northern Guatemala. Costa Rica, with the highest peaks, has a highway rendered useless during most of the eight-month rainy season. In addition, most of the heights are shrouded in fog throughout the year; bright sunlight is uncommon. Such, then, is the barrier to direct land communication.

Elsewhere, Central American geography is completely different. From the mountainous regions, extending toward the two coasts, the land slants down toward sea level in a gently rolling fashion, finally becoming flat along the Pacific and Caribbean. In the lowlying coastal areas temperatures are high, air sultry, the climate strictly tropical. Lush jungle foliage, verdant plants, strange animals and insects, and hours of relentless sun, all characterize these regions. Population is relatively sparse and, in deference to the heat, indolent. Only at the large banana plantations or in the sugar cane field is activity likely to proceed except at a slow pace. The entire sub-continent is subject to severe, steady rain. Even in the highest elevations the rainy season generally extends from mid-April or May into November, and few days pass without at least a little rain. In the higher regions, annual rainfall will near 75 inches. Toward the seas it will easily pass 160 inches. Indeed, parts of Guatemala average 195 inches of rainfall a year. While this has a certain nuisance value, it is of considerable importance for other reasons. The basic agricultural economies are geared to the rainy season, without which crops wilt and die. Early rains, for example, have been known to bring the coffee plants into blossom prematurely. A dry spell may then destroy nearly all the plants. And an occasional rainy season may be dry enough that the agricultural products are poor as a result. At the other extreme, excessive rains can substantially damage or even destroy a year's crop. This is a periodic occurrence in the banana industry. High winds, tropical storms, and days of unrelenting rain may completely inundate acres of bananas, ravaging the harvest. Complete recovery may take as long as two or three years.

Such realities can be offset by a variety of features which contribute to the geographic beauty of Central America. There are literally dozens of volcanic formations, most of them readily accessible to travelers. Included among these are El Salvador's Izalco, the "Lighthouse of the Pacific," visible for miles from the Pacific. Poás, in Costa Rica, reputedly boasting the world's largest crater, is visited by those hardy enough to make a four-hour hike through the countryside. Each of the other republics can boast of at least a few volcanoes. Many are still active. Izalco caused considerable damage with an eruption in 1947, and Nicaragua's Cerro Negro took lives in the late 1940's. Not a few of the volcanoes are situated near mountain lakes which are untapped tourist attractions of considerable charm. Many, only a few hours' travel from one of the national capitals, lack only the investment of ambitious businessmen to become major tourist attractions. Others dot the countryside, including Lake Nicaragua, second largest lake in the hemisphere south of the United States. Roughly twice the size of the Great Salt Lake, Lake Nicaragua is, along with its sister, Lake Managua, one of the more attractive sights of the region.

Although these geographic facts have evident importance, population itself is a vital factor. Representing a variety of racial and national strains, ten million people live in Central America. Whites, Negroes, Indians, mulattoes, mestizos, and all imaginable combinations of cross-breeding are found in the area. Contrary to popular opinion, the racial complexion of the different countries is far from uniform. To the north, for example, Guatemala has a 62 percent Indian population. Many are unacquainted with the barest elements of modern life. They continue to worship their ancient gods, speaking an Indian dialect, not Spanish. On the other hand, Costa Rica's population is 97 percent mestizo, of which the greatest part is pure white. This region was never densely populated, and as a result of Spanish colonial policies, most of the indigenous elements were wiped out or relocated elsewhere. Today there may be fewer than seven thousand Indians in the country.

Between these extremes lie the other countries. In most, the predominant strain is mestizo, a mixture of European and Indian blood. In El Salvador 78 percent, in Panama 65 percent, and in Nicaragua 69 percent of the population is mestizo. The pure white percentage is generally around fifteen, with the Indian element roughly comparable. Pure-blooded Negroes are not numerous and tend to live in concentrated areas. Most were brought from Haiti or Africa generations ago to contribute their labor at rock-bottom prices. In Panama, for example, thousands of Negroes were imported from Jamaica, Haiti, and neighboring islands at the turn of the century to build the Panama Canal. Their labor was extremely cheap, and they withstood better than others the rigors of physical labor under tropical conditions. To the north this same procedure was adopted, although on a smaller scale, at banana plantations and palm oil installations. With this diversity of racial backgrounds, there is a relatively low amount of intolerance. Discrimination is not unknown, to be sure, yet it is less a factor in the social structure of Central America than in other parts of the world. Intermarriage began centuries ago between Spanish colonists and soldiers and the Indian girls. This rapidly became an accepted practice, and no stigma was attached. Consequently, the people have lived in this fashion for several hundred years. Today the lot of pure-blooded Indians and Negroes is greatly inferior to that of mestizos or Europeans, although not generally as a direct result of intolerance. This inferior social position, particularly that of the Indian, is the result of other factors.

After years of servitude under Spain, the Central American Indians retreated to a secondary position. Most retired to less accessible or somewhat undesirable parts of the land. In Guatemala they live high atop the mountains, scratching out a meagre existence. Elsewhere they have also drawn away from the centers of population, effectively bypassing the mainstream of modern life. Rather than venture out among the city people or the land-owning mestizos they instinctively avoid all contact with other groups, living an extraordinarily narrow existence with fellow natives. Through the years, the Indian has fallen even farther behind the rest of the population. If he goes to market in one of the more populous areas, he is bewildered, frightened, and in the end possibly duped of his goods. Under such circumstances, the Indian exists on a social level inferior to the bulk of the population. This is no result of great intolerance on the part of others, however. Like the Indians, the Negroes generally lead a subordinate existence. Here, intolerance is more evident.

In Panama, the treatment of the Negroes has been a problem for some years. This is dealt with at greater length in Chapter Seven. Suffice it to say that they have not been able to integrate themselves satisfactorily into society. This despite their willingness and desire to improve their status, a willingness utterly lacking in most Indians. Panama excepted, the Negroes have banded together because of economic factors and from social choice to form small groups from which there is no great desire to mix with others. On the part of the mestizos and whites, the Negroes as a group are viewed with condescension. Individually, however, there is less discrimination. In most of the capitals there are colored lawyers, businessmen, and legislators active in the life of the city. For an ambitious and intelligent young Negro, the obstacles to advanced education and a professional career are ones of poverty and financial need, not racial persecution.

The potential economic role of Central America will increase greatly in the next few years as the result of a general population expansion, among the most rapid in the world. According to a 1950 survey by the United Nations, this population is increasing at the rate of 2.3 percent annually. This will bring the population far past the twenty million mark by 1980. Few things could potentially be more fortunate, in view of the low population density. In El Salvador the density is 161.1 per square mile. None of the other five is even half so densely peopled. In future terms, this means that the many untapped economic resources may be developed by an augmented population. This, however, is dependent upon successfully coping with the existing handicaps of an overwhelmingly rural population. Nearly 70 percent of the population is rural. Consequently, society is generally oriented along non-urban lines, and no government can escape the fact. Rural life has characteristics bearing upon the education, culture, political participation, and the very nature of the people. Such factors as isolated, unevenly distributed population centers, inefficient use of total land area, and rigid social structure have led to the existing system of agricultural units of production. No more than a few hundred families own the great bulk of land. For them, Central America is a region of wealth and prosperity. But the vast majority is subordinated to these few and leads a weary life of drudgery. More than 70 percent of the population earns two hundred dollars or less annually. This points up the striking contrast of wealth and poverty so characteristic of these countries. The rich control the money and show little willingness to reinvest it. New opportunities are consequently closed to the peasant. Untapped natural resources remain a potential of what could be; government programs of public works and economic improvement are crippled by consistent refusals of the large landowners to reinvest their money, to open new vistas of progress.

In rural areas the family group is universal. Authority is basically patriarchal. From generation to generation there is little change. Childhood is a brief part of life. From the age of six or seven, children are expected to participate in the endless task of family-feeding. There is no time or opportunity for childhood games or youthful fantasies. Children work in the fields alongside their parents, brothers, sisters, and other relatives. Little attention is given to education. It is compulsory from the age of seven, to thirteen or fourteen, but seldom enforced. Home pressures contribute to poor attendance. After perhaps a year or so of study a child is taken from school by his parents, the process assured by bribing the teacher to remove his name from the class roll. In many areas, the school may be several miles from the home of the child which raises higher barriers. As children grow up, marry, and pursue life, their attitude is one of complacency, not defiance. The rural people accept their lot, hard though it is. They ask no more than adequate food and a minimum of sickness. The world is accepted as it is. There is no desire to dominate life, but rather to come to terms with it as fully as possible. Manual labor is considered by rural people the most honorable form of work; persons who do not pursue an agricultural existence and those trying to change the way of life are regarded with scorn.

A characteristic of rural areas is the system of land holdings. Like many of the things discussed above, this is subject to variation from country to country. In general, it is true that land holdings are either quite large or extremely small. The large holding is the *latifundio,* frequently several thousand acres large. Nathan L. Whetten once wrote that these expanses are often held for purposes "of prestige, not economics." The owner of the *latifundio* usually keeps out of production large portions of the land, and he rarely reinvests much of his income in improvement. Labor is paid a beggarly sum, and its efficiency is correspondingly low. The unbalance between labor and capital is a serious factor in maintaining the inequitable wage system. On each *latifundio* the owner is absolute ruler. His word is law, and those who defy it find themselves without home, job, or food. At the other extreme is the small holding, the *minifundio*. This is usually a poor chunk of land. It may be on a mountainside, where the problem of erosion must be dealt with but never is. There is barely enough space to cultivate the staples with which the owner must feed his family. Year after year the same crops are cultivated, and the soil becomes understandably poor. In a matter of time the family gathers together its few possessions and trudges a few miles to a similar location. Seed is inferior and crops sparse. Planting and harvesting methods are primitive, time-consuming, and ineffective. Even plowing is often done by hand—scratching or digging the surface, dropping in the seeds by hand, and covering the space with tired topsoil. Such an existence is almost as complete an economic slavery as that to which the *latifundio* laborers are subjected.

The effect of the population, then, is a factor to be dealt with by each individual government. Future economic development depends upon the rural population and, under existing conditions, it seems almost prohibitive. As for political activity, the problem is also imposing. To much of the rural population there is nothing less interesting than politics. It is viewed with suspicion as an evil, incomprehensible specter conjured by the urbanites, who are generally distrusted. Particularly by those living on small land holdings, there is great distrust of the outsider. And those living on *latifundios* are less members of the country than of the individual plantation. Their whole life revolves about the events of the *latifundio;* speeches and politics seem remote, unreal. With such attitudes, future leaders have many obstacles to overcome. Yet they must be conquered if economic development and political maturity are to come.

HERITAGE OF DARKNESS

Few parts of the world have struggled with more energy and less success in the search for representative democratic government. All of Latin America has pursued the reality of free government while everywhere it has been more chimera than fact. There are many aspects of this continuing quest for political maturity. None is more important than the Spanish political heritage. After the conquest, a system of rigid civil authority was instituted. On no level was there individual participation. Spanish government was highly centralized. The natives, lacking self-government, lived under absolute despotism, obeying the royal edicts from Spain or, more often, the monarchical regents in Central America. There was a pervasive atmosphere of suppression; democratic government was something alien. Colonial rule was usually administered by a viceroy sent from Madrid and, in cases of sudden trouble, there was no time for royal consultation. From this beginning grew the tradition of "personalism" which lives today.

When the Central Americans threw off the Spanish yoke in 1821 there was no basis for democratic government. All that had been observed and experienced was of authoritarian nature. Constitutionalism was unknown, democratic institutions unheard of. There were few men with the education, ability, or following to unify the region once independence was won. Various attempts at Central American federation failed. Even in the individual countries people were split by warring factions. In the absence of traditions of legitimacy, those men with personal following and ambition—and there were many—pursued power by the only means at their command, violence and revolution. The result was over a century of fratricidal strife. There was an almost total absence of political parties. Instead, political affairs revolved about a personal leader to whom the people might rally.

The Latin principle of caudillismo is a prevalent political phenomenon in Central America. The caudillo is a personal *jefe,* or "boss." Often the representative of a small geographic section, he is followed passionately by a small coterie of followers, almost entirely on the basis of personality. Central Americans think in terms of the personality; policy is generally secondary and may be formulated once power has been won. Often the caudillo is a magnetic, charismatic individual. He wins converts to his cause by making occasional public appearances at which he paternalistically listens to individual problems and complaints, issues sweeping promises, fills the listeners' hearts with fervor and their stomachs with cheap liquor, and rides off with even greater popularity. Caudillismo has been a major reason for the century-long instability of these six states. Through the years, it has become intimately connected with two other principles of authoritarianism—personalismo and continuismo. Once a caudillo wins access to power, he immediately turns to personalismo as the instrument upon which to anchor his future. Supporters and sycophants are brought into public office, national administration is overloaded with his supporters, and their tenure is dependent upon personal fidelity to the caudillo. Nepotism is widely practiced; even remote members of the official family receive jobs of one sort or another. Once the caudillo has firmly entrenched his backers in positions of control, he can turn to the problem of establishing his continuation in office. Thus he invokes continuismo.

Even the most dictatorial rulers make a fetish of cloaking their despotism in the mantle of freedom and democracy. To the outer world a picture of a bucolically happy peasant democracy must always be given, even if no one is deceived. A regime coming to power following a coup d'état will usually call itself a "provisional" government pending the "stabilization of conditions and quelling of public disorders." Opposition is repressed and electoral machinery placed in the hands of the revolutionaries. Then a vote is held, often with the official candidate unopposed. Later elections may be conducted to "affirm the will of the people." A personal twist to the process was developed by Tiburcio Carías in Honduras. He arranged for the subservient legislative organ to draft a new constitution, extending his presidential term several years more. This was repeated when the law limiting presidential terms to six years was waived in his case, that he might continue at the service of the Honduran people—all without any referendum from the people.

The fiction of legitimacy is further buttressed by constitutions calling for complete separation of powers. Unicameral assemblies—only Nicaragua has two legislative bodies—are entrusted with a carefully ennumerated list of duties. In practice these legislatures are rubber stamp institutions with no real authority. Accustomed to receiving orders from the presidential palace, they treat these instructions like commandments handed down from on high. In the rare instances when the legislators have a chance to exercise significant authority, they are either unable or unwilling to do so. Under such personal government, constitutional traditions have never developed beyond the formative stage. No Central American country has survived its 135 years of independence without a fistful of constitutions, most of them scrapped or rewritten by an insurgent band of revolutionaries. Constitutional statutes and laws rarely fulfill their function of permitting and facilitating a smooth process of government and democratic succession. Almost without exception they have prohibited a president from succeeding himself without the intervention of a term served by another person. This has either been ignored, revised, or else circumvented by the selection of an "official" candidate pliable to the wishes of the outgoing executive.

Another important crutch of the dictatorial government is the "state of siege," or "state of emergency." Most constitutions have a catch clause permitting unilateral executive declaration of a national state of emergency during which all civil liberties, guarantees of personal freedom, constitutional rights, and exercises of individualism are suspended. The government rules by executive decree, unilateral decisions emanating from the ex-caudillo. Martial law may be declared, often a signal to turn loose bands of ruffians which roam the city, attacking and beating anyone who crosses their path. For the opposition, hounded and persecuted though it may be, this prolonged state of emergency can be met in only one way —revolution.

Constitutional means of opposition usually end in failure. When elections are finally held, they are conducted by election boards manned by supporters of the regime. Campaigning is restricted, and opposition meetings are often forbidden under the justification of preventing political disturbances. Candidates are harrassed at every turn. They may even be declared ineligible for the election. The open cynicism of election officials is startling. On election day, voters may be intimidated if they show signs of opposition to the government. The secret ballot is only occasionally employed. Even if all the above procedures are ignored, it still lies within the power of election workers to falsify returns in favor of the official candidate. With only these men reporting the results, the opposition has no assurance that the returns will have any validity. In the face of all this, the common answer is revolution.

Nowhere has the practice of violent change been more openly espoused than in Latin nations. In Central America, any government is fair game for revolutionaries. This is perfectly in keeping with the curious ethics of politics there. In the same spirit a government persecutes the opposition at every opportunity. The opposition, if building military strength for a revolt, bides its time until the moment seems propitious, then strikes. The government, in fighting back, rarely expresses ethical resentment against the opposition. Most regimes would admit that, if they were too weak to suppress a revolution, then indeed the rebels would deserve a chance in power. Nicaraguan dictator Anastasio Somoza expressed this philosophy once after narrowly escaping an assassination attempt, something highly unprincipled in the great game of politics. "Hell, it's no crime to overthrow a government in a fair fight, but murder is something else." This revolutionary habit has long been the traditional means of reversing election results. Thus a vicious circle has developed denying the growth of democratic practice. Power is used to justify fraud since, once a government leaves office, it lacks constitutional means of regaining power. This very refusal prolongs the system. After a few years, the opposition determines to follow the same pattern once it is in power, and so the cycle is repeated. And the people, too often unaccustomed to democratic procedure, accept the situation calmly.

Concomitant evils are graft and corruption. Even the staunchest supporters of the president receive ridiculously low wages. If they are to live at more than subsistence level, they must rely on financial aid from the public monies. Custom has dictated that a government worker's existence depends upon various unofficial supplements to the salary itself. Often this is done quite openly, and the practice extends throughout the hierarchy. On the top level, a cabinet minister may negotiate a series of contracts directly beneficial to private enterprises of which he is a major stockholder. Most high officials are also quick to use the influence of their position for personal financial profit in the form of discriminatory or beneficial commercial agreements and tariff walls. At the other extreme, the porter or office boy so common to most government offices may well accept a small tip from a visitor in order that he may see the office chief before others who may be waiting. Government hierarchy is honeycombed from top to bottom with such procedures.

One of the most serious effects is that exerted on political parties. The usual idea of Western democratic political parties is almost totally absent in the Central American republics. There is no system of traditional parties. The great majority are small personal machines created for the express purpose of promoting one individual. Once this man leaves power, is defeated, retires, or dies, the party disintegrates. Such men as Castillo in Guatemala, Osorio in El Salvador, Ulate and Figueres in Costa Rica, Remón in Panama, and Lozano in Honduras are, or recently were, in power supported by a party created with one idea in mind—to elect the man or, by some other means, to put him in power. Often these parties bear long, involved titles. Typical are the National Liberal Party, Patriotic Front Coalition, National Liberation, and National Popular Alliance. Such parties dedicate themselves to the destructive opposition of rival political elements. Execrable insults flow back and forth, even in countries with a controlled press. The slightest possible incident is blown up into absolute proof of a dastardly scandal perpetrated by the government or a rival political faction. A Costa Rican newspaper once headlined "HONDURAN GOVERNMENT OVERTHROWN IN POPULAR REVOLT." It was later explained that government-supported candidates were trailing in the early returns of a small local election.

Positive criticism or formal programs of action are almost non-existent. A party, if it may be referred to as such, is concerned solely with tearing down the opposition. Its own plans are nebulous. The attitude seems to dictate that there will be plenty of time to make plans once actually in office. The platform, if indeed one is issued, will be filled with half-truths, platitudes, generalizations, and promises of something for everyone. Even in recent years exceptions have been rare. Parties have been founded with the purpose of forming a permanent stable political organization. One of the most recent attempts was that of Costa Rica's José Figueres. Yet the permanence of his effort seems questionable too. Under such circumstances, the only sort of party which can continue to operate effectively is a highly disciplined extremist organization. The Nazis had local parties until they were weeded out following Pearl Harbor. The Central American communist parties are the only such groups at present, and they withstand all attempts to wipe them out, although in several cases their activities have been drastically reduced. Although the communist parties receive orders from abroad, they are composed primarily of nationals and thus have a certain initial respectability. As they can provide well disciplined, carefully trained administrators, the Communists are often able to move into government posts. This was notably true in Guatemala, where two successive regimes relied heavily upon the administrative and political skills of the thoroughly trained Communists.

No political tradition is older than that of army domination. Since the 1821 break with Spain, the republics have conducted affairs with active participation by the military. Even in recent years, with military coups diminished somewhat since the nineteenth century, the army is the key factor in any disturbance. Governments universally rest upon the backing of the army. Without this there can be no assurance that the regime will survive from one day to the next. In El Salvador, the last two presidents have been military officers, firmly supported by the military. The Somoza regime in Nicaragua is backed by the National Guard. In Honduras, the army was loyal to General Carías for sixteen years and then transferred support to his hand-picked presidential successor. Guatemala's Castillo, as army officer, won his 1954 uprising only when the regular army officers refused to fight for communism-tinged Jacobo

Arbenz, himself a former officer. And in Panama, only four years ago, the chief executive, José Remón, was the former chief of national police, Panama's only military force. The record fails to reveal any general trend in army action. Frequently it has proved loyal to the existing government, bound as it can be by the high wages and plush living conditions with which civilian presidents ply them. At the same time this may be of no use, as in Guatemala in 1954. The army may well decide to sit out any planned revolution, in which case the regime has little chance of survival. Other times it will rally to the support of a new rebel, throwing its weight against the government it is sworn to uphold. Only a small circle of ranking officers need be influenced, and the subordinates follow unquestioningly. Thus the army is the one indispensable tool with which the regime must cope. Many governments have existed only at the whim of army leaders, an insecure tenure at best.

Students are another potent force in political affairs. Universally, students are young adults with energy and spirit to burn, often motivated by the highest form of idealism. In Latin America, this combines with natural Latin volatility to produce a dynamic, incendiary, and often irresponsible person. As a former representative of the United States National Student Association, the author has met, traveled among, and argued with these people for countless hours. Many are quite sincere. However, they look around and see the social and political inequalities of their country. The automatic response is to rectify all wrongs at once. And so the students take it upon themselves to be the conscience and guide of the nation. In their misguided enthusiasm they become involved in political rallies, defy government troops from the sanctuary of university walls—where the military are traditionally forbidden to enter— and only rarely do positive good. Nonetheless, they do have at least a strong nuisance value and, occasionally, may be instrumental in some important political event.

A final force which often goes unrecognized is that of the commercial interests. With the growing urbanization of the Central American capital cities, the old *latifundio* owner is slowly wielding less political power. His position is being supplanted by the city business interests. Only the shrewdest and most secure regimes are able to take personal control of business. The others—the great majority—are obliged to deal with the merchants. This gives commercial people a role that is often powerful and frequently at odds with the wishes of the populace. The most recent example is the commercial pressure brought on the Panamanian government to influence the 1955 Canal Treaty with the United States. This will be demonstrated in Chapter Seven. The important thing is to recognize the hidden but sizeable role played by business interests today, without any reference to foreign enterprise.

"The fundamental fact upon which the *de facto* governments or outright dictatorships of Latin American postulate their existence is a semantic subtlety by which they maintain the outward semblances of a free democratic system for export purposes while a thoroughgoing despotism holds sway within their borders."[1]

In such words does an outstanding liberal commentator speak of Latin American—and, inclusively, Central American—dictatorial governments. One of the most outspoken critics of despotic government, Arciniegas has observed that the fundamental conditions of democracy are nullified where critics and opposition are silenced, elections fraudulent, radio and press censored, and rival organizations outlawed. Despotic governments repeat the promises the people want to hear but continue the pursuit of repression, corruption, and authoritarianism. Opponents are jailed, exiled, or bribed into ineffectiveness.

Central America has become synonymous with political instability and revolutionary government. The colonial tradition has led to the continuation of anarchy and despotism. Persecuted majorities continue to fight dictatorial minorities with limited success. Where minority government may be less repressive, people are occasionally aroused by promises of democracy, elections, and representative government. Governments continue to mouth the principles of democracy as the vanguard of regional progress. When words conflict with deeds, however, confusion and doubt are engendered. An attitude of cynicism and mistrust results. To Arciniegas and others, all this is even more odious since they feel Spanish America was conceived in the ideals of freedom no less than the United States. To be blunt, this is absurd. An examination of the historical background of the area, even as cursory as that which preceded, reveals the lack of liberal democratic principles. This area was founded in the spirit of the Spanish monarchy and the Inquisition. From the very first, authority was repressive, despotic, and brutal, with individualism thoroughly discouraged. Private conscience was not a factor. Only unquestioned decisions of the throne or its representatives carried authority. Woe to him who dared reject it. This atmosphere continued for more than three hundred years. Only then was royal rule thrown aside. During 135 years of independence there have been only glimmerings of true democratic spirit. These have been extinguished periodically by the flood of caudillismo, dictatorship, revolution, and the flaunting of human rights.

In view of these historical facts, the presence of traditional liberal political ideals seems the thinking of a wishful imagination. Certainly there is little indication of long-existing democratic principles. To say that the area was first conceived in liberty is to ignore that democracy is a commodity the Spaniards never brought to the New World. Where such ideals do exist today, they are not the result of past history. No doubt many nationals today nurse the ideals of democracy. These principles, to those who have come into contact with them, are cherished as well they should be. Among these people are teachers, journalists, workers and leaders. Unfortunately, these people form a tiny segment of the population. For every one of these men there are at least four others to whom the most elementary liberal political ideas are foreign. The basic fact that the Central American population is over 50 percent illiterate* is in itself a strong explanation. Geographic and economic factors are also strong contributors. So isolated are many of the country people that they are almost never reached by city folk and ideas, let alone political participation. Rarely is a political candidate seen, and then probably only a minor local official. The land-holding system heightens the isolation of the individual. Thoughts of democracy and freedom are severely handicapped under such circumstances. To the extent that any human being must have hidden desires for individual freedom and exercise of opinion, Central America has many democratic sympathizers. In any more literal sense, however, the great mass of the population is much too inert to constitute an articulate democratic majority.

In Central America, few men have been more criticized than the military rulers and dictators with which the area has been plagued. It is often said that these men, from their arrogance toward democratic procedures, are totally unrepresentative of public opinion. This is one of many popular illusions that should be thoroughly debunked. It is not unusual for a caudillo to have the unquestioned support of the majority of his people. He may have first won office as a representative of free and

*Figures are unreliable to the point of absurdity. This one is probably less than the actual percentage.

liberal political ideals. He may indeed be a vociferous orator in favor of democratic principles. Having taken office, he may also pose as an advocate of progress, and in time bring material benefits to his country. Subsequent chapters will deal in some detail with two notable figures who fit this pattern—Tiburcio Carías of Honduras and Anastasio Somoza of Nicaragua. Carías, for half a century a dominant figure in Honduran affairs, was for sixteen years his country's president. During these years a number of measures were introduced and developed which advanced Honduras in different ways. These were quite inadequate in view of his long administration, although there is no real question that he was the most popular politico in Honduras during his earlier years in office.

Nicaragua's Somoza is somewhat different. Although running in several elections after becoming chief executive in 1937, General Somoza was never openly opposed by a strong anti-government candidate. There were a large number of Nicaraguans, even excluding political exiles, who hated him with undying bitterness. They would have stopped at little to remove him from power. Several assassination attempts were made prior to the fatal attack in 1956. At the same time, Somoza was genuinely popular with many Nicaraguans. To those who never crossed him politically, General Somoza was generally liberal. Public liberties and individual freedoms were generally respected, while business flourished. Open and honest elections in Nicaragua would very likely have returned him to office. Even more surprising than this is the affection in which he was held by many. This belies some of the more common generalizations about Central American despots. As Chapter Five reveals, Somoza undeniably accomplished much in many fields, regardless of the degree of democracy he permitted.

Such examples suggest a conclusion which many have chosen to ignore. Under the retarded circumstances of Central American life, dictatorship—if competently administered and genuinely concerned with national progress—has an important role to play. Of course, any government resting on military strength in place of public opinion earns opprobrium. Unless democratic elections, civil rights, and political liberty are completely untrammeled, a government leaves much to be desired. Yet these conditions are so retarded that they can scarcely mature while material circumstances are so shockingly inadequate. There is, it seems, a role of value for the authoritarian government. This is not to suggest the thesis that backward sections must pass through a period of dictatorship on the path to political enlightenment. However, the situation in Central America is significantly different from that of, for example, Indonesia, or other fledgling Far Eastern nations. There, history records peoples being subservient to foreign powers through centuries of domination. Only since World War II have such countries won their independence and vented nationalistic passions.

In Central America, colonial rule was followed by a pattern of authoritarian government administered by countrymen of those subjected to the rule. To be sure, there are voices raised against United States dollar diplomacy and economic imperialism. Even without this, a state of extreme political insecurity continues. The absence of improper interference from abroad does not solve the critical problems of government and economy. This lends credence to the belief that true democracy is severely handicapped, if not completely handcuffed, by the extraordinarily involved economic complexities. Key to this analysis is the factor that is too often overlooked: the low standard of living. The great bulk of the population is gnawed at by sheer hunger, not a passion for democracy. The Central American peasant thinks of one thing, feeding himself and his family. His whole life is a continuing battle to fill the stomach, not always a winning struggle. When we call Central America underdeveloped, it does not mean the lack of machine-line industry, a car in the garage, a recreation center for the children, and a radio in the house. Central Americans live on the brink of starvation. Hunger is a familiar specter. In rural areas it is rare to see an overweight person. There is too little food. Poverty, illness, poor crops, disasters of nature, all these sweep up the peasant in the continuing grim battle for existence. Only rarely does he lose, but the possibility is omnipresent. The hunger for democracy and representative government can only be treated when physical hunger itself is curbed.

Of Central America's twin problems of economic wellbeing and political competence, the first must receive priority. A starving traveler lost in the desert will submit to another in order to be led to the oasis. He will not wait for someone promising equal treatment or democratic government at the oasis. In such circumstances, there is a place for absolutist government in the scheme of things. Somoza of Nicaragua is again an excellent example. In two decades he did for Nicaragua what more than a century of irregular governments found impossible. If his political regime was far from democratic, it was scarcely more undesirable than the endless succession of revolutionaries, military leaders, and outright bandits who stole power from one another, generation after generation. It may well be that, if Nicaragua seems ready for true democratic government today, it is a result of the material progress achieved by the Somoza regime.

This is not an isolated case, for there are other examples. In Guatemala the thirteen-year regime of Jorge Ubico brought a number of improvements. These were admittedly inadequate and, in 1944, he was overthrown. However, Ubico had helped create an economic situation under which a greater desire for democratic ideals was aroused. Indeed, his regime was followed by nearly a decade of continuous government, including a free election, until communist infiltration upset the picture. In Panama, a number of critical matters were alleviated economically during the brief government of strongman José Remón. These in time may well have led to an atmosphere more conducive to the encouragement of political freedom. His death at the hands of assassins interrupted the general trend.

The point is this: Central America cannot enjoy freedom and individual liberty until democratic ideals become a reality to the people. This in turn can come only when the basic problems of subsistence and living conditions are met. So inculcated are the people to authoritarian and disciplined rule, that they are most likely to find economic satisfaction under strong governments. Country after country gives evidence of this reality, bitter though it may be. In Guatemala, the revolutionary military government of Castillo, while dedicated to democratic government, improved the economic situation with the authority of an increasingly insistent regime. El Salvador, enjoying its greatest prosperity in years, has not freely elected a president in ten years. Nicaragua is economically the soundest country of all the isthmus, after a full generation under the Somozas. Honduras lost its small measure of prosperity when it failed to elect a president by constitutional means. In Costa Rica, by far the most democratic, a series of government scandals added to generally poor administration created economic conditions the new government has yet to alleviate. Panama, finally, is thriving on the fruits of the economic policies and contractual negotiations of former police chief Remón.

So deeply rooted are the ways of political chaos and anarchy in Central America that no rational, progressive leader has more than a narrow chance of success. Only the strong personality can gain the necessary time and means to establish political stability and meet the crying material needs of his country. Once the worst of these are fulfilled, democratic leadership has a substantial opportunity to achieve genuine political freedom. No matter what the volume of writing, the number of speeches, the behind-the-scenes maneuvering, the cries for liberal leadership and an end to authoritarian government—Central America is first a land of illness and hunger.

Wealth and Poverty

Rich, fertile land is a geographic endowment of the Central American isthmus. There is no need for reliance on one or two products alone. Yet with mineral deposits limited, the emphasis must naturally be placed on agricultural products. The region has traditionally exported raw materials to the industrialized nations, importing manufactured goods. The result has been an economic unbalance of trade which increased harvests have not removed. Disparate economic conditions have multiplied through the years. Despite dormant wealth, the republics of Central America exist in a state of poverty. Most people are deprived of the most elementary services civilization has to offer.

While prices are high and continue to rise, inflation is steep, and real incomes are falling. Government financing, something unheard of until the postwar years, is often ill-planned and inflationary. Facts show that state planning has failed with a discouraging consistency over the past years. Government intervention—notably under Figueres in Costa Rica and now in the other republics as well—has succeeded in establishing a complex hierarchy that consistently fails to improve the lot of the people. As government gradually becomes a major business of a nation, the capitals become increasingly overcrowded from the influx of people from the countryside in search of an urban existence on higher than subsistence terms. Most are sorely disappointed. The general failure at official planning has increased budgets, swollen national debts, and brought a greater reliance on the government than ever before by those dependent upon it directly for a livelihood. Measures have unhappily proved impossible of realization and aggravated the grave state of economy and trade. With private financing usually limited and extremely conservative, government participation in matters of exchange and finance has even greater impact on prices, taxes, the rate of exchange, and money supply.

The rush to assume the trappings of a modern, twentieth-century government shrouds a general inability to grasp the problems and machinery inherent in this kind of state.

National economies in this area have traditionally relied on one or two products as the staple of international trade. El Salvador's chief export, coffee, accounts for more than 80 percent of her outgoing goods. In Guatemala the figure is 77 percent. Panama and Honduras, their economies tied to bananas, send at least half of their total exports from banana plantations. Costa Rica and Nicaragua are only a little less hampered. With this dependence on one or two crops to provide the necessary income for expansion, development, and the importation of finished products for the home consumer, there is a dangerous reliance on the international market. High prices in coffee, bananas, or cotton can temporarily swell national income. Comparable decreases in the price level—over which the exporting countries have little control—throw finances into a crisis. Confronted with the apparent impossibility of stabilizing international prices by leveling future demand in accordance with supply, the countries can do little more than expand their agricultural output in these critical products while prices are high. Yet the rate of progress in the last decade has been slight. Terms of trade have been advantageous, yet economic productivity has remained much the same. Increased productivity is crucial for increased per capita national income. There are exceptions, of course. Nicaraguan cotton has climbed amazingly in recent years, after having been a minor commodity. And Salvadoran coffee production has risen slightly. Yet, on the whole, there has been almost no increase in the physical volume of Central American exports since 1947-8.

The terms of trade are but one of several economic factors. They give little value to sheer volume, which is often a major determinant of international prices. They also exclude the quality of the product, particularly in the case of industrial products. Thus, in the absence of increased production, the hope must be for continued high prices. The value of the export dollar has quadrupled in the last forty years. Had it been otherwise the republics would have suffered severe economic dislocation. The postwar rise in coffee prices has been particularly spectacular. The 1955 price was more than four times as high as in 1944. On such uncontrollable rises in international prices rests the economic prosperity of these countries. Recession and retrogression is a present danger.

One of the most familiar complaints heard from Central Americans is criticism of highly industrialized countries in paying too little for raw materials. If the United States, Great Britain, and West Germany, for example, were to pay higher sums for raw materials, these republics would have greater flexibility in expanding their economies and general productivity. This, in turn, would be advantageous to industrial nations. This is supplemented with the statement that too much is charged, in turn, for the shipment of industrial products. In short, the industrial country should pay more for raw materials while lowering its own prices on finished commodities. This is complicated by an insistence on levying higher duties on incoming products. This is rationalized by the argument that Central America cannot compete against highly efficient mass production goods without the aid of a high protective tariff. This is more noticeable in such small regional industries as shoes, leather goods, liquor, cigarettes, and processed foodstuffs. The contradiction is obvious. In the first place, if foreign companies pay more for raw materials and charge less for the end product, profit becomes impossible. Furthermore, if import regulations hike duties, no foreign producer can meet the higher duties while charging lower prices. Costa Rica has been particularly guilty of this curious economic theory, and it has backfired outrageously. Foreign imports have been reduced, business has declined. Imports are priced far out of the range of average Costa Rican pocketbooks. Most citizens either buy inferior Costa Rican products or else do without. Costa Rica has stubbornly insisted its theory is sound, but both in practice and in principle it is badly flawed.

With Central America increasingly plagued by such problems, the solutions must come from the individual countries, their resources, and native genius. Economic production must rise, both through improved production techniques and individual industry. A concomitant problem is the balance between specialization and diversification of industry. A series of economic reports has recommended without exception the creation of small light industry throughout the area. Particularly with lower individual tariff walls, the region could be serviced by its own small industries. At present, there has been little effort to develop these potentialities. Certainly national trade barriers remain formidable. Countries prefer to buy a greater volume of foreign goods through specialization in one or two commodities. They rely upon foreign exchange currency received from the exportation of these crucial commodities; from these funds are purchased consumer products and capital goods. The same money services foreign investments.

Light industry itself faces serious problems. Large scale production and small unit profits are not necessarily effective. A factory in any one of the republics can produce enough in a period of weeks to meet demand for nearly a year. Present efforts aim at the lowering of mutual walls. In this way, Honduras, for example, might set up a paper factory supplying the entire region. Other nations could be represented by small factories devoted to other products. Until tax measures permit this, however, the high initial investment in even a small factory can scarcely be repaid. Yearly profits would be small indeed. Today there is neither mass production nor the demand of a large mass market. Commercial values are also an obstacle. Central American merchants are embued with a set of commercial values completely foreign to Europeans and North Americans. They are notably indifferent to the long term effects of any one transaction. Each sale provides a new opportunity for great profit. Wherever possible, one party will take advantage of the other. A businessman may swindle a customer today, although the customer will cancel a valuable order the next day as the result. Always the merchant sells as high as possible, buying as cheaply as he can. There is little interest in mass production for wide demand. The merchant of Central America is little impressed by the promises of selling cheaply on a large scale. To him, each sale is an individual opportunity to make a killing. He cannot be convinced that small profit and high volume can produce a substantial profit.

Perhaps the most crippling of all regional economic practices is that of reinvestment—or, rather, lack of it. While consumption levels should be allowed to rise, investment must be encouraged. There is a fierce need on the part of the wealthy to put more of their savings into productive undertakings. In response, the well-to-do invest either in real estate or, even more frequently, in foreign enterprises, tying up their money in solidly conservative commitments from which the countries themselves cannot benefit. Government financing, attempting to lead the way in development and financing itself, has tended to pursue inflationary policies. Home inflation and the normal amount of political disturbances only force the more prosperous to extend their investments to secure enterprises, continuing, in turn, to withhold capital from their own countries. The circle is unending unless interrupted by political chaos or economic collapse.

Subsequent chapters deal with the six countries individually, while the concluding passages will pose some of the more ticklish problems and suggest whatever solutions might alleviate existing conditions. For the present, several characteristics should be re-emphasized and borne in mind while considering the individual republics. Although each nation has its own endemic peculiarities, it stands in juxtaposition with its neighbors. To a varying extent, these countries are passing through critical times. Past events have often borne such bitter fruit that today's conditions seem but a continuation of the rough-hewn tradition of revolutionary politics, disregard for constitutional practice, flaunting of public opinion, and reliance on the omnipotent strong man. Yet the crisis is today more severe than ever before. To the United States, the gravity stems in large part from the presence of the international communist movement. The discarded idea of the popular front, of socialism through representative government, is being re-adapted and twisted to fit local conditions. The relaxation of international tensions certainly improves the atmosphere in which Central American Communists conspire against their respective governments.

The Central American himself, however, is the direct target of the present crisis. For years, he has lived amidst poverty, misery, illiteracy, and the very lowest conditions of human servitude. It is more than a little surprising that this has not long since passed into personal and moral degradation. Now, after years of backsliding, the danger is acute. No bonfire can flicker unguarded without becoming in time a conflagration. In 1954, the entire sub-continent escaped utter anarchy by the narrowest of margins. Since then there has been nothing to halt the erosion of spirit, body, and soul. The accumulations of over a century of exploitation—first from abroad, now primarily from the interior—have increasingly weighed down the ten million population. Unless the widespread causes of suffering are remedied, by both emergency and long-term measures, no one can prophesy the magnitude of the inevitable disaster. The critical moments are arriving—the tide of Central American history is sweeping toward desolation, if not complete destruction.

Chapter Two

GUATEMALA

AMID THE LUSH GREENERY of Central America, two hours' flying time from the Panama Canal, lies Guatemala. In appearance, it is a sleepy republic far removed from the outer world. To the north, a high plateau extends to Mexico and the Caribbean. In the south, a dense jungle sweeps toward a series of high lakes and volcanoes. This is the country that, in the last decade, has experienced the most violent outbursts of all Central America. Since World War II Guatemala has seen a communist government come to power and insinuate itself into the social fabric. Only after a tumultuous upheaval has the republic returned to a kind of normality. Communist designs on Guatemala, although temporarily diverted, have affected the country profoundly. There has been no true return to the past. Many families retain the memory of loved ones tortured or executed by the Red regime. Others today suffer reprisals from the existing government for suspected transgressions before the fall of communism. For the United States, Guatemala is living proof that the tentacles of international communism have reached to its very back door. And to the Communists, many valuable lessons are apparent. Future subversion in Central America will be planned in accord with Guatemalan successes and failures.

The bulk of recent Guatemalan history is the tale of Red infiltration, expansion, consolidation, and ultimate defeat. Yet there is more, for Guatemala today is attempting to look ahead, to formulate plans that will lead it further away from the tragic experience of communism. While the communist experience is fresh in national memory, it is also important to follow what has happened since then. Ultimate survival and progress may well be predicated upon this search for the path to economic development and legitimate political existence.

COMMUNISM GAINS A FOOTHOLD

Ever since its independence was established in 1839, Guatemala has suffered recurrent revolutions and dictatorial regimes. In 1931 a feudalistic government under General Jorge Ubico began paving the way for communist subversion, creating circumstances under which communism was first to assert itself. One commentator has said that the Guatemalan custom of despotism reached a "savage climax under the megalomaniac General Jorge Ubico."[1] Suppressing opposition ruthlessly, he employed a secret police force to assure his uninterrupted rule. Elizabeth Velsmann wrote that "if Guatemala resembled a prison, it was an efficient one."[2] Admittedly, there were certain material improvements. The pathetically inadequate education system was expanded. Roads were built—narrow, rough, unusable in the rainy season—but nonetheless an advance over previous construction. And, thanks to an agreement permitting free entry of Guatemalan coffee into the United States, economic prosperity managed to keep the country from sliding backward. But for all this, the country was sunk in a morass of inefficiency, personal graft, and government corruption which could not continue indefinitely.

Finally, in 1944, Ubico's model prison became a rebellious one, and the warden was unable to meet the inmates' demands. As criticism snowballed, businessmen, lawyers, and students led the growing wave of protest. They marched to the National Palace. Ubico promptly declared a state of siege in Guatemala City, soon extending it nationally. In the capital, people closed their shops, businesses were shut, movie theatres locked their doors, and the university suspended classes. Faced by growing opposition and army discontent, Ubico surrendered power to a three-man junta headed by Federico Ponce. Named provisional president on July 4, 1944, Ponce promised elections at an early date. After forcing Congress to approve his presidency, Ponce proceeded to emulate Ubico. He reinstituted press censorship. One journalist who published critical editorials was murdered. Intent upon consolidating his position, Ponce followed Ubico in reverting to the strongman tradition. Ponce had failed, however, to reckon with the public. The overthrow of Ubico had freed a Pandora's box of hidden aspirations and dreams. Ponce was not the man to handle the situation. A small group of army officers led university students in an attack against the government on the morning of October 19. By a stroke of luck they scored a hit on the main government ammunition arsenal, and after that victory was swift. By afternoon Ponce had taken refuge in the Mexican Embassy. With a loss of one hundred men, the young military leaders had won control of Guatemala. This was the moment that marked the transition from right-wing despotism to something else. Few anticipated the swing of the pendulum as it started toward the extreme left. Elections were immediately scheduled and, much to the surprise of most observers, held as planned at the close of 1944. The temporary government put forward the candidacy of Dr. Juan José Arévalo. It was under his presidency that the Communists first gained a foothold.

A virtual unknown, Arévalo was a forty-two-year-old professor who had spent the previous ten years in Argentina lecturing at the University of Tucumán. He had the advantage of being disassociated with all political parties and personages. Quickly capturing the fancy of the populace, Arévalo proved an excellent campaigner. His vigorous two-hundred-pound frame became familiar during the two-month campaign. Scattered opposition argued that his years of absence had given him Argentine citizenship, and he was ineligible to run. Ignoring these charges completely, Arévalo proceeded to win the election overwhelmingly. Different tallies gave him from 85 to 92 percent of the vote, and on March 13, 1945, he became President of Guatemala.

The new President was in the curious position of being free from political obligation. Though elected following a revolution, he was disengaged from the revolution itself, free to follow his own course without prior commitment. Arévalo himself acknowledged this position. On September 1, 1945, he said in a radio message from the presidential study,

> My personal position in the government is clear and definite. I do not belong to any political party nor to any social class. I realize fully the position of a democratic president, one who does not consent to decrees nor those who foment them. . . . The first duty of a president is to save and integrate all the forces of which the nation is composed. . . . I have an absolute faith in all Guatemalans. There are no longer distinctions, preferences, exclusivity. There is no more than one direction [toward] national dignity. . . . Let us be spiritually strong and we shall maintain the pace toward it. And

if the task is fatiguing and hard and painful to us, we will continue in it because that very fatigue, hardness, and pain will not be experienced again— by our children and our children's children.[3]

In view of this, Arévalo's six year term appears devoid of accomplishment. No one has quite succeeded in pinning down Arévalo's politics. Perhaps this indicates to a certain measure the lack of a positive program. In a radio address on February 15, 1945, the president-elect placed Guatemala in a revolutionary period, a time of flux, of experimentation and of development.

Guatemala has stopped being a democratic masquerade in order to convert itself to a democracy. Thus, with this new social reality and with this new moral investiture, we can continue without blushing or being abashed. . . .

The government of Guatemala is aware of certain prejudices of the social order. The workers, the farmers, are seen with distrust, perhaps even with scorn. . . . There has been a fundamental lack of sympathy for the workers . . . now we are going to install a period of sympathy for the man who works in the fields, the factories, the shops, and in commerce. We are going to re-evaluate civically and legally all the men of the Republic.[4]

Arévalo called his philosophy of government "spiritual socialism." Just what this embraced has never been clear. The President announced that his socialism recognized the inherent inequalities of man, and that it demanded the spiritual liberation of all men. "We aim to give each and every citizen not only the superficial right to vote, but the fundamental right to live in peace with his own conscience, with his family, with his property, and with his destiny."[5] In later years, many have referred to Arévalo as an out-and-out Communist. There are some grounds for the supposition. During his presidency the Communists burrowed into the vitals of Guatemalan life. He was aware of their presence and made only half-hearted efforts to uproot them. But in spite of this, the author is inclined not to believe Arévalo was a Communist. That he was a leftist is unquestioned. No one can deny that he ignored the communist threat during his six years in office.

Yet it would be preferable to believe that he was simply incapable of taking positive action of any sort, whether concerning communist infiltration or some other phase of national policy. His years in office reveal no accomplishments of real significance. Unlike his successor, Arévalo frequently donned the garb of anti-communism. He once wrote that "Communism is contrary to human nature, for it is contrary to the psychology of man . . . basic theories of communism . . . [are] impossible of realization as long as man is man. Here we see the superiority of the doctrine of democracy, which does not seek to destroy anything that man has accomplished but humbly seeks to 'straighten out the crooked paths.' "[6] In the final analysis, the important fact is not the question of Arévalo's communism or anti-communism. What does matter is the extensive infiltration of the Reds during his administration. Regardless of his politics, this is something which cannot be excused, and for which Guatemalans are never likely to grant forgiveness.

According to communist doctrine, the key to revolution is organizational strength. Lenin wrote, "give us an organization of revolutionaries and we shall overturn the whole of Russia." Guatemala was no exception. There, as elsewhere, the Reds directed their energies to the construction of a monolithic organization of conspiracy. Communist expert Bertram Wolfe has written of the revolutionary ideal succinctly: "They would penetrate everywhere, gather news, spy out information, report on moods, carry commands, recruit the best in every locality and bind them closer to the movement. They would acquire influence over the working class . . . blowing every spark of class struggle and popular indignation into a general conflagration."[7]

The earliest evidence of communism came with the founding in 1944 of the first Guatemalan labor union. The Confederación Guatemalteca de Trabajadores (CGT) was created in response to dissatisfaction with the paternalistic authority of the landowner over the worker. Leadership at this stage was negligible, and there was nothing to indicate communist participation. This lack of leadership fostered a vacuum in which Communists were quick to press their opportunity. Following shrewd advice from Mexican marxist Vicente Lombardo Toledano, Guatemalan Communists swiftly reached for positions of influence. Past training in organizational matters, primarily in Mexico, had prepared them well. This knowledge of organizational techniques was a precious commodity in Guatemala, and Communists were quickly lent for service. They soon claimed many posts of leadership in the CGT, and their influence grew by leaps and bounds.

The Communists also helped form a students' party, the Frente Popular de Liberación (FPL), and at the close of 1944 the Sindicato de Trabajadores Educacionales Guatemaltecos (STEG). From the start they began to solidify their positions. Content at first to work behind the scenes, they were conciliatory, hardworking, and generally helpful. Political subjects were skirted, communist dogma played down, and political theory discussed in philosophic terms. The evils of capitalism drew considerable criticism. In March of 1945 the Communists opened Escuela Claridad, an indoctrination school in conjunction with the CGT. Salvadoran Communists Abel Cuenca and Virgilio Guerra were directors. Teachings there turned to discussions of yankee imperialism and capitalist decadence. Marx was studied slavishly. The first dispute over communist tactics arose at mid-year, when non-communist factions of the CGT objected to continued operation of the school. The union's future seemed in jeopardy, and shutting down the school might silence government criticism. A minority of Communists agreed, fearing an outburst of public opinion, opinion that might be steeled against future communist activity. This point of view, as it turned out, gave an exaggerated value to Guatemalan public awareness.

The issue itself was not intrinsically significant, except as the first serious obstacle to the Reds. After hesitating, they forced the issue and succeeded in maintaining the school despite opposition. In November, 1945, the issue finally came to a head, and the CGT leadership definitely decided not to close the school. At once the non-Communists splintered from the CGT and formed the Federación Sindicalista de Guatemala (FSG). Of the defecting member unions of CGT, the only important one was the union of railway workers, the Sindicato de Acción y Mejoramiento de los Ferrocarrileros (SAMF). But, while the Reds hated to see the departure of SAMF, they were reconciled to it. Having thus passed their first real crisis, Communists faced the future with greater confidence. With authority in the only important labor federation, they had consolidated control within a short time. Collective leadership had gone to the Communists.

The center of the controversy, Escuela Claridad, finally was forced by the government to close in January, 1946. Arévalo's interior minister cited as grounds a constitutional provision forbidding "political organization of a foreign or international character." Results were, from the government standpoint, ineffective. Small "study groups" continued to train Guatemalans in marxist ideology. The number of secret units increased, and a nucleus of young people was built. Throughout their Guatemalan adventure, the Reds never slackened efforts to prepare through indoctrination as many native Guatemalans as possible in communist ideology. These trainees were the ones to pose in the mantle of nationalism a few years hence while actually following the communist line. Having created the groundwork for a well-trained monolithic organization, the Communists turned to the second stage in their subversive ideal: the consolidation and expansion of control. The principal task on hand was to subvert the independent FSG, which had left the Red-dominated CTG in late 1945. They planned to gain control of the railway workers and, through them, the parent organization, the FSG.

In 1946 a young ambitious man named Manuel Pinto Usaga apparently adopted communist doctrine for the sake of personal advancement. In February, 1947, he signed a document establishing the integration of the FSG with the CGT. This so-called merger, actually a subordination of his group to that of the Communists, was legalized as the Comité Nacional de Unidos Sindicatos (CNUS). The announced goal was coordination of overlapping activities and administrative efficiency. The practical result was further centralization of communist authority. Satisfied with their labor organization, the Reds visualized the next step on the road to power as the formation of an official political party. Thus the Vanguardia Democrática was created on September 20, 1947. Precursor to the Guatemalan communist party, Vanguardia was the first communist political organization with hierarchical organization and bureaucratic channels of policy-making. Red leader Manuel Fortuny later recognized September 20 as the date of the founding of the communist party in Guatemala.

Fortuny, congressional secretary following the 1945 elections, trod gently in succeeding months. It was some time before he felt free to establish a genuine "communist party," one referred to as such. Two years after the formation of Vanguardia Democrática, he rechristened it the Partido Comunista de Guatemala (PCG). From that time—September 28, 1949—the communist party was a full-fledged member of the national political scene. Continuing party consolidation hit a serious snag shortly after Fortuny founded the PCG. Victor Manuel Gutiérrez, an important labor leader, personally created the Partido Revolucionario de Obreros Guatemaltecos (PROG). The result was a double communist organization in Guatemala—the PCG under Fortuny and the PROG under Gutiérrez. Both men were avowed Communists, both were in accord with basic Red policies. The tactical orientation of the two was quite different, however. Daniel James describes Fortuny as a "Russia

Firster," an internationalist following Moscow directives assiduously. Installation of the party in power in Guatemala would be another step in the march of international communism against the Western world. On the other hand, Gutiérrez was a "Guatemala Firster," an ardent nationalist concerned more with communism as a remedy for Guatemalan ills. Opposed to close bonds with Moscow, he was willing to follow their advice, but to him it was advice, not command.

By mid-1950, then, there were not one but two communist organizations. At first there were no moves to rectify the matter. Both PCG and PROG went their separate ways, ignoring one another. When conflict was impending, they backed away from a clash. Nonetheless, the *modus vivendi* was necessarily shaky. Mexican communist director Toledano, apparently on orders from Moscow, "visited" Guatemala for a vacation, talking with both Fortuny and Gutiérrez. He failed to bring the men together, and hopes for mediation shattered. Rapprochement became imperative. Further delay brought growing friction which was likely to ignite inter-party strife. In November, 1950, Gutiérrez attended the Red-sponsored World Federation of Trade Unions Congress in Berlin and went from there to Moscow. He toured the satellite countries as well as the Soviet Union, returning to Guatemala after two months. What or who convinced him to join forces with Fortuny we do not know. In any event, he released a proclamation to the members of PROG on January 25, 1951: "Announcing the dissolution of the Revolutionary Party of Guatemalan Workers, we wish to make it quite clear that the members are absolutely free to choose their political affiliation. But the Central Committee takes the liberty of recommending that comrades join the Communist Party of Guatemala."[8] Thus the two communist organizations were one. Gutiérrez entered the ranks of PCG and brought his followers along. He could claim to have given a free choice to the disbanding PROG, but he obviously had acted on a Moscow directive, and the membership of PROG complied faithfully. One month later, *For a Lasting Peace, For a People's Democracy!*, the official cominform newspaper, editorialized that "The act of the Revolutionary Workers' Party of Guatemala [PROG] is a striking demonstration of the correct attitude ... and of the deep understanding of the historic need to strengthen and develop the Communist Parties as the militant staff of the working class and all working people, of the entire national liberation movement against foreign imperialism."[9]

The second congress of the PCG revised its name once again in late 1952. It became the Partido Guatemalteco de Trabajo (PGT) and continued under that name until the 1954 revolution. The change was made to fit local conditions. Party theorist Alfredo Guerra Borges, secretary of the central committee, has since explained that it was adopted to avoid the emotional and legal handicaps of the word "communist." The Reds could avoid association with communism in the eyes of the masses by using another name, and "labor" seemed adequate and safe. As the Labor party, the Communists were also in a position to dodge Constitutional Article Thirty-two. This prohibited registration of any political party with foreign or non-Guatemalan tendencies. The January, 1953, congressional elections could scarcely be entered by the "communist" party, regardless of government orientation. But as the "labor" party, nothing could be more simple. The "new" PGT was free to associate with other organizations, campaign as a legitimate national political party, appeal to the masses on non-marxian terms, and further tighten the communist noose.

As is the case in most political movements, the personalities and individuals involved were highly important. In Guatemala, party workers and leaders alike were divisible into two groups. There were many professional Communists, non-Guatemalans, who had no dedication to Guatemala but only to the international cause of communism. These included Mexicans, Salvadorans who had survived their ill-fated revolt in 1932, and even Balkan adventurers. Thorough-going "Bolsheviks" in every sense of the term, these were battle-scarred veterans of the eternal Red war against capitalism. These were not idealistic, fuzzy-cheeked youths, but practical, hard-headed political experts. They were the men who first gave impetus to the Red drive during the hesitant existence of the movement in the early 1940's.

Native Guatemalans formed the second group. Most had been trained in the Escuela Claridad or small study groups; they were, in many cases, sincerely convinced that communism was the answer to Guatemalan difficulties. Extremely young, they formed the most pliable segment of the population and were the easiest for hard-core Reds to mold in the proper image. In 1945, Fortuny was the oldest, although not yet thirty. Many others were barely out of their teens. Young self-styled intellectuals of the lower middle class, they were students, teachers, lawyers, and often former employees of foreign enterprises in Guatemala. They were indeed ripe for the subtle communist suggestion that marxism would soften and then dissolve completely the rigid and archaic social system of Guatemala. Frustrations of the preceding decade left the minds of the youths particularly impressionable. Desperately searching for something better, they felt their hopes buoyed by the promises and blandishments of communism. Experienced instructors in the study groups listened patiently and with sympathy to the plaintive queries of the depressed young men. The U. S. State Department, in its White Paper, credited the study groups with making "international Communist agents of a nucleus of young men in the revolution . . . matters soon progressed to the point where the clandestine Communist party was successfully organized with these younger men. . . . Its members hid the conspiracy by continuing to present themselves to the public as leaders of the pro-Government revolutionary parties. . . ."[10]

Most influential of the Red bosses were Fortuny and Gutiérrez. Fortuny, who eventually became the communist leader in Guatemala, was born in 1916, living through the years of Ubico's dictatorship in Guatemala while others were preparing in Mexican training schools. A one-time law student, former radio newscaster, and ex-employee at the British Legation, he first gained public prominence in 1945, when he won election as congressional secretary. It was during the time he held this post that he founded the Vanguardia Democrática and the Partido Comunista de Guatemala. After the 1952 merger with PROG, he became secretary-general. From that time, Fortuny was the top Guatemalan Communist. His only serious rival was Gutiérrez, who for a time seemed about to eclipse him. Six years younger than Fortuny, Gutiérrez advanced through the labor union while Fortuny was pursuing a political path. He quickly became the head of the labor union (CGT), and after his 1946 election to Congress as a non-Communist, expanded his role to include both labor and political matters. Once he disbanded PROG in 1952 and joined Fortuny, Gutiérrez was destined to play a secondary role, for Fortuny successfully packed the six-man party secretariat with his own followers.

Party organization has never been completely revealed, although more than four years have elapsed since the overthrow of Guatemalan communism. We do know that the secretariat directed the party and issued all decrees to the organization. To bolster the communist claim for quasi-representation, a twenty-one-member central committee was elected to the party congress, with authority to conduct party business when the congress was not in convention. The committee was actually a rubber stamp body and never failed to approve decisions handed down from the secretariat. As is always the case with communism, policy came down from the top.

The Arbenz Administration and Communism

The ascension of Colonel Jacobo Arbenz to the presidency was an important event in the communist advance. To Arbenz clings more guilt than Arévalo in permitting Red subversion. When he became president, in March, 1951, Arbenz had the means at his disposal to smash the communist menace. It would have been difficult, clearly, but the possibility existed. Instead, Arbenz pursued the same course as Arévalo, going even further in aiding the conspirators. Like Arévalo, Arbenz was never a Communist, although never declaring himself an anti-Communist as had his predecessor. Arbenz was an enigmatic figure in 1951, as he is even today in exile. Born in 1913, in Quezaltenango, Guatemala's second city, he won a scholarship to the national military academy, the Escuela Politécnica. Winning the second highest honors in the history of the school, he went on military duty and served in various Guatemalan departments (states), receiving promotions at an unspectacular rate. While a lieutenant he married María Christina Vilanova, and that wedding had much to do with his later political orientation.

The daughter of a wealthy coffee-planting family, Señora de Arbenz married without her parents' approval and was disowned. Accustomed to a more luxurious living standard than that possible on a junior officer's pay of sixty dollars a month, she determined that her husband would reach high position. Her ambitions for Arbenz were perhaps greater than his own. The young officer became increasingly aware of social injustices which he felt continually dogged his footsteps and became an avowed enemy of the upper classes. General Ubico was despised as a feudal overlord without interest in the people. Arbenz' personal feelings pushed him toward an inflexible position. Prodded continually by his wife, he became involved in the conspiratorial manipulations culminating in the overthrow of Ubico, and then in the brief tyranny of Federico Ponce. Once Ponce was defeated, Arbenz joined Colonel Francisco Arana and a civilian, Jorge Toriello, in organizing elections and drafting a new constitution.

During the Arévalo government, Arbenz prepared for the 1951 elections. As defense minister, he was able to create a personal machine through patronage and army support. Before long there were many arbencistas in the bureaucracy. At the same time Arbenz became the recipient of a flood of communist propaganda, much of it passed on by his wife and by communist intellectuals—especially Fortuny. Señora de Arbenz, versed in marxist ideology, advanced its tenets to her husband in reply to his dissatisfaction with the conditions of poverty and inequality. She had little difficulty in convincing her military-minded non-intellectual husband of the intrinsic value of marxism. To Arbenz, marxist doctrine seemed an answer to the rigid social stratification and upper-class discrimination existing in Guatemala. Before long he was a regular reader of *La Unión Soviética*. Arbenz, in short, was duped into valuing communism as a panacea for national ills. While not unintelligent, as his academic record shows, he was no deep thinker. Failing to examine marxist doctrine critically, he gained a quick superficial knowledge of it and adopted the dogma as his own. His wife continued to invite communist personalities to their home; Vicente Toledano turned up at the Arbenz' with surprising frequency, and Fortuny, Gutiérrez, and Pellecer were among the Red leaders who were regular guests. Considering his background, it is easy to understand how Arbenz was led to accept communism.

President Arévalo, in the meantime, was constitutionally unable to succeed himself in 1951, and there was prolonged jockeying for position by the two possible candidates, Arbenz and Arana. Arana, a stout, jovial, and highly popular man, was chief of the armed forces. While nominally dividing military power with Defense Minister Arbenz, he was actually in complete control of the army. His popularity and the coldness of Arbenz' personality seemed to assure Arana's candidacy and election in 1951. Repeatedly urged by advisers to seize control by a military blow, the staunchly democratic Arana determined to wait for the election. This was literally a fatal mistake.

In July, 1949, advised of a supply of anti-government arms cached near Lake Amatitlán, Arana investigated personally, accompanied by an aide and a chauffeur. Arbenz was told of the trip. Near a bridge by the lake, Arana's car was ambushed, and he was riddled with submachine gun bullets as he stepped from the car, dying instantly. The driver managed to return to the capital and charged that the assassins had driven away in the car of Señora de Arbenz. After several days of incommunicado questioning by the government, he meekly retracted his statement. The army rose in immediate protest and marched to the Presidential Palace demanding the resignation of Arévalo and his cabinet, including Arbenz. The next thirty-six hours were chaotic. The army revolt was poorly organized and executed; its very spontaneity robbed it of any possible success. Many forces remained loyal to the government. Arbenz' forces finally quelled the disturbances and the government remained in power. This was but another "incident in the revolutionary life," commented Arbenz afterwards.

With Arana dead, Arbenz was assured the presidency. On February 6, 1950, his candidacy was announced by the Partido Acción Revolucionaria (PAR) and the Renovación Nacional (RN), staunch Arévalo supporters. Two weeks later Arbenz accepted the bids, agreeing to support the PAR platform. This was a loosely written, eighteen-plank nationalistic platform urging land reform, equal distribution of tillable land, and opposition to the penetration of foreign interests. On the twenty-first Arbenz resigned as defense minister and began an active campaign.

The November election pitted Arbenz against three men, none offering serious opposition. The closest approach to a formidable candidate was General Manuel Ydigoras Fuente, a conservative of the Ubico regime. He was conveniently exiled when the campaigning became heavy. Minister of Health Victor Manuel Giordani ran for the Frente Popular de Liberación (FPL), spending his campaign denouncing Arbenz in vituperative language before sparse crowds. And Dr. Jorge García Granados formed his own party and ran on his record as president of the 1945 constituent assembly. He asserted his certainty that he was not a darkhorse candidate and honestly expected to win, no matter what observers thought. Of course, the election was a runaway for Arbenz, who doubled the vote total of his three opponents. Ydigoras also outdistanced the other two.

Before fifty thousand spectators in the national stadium, Jacobo Arbenz took the oath of office on March 15, 1951. Over thirty special delegations from abroad were present. After a short speech, outgoing President Arévalo transferred the blue and white silk presidential sash to Arbenz. At thirty-seven, the youngest of all American presidents, the new chief of state harangued the crowd in a flaming speech of hollow rhetoric and sweeping half-truths. Of his proposed program he said:

"Our government proposes to start down the road of economic fulfillment for Guatemala, toward the following three fundamental objectives: to convert our country from a dependent nation with a semi-colonial economy to an economically independent country; to convert Guatemala from a country bound by a predominantly feudal economy into a modern, capitalistic one; and to make sure that this transformation carries at the same time the greatest possible elevation of life for the great mass of the people." No indication of his future intimacy with communism was suggested in the address, and he concluded that "we will make of Guatemala a prosperous, modern country, a model democracy, and . . . we will achieve for our inhabitants greater well-being and prosperity. Our motto will always be: Forward to a Better Guatemala."[11] These are the words of a man who four years later was, in the words of James, "one of the chief architects of the . . . Communist revolution."

From this day forward, the Communists had in the youthful president a major ally. The bonds between the two were powerfully forged. Arbenz, never a card-carrying Communist, followed the party line on important matters. Few people today are sure whether he was merely a weak man swayed by wife and friends, or something else. Arbenz repeatedly commented on his power to expel the communist party from his administration and Guatemalan affairs, but was never "ready" to do so. Perhaps this was true at first. As the months passed, however, Arbenz fell increasingly under their control and was soon heavily in their political debt. By 1954, the author has suggested, the Communists "would have broken his efforts on the altar of international communism."[12]

The Communists were openly elated with Arbenz. Manipulation of the president, of all persons, was an unheard-of stroke of fortune. On February 20, 1954, communist propagandist Guerra Borges explained the Red position: "We Communists . . . loyally support the Government for the simple reason that its policy continues to reflect the interests of the majority of Guatemalans and the national interests. To this end the Communists are dedicated."[13] The reader might substitute for "majority of Guatemalans," the phrase "majority of Communists." For the Reds indeed supported Arbenz for precisely that reason: the policy of the government continued to reflect the best interests of the communist party.

Under the Arbenz administration, communism increased its grip on different phases of public life. These included the courts, legislature, propaganda media, and the much-discussed agrarian law. The Guatemalan Supreme Court was used only once to advantage by the Reds; yet that instance was important and clearly indicated its subservience to Arbenz and the Communists. In the early days of 1953, as a result of the controversial Agrarian Reform Law (see below), a farmer named Ernesto Leal Perez appeared before the Court, asking an injunction preventing the seizure of his land. Purpose of the case was to test the constitutionality of the law. Perez' backers hoped for an opinion that would nullify the law, based on Constitutional Article 172 relating to abuse of executive power. Their hopes were justified when the Chief Justice and three associates upheld the petition for injunction. The fifth opposed it. Instructions also went out to lower courts ordering particular care in all disputes emanating from land expropriation under the new law. President Arbenz, named as defendant in the case, was asked to present a full report on land seizures within twenty-four hours.

Arbenz responded promptly. Instead of reporting to the Supreme Court, he appeared before the Legislative Assembly. Rejecting the Court request, he called the action a usurpation of executive prerogative and claimed total executive immunity from judicial action. This principle, at best highly questionable, was supported by immediate legislative action. The Assembly condemned the Court and, by a forty-one to nine vote, with six abstentions, dismissed the errant judges. Acting on its constitutional right to appoint and remove Supreme Court justices, the Assembly chose more tractable individuals. They would presumably not be so impolitic as to accept a petition for injunction.

Twelve hours of debate were consumed in arguing the extraordinary action. Gutiérrez declared that "a people cannot live subordinated to a constitution. . . . The duty of congress is to support the president of the republic in this historic case because to accept the recourse to injunction would signify the overthrow of the agrarian reform law."[14] Ernesto Marroquin Wyss, an avowed Communist, was even more outspoken. Calling the injunction petition an attack by "feudalistic and imperialistic" interests against President Arbenz, he cried that "we have arrived at the time for complete liquidation of the reactionaries." Congress admittedly had authority to dismiss the justices. Removal of a judge from the highest judicial bench was authorized in cases of criminal intent or "notorious bad conduct or manifest incapacity," according to the constitution. This was the only legal basis for dismissal. But no charges were ever brought against the four dismissed judges. If there were indecent standards of conduct, the guilty should have been prosecuted. After being ejected, however, their case was quickly forgotten.

The bar association of Guatemala leapt to the attack and passed a resolution that the dismissals "flagrantly violate the articles of the constitution that guarantee the right of injunction." A bill of grievances charged Arbenz with constitutional violations, and the Legislative Assembly was condemned for improper action. Widespread protest strikes also followed the dismissals. Seven thousand students and anti-government partisans marched to the national palace to object. Street fights broke out; windows and lights were smashed. Enraged youths burned copies of the constitution in front of the palace. The demonstration ended quickly when the palace guards fired on the crowd, killing one and wounding several. President Arbenz' only public statement called on the opposition to accept the decision. He was determined, he said, to pursue the good of the people and had no intention of deserting the revolutionary cause because of reactionary attacks. He was "very tired" of the whole affair. More than a few of the citizens themselves were "very tired" to hear their president say, in effect, that he knew best what was good for them and would pursue the course of his judgment regardless of the constitution or public opinion.

The fifty-six-member Legislative Assembly was also a pliable tool in communist hands. Its attitude was so innocuous that many important issues never came before it. Nonetheless, there is ample evidence of its pro-communist orientation, despite the fact that there were never more than four avowed Reds sitting in the Assembly. In one instance, the legislators paused for a minute of silence honoring the "buen amigo, José Stalin," who had just died. Red leader Gutiérrez offered the motion. Manuel Pellecer called the Soviet tyrant a true champion of democracy. His opening remarks referred to Stalin as a benefactor of mankind. One of the few vocal anti-Communists rose to speak, and referred to Stalin in his opening remarks as a modern Nero, Genghis Khan, and Ivan the Terrible. His words were drowned out by a roar of protest, and when order was restored the chair ruled him out of order.

In the same month (March, 1953), the Assembly responded to unofficial presidential prodding by one of the most petty acts imaginable. Spruille Braden, former United States diplomat and Latin American expert, attacked the Guatemalan government in a speech to the Great

Issues course at Dartmouth College. Charging that ex-President Arévalo had delivered the country into the hands of Communists, he spiced his address with several accurate but inflammatory statements. The Legislative Assembly adopted a resolution cancelling the 1945 award to Braden of the Order of the Quetzal, a high Guatemalan honor. Arbenz, approving the action, called Braden disloyal to democratic principles in denouncing the Guatemalan government.

Probably the most important piece of legislation during the Arbenz government was the highly controversial Agrarian Reform Law, which provoked great public dispute, as well as the removal of the four Supreme Court justices. The reverberations from this legislation were heard for months afterward, and it was still a matter of dispute when the Arbenz government was toppled by revolution. The heart of the bill was an effort to rearrange the agricultural land-owning situation. As early as 1949, Leo Suslow had commented that an agrarian program was one of Guatemala's primary economic needs.[15] He recommended a program of governmental expenditures to co-ordinate an agrarian program to teach techniques of hygiene, nutrition, sanitation and production. As he noted, revision of the antiquated land system had been slow in coming. Under Ubico, the peasants were landless and continually exploited by the small group of land owners. The ignorant Indian worker, shackled to a system of bondage, had no recourse but to accept the situation and almost literally scratch out a minimal existence.

In 1949, the Communists began agitating for reform. Gutiérrez and railway chief Pinto Usaga drafted proposals for congressional action, and a bill was developed by a legislative committee headed by Gutiérrez himself. Arbenz announced his support before his election and, after taking office, issued several public statements reiterating his approval. In early 1952, he addressed the Legislative Assembly to urge adoption of reform. The proposal demanded redistribution of all estates seized from Germans during World War II. The government was to redistribute all land on private estates worked by a sharecrop system. Uncultivated land on estates of over 220 acres, where less than two-thirds of the estate was under cultivation, also was subject to expropriation and redistribution. Some three hundred thousand families were to receive land under the law. The program was to be financed by an issue of government bonds, both internal and external.

Reaction was immediate. Leaders of the five-hundred-member National Association of Agriculturists warned the bill would create severe economic dislocations. Peasant uprisings would be inevitable. Others spoke of likely riots in the capital, and a few hotheads cried that civil war was near. Both supporters and opponents of the measure were apprehensive. The Association of Agriculturists, all landowners, offered an alternative to the government reform. Suggesting the opening of tracts of land in northwest Guatemala, they claimed that improved transportation and communication would make the plan workable. The government disagreed. Too much government financing would be needed; previous resettlement plans—on a smaller scale—had failed, and there was no time to wait for implementation of such a program. Minister of Economy Roberto Fanjul said that "it would be dangerous to postpone it [reform] because the peasants are aroused and if we do not do it now they will take the law into their own hands with bloody results . . . our main interest in passing the law quickly is to stave off serious trouble with the peasants."[16] President Arbenz, in a typical display of inflexibility, announced that he would rather fight the opponents of the bill on military battlefields than yield its fundamental principles. If the opposition would not or could not curb its criticism, war would result.

On June 15, 1952, the Agrarian Reform Law was passed by the Assembly and sent to Arbenz for his signature. In addition to the features described above, it offered recompense to owners of expropriated land. Payments were to be made in government bonds redeemed over a twenty-five-year period. Small landowners were to take comfort in the provisions of Article 10 which exempted estates more than two-thirds under cultivation. Ultimate administrative authority ("the supreme executive organization of the Agrarian Reform") was granted the President. He had complete authority in any disputed expropriations or compensatory payments. As such, the President was placed above the Constitution. This was all grist to the communist mill. In July, the cominform paper editorialized that the "Communist Party of Guatemala leads . . . the democratic forces fighting for the agrarian reform," winning "not land purchase but complete expropriation and its distribution." For the Reds, the important thing was the extension of domination across the countryside. Satisfaction of peasant aspirations was entirely secondary. Adoption of the law created the National Agrarian Department (DAN) to administer the measure, with subordinate regional and local agrarian committees to execute its orders. This was but another opportunity for the Communists to infiltrate the Guatemalan social fabric.

Director of the DAN was a non-Communist, Alfonso Martínez, but he was a close personal friend of Arbenz and rumored to have arranged and possibly executed the ambush of Arana. His deputy was a Communist, Waldemar Barrios Klee. Another Communist, Major Mario Sosa, was Inspector General. Of the nine members of the managing National Agrarian Council, three came from the CGTG* and the newly formed leftist peasants' organization, Confederación Nacional de Campesinos Guatemaltecos (CNCG). Sub-councils, representing roughly one thousand people per department, were composed of members of the DAN and labor and peasant organizations. Normally, two or three of the five members were fellow-travelers or Communists. Thus gaining control of DAN machinery, the Reds bolstered their influence once more. And their determined insistence on the legislation enhanced their position of favor with President Arbenz. Fortuny exulted that "We Communists recognize that, due to its special condition, the development of Guatemala must be accomplished for a period through capitalism . . . [however] it is no longer historically inevitable that the people . . . must pass through long capitalist periods."[17]

The Agrarian Reform Law, then, was another example of the Assembly almost mutely accepting the program of the executive and enacting it into law. In Guatemala, as elsewhere in Central America, there was no tradition of legislative independence. For years the Assembly had been a rubber stamp body, acting on the whim of a dictator. So it was that the Communists subverted the Legislative Assembly with consummate ease.

Another important tool in Central American politics is the collective news-gathering agency. Despite relative public unawareness, propaganda media have through the years been vital pillars of any government. The Communists were quick to realize this. Both governmental and private sources of dissemination fell to the Reds. In June, 1950, the Communists founded a weekly, *Octubre*. The maiden issue featured anti-yankee articles under a masthead bearing the hammer and sickle. The initial issue carried exaggerated praise for the Soviet Union, and Gutiérrez was

* In October, 1951, after absorbing several small previously independent labor groups, the CGT was renamed the Confederación General de Trabajadores de Guatemala (CGTG). It remained essentially the same organization, but in expanded form.

the first director. To underscore its beliefs, the paper held a communist meeting of some two thousand persons to celebrate the first issue as it rolled off the presses. June 21, 1951, a comparable gathering of Communists and sympathizers commemorated the first anniversary of *Octubre*. Variedades Theatre was used for the meeting, city officials having granted its use in accordance with a regulation requiring owners to offer their theatres to the government for twice-monthly use for "cultural acts." The stage was backed by enormous pictures of Lenin, Stalin, and Fortuny.

Diario de Centro América, long the official government organ, moved to the left following the election of Arévalo in 1945. Its editor, for some time one of the six members of the Secretariat, was Alfredo Guerra Borges. This was supplemented in time by a party daily, *Tribuna Popular,* which began publication in August, 1953. Guerra Borges was its editor, as well. The semi-official *Nuestro Diario* never won widespread circulation, but was for a time edited by Communists. TGWA, the government radio, spread daily propaganda and lies for the Reds. The United States was continually attacked. Opposition to communist aspirations was violently condemned. As early as April, 1945, the staff had communist members, thanks to the appointments of Arévalo. Later, party propagandist Pedro Geoffrey Rivas became manager of the station's board of directors, and in the following years the board included several other Communists. Arévalo also gave Fortuny an important post in the Department of Press, Propaganda and Tourism, an official part of the government. Mario Silva Jonama, an experienced agitator and agent, followed Fortuny into the organization in 1949 and in time became undersecretary. Humberto Alvarado, yet another Red, directed the department after 1950.

Typical of communist propaganda was a huge cartoon in *Diario de Centro América* on January 15, 1953. It pictured a gigantic figure, labeled "democratic forces," supporting the people with votes in their hands. Prostrate under the figure was a formless face labelled "anti-Communist." One of the bloodstained hands clutched a dagger.

It is true that there were anti-Communists in press and radio. Some of these were vocal throughout the years under Arbenz. Yet, try though they might, they were unable to raise their voices over the barrage of pro-communist, pro-Arbenz propaganda. The U. S. State Department felt justified in announcing on January 30, 1954, that Guatemala was engaged in an "increasingly mendacious propaganda campaign." Its report concluded that "The official Guatemalan press and radio offices, to which President Arbenz has appointed a group of dedicated propagandists of communism . . . have a long record of circulating false charges, typically communist in their technique, against the United States, the United Nations, and particularly those countries which have been actively resisting communist aggression."[18]

ANTI-AMERICANISM: AN OUTWARD LOOK

For the better part of a century, nationalistic forces have run rampant through Central America. During this time the United States has committed countless blunders in the area. Today, the residue of resentment is a regional characteristic. Years of exploitation, insincerity, intervention, and outright bungling have left their imprint on the temper of the people. Consequently, emotional appeals can and still do succeed in arousing latent resentment against the United States. For Arbenz and the government officials, anti-Americanism was a rewarding policy. The President, as have so many other leaders through the pages of history, found an advantageous practice in attacking an external power, in constructing what the Chinese call a "paper tiger," one sufficiently menacing to divert the attention of the people. As internal dissatisfaction mounted, Arbenz tried increasingly to turn national resentment against the United States. Such diversionary tactics, invoking the specter of fear, distracted the people from internal problems. In Guatemala, the United Fruit Company provided an ideal target. The Reds were not so inept as to overlook its potentialities.

The United Fruit Company of Boston (UFCO), founded in 1871 as a small trading company dealing in bananas, has expanded into one of the major international enterprises. Its empire in Latin America is unrivalled. With major investments in a dozen republics, it has recently spread to Europe, as well, and deals in many commodities besides bananas, including sugar, cacao and palm oil. The Guatemalan division of UFCO first opened in 1906, and the government leased acreage to the company on the Caribbean coast—the Bananera division. In 1936, a second division was added, in the Pacific region of Escuintla. Terms of the 1936 agreement, negotiated by General Ubico, were later called by the Communists an imposition by the United States company. But Archer Bush, a stern critic of UFCO policies, admits that Ubico insisted the laborers be paid a daily wage of fifty cents rather than one dollar.[19] He wanted to hold prices down to the level paid by private Guatemalans in related labor. The 1936 contract granted UFCO concessions including exemption from internal taxes, and import-free machinery and construction goods, as well as the privilege of establishing various "marginal" facilities for employees. Bear in mind that these concessions were willingly accepted by General Ubico, the legally-recognized chief of state. The company did not coerce the government in any way.

The flames of dispute were fanned by expropriatory action by the government in 1953. The original expropriation, promising recompense, applied to the Pacific holdings of the company, at Tiquisate. The government seized 233,973 acres. This figure later rose to 413,573 acres, when additional land was taken from the Bananera division. The action touched off a round of arguments, protests, claims, and counterclaims, and the atmosphere was one of increasing acrimony and rancor.

Despite earlier denials of expropriation by government authorities, the seizures were not entirely unexpected. In a speech to the Assembly in March, 1953, the President assured that he would neither expropriate UFCO properties nor expel the company from Guatemala. At the same time he warned that impending negotiations to renew contracts for the Tiquisate plantations had to be consummated quickly. A violent storm in September, 1951, had destroyed much of the Pacific division, resulting in a long lay off for many workers. The government unreasonably insisted, in early 1952, that, when these workers returned, they should be paid unearned wages for the inactive interim period. This totalled some seven hundred thousand dollars; UFCO refused to pay. A forced auction was scheduled to sell the company's buildings and equipment on March 5. Faced with implacable government opposition, UFCO capitulated and agreed to terms.

Expropriation itself was the central issue in the dispute between the government and UFCO. The Guatemalans justified expropriation under terms of the Agrarian Reform Law. Among the articles of the law was one referring to large uncultivated holdings. Land seized at Tiquisate was uncultivated, and the expropriation was perfectly consonant with the existing law. However, in later months, acreage was taken from UFCO which was actually under cultivation. Unable to justify the action in constitutional terms, the government blandly denied the seizure of cultivated soil.

Several points at issue are important. It would be false to assume that the government was entirely to blame. UFCO made several strikingly near-sighted decisions which contributed to the basic disagreement. In the first place, terms of the existing 1936 contract were clearly inadequate. Guatemalans, with complete justification, could state that UFCO gave inadequate financial compensation to the government for concessions granted it. Duties and taxes totalled one-tenth of UFCO annual profits. When Arévalo requested a new arrangement, he was coldly rebuffed. With the contracts several years short of expiration, UFCO had no legal obligation to renegotiate, and refused to do so. This policy proved disastrous in the long run. In time, UFCO recognized its short-sightedness and offered new terms. By then, however, Arbenz was in power and the Communists exerted much more influence. Renegotiation was out of the question. A ripe harvest of propaganda was the Communists' for the taking, and xenophobic appeals to the populace seemed more worthwhile to the government than arranging new contracts for the benefit of the people.

UFCO relationships with the railways were another painful subject to Guatemalans. This was based on the relationship of UFCO to International Railways of Central America (IRCA). In 1936, UFCO purchased a large chunk of IRCA stock—just under 50 percent. At first, UFCO intended to build a Pacific port to ship bananas from its Pacific division. This would have cut deeply into IRCA business on the railway between Puerto Barrios, on the Atlantic, and the capital. The agreement of September 17, 1936, stated that UFCO would not build a Pacific port. In exchange, it would pay IRCA a shipping rate below existing price levels. The rate was overtly preferential. As a result, IRCA retained its UFCO business, without the competition of a Pacific port. UFCO was saved the expense of building it and also received preferential shipping treatment.

Price discrimination irked the Guatemalans, but even worse was the fact that foreigners controlled the major railway in the country. The highways, of course, were not foreign controlled, but none crossed the country from Pacific to Atlantic. The railway was the only means of traveling from one side of Guatemala to the other. National pride—always touchy—was rubbed raw by continual communist carping on this manifestation of "yankee imperialism."

The government finally intervened by seizing IRCA assets on April 1, 1953, claiming non-payment of charity taxes. The railway owners denied the applicability of any such tax; no evidence has ever contradicted the opinion that this was a trumped-up charge by which the government could examine the company books and determine its ability to pay taxes. In early 1954, the government issued a demand for the payment of $10,500,000 in back taxes—"charity taxes," they announced. A strike in the fall of 1953 also confused the issue, and in time the government set up a receivership. It was after this action that the demand for back taxes was made. As had been the case in the UFCO dispute, payment for concessions was based on outdated contracts that had paid the government, through the years, a ridiculously low sum. Once again, United States capitalists had, by short-sighted financial policies, jeopardized their own future and at the same time given the government another issue to exploit in the continuing anti-yankee campaign.

Even more important to the Communists and to the Arbenz administration was the issue of UFCO's labor policies. UFCO paid its banana worker more generously than his counterpart working for Guatemalan employers. However, the banana industry is a changeable business; the position of the common laborer is perilous, his job status very tenuous, at best. Banana farming is a shifting enterprise, for no plantation can survive longer than one generation. The onslaught of Panama disease or lack of crop rotation inevitably exhausts the soil, and new lands must be cultivated. This transitory form of agriculture works obvious hardships on the worker. Changes of location and part-time labor are not designed to give the laborer much security. And so, in compensation for this, the worker demands higher wages and increased marginal benefits from the employers.

UFCO has resisted labor organization throughout Central America. In Guatemala, the late 1940's and early 1950's brought an increasing demand for organization. The Communists naturally contributed to this movement, hoping to drive a wedge between company and employees, thus exacerbating national passions and increasing anti-U. S. feeling. While there was no official UFCO recognition of labor, the company was forced on different occasions to deal with labor leaders. A major strike in 1948-9 demanded increased medical care, new housing, and a $1.50 daily wage. The company relied that profits were too small to finance the proposals. The workers struck, and UFCO instituted a lockout. The Arévalo government intervened and, when the courts decided in favor of the laborers, insisted on partial concessions from the company. In succeeding years, there were other, though smaller, strikes and protests. An atmosphere of ill-will developed between labor and management. The intractability and intransigence of company officials created almost as much rancor and misunderstanding as the well-organized attacks of communist propaganda.

In all fairness, however, UFCO had elements of justice in its position. Certainly the welfare of the workers was not ignored. The lot of the banana worker was better than that of other Guatemalans working outside this industry. Housing conditions provided modern sanitation, sewage disposal, plumbing, electricity, and disease-prevention. No Central American observer need be reminded how scarce are these commodities elsewhere. The modest physical surroundings of the workers were plain but pleasant. A few miles from a UFCO village are the miserable grass-roofed huts in which other laborers live. The contrast is unforgettably vivid. Banana workers were also treated, inoculated, fed, and cared for in hospitals and dispensaries at no extra charge. Schools were built and administered for children of the workers. In 1953 alone, 5,397 pupils attended company-established schools taught by 103 company-paid teachers. Commissaries supplied food at lower prices than Guatemalan markets. Yet there was no compulsion, and workers could buy their food elsewhere. Entertainment, movies, recreation, and churches were all provided, as well.

As for wages, the average Guatemalan banana worker today receives almost a thousand dollars a year. The annual individual Guatemalan income in the 1950's is barely three hundred dollars. Thus the UFCO employee receives an average of three times as much pay. This disparity is so favorable that, even today, officials feel justified in rejecting demands for increased pay.

No action was fought as bitterly by the company as the expropriation of its plantations. Officials pointed out that, for them, lands under cultivation were only a little more important than untilled ones. For in a few years, existing lands would have to be abandoned and new sites established on the uncultivated lands. Thus the seizure of uncultivated lands was damaging to future prospects. Only by maintaining these fields at all times could UFCO hope to continue successful operations. Without them, one bad plague of Panama disease—which completely kills the plant it attacks—could wipe out UFCO holdings. Tropical storms—often flooding or blowing down fields of bananas—would have the same result. A 1951 storm near Tiquisate destroyed the year's crop there. UFCO's final point was that the expropriation was totally unnecessary. Coffee, not bananas, was and is the major source of economic strength in Guatemala. Bananas provide the principal, but less important, economic assistance. In the last analysis, the enraged attitude of the company officials usually boiled down to a dogmatic belief that "they can't do it to us!" When "they" did, company officials were dumbfounded.

Realizing that it had no recourse in Guatemalan courts, the company applied to the U. S. Department of State. On March 23, 1953, the Guatemalan ambassador in Washington was handed a note requesting adequate compensation for UFCO as soon as possible. Two months later an official memorandum from the Guatemalan government rejected the request. It argued in favor of Guatemala's legal right to seize property on the basis of sovereignty. A second Washington request, more forcibly worded, went ignored for a period of six months. On April 20, 1954, the United States officially demanded $15,854,849 as compensatory payment for the expropriated acreage. Foreign Minister Toriello refused to accept the note. He called it "another attempt to meddle in domestic affairs of Guatemala," and attacked the U. S. position fiercely. The dispute was temporarily suspended, and the June fall of the Arbenz government put an end to the case, for the time.

In review, there are things to be said for both sides. The Guatemalan government had a legal right to expropriate land, and there were many causes for doing so. On the other hand, the method of approach and, finally, the refusal to pay adequate compensation, were both morally and legally wrong. As for UFCO, while it had provided many benefits for the workers, it was not unreasonable to grant further concessions, as well as negotiate a new contract with the government. Past years of paternalistic authority and downgrading of nationalistic dreams and aspirations piled up a mountain of resentment and rancor. The bondage of half a century—for such was the usual Guatemalan interpretation—had to be erased as a matter of national pride. UFCO inability to recognize this fact was but another factor contributing to the communist drive for power.

ATTACK AT CARACAS

The peak of "anti-imperialist" outpourings was reached at the Tenth Inter-American Conference convened in Caracas, Venezuela, in March,

1954. Never before had the United States been so viciously attacked by a Latin nation. Denunciations were bitter, vitriolic, and prolonged. The Communists not only put the colossus of the north in its place, but diverted popular attention back home. Criticisms were eagerly repeated and discussed in Guatemala. Guatemala went to the conference with one idea—exploitation of the historic Latin resentment of the United States. Headed by Foreign Minister Guillermo Toriello, the Guatemalan delegation quickly realized it had an incomparable sounding board for its propaganda and determined to exploit the opportunity fully. Flaunting their defiance of the United States outspokenly, the Guatemalans became heroes at home by their display of bravado. Expecting an anti-communist resolution from the United States, they cared little about the outcome. They knew the U. S. could probably force adoption of any resolution it wanted, but no such agreement was expected to change the nature of things inside Guatemala.

The United States position was not as simple. The North American delegation, led by Secretary of State John Foster Dulles, intended to spotlight Guatemalan communism and at the same time pass a stern anti-communist resolution. The U. S. was handicapped by personal factors, however. John Moors Cabot, Dulles' top Latin American expert, had just resigned as Assistant Secretary of State for Inter-American Affairs, reportedly due to differences with Milton Eisenhower over economic aid to the area. He accompanied Dulles only in the role of advisor, and his newly-named successor, Henry Holland, was an unknown quantity. At the same time, Dulles miscalculated badly the climate of opinion. He failed to realize, despite repeated warnings, that the republics of Central and South America were relatively unconcerned with communism and wanted a small-scale Marshall Plan, or at least some form of increased economic assistance. This fact was not recognized by Dulles until the conference had been in session several days and was not, unfortunately, the first indication of Dulles' lack of understanding of Latin American relations.

Toriello launched the Guatemalan offensive in his first convention speech on March 5, 1954. In a wide-ranging, unrestrained attack, he lashed out at U. S. policy as that of "the Big Stick, tarnished dollar diplomacy, and the landing of the Marines in Latin American posts." His fifty-five-minute address said many of the things other Latin delegates hoped to hear but dared not say themselves. The official Guatemalan information bulletin headlined "TORIELLO PLEADS CAUSE OF UNDERDEVELOPED COUNTRIES," and the foreign minister was praised for raising important questions despite the oppressive "steamroller atmosphere." Denying Guatemala's communism, he asked why this was the U. S. characterization. The answer he provided promptly: "The answers are plain and simple. The plan of national liberation which my government is executing had to affect the privileges of foreign enterprises which were holding back the progress and economic development. . . ."[20] As for the proposed U. S.-sponsored resolution against communism, he declared that this meant any government in Latin America touching interests of foreign companies controlling basic resources would be called communist. The result would be foreign intervention. Guatemala, categorically opposed to a resolution trampling on the principles of democracy, would fight it with determination.

The speech was enthusiastically received. There was a warm ovation —the greatest of the conference. The Guatemalan information bulletin triumphantly bragged that "There was no doubt that Guillermo Toriello . . . had voiced the deepest aspirations of millions for democracy, justice, and peace between nations."[21] Secretary Dulles responded immediately with a press statement, warning that he would discuss the issue of international communism without having the issue "obscured by an abusive attack upon the United States." He was anxious to see Guatemala's position toward the intervention of communism when that part of the agenda was reached. He charged Toriello with opposing any declaration against international communism: "We are confident this conference . . . will go on to declare that domination and control of political institutions of any American State by the international Communist movement would constitute intervention by a foreign political power and be a threat to the peace of America."[22]

Two days later Toriello issued a counter-statement, denying Guatemalan opposition to any anti-communist resolution. He refused to concede that Guatemala's stand on communism would be tested when the item was reached on the agenda. Though he made many pronouncements and took part in various committee meetings, the Toriello magic slowly slipped away. He continued to be lionized by Caracas society; his prominence in the conference itself was a different matter. On March 9 he alienated other delegates by walking out of a plenary session when Dominican Minister Joaquin Balaquer sided with the United States.

Calling for an end to anti-Americanism, he criticized countries that helped Soviet Russia but only attacked the United States. Toriello snapped at reporters that he had "more important things to do than to hear such people in the ridiculous and stupid role of discussing democracy."

Secretary Dulles hoped to enlarge the 1947 Treaty of Rio de Janeiro, making subversion and communism a cause for hemispheric conferences. In this event, there would be a call for action in accord with existing treaties. The object was to cloak with collective intervention measures necessary to eradicate communist governments, whenever they might arise. Despite Latin fears that the resolution would bring heavy abuse, the United States pushed it. After a fortnight of backstage maneuvering and heated discussion, the declaration, informally called the "Dulles Doctrine," was passed by a vote of seventeen to one. Guatemala opposed the declaration, with Argentina and Mexico abstaining.

The resolution, officially called the "Declaration of Caracas," denounced international communism as incompatible with the concept of freedom and constituting a threat to inter-American security. Calling for collective action in time of need, the critical passage argued "That the domination or control of the political institutions of any American State by the international communist movement, extending to this Hemisphere the political system of an extracontinental power, would constitute a threat to the sovereignty and political independence of the American States, endangering the peace of America, and would call for a Meeting of Consultation to consider the adoption of appropriate action in accordance with existing treaties."[23]

Machinery was set up to meet seizure of a republic by a foreign power. Each American government was to fight communist activities internally, exchanging information with one another. Consultation was provided for in cases of apparent communism. This was to precede action, and was a Colombian amendment designed to placate fears of abusive intervention. "This declaration of foreign policy made by the American republics in relation to dangers originating outside this Hemisphere is designed to protect and not to impair the inalienable right of each American State freely to choose its own form of government and economic system and to live its own social and cultural life."[24]

Passage of the resolution was hailed in the United States as a triumph for the Dulles diplomacy, a "striking victory for freedom and self-government in this part of the world."[25] The Latins were less sanguine.

One delegate was quoted by the *New York Times* as saying that if "the U. S. wanted to badly enough, it could have a resolution passed declaring two and two are five." Another representative said that "you don't always have to see the sun, but you know it is there."[26]   The United States, certainly, gained no prestige in Latin America from the conference. In addition, much good will was lost. A Brazilian delegate claimed the United States had reached its lowest ebb in its role of hemispheric leader of democracy.

For Guatemala, its purposes were achieved: increased prestige abroad, added popularity at home, the communist position stronger than ever, and the government locally hailed in the press. Guatemala City dailies cheered Toriello, the brave patriot, for having unmasked U. S. policy. President Arbenz told a large rally in Guatemala City that, "Some of the legal positions maintained by us were defeated, but Caracas constituted a victory for our delegation, because it defeated the forces of imperialism and feudalism that raised the banner of anti-Communism in order to intervene in the affairs of the Latin American nations. . . . I am convinced that Guatemala is not alone in the fight against the forces of imperialism."[27]   The Communists hoped to isolate the United States from the other American republics, and thus destroy the most severe threat to their power. They were unable to do so; yet they succeeded in creating widespread suspicion and mistrust of U. S. motives. Transformation of emotional hate of "yankee imperialism" into communist partisanship was one of the means by which the Reds intended to gain complete power. They were only following the line laid down by Stalin in 1924.

From Terror to Liberation

In the spring of 1954, the Arbenz government became the object of a war of nerves from rebel forces in Honduras. Led by an obscure little exile, Lieutenant Colonel Carlos Castillo, the anti-communist forces prepared for invasion. Headquarters were in the Honduran capital, where Castillo begged and cajoled for all the arms and financial aid available. Throughout the early months of 1954, he issued repeated appeals to the Guatemalan populace for support, promising the overthrow of communism before year's end. Increasingly unsure of his position, President Arbenz instituted a wave of political arrests and brutal beatings. The Communists anxiously joined in the wave of violence. Popular opinion finally began to rise against the government. Reprisals and physical violence were unparalleled in the annals of Central American politics. In a now-famous interview, *U. S. News & World Report* questioned two victims who managed to survive. Dávila Córdova told how he was seized one evening as he closed his law office and driven blindfolded in a car to Civil Guard headquarters.

Q. What kind of tortures?
A. They applied electric shocks to my body. They applied a steel band to my head which caused such pressure on my brain that I lost consciousness.
Q. Where were these things done?
A. These tortures were applied every three or four hours in a special room at . . . Civil Guard headquarters, where they took me from my cell. . . .
Q. Were others arrested and tortured?
A. When they finally took off the blindfold, I saw that five other prisoners had come with me and that they bore on their bodies horrible marks of the tortures they had undergone. On one of these men, Horacio de Córdoba Monzón, the injuries were so bad that he could not walk, because his feet were completely useless.[28]

The stark terror continued into the late spring. Arrest, conviction, torture, reprisal—all were common in Guatemala. Under the direction of Civil Guard Chief Rogelio Cruz Wer, the police were merciless in treatment of prisoners. Photographs of mutilated, tortured victims were found after the fall of Arbenz. Atrocities were unspeakable. Veteran newsmen who visited Buchenwald and Dachau in the last days of Hitler's Third Reich testified to the brutality of the Guatemalan security forces. One wishes that the countless Latins who have argued that the Arbenz regime was "democratic," might have seen these examples of barbarism.

Lashing out blindly at all within its reach, the regime expelled NBC broadcaster Marshall Bannell and *New York Times* correspondent Sydney Gruson on February 2 for slanderous defamation and inaccurate reporting. Actually, Bannell had denounced Soviet subversion. Gruson, ousted for having "defamed and slandered this republic and its Government," was blamed for a dispatch calling Arbenz a prisoner of the Communists. Yet the story had been cabled to New York in November, two months before anyone noticed the supposed "insult." Foreign Minister Toriello responded to an outspoken wire of protest from the Inter-American Press Association by claiming that freedom of the press was still existent. Meanwhile, independent Guatemalan newsmen, wearing black ties of mourning, accompanied Bannell to the Guatemala City airport.

In the midst of rampant terrorism, the outer world was told on May 17 that a shipload of arms was on the high seas to Guatemala from Stettin, Poland. Loaded with two thousand tons of weapons and ammunition, the freighter *Alfhem* had steamed through the Skagerrak, and after twice changing course, first from French West Africa and then the Dutch West Indies, docked at Puerto Barrios, Guatemala. The cargo —"steel rods, optical glass and laboratory supplies"—was unloaded on a dark night under the personal direction of Defense Minister José Angel Sánchez. The weapons, reportedly mortars and rifles, were shipped to the capital. The news exploded like a bombshell. In the United States, Rep. Patrick Hillings said the report made it "imperative that we deny the use of the Panama Canal to suspicious vessels."[29] Secretary Dulles told his news conference that arms could build a communist stronghold near Panama, endangering "the peace of America." The United States, he said, was ready to act in accord with its fellow members in the Organization of American States to prevent war. And Guatemala's Latin compatriots were equally startled. In New York City, General Antonio Seleme, the Bolivian military attaché, suggested a U. S. air base in the Bolivian Andes as an additional defense of the Canal. Panama's Washington ambassador, Roberto Heurtematte, said that "through similar military assistance Russia converted her neighbor countries into satellite police states."[30]

Even the shortsighted Arbenz realized the magnitude of the action and acted hastily to calm his neighbors. Toriello tried to laugh his way way out of a corner in an interview with Edwin A. Lahey. Asked about charges that Guatemala was communist, he said "that's a lot of baloney," and added that Guatemala could buy no arms from the U. S. Questioned about the origin of the military equipment, he sidestepped the issue with "I'm only the Foreign Minister, not the Defense Minister." The United States speeded additional arms to Honduras and Nicaragua, redressing the Central American balance of power. At the same time it called for a foreign ministers' meeting to chart multilateral action. After a brief delay for diplomatic amenities, it was scheduled for early July in Montevideo, Uruguay.

At home, Guatemala continued to retrieve its miscalculation as well as possible. The President suggested a personal meeting with President Eisenhower. Toriello met with U. S. Ambassador Peurifoy to ease tension with the United States. He insisted that all the diplomatic problems were directly attributable to the UFCO dispute. If only that could be settled, "everything would be different." But an unidentified foreign service officer framed the U. S. position succinctly: "If the Guatemalans paid the United Fruit Company's full $16 million claim tomorrow and decorated every last United Fruit official with the Order of the Quetzal, we wouldn't be one whit less concerned about the danger of Communism in Guatemala."[31]

Ever since June, 1954, there has been an exceptionally widespread feeling among all Latin Americans that the United States, with Secretary Dulles in the direct pay of UFCO, intervened against a popular democratic government because of imperialistic economic interests. They fortify their opinion with amazing statements since published by Toriello and Arévalo in a pair of books denouncing "yankee imperialism." It is superfluous to repeat the innumerable proofs that Guatemala under Arbenz was communist, undemocratic, and almost totally cynical. And while the United States did intervene, it was strictly for political and not economic reasons. Most Latins refuse to accept the fact that the United States was badly troubled by what was obviously a communist regime. It had taken no action for more than twelve months after the expropriation of UFCO properties. Only when the communist threat became acute did the United States become active. Despite longstanding resentments, no intelligent Latin in possession of the facts can honestly attack the United States for interfering in the name of economic interests.

In June, 1954, impatient for the expected internal army revolt, Colonel Castillo launched his invasion from Honduras, and the battle was joined. For weeks Guatemala had protested to the Honduran government about the formation of Castillo's troops. The government of President Gálvez, aroused over Guatemalan infiltration of Honduran banana laborers and general communist meddling, coldly refused to recognize the existence of any such revolutionary group. The government of Gálvez was criticized for this position, often called a tool of the United States. The truth of the matter is that the continual intervention by Guatemalans in national affairs of the other republics was so blatant and inexcusable that, after a certain point, Guatemala was anathema to her sister republics. All, including Honduras, were anxious to retaliate in any way possible against the Arbenz regime.

Responding immediately to the attack, the Arbenz government dispatched troops to meet the rebels, taking the case to international agencies.

Toriello wrote the United Nations, demanding an emergency session of the Security Council to stop "the aggression in progress against Guatemala." The Council complied by hurrying into session on June 20. The Soviet Union blocked a move to transfer the question to the Organization of American States; then the Council adopted a resolution calling for a cease-fire. The Guatemalans simultaneously appealed to the OAS, as well, requesting an examination by the Peace Committee. In appealing for UN aid, the government made another grave blunder, this time by calling on the Soviet Union for aid. Russia had always "come forward resolutely against aggression," according to Toriello. This served no purpose; the case continued before the Security Council. The Western hemisphere was uniformly amazed by the appeal. For the U. S. Dulles could announce with complete candor that Foreign Minister Toriello "openly connived . . . with the Foreign Minister of the Soviet Union. The two were in open correspondence and ill-concealed privity."[32]

While the Security Council was debating further action, several American republics requested from the Council of the OAS a special ministers' meeting. Their statement declared: "Our governments view with increasing concern the demonstrated intervention of the international Communist movement in the republic of Guatemala. . . . The recent outbursts of violence in the area intensify considerably this concern and pose an urgent need to hold a meeting of the organ of consultation."[33] The Peace Committee, in the meantime, was scheduled to leave for Guatemala City on June 27 for a report to present to the meeting of the American ministers. Their plans were cancelled when President Arbenz resigned the same day.

The five hundred to one thousand heterogeneous soldiers of Castillo gathered in Honduras for some six months before launching their invasion. Their commander had hoped to force internal revolt in the form of army rebellion. But the Guatemalan Army, one of the most powerful factors in national affairs, chose to remain aloof until the very end. Its apparent unwillingness to take the initiative led Castillo to attack in June. His forces were armed almost entirely by the United States. This has been denied repeatedly by U. S. officials. Yet there can be no serious doubt of U. S. intervention. Castillo was not a wealthy man and certainly could not raise enough money to buy the arms with which he eventually attacked. For weeks before, it was no secret in Tegucigalpa that U. S. arms were going to Castillo. Visitors in the city reported the rebels training, drilling, and irritably killing time until they went into action. A few even saw scattered ammunition boxes with United States seals. Even with these arms, however, Castillo was outgunned and outmanned by the regular Guatemalan Army, nearly ten thousand strong. While his troops groped through southern Guatemala searching for government forces, events in Guatemala City moved quickly toward a decision. It was only after a series of semi-comic palace intrigues that Arbenz was ousted and replaced by Castillo.

Sunday afternoon, June 27, U. S. Ambassador John Peurifoy, one of the key figures in behind-the-scenes manuvering, received a summons to visit army chief of staff Colonel Carlos Enrique Díaz. Traveling through shuttered streets with a pistol under his coat and accompanied by a member of the embassy Marine Guard, he met Colonel Díaz and other army officers. Almost three hours of discussion followed; Díaz said that army morale was low, and he wanted to stop the fighting. He suggested the formation of a junta abolishing the PGT and expelling the Communists from Guatemala. Peurifoy approved but insisted that the Communists had to be completely uprooted. Díaz' previous association with Arbenz left the ambassador skeptical of his motives.

Heartened by the cautious encouragement, Colonel Díaz and two assistants went to the National Palace for an interview with the President. They insisted that Arbenz resign. The usually stoic President lost his composure and flew into a rage, arguing vehemently against his fellow officers. During the meeting he received news of several cabinet resignations. His communist advisers, even Fortuny, were unavailable for advice, having deserted him. Faced with an impossible situation, abandoned by associates and Communists alike, he had no choice but to step down.

Later that same evening, Arbenz addressed the nation by radio for the last time. Alone in his personal disaster, the embittered President addressed the country with uncharacteristic emotion: "I say goodbye, my friends, with bitter sorrow, but still firm in my convictions. Preserve what has been so costly; ten years of struggle, tears, and sacrifices, of democratic gains, are many years to gainsay history. I have not been confronted by the enemy's arguments, but by the material means for the destruction of Guatemala. With the satisfaction of a man who believes he has done his duty, with faith in the future, I say: Long live the October Revolution! Viva Guatemala!"[34]

Colonel Díaz followed immediately, pledging a fight against the rebel forces. At 4:00 A.M. Monday morning he awoke Peurifoy, accompanied by fellow junta member José Angel Sánchez, asking the ambassador to contact the rebels and negotiate a cease-fire. Peurifoy at first agreed but hours later learned that Díaz was letting fleeing Communists scatter in all directions. Díaz obviously hoped to maintain the Red government in some semblance.

Another meeting at 2:00 A.M. Tuesday morning brought Peurifoy from his bed to Díaz' home once more. Again riding armed through silent streets, he was met by Díaz and Sánchez. Col. Elfego Monzón, the third member of the junta, was absent. Peurifoy, hopeful that Monzón at least was sincere, insisted that he be called before the discussion began. After calling Monzón, Díaz and Peurifoy talked for a few minutes. Noise in the adjoining room caused Díaz to excuse himself briefly and leave the ambassador. Sounds of a brief argument carried through the door, and then Monzón suddenly stepped into the room. "My colleague has decided to resign. I am replacing him," were his first words. Sánchez was also ousted. Peurifoy, pleased with the turn of events, agreed to arrange a conference between Monzón and Castillo. The two colonels met the following afternoon, June 30, in San Salvador.

Negotiations hit a snag, and after several hours of haggling the announced cease-fire had to be extended. On the next day, Friday, July 1, Peurifoy received reports that Monzón was withdrawing after a collapse of negotiations. He immediately flew to San Salvador, muttering as he left that "we will get this straightened out." Arriving in an outlandish checked jacket and green Tyrolean hat, he sat down with the two men at once and, in a short time, they agreed to stop the two-week-old war. Determined to wipe out communism, they established a five-man junta including Monzón and Castillo. After fifteen days a temporary chief would be elected by the junta.

Terms of the peace pact outlined four goals. Castillo's forces were incorporated into the regular army. The new junta took full legislative and executive powers, maintaining command of the army. Third, the junta was empowered to abolish the constitution or suspend certain articles. And lastly, national elections were promised once the constitution was revised or a new one enacted. In Guatemala City, Castillo was received by a crowd of over fifty thousand lining the streets along his approach. Addressing the cheering throngs in the main plaza, he promised "true justice for the workers and all sons of this . . . land." He referred to

Arbenz and his aides only briefly: "These men are criminals . . . responsible for torturing and killing many people."[35]

Approval and encouragement followed from the United States. John Foster Dulles announced that, "As peace and freedom are restored . . . the United States will continue to support the just aspirations of the Guatemalan people. A prosperous and progressive Guatemala is vital to a healthy Hemisphere. The United States pledges itself . . . to help alleviate conditions in Guatemala and elsewhere which might afford Communism an opportunity to spread its tentacles throughout the Hemisphere. Thus we shall seek in positive ways to make our Americas an example which will inspire men everywhere."[36]

PUTTING THE PIECES TOGETHER

The first task facing the new government was recovery of political calm and national stability. Castillo devoted himself tirelessly toward this objective, but his regime was soon shaky. A wide variety of problems frequently swept up his government and carried it along powerless. Weeks after the temporary junta took power, Castillo was installed as temporary president, and in time the junta was completely dissolved, leaving Castillo indisputably in command. Early in October, 1954, he announced elections to decide whether he should retain power. To reduce "unnecessary paper work," the elections were to be conducted orally, with voters telling election boards their choice. Secret ballot was ignored. The voters were given two assignments: first, to choose members of a constituent assembly to draw up a new constitution, and second, to decide whether to continue Castillo in power. Delegates to the assembly were members of the new-born National Anti-Communist Front; there were no opposition candidates. Officials would ask voters if they wanted Castillo to continue in office for a term decided by the assembly. Voters could answer yes or no, but if no, had no alternate candidate to select. Terms of the plebescite obviously assured Castillo's "re-election." Despite this undemocratic procedure, Castillo was genuinely popular in Guatemala and was returned to office overwhelmingly. In November, following the election by one month, the pro-Castillo constituent assembly set the term of office to extend until March 15, 1960, giving Castillo nearly six years to accomplish his goals in Guatemala.

The pressing need was still for tranquility. Despite the legitimatizing effect of the plebescite, Castillo was faced by hostile elements, notably ambitious right-wing landowners envisioning a return to the days of conservative dictatorship. On January 22, 1955, with the moral support of these men, a small band of conspirators attempted to overthrow the government. Gathering at Aurora airfield, some hundred men attacked through the main gate, only to be confronted by two tanks and government forces, which opened fire. The Interior Ministry later announced that the government had known of the conspiracy for several days and had preferred to stop the rebels in the very act of revolt. Some half-dozen men were killed and several others wounded before the conspirators surrendered. Ringleader of the attempt was Colonel Francisco Cosenza, former ambassador to Italy and one of numerous arbencistas still in Guatemala. A long-time friend of the deposed president, he planned the attack and, when it failed, fled to the Salvadoran Embassy for diplomatic asylum. Castillo's popularity wore well, and the arbencistas and other dissident groups were without widespread support. A state of siege was imposed for a few days, and an early curfew cleared the streets of the capital.

Perhaps the most startling development was the implied involvement of Colonel Monzón, who had helped engineer the end of the Arbenz government from the inside. Having been squeezed out of the governing junta some months before, he remained highly popular, especially with the army. Regular army officers had resented the intrusion of Castillo's irregulars into the ranks, and Castillo was both apprehensive and jealous of Monzón's popularity. Previous efforts to give Monzón a foreign diplomatic post had been rebuffed. Fearing his popularity, Castillo hesitated to force the issue. After the plot, however, government sources let it be known that Monzón had been immediately assigned to a South American diplomatic post. Aware of his earlier refusal, reporters pressed the issue. The government would say only that the colonel was a "focal point of dissension." They refused to involve him in the abortive plot. No one could prove any definite connection with the conspirators. He was known to have been on good terms with several of them, but this was implication, not proof. In the end, Monzón was forced, much against his will, to accept the foreign diplomatic assignment. His wife testified that he was accompanied by armed guards from his home to the airport and placed on a southbound plane.

Although Monzón was gone, the battle for survival and stability continued. On May 1, Herbert Matthews cabled the *New York Times* that the government was at last emerging from the tempestuous post-revolutionary chaos, with both remaining arbencistas and right-wing conservatives beaten off. In pursuing a middle-of-the-road course, the liberation leader had managed to buttress his position by winning at least tacit approval of regular army officers who had turned their backs while the Communists subverted national life under the Arbenz administration. Traveling through Guatemala continually, Castillo worked to build up his personal popularity, particularly in more remote areas.

When Castillo first took power, he was confronted with virtual government bankruptcy. Widespread looting by the Communists and by Arbenz left the national treasury empty. Arbenz himself deposited some six million dollars in Swiss banks after fleeing the country. The communist treasure was also large, with the Reds taking it to finance future adventures and a possible return to power. Castillo was thus barely able to operate a government at all and could scarcely consider plans to attract more capital or alleviate widespread unemployment. Finances haunted him continually in his fight for political and economic recovery.

Besides operational government expenses, Castillo had the pressing debt of back pay to the irregulars of his tattered Army of Liberation. And, after returning to the capital, he had promised indemnification for the victims of the senseless reign of terror that preceded the communist defeat. At first, he appealed to the moneyed landowners to contribute to a one million dollar fund. Landholders responded by proposing a tax plan including both wealthy and poor. Castillo, pursuing a middle way as always, ignored the outraged protests of friends and supporters and studied the suggestion. Almost simultaneously, he discovered that strong financial support was being given anti-government conservative politicians by the same rich businessmen and agriculturists.

Thoroughly aroused, he levied a capital tax calling for payment valued at 3 percent of property assessed at over five thousand dollars. It also provided for a tax of 1 percent on business capital over five thousand dollars, 10 percent of the average monthly earnings of professional men, one dollar a head from cattle owners, and ten thousand dollars from large sugar mills. Estimating total needs at $6,200,000, Castillo allotted funds for new roads, workers' housing, and repair of hurricane damage At the same time, promised aid from the United States was slow in coming. The expected flood of financial assistance was a bare trickle. The words of shining optimism from Secretary Dulles in June, 1954, were not followed by actions. President Eisenhower himself had spoken of making Guatemala an anti-communist showcase. Initially, $6,425,000 was promised. Little more than half that amount reached Guatemala in the first eighteen months of Castillo's government. This sum was contributed with strings attached. No money would go to Guatemala until the U. S. received specific explanations as to its use. Even then, the money had to be matched by Guatemala. The amount for roads was set at $4,425,000, providing Guatemala would add $1,500,000 more. In the early Castillo days, unfortunately, there was no matching money available. The $6,500,000 first contributed barely equaled the amount of back wages owed government bureaucrats. Daniel James editorialized that the donation was "as helpful as feeding aspirin to a man with appendicitis." Total Arbenz and communist looting was estimated at $20,000,000. The U. S. contribution, by comparison, was a drop in the bucket. For Castillo, U. S. declarations of friendship were hardly adequate. Only in 1956 did U. S. financial aid begin to arrive in significant quantities.

Economically, few measures have been more important than land reform. The prestige of both Castillo and the United States was riding on this program, always inviting comparison with the work of the communist-controlled DAN. Arbenz' legislation was in operation for two years. An estimated fifty-five thousand families were moved onto plots of their own, many taken from UFCO, a lesser number from large landowners. Most settled on ten-acre plots, and selection was contingent upon political obedience. The Arbenz government retained a lien on land titles and, after the death of the owner, lands would revert back to the government, presumably to be sold. These families took over both uncultivated and cultivated land. Bloodshed and violence often resulted, with many illegal seizures. Landless Indians, hearing of the reform, would take land and claim it as their own, exercising squatters' rights.

After the revolution, large landholders reversed the procedure and snatched back all the land available, often sending squads of "bully boys" where intimidation was necessary. Castillo, finding nearly eighteen thousand people unemployed in June, 1954, put jobs before farms and began his ambitious road-building program (see below) with unemployed labor. He refused to abolish the Arbenz law precipitously, and the government dispossessed no Indian peasant from land unless new property was available for him. At the same time, the President called upon U. S.

farm experts for advice. He explained the attitude of his government toward the issue:

The Communists had their land reform, but ours will be better. To make sure that it works, I have asked the American Department of Agriculture for . . . experts. . . .

We have laid down the principles and it is up to the Americans to help advise us how to apply them. The first principle is that the farmer gets the land for keeps. There are no strings. The Communists pretended to give land outright, but actually they only gave a deed of lifetime use. We want a nation of small owners, not state share croppers.

The Communists "reformed" the easy way, by grabbing land that was already cleared. We shall let the squatters keep some of the land already seized. But mostly we shall open up new frontiers. Fresh roads built with American help will penetrate the wilderness. We have plenty of unused land waiting for settlers.[37]

Not until March, 1956, was the land reform law completely revised. Castillo announced in an executive decree that the plan intended to settle landless peasants on government-owned lowlands, where prices for homesteads were low. At the same time, combatting Indian reluctance to leave the mountains after living there for centuries, additional lands in the highlands were provided, in most cases by expropriation of unused portions of large estates. The new law protected ownership by giving outright possession and forbidding resale without government permission for twenty-five years. This latter provision would prevent landowners from buying their land back from the peasants. Technical assistance, low-cost housing, and easy credit were included in the comprehensive plan, and agricultural education was set up in hopes of improving farming methods.

Financing the reform was part of a mammoth five-year economic development program costing $250,000,000. The new program, announced as the reform went into effect in March, hoped for some $50,000,000 from the United States. Additional funds for the reform program came from a new tax outlined by the agrarian law. Untilled sections of large farms would be taxed while left unproductive, the tax increasing 25 percent a year for five years. The obvious object was to force large landowners to farm their land, rather than hold some of it as a long-term investment. Effects of this program could well have revolutionary results for Guatemalan agricultural life. If successful, it would raise the entire national economy to a higher stratum.

Unfortunately, preliminary results have been poor. As 1957 drew to a close, the program was bogging down. Some thirteen thousand families had applied for land as early as mid-1954. But three years later, even the government claimed only seventy-four hundred had received plots under land reform. And while families were to receive fifty acres instead of the ten granted by the Communists, only one in six have actually received a full fifty-acre plot of land. Of the other six thousand, most are illegal squatters who still operate and live on land seized during the first post-revolution confusion. Roughly 2 percent of the Guatemalan population still owns 70 percent of the land. The government also found itself with less land than anticipated. UFCO transferred some hundred thousand acres to the government, which retained 134,000 acres seized by the Communists in 1953. This is still proving inadequate. A clearing contract was recently let for $525,000—roughly 20 percent of the national budget. Under the agreement, however, the company will clear only five of each fifty acres, a slow pace indeed, and one more suited to private capital. At this point, the government cannot point with pride to the achievements of land reform. Future prospects are better, but the problem of land distribution will not wait indefinitely.

Land reform, obviously, was not the only economic problem to be dealt with, and the others were lumped together under a Council of Economic Planning created in November, 1954. Castillo discussed its work in an interview with *Latin American Report* in June, 1956. The Council of Economic Planning, he commented, was "charged with preparing a basic five-year plan. After six months of specific research . . . the plan emerged as a reality. Covering the period from 1955 to 1959, the plan deals with works on public roads, development of agriculture and the native economy, light and power systems, budgetary reorganization, taxation, and technical coordination among the various agencies. With this blueprint to advance the systematic economic development of the country, it is felt that solid foundations have been laid for the welfare of the Gutamalan people."[38]

Guatemala's greatest dollar-earning product, coffee, has been one of the central problems of the Council. Like other coffee growers, the Guatemalans have ridden for years on the increasing international price for coffee, without expanding their production. This attitude is gradually changing. Idle land is being planted and fields increased. Greater care is given to the process of planting and to the seeds themselves, in hopes of bettering the product. Most growers are also centering production around the heart of the estate, in lieu of scattering plantings in remote, non-contiguous fields.

At the same time, coffee growers are complaining bitterly about the inadequacy of transportation. Feeder roads are needed in Guatemala if the products of the *finca* are to go to market, and then abroad. Low-cost transportation is vital. While the government is actually engaged in a major road-building effort, it does these planters little good. By the end of 1958, the so-called "Big Three" were nearing completion. These are the Atlantic Highway, running from the Caribbean port of Puerto Barrios to Guatemala City; the Pacific Highway, from the Mexican to Salvadoran border; and the Inter American Highway, between the same borders through the capital. While these are important, they will be of primary value to the tourist business. Whether or not this will bring more revenue than would feeder roads from farm to market remains to be seen.

The reviving agriculture was given a serious blow by the corn shortage of 1954-55, when production fell short of demand. After a second shortage appeared in 1955-56, the United States shipped corn to Guatemala. Guatemala's usual eight to ten million hundredweight of corn production was drastically down, just at a time when the ten million hundredweight demand was increasing with the 3 percent annual population rise. U. S. corn shipments began arriving on March 25, 1956, and were valued at $2,500,000. This was financed from the $15,000,000 in economic aid appropriated by the United States, including $5,000,000 earmarked for scarce commodities. Despite individual problems and setbacks, the key to Guatemalan agricultural wellbeing lay in the $250,000,000 economic development program mentioned above. Its five-year aim—roadbuilding, communications, public health, electrification—was well set forth. The major question was that of financing. Organs of international cooperation loaned $32,400,000, and the U. S. committed itself to $21,400,000 for further road construction. The remaining 75 percent was to be financed by internal income. Whether this can be done is an important question for Guatemala.

Foreign investors are discovering a "new deal" in Guatemala with the expulsion of the Arbenz regime. President Castillo promptly offered friendship to foreign investors. UFCO's Pacific division, Compañía Agricola de Guatemala, relinquished its claims on the hundred thousand acres seized by the Communists, receiving in return a promise of non-discriminatory legal treatment. "The best pattern for the future is for our farmers to take over the land and grow the bananas for themselves, with the big companies selling them insecticides and fertilizer and giving them advice."[39]   These words of Castillo probably were received with less than enthusiasm by UFCO officials, but they were pleased to be receiving reasonable treatment once more after years of official opposition. Further negotiations were completed in spring of 1956.   While offering 120,000 acres of holdings near the mouth of the Motagua River to the government, UFCO agreed to pay a tax of 30 percent of its annual profits from the Atlantic division.   This was almost identical to the understanding reached earlier by the Pacific division.   The new contract, which immediately went into effect, is to last until 1981.   The old contract, of course, stated that UFCO paid no tax or duty other than two cents on each bunch of exported bananas plus a fourteen thousand dollar annual fee for land rental.

Business with other important foreign investors was pursued at great length.   Negotiations extended well through 1956 between the government and International Railways of Central America, as well as Empresa Eléctrica de Guatemala.   The talks with the railroad sought modification of complicated existing laws, combining and condensing into a new bill. The highly confidential talks neared agreement very slowly, due in part to a dispute over several million dollars in tax cases.   Final agreement was a compromise of conflicting views.

Of most immediate importance to Guatemala was the discussion with Empresa Eléctrica.   Like other Central American countries, Guatemala is sorely in need of additional electric power.   Empresa, a subsidiary of American and Foreign Power Company, has been negotiating with the government since December, 1954.   Supplying the central zone of Guatemala with power, it offered to invest over sixteen million dollars in expanding its capacity from the present 21,000 kilowatts.   An estimated 30,000 kilowatts are now needed.   Guatemala, impressed by the Salvadoran electrical system and plant recently put into operation, insisted on increased investment.   Empresa reportedly has been willing to include a thirty million dollar plan to expand generating capacity and install the first Central American nuclear power plant in 1959.   But no definite agreement has yet been reached, despite long months of discussion.

A final but very important step was revision of existing petroleum laws, which discouraged foreign investors from the initial outlay of bringing in equipment and personnel to pioneer Guatemalan oil fields.   Castillo decreed all Guatemala open to exploration by reputable firms. Relying upon expert technical advice, he employed a team of Venezuelan technicians who recommended the measures adopted. This temporary decree was replaced in July, 1955, with passage of a new petroleum law requiring fifty-fifty profit sharing between the exporter and Guatemala. Bids were accepted to begin operations. Ninety-two separate applications reached the government, with twenty-nine different companies asking concessions for exploration. These included California Standard, the Texas Company, Standard Oil, Sun Oil, Atlas Petroleum Company, and Central American Oil and Mining Company. With an application fee of five hundred dollars, the government received $46,000 before granting a single concession. Applications are now under study by government officials and foreign technical advisers.

Castillo, when asked if he thought oil would answer all Guatemala's economic problems, said: "Oil is a potential wealth whose exploitation could result in new sources of well being for the country. Nevertheless, the answer to all of Guatemala's problems lies in a plan of development. . . . The government, concerned with promoting adequate and sane exploitation of all natural resources, gave special importance to the possible exploration and subsequent exploitation of oil. With this in mind, it formulated the Petroleum Code, which adequately guarantees the interest of the state, of private citizens, and of the petroleum industry."[40]

Return to Crisis

As Castillo's presidential term lengthened, doubts increased about his government's orientation. Abroad he was still admired as the doughty communist-fighter he was. Various errors in judgment or undemocratic actions were viewed as those of an inexperienced politician. Born in Santa Lucia Cotzumalguapa on November 4, 1914, he entered the military academy in the capital, began his army career, later serving as commandant of the school during the Arévalo administration. Strongly opposed to that and the following regime, Castillo had administrative experience only as the commandant. Extremely soft-spoken, Castillo was moderate to the point of mildness. But he could be an unrelenting individual when aroused. Undemocratic leanings showed themselves on several occasions. Legal suggestions of dictatorship were written into the new constitution in early 1956. Article 77 guaranteed civil rights except "in the case of activities against the security of the state, perturbation of the peace, public calamity or invasion." This law categorized five different emergencies. All could be declared by presidential decree except the most severe—total war—which required legislative approval. Thus, on any pretext, the president could suspend writs of habeus corpus, impose press censorship, instruct police to fire on demonstrators, and outlaw all political parties.

Early in his regime Castillo had used a secret National Defense Committee Against Communism to help root out remaining Reds and arbencistas. This group, given power to search homes and make wholesale arrests without a warrant, ranged far and wide over the countryside for months. Its operations were not unlike the Ku Klux Klan. Gradually, the jails filled. Castillo, alleging that he needed such an organization to uproot communism, nevertheless was persuaded to relent, largely because of the practical reason that jails were overflowing. Some forty-five hundred vigilante victims went free. For a long time, criticism was light. After passage of the Law of Public Order, for example, which made a crime of "speaking ill of the President," *Prensa Libre* editorialized that "an unpopular government could use the law to maintain itself. . . . This law looks like it had been written by Generalissimo Trujillo. . . ." At the same time, Castillo was not criticized directly, for he was a "tolerant man, but let us remember that we are legislating not only for now but for the future as well—and the future may bring a capricious or oppressive President."

A sudden outburst in June, 1956, re-aroused doubts as to government orientation. Guatemalan students were involved, and trouble started on May 1, Guatemalan Labor Day, when three law students grabbed the microphone at a labor gathering and turned it into an anti-government demonstration. The government looked askance and prepared for the next national celebration—that of the fall of Ubico on June 25. A sub-secretary of the Interior Ministry said, "we are waiting for the Communists—we'll show them on June 25." And Mario Lopez Villatoro added that "what happened on May 1 will not happen on June 25."

On Saturday, June 23, pamphlets allegedly published by the leftist National Civic Committee were distributed throughout the capital. There was tension all day. Late Saturday the cabinet met and revoked permission for a student demonstration on Sunday. It declared a state of alarm and suspended thirteen constitutional rights for thirty days. The emergency decree claimed that the Communists were meeting to carry out "actions designed to spread panic and disorder in the country and thus prepare a propitious atmosphere for the development of their subversive intentions." Early Sunday morning a group of students met to begin a parade honoring María Chinchilla, a school teacher instrumental in the 1944 overthrow of General Ubico. Over four hundred students and workers gathered to begin the march to her grave. Police attacked with clubs and rifle butts to disperse the crowd. The entire city was angered by the intervention. José Trinidad Uclés, president of the Asociación de Estudiantes Universitarios (AEU), met with Castillo on Sunday night to protest, but the President gave no satisfactory reply.

Monday, a large group of students assembled at noon to discuss the incident. After a heated meeting it was decided to demand government abrogation of the state of alarm. AEU also decided to go on strike if demands were not met within twenty-four hours. A committee of three withdrew to draft a manifesto. At 7:00 P.M. the students reconvened, approved it, and decided to read the protest in Central Park despite government warnings not to congregate in the streets. A few students were opposed to open defiance of the government, but the majority favored a reading. At 8:18 the meeting adjourned and five hundred students began marching toward Central Park. Despite a police warning that "we will sweep you off the streets by whatever means we have," the students were confident. They marched and sang the national hymn. Students were five blocks from the park on Sixth Avenue when met by police. Witnesses are divided on what happened, but the best knowledge seems to be that police fired on the students without any indication of student violence. Shots fired in the air failed to stop the marchers, and police turned their fire onto the column. Uclés, in the meantime, was foolishly trying to read the manifesto on the street corner. Casualties increased, students dispersed, and the incident was ended. However, one student died on the spot and three others later that night. None were considered Communists. Estimates of the wounded varied from 18 to 27; 168 were arrested and 17 exiled to Honduras in a matter of hours. The latter included Mario Monteforte Toledo, editor of the opposition socialist newspaper *Hoy,* who was accused of writing editorials calculated to "incite sedition and the overthrow of the government."

Monday night the government declared a state of siege, placing Guatemala under martial law for thirty days. Police charged that after the restoration of order, eight revolvers, three hand grenades, and assorted knives were taken from the students. All students denied the charge, blaming the police for opening fire on demonstrators while they marched peacefully, unarmed. The government soon added that in view of communist activities, there was need for "immediate repression with the adoption of severe and drastic measures." The state of siege suspended all constitutional rights, censorship was ordered, and the army established a 6:00 P.M. to 9:00 A.M. curfew. Arrests and expulsions continued through the week. On Wednesday President Castillo stated: "My choice is either to surrender Guatemala again to the Communists or to crush them wherever they raise their heads. I have chosen to hold Guatemala. . . . The state of siege will be maintained to . . . eradicate agitation and complete the capture of those responsible. . . ."[41] Later, student meetings with Castillo brought the release of most imprisoned students. Police involved in the shooting were not, of course, dismissed. Castillo later told interviewers that he "had to choose between allowing chaos or . . . acting rapidly and energetically to guarantee security and life by suffocating this subversive attack."[42]

Briefly, there is little question that AEU was justified in protesting the original beating of students, and later, the arrest of students and suspension of constitutional liberties. It was both foolhardy and illegal to defy the government by marching to Central Park, however. Even so, there was no real justification for police brutality in firing on the marchers. Efforts to justify its position by the government were unsuccessful. The episode was a clear example of a jittery government hopping at the slightest sign of difficulty, then passing it off as a communist plot. Castillo was slowly finding Guatemalans less and less impressed by his cries of communism whenever opposition reared its head. Castillo never realized that the presence of some Communists did not mean they were conspiring under every bed.

The one firm bulwark of support for Castillo throughout all difficulties was the Catholic Church. After some eighty years of anti-clerical rule, the Church was for the first time beginning to enjoy favorable government attitudes. Castillo relied upon it for much of his support. During the Arbenz regime the Church fought the Communists under the leadership of Archbishop Mariano Rossell y Arellano. The Archbishop, a man of "remarkable courage and moral authority who is yet humble and *simpatico*,"[43] led a continual attack against the Communists. When Castillo came to power, Guatemala got a government tolerant of Church activities. Catholic newspapers appeared, deputies were elected to the constituent assembly, and on the first anniversary of liberation Castillo decorated the Archbishop with the Order of the Liberation. There was but one occasion when there was disagreement between the two. In mid-1955, when the "Committee of 17" was drafting the new constitution, Rossell y Arellano wrote asking pre-eminence for the Church. He threatened that the Church would assume a "position of estrangement" if not made the state religion. Castillo called a press conference, announced that such pre-eminence negated democracy, and added that Catholicism was already pre-eminent.

Castillo won his argument. Article 51 of the constitution guaranteed "free exercise of all religions." While this rejected the Catholic position, it at least assured religious freedom. Article 50 preceded it by stating that religious institutions could "acquire and possess properties . . . provided they are devoted exclusively to religious ends. . . ." All this prodded the Catholics into greater activity, and their influence was strong. Most hoped to expand programs of social recovery. To Daniel James, the Church appeared a positive force for progress, as "the State is letting the Church breathe again."[44]

Labor elements began to assert themselves in May, 1957, threatening through their Trade Union Council to stop co-operating with the government. The Council, supported by the ORIT and AFL-CIO, issued a May Day proclamation attacking Castillo's administration: "Conditions in the countryside, in industry, and in commerce are similar only to the anguished times of need we went through before our glorious revolution of October, 1944 . . . unless labor gets back the legitimate gains given to it by the 1944 revolution, we may have to decide upon a recess of all union activities."[45] Three points were criticized. First, the government elimination of a labor code clause permitting re-instatement of workers unjustifiably dismissed—a measure recently enacted—was to be reversed. The Council also asked that the operation of labor courts be speeded up and not oriented toward the government. Finally, decrees barring public employees from organizing and from striking were called "monstrosities" that made the labor struggle "almost untenable."

There was no immediate official reaction, but within a month pro-labor measures were initiated. A minimum-wage law was granted giving the government power to impose minimum wages whenever necessary. Although not invoked at first, it was a sweeping power that later was held over landowners' heads to reduce the continual change of wages. This wage law called for the unionization of farm workers through the Syndical Council of Guatemala. Despite opposition of the General Association of Agriculturists, rural workers thus were organized for the first time. In addition, a long-tabled legislative proposal for increased property taxes was brought back to life, calling for increased taxes on property recently improved by new public works.

By the middle of 1957, Guatemala was beginning to show favorable economic signs for the first time. The accumulated injection of almost $90,000,000 began to be felt. Unemployment was on the decline, investments had increased, and the search for oil was proceeding on an unprecedented level. Roads and buildings were dotting the countryside, and foreign technicians were working for the improvement of agricultural techniques. Bank deposits had reached $100,000,000, and savings were $10,000,000 compared to $3,000,000 only three years earlier. A record high of $129,000,000 was in circulation. The 1957 coffee crop brought over $100,000,000 in extra captial that was promptly poured into new projects. Long-time observers of the Guatemalan scene could not remember such prosperity. Castillo's measures were finally taking hold. Increased political stability was permitting the unprecedented economic progress. Then, in late July, one well-placed bullet upset all calculations.

On the night of July 27, 1957, Castillo and his wife walked down a long corridor in the Presidential Palace toward the dining room. A member of the Presidential Guards, Romeo Vásquez Sánchez, snapped to attention, brought his rifle to his shoulder, and shot the President through the heart. Moments later he shoved the muzzle toward his head and fired into his skull. Castillo already lay dead in the hallway. Vice-President Luis Arturo Gonzalez took office the next morning after a nocturnal session of Congress. The army was called out, troops patrolled the city, and the regime prepared for uprisings or an invasion from abroad. The transition was surprisingly smooth, and there were few incidents to disturb the city. Gonzalez received pledges of support from the armed forces. The next day Castillo lay in state at the National Palace as crowds shoved past the coffin to pay their final respects. Later investigation revealed the assassin to be a fanatic without political connection with either communism or other anti-Castillo elements. But the incendiary nature of Latin politics had claimed another victim. The loss was a costly one. It left a tremendous vacuum, for there were no members of his administration to whom succession was clear. Despite the initial strength of constitutional succession, no one expected acting president Gonzalez to stay in office until 1960. Gonzalez soon announced elections on October 20 to select a new president. Three men entered the race. From government ranks came former Supreme Court Chief Justice Miguel Ortiz, fully supported by the administration as Castillo's heir. Sixty-two-year-old Miguel Ydigoras, a high official under Ubico and losing candidate for president against Arbenz in 1951, was supported by extreme right-wing groups, and staged a vigorous campaign in the outlying areas. His strength was clearly in rural constituencies. The third candidate, Miguel Asturias Quiñónez was entering politics for the first time, and his chances were slim. The left-wing Revolutionary Party had hoped to run his leader, Mario Mendez, but government decrees prevented his participation.

Unofficial returns gave Ortiz a long lead, and he immediately claimed the presidency. The vote was 198,131 to 128,323. Quiñónez was far in arrears. Ydigoras promptly charged fraud and threatened "rivers of blood will flow" if Ortiz took office: "We shall march, people of Guatemala." Ydigoristas and left-wingers marched to the National Palace and demonstrated violently. The government announced a state of siege and sent troops fanning out through the city, but rioters were not to be denied. Several days of continual incidents and rioting followed; on the third day the army stepped into the breach and named Second Vice-President Guillermo Flores Avendaño as chief of state. "The last election is vitiated, because there was no full guarantee to the citizenry of the legitimate exercise of its rights. . . . A new electoral event will normalize the political activities of the country."[46]

New elections were called for January 19, 1958, and government direction during the interim period was not noticeable. Preoccupation was entirely with the forthcoming vote and succession of power. Once more Ydigoras was a candidate, and backed again by conservative and business interests, made a strong bid for votes. Thirty-seven-year-old José Luis Cruz, an original member of the Castillo military junta, and now ambassador to Washington, returned as candidate of a middle-of-the-road coalition that included support of the former Castillo grouping. He promised to continue Castillo policies. The previous agitation over Ortiz, who was only a minor figure, caused the Castillo group to drop him, and he soon faded into the background. The Revolutionary Party was able to enter its leader Mario Mendez as a result of court action setting aside government prohibition of his candidacy. There was considerable doubt as to the influence of communist elements in the party, although non-communist Mendez claimed that his party had purged Red sympathizers.

A close tabulation finally showed Ydigoras the winner with 140,802 votes. Mendez received 98,238 votes, and Cruz 97,668. Despite the clear-cut victory for Ydigoras, he lacked a plurality, and the election was thrust into the legislature where Castillo supporters were expected to return Cruz to office. Amid cries of electoral fraud, observers forecast civil war if Ydigoras was denied office. It is to the credit of Cruz that he instructed members of Castillo's old Movimiento Democrática Nacional to fall in line behind Ydigoras, whose votes had been 41 percent of the total. Cruz and Ydigoras agreed on the need for national unity. On a more practical level, the MDN received several cabinet posts and Cruz was promised another ambassadorial position. The final vote in Congress gave Ydigoras forty votes, Cruz eighteen, while seven were blank.

On Sunday, March 2, 1958, Miguel Ydigoras was sworn in as President by Julio Prado, President of Congress. Ydigoras was pictured by many as a dictatorial type, and many had misgivings. Born in 1898, he became a career officer and, until 1944, never took part in political affairs. After serving as governor of two departments, however, he was forced to resign following the anti-Ubico revolution of 1944, and he remained abroad until 1950, having served as a diplomat in both Washington and London, where he attended the London School of Economics and Political Science. After his 1950 loss to Arbenz, he went into hiding once more. After Castillo took power he was sent to Colombia as ambassador, returning only in August to enter the race precipitated by Castillo's assassination.

Elected primarily with the support of landowners and members of the upper middle classes, he insistently reiterated his belief in democratic methods. Aides claimed that the years in exile had mellowed the man, although in manner he remained curtly precise. After the inauguration he took great pains to dispel fears about autocratic procedures. A trip to the United States was made precisely to assuage doubts about his political orientation. As Guatemala looked forward with very guarded optimism to the days that would follow, Ydigoras asserted his complete dedication to democracy. Whether or not he was sincere was not immediately evident, but in a pre-inauguration "prayer" he addressed Guatemala with a pledge to maintain basic freedoms: "During the recent electoral campaign I was accused often of aspiring to be a dictator. I have always rejected this unjust accusation because what I want most is to rule the country with freedom and respect for the laws."[47] Only the experience of his new government would be able to bear out his statement. Guatemala was waiting for proof.

Chapter Three

EL SALVADOR

NESTLED BETWEEN THE mountains of Honduras and the jungles of Guatemala is El Salvador, smallest and most densely populated of the Central American states. The only republic on the isthmus lacking a Caribbean coast, El Salvador has for some years been the rallying point for supporters of regional union and increased Central American political maturity. Many significant efforts for unification have originated from the small country. Most existing regional organizations make their head-quarters in the capital city, San Salvador. Today, the very offices of the secretary-general of the Organización de Estados Centroamericanos (ODECA) are operating in San Salvador.

While leading the vanguard of regional economic and political co-operation, El Salvador has repeatedly lent its offices in mediation of various regional disputes. Several times in the last chaotic decade, only Salvadoran conciliation has prevented the powderkeg that is Central American politics from exploding. Increasingly, its neighbor republics have turned to it in time of danger for advice or assistance in softening grave situations. The reasoned approach of El Salvador has been the very antithesis of the usual breast-beating Latin volatility.

Yet, paradoxically, Salvadoran internal politics have remained unpredictable. After the last revolution, in 1948, national stability seemed just around the corner. For the next eight years political unrest was at a minimum. And then the 1956 presidential elections evoked once more the familiar picture of an outgoing leader handpicking his successor, handcuffing the opposition, and thus perpetuating the government, though in new and less familiar garb. And the assumption of power by the new chief of state has brought no guarantee of maturing political awareness.

Crowding 2,122,000 people into a nation the size of New Jersey, El Salvador has the densest Central American population at 161.1 per square mile. Relying largely upon the revenue of its coffee exports, it is another one crop country, so typical of the geographic region. Its economic resources, of course, include other products, such as cotton and corn. Small quantities of minerals—primarily gold and silver—are also found. However, as we shall see later, the economic wellbeing of the country is dependent upon coffee; all plans and projects aimed at development are based on this premise. There is no alternative.

Such is the general outline of El Salvador today. Small, populous, a stabilizing influence on regional affairs, this coffee country is faced with a series of national problems, the gravity of which must not be underestimated. At the same time, its future prospects seem as bright as any other Central American republic. Events of recent years suggest an upswing in national fortunes. With enlightened leadership and economic luck, El Salvador may well lead the way for its neighbors, if any are to arrest the backsliding of the last decade.

ECONOMICS—FROM INERTIA TO ACTIVITY

Since 1931, El Salvador has been ruled to varying degrees by military authorities. There have been a few brief governments of pacific and purely civilian orientation, but the army has maintained a sizeable share of power, wielding its influence continually in national affairs. During this time economic development slowed to a standstill. Until the revolution of 1948, these were indeed unproductive years. The man first responsible for this pattern came to power a quarter of a century ago by means of the usual anti-government coup. He was Maximiliano Hernández Martínez, one of the more unusual figures of contemporary Central American politics. Martínez, heading a military government, based his appeal on a continual succession of magical formulas and imaginative impossibilities. Ignoring the educated Salvadorans, he appealed directly to the poverty-stricken peons who, in their ignorance, gave him the support necessary to remain thirteen years in power. Himself a mestizo like most Salvadorans, Martínez became a complete dictator. For thirteen years no Central American country, not even the Guatemala of Jorge Ubico, was dominated so thoroughly by one man. Few were as bloody as Martínez.

A Theosophist, Martínez captured the minds of the peasants in various ways. He devised unheard-of methods of corn planting which fascinated the agricultural workers although growing no more corn. He filled green, yellow, and blue vials with plain water and set them in the sun on the roof of the Presidential Palace. After a period of "aging," these vials became potions guaranteeing relief from rheumatism, heart disease, or dysentery. Before any of his schemes became an obvious failure, the tyrant would concoct a new one, surpassing all the others in captivating the uneducated mind. Called "a Merlin, a wizard," by Germán Arciniegas, the dictator also buttressed his position with control of the military. At opportune moments this burgeoned into bloody suppression. Uprisings were frequent and were dealt with cruelly. He once was quoted as saying "it is a greater crime to kill an ant than a man, for when a man dies he becomes reincarnated, while the ant dies forever." The worst blot on his record is the suppression of a 1932 revolution. Officially, a communist plot by Mexican agents was put down with the loyal support of all patriotic Salvadorans. Actually, poverty-blighted peasants agitated for land reform and were shot by landowners for their trouble. This touched off a general bloodletting in which the government intervened. The most accurate guess estimates nine to twelve thousand were killed as a result of the grisly suppression. Periodically re-elected against token opposition, Martínez had his own way until 1943. Then a young doctor, Arturo Romero, began to organize anti-Martínez forces. A revolution was put down in December, 1943. The fleeing Romero was badly injured by machete wielding border guards unaware of his identity.

Taken to a hospital, Romero became the center of a tug of war. The authorities wanted to keep him, while friends and supporters hoped to free him from virtual imprisonment. By the time Romero was released, the dictator had instituted a policy of execution, hoping to quell increasing opposition. Wide reprisals followed the slightest breach of public order. To critics, he replied, "let my enemies reincarnate when I am dead." In May, 1944, the eccentric dictator was finally forced to resign when a nation-wide strike paralyzed life completely. At first, he relinquished his position to an acquaintance, General Andrés Ignacio Menéndez, retaining a share of power himself. In the subsequent years he lost all support and was exiled.

The next four years found a succession of men passing through the presidency rapidly—a chief justice, a police officer, and a Falangist. In 1948, the army united under the leadership of a four-man "Council of Revolutionary Government" to unseat General Salvador Castañeda Castro. Most of those in positions of influence today in El Salvador were prominent members of this revolutionary group. The four-man junta spent some eighteen months solidifying its position and tempering the national sentiment. In the elections of March 26, 1950, Lieutenant Colonel Oscar Osorio, one of the junta leaders, was placed in the presidency. His election was unopposed. Firmly entrenched and well supported by his party, Osorio initiated what he hopefully called a period of honest reconstruction. At the time, few observers realized how well he might fulfill the prophecy.

Before election, the story of Oscar Osorio was not an exciting one. Like many Salvadorans before and since, he attended the military academy and, upon graduation, began active army service. Advancing through the officer ranks, he succeeded in evading Martínez' sporadic thrusts at opposition within the army. When the military overthrew the existing government in 1948, Osorio was a member of the ruling Council of Revolutionary Government. By the time elections were held, he had asserted his leadership of the Council and ran as the official candidate of the PRUD—Partido Revolucionario de Unificación Demócrata. Opposed by Colonel José Asencio Menéndez, Osorio won by a vote of 345,239 to 266,271. In view of his backing from PRUD and army leaders, the margin of victory was unspectacular.

On assuming the presidency in September, 1950, Osorio set out to remedy pressing national problems, all of them deteriorated by preceding years of inaction. The list of needs was not short. Economic development, power and electrification, highways, housing, national finances, a balance of imports and exports, communist infiltration from Guatemala, and unionism—all these problems confronted Osorio. His immediate and most determined action was directed toward economic development.

El Salvador is decidedly agricultural. Sixty-two percent of the population is rural. Of its different products, none rivals coffee in importance. Eighty to 85 percent of its exports are coffee, and without this the balance of revenues and expenditures would be non-existent. Like other coffee producers, El Salvador shared in the post World War II prosperity as coffee prices climbed to record highs on the international market. At the same time, the quantity of coffee produced remained nearly the same. National coffee growers grew alarmed at the danger of an international price decline, bringing with it decreased income.

Such was the coffee situation when Osorio assumed power. With 71 percent of Salvadoran land under agricultural cultivation, there was little chance of expansion. There was simply no land on which more than the existing 118,800,000 coffee trees could be grown. Under the Coffee Defense Law of 1933, a commission had been established to deal with the industry. Composed of private coffee growers and government officials, the commission had skidded into a trough of inactivity. President Osorio promptly gave new impetus to the commission. Government appointees were instructed to participate in its affairs enthusiastically. Government funds were diverted to bolster the organization and industry financially. United Nations experts were called in to make suggestions, and coffee growing techniques were improved. United Nations assistance was accompanied by further government action. In August, 1954, the Ministry of Agriculture and Cattle announced the study and imminent creation of an Institute of Investigation of Coffee. Designed to regulate and improve coffee production in El Salvador, it was to rely in large part upon suggestions and advice of members of a UN commission. The government announced its intention of putting the Institute in operation by the beginning of 1955. It was actually months later before the Institute opened.

Despite adverse natural phenomena, the coffee industry flourished. The 1952 crop was threatened by a *chacuatete** invasion; fortunately, at the last moment the menace disappeared. The following year, in July, the president of the Central Bank of El Salvador, Luis Alfaro Durán, stated in an interview that the coffee harvest for 1953 would be very poor. With little rain, the coffee plants had flowered prematurely. The only hope for coffee growers was possible compensation from high international coffee prices—if they didn't fall. In late September, just when the rainy season usually ends, the country was hit by a violent, prolonged storm. Highways, railroads, and telegraph lines were damaged. The rains, continuing in early October, raised rivers to a dangerous level. Many coffee fields were inundated. Winds were clocked as high as seventy miles per hour. Strangely, financial damage was slight. The inflated international coffee prices held steady, and coffee growers suffered little.

Notwithstanding flooded fields, the harvest in 1954 was larger than

* A disease destroying coffee plants, ruining a year's output entirely.

ever. On July 21, 1954, the Dirección General de Estadísticas y Censos de El Salvador announced that the annual volume of coffee harvested was up. Volume for the 1954-55 crop was estimated at 1,600,000 quintales† of 46 kilos, as compared with 1,200,000 quintales in 1953-54. The percentage increase was over 30 percent in the west, 20 percent in the east. Even in the central regions, where the 1953 rains had been most severe, there was a 5 percent increase. And this estimate proved substantially correct, despite the Brazilian coffee crisis at the end of the year which slightly reduced the anticipated volume of sales. All these efforts—both government and UN oriented—produced gratifying results. In 1953, El Salvador sent 134,741,334 pounds of coffee to the United States with a value of $64,367,828. By 1955, the net quantity was 174,900,000 pounds, valued at some $83,549,730. This was a financial increase of about 30 percent in less than three years.

The susceptibility of the national economy to fluctuation in international prices remained great, however. On November 30, 1954, Foreign Minister Roberto E. Canessa explained the position of the coffee producers at the convention of the National Coffee Association in Boco Raton, Florida. North Americans must realize, he noted, "that the coffee growing investor, even after risking his capital for five years, has to take still more risks in order to obtain superproduction of his product. . . . When you undertake a campaign to lower the price of coffee [in the United States], what you are doing is limiting, in effect, North American exports to Latin America."[1] Without the revenue of profitable coffee production, a country like El Salvador lacks the basic capital to deal significantly with North American business.

Apprehensive of the obvious dangers of a one-crop economy, the Osorio administration sought diversification of agriculture. Aided by abundant low-cost labor and low production costs, other products were encouraged. Corn became the second agricultural product after coffee. Sugar increased in importance, with several refineries devoted to the preparation of sugar for local consumption. At the same time, a United Nations commission studied means of improving the economy. On December 10, 1952, the head of the UN commission recommended limited industrialization as the best means of elevating the economy. Dr. Bertrand F. Hoselitz, of the University of Chicago, announced that development of Salvadoran industry was feasible, notably in the field of

† A quintal is the Latin equivalent of a hundred-weight.

textiles and construction materials. There were two principal elements, as he saw it. First, "the introduction of more efficient methods of production and the use and distribution of available resources." Second, promotion of the "highest possible grade of integration and economic collaboration with other Central American countries," permitting a regional division of labor. Gradual expansion of the tourist industry and economic direction by the government were added possibilities for development.

Six weeks later in New York City, Dr. W. J. Feuerlein, chief of the Auxiliary Technical Aid organization of the United Nations in El Salvador, also advised industrialization as the key to higher living conditions. Noting the agricultural predominance in the economy, he said that even highly increased agricultural production would be insufficient for the needs of the republic, "there is simply not enough land for the size of the population." The very size of the population, he felt, was large enough to contribute effectively to industry. With mineral resources limited, the emphasis would be on light industry—general textiles, kitchen utensils, and construction materials. He concluded that while the mission of his group would end in March, several members would remain to help carry out recommendations.

One of the administration's responses was a concerted effort to create a domestic market for coffee bags. For years a small local factory had manufactured these bags, almost all of which were sent abroad. The government built an addition to the factory and urged national coffee producers to use local coffee bags exclusively. Employing over four hundred nationals permanently, and others on a part-time basis, the factory has now increased its production to well over 1,200,000 bags annually.

Over a year later, in July, 1954, the government reached an agreement with the United States giving additional propulsion to its program of increased productivity. This agreement established a cooperative program of productivity through which El Salvador would develop its resources of industrial production. Interchange of technicians, trainees, and experts would presumably help raise Salvadoran knowledge of industrial and productive techniques. The United States agreed to give technical aid in the study and planning of additional factories as well as selection of machines and training for its maintenance. The program also established a center of industrial production to serve as an organ of the Salvadoran government, with authority over the administration program of productivity on a cooperative basis.

To further rural living conditions and public health, the Osorio administration proposed on February 18, 1953, the founding of a rural credit bank. This proposal, after months of study by the government, was presented with the strong support and personal encouragement of President Osorio. In announcing the projected bank, Minister of Economy Jorge Sol Castellano attacked the problem of rural conditions. The Rural Credit Bank was to work in collaboration with the national Central Reserve Bank, operating with an initial capital of five million dollars. Through financial and technical assistance, it hoped to promote rural production and related agricultural efforts, with particular attention to the individual small scale farmer. While the Bank was being organized, Sol Castellanos formed advisory committees for small industries, including the soap, shoe, cigar, and hat factories. These groups worked closely with manufacturers to stabilize national prices, strengthen economic stability, and raise the public standard of living.

Beyond the rural credit bank, the most highly publicized economic plank of the Osorio administration's development drive was the Program of Economic Development and Social Wellbeing. Proclaimed shortly after Osorio's inauguration, it decreed the establishment of the Salvadoran Institute for the Promotion of Production. The autonomous organ channeled public and private efforts toward greater national riches, in hopes of building a more efficient production in accord with the country's needs. The new Institute was to promote activities in the fields of agriculture, mining, and fishing. A small investment bank, subsidiary to the Institute, was set up to promote national investment. It began with three and one half million colones capital (approximately $1,400,000), and was progressively augmented by the government as new circumstances required. The Institute had full liberty in its operations, for its founding law granted complete autonomy. The Directive Council, entrusted with administration of the Institute, was composed of both public and private figures. The Program of Economic Development also outlined plans to increase the Salvadoran fishing industry, surprisingly important to the economy in view of the short, 160-mile Pacific coast. The government, supporting the industry earnestly, developed a series of technical studies to determine the true potential of fishing in Salvadoran coastal waters. Forms of fish cooperatives were also studied by members of the Ministry of Labor and Social Progress. An impractical plan of increasing the importance of fish to the national diet was short-lived.

The third project outlined by the Program was national tourism. A Junta Nacional de Turismo was created under the Ministry of Economy, with a view to improving facilities and disseminating tourist information, particularly in the United States. The success of this program is highly suspect. The same obstacles are faced by other tourist institutes. Costa Rica has found its institute unsuccessful. However, in the absence of extensive Indian ruins or natural wonders other than Izalco Volcano, the tourist organization hopes to publicize El Salvador's attractions as quiet, out of the way rest spots which are undisturbed by the usual effects of heavy tourist onslaughts, as in Mexico. New parks and improved highways are being planned.

The three H's—health, housing, and highways—were also attacked by the Osorio program. Prospects for improved public health were encouraged with the January, 1945, announcement of plans to construct a National Medical Center in San Salvador. It was planned by the Corporación de Alojamientos, a branch of the IBEC (International Basic Economy Corporation) in New York City. The IBEC was in turn a branch of Casa Rockefeller, receiving its funds from the Rockefeller source. The Corporación planned the buildings and arranged technical aid. At this writing, the National Medical Center is reaching completion. Designed to control 40 percent of all medical cases in the country, it has a Central Hospital building of nine stories, with adjacent, smaller structures housing research and administrative personnel. The cost was amortized over a six year period by an issue of government bonds valued at three million colones.

Housing was one of the more highly vaunted Osorio projects. In September, 1953, the government launched a bond issue of eleven million colones to finance construction of housing in Valle La Esperanza, an area destroyed in May, 1951, by an earthquake. Further low-cost housing eventually followed, although its significance was exaggerated by government spokesmen. Housing at different times was shunted aside in deference to other plans. Many of the buildings erected were temporary prefabrications, and others never left the drafting board.

Highway construction was a major part of Osorio's plan of economic development. Despite the fact that the Salvadoran road net was, and still is, the best in Central America, with over two thousand miles of roads crisscrossing the tiny republic, construction continued on new routes. The countryside was linked more closely to the markets of San Salvador, Santa Ana, San Miguel, and smaller business centers. At the same time, the Inter American Highway, in large part only a dirt road south of the capital, was improved and surfaced. By mid-1956, only a few miles north of the Honduran border remained unsurfaced. The highway in the north, deteriorating from years of usage without repair, was also re-patched in many places.

If any one work will in future years be identified with the Osorio government, that will be the power dam and plant on the Lempa River. This was, above all else, the outstanding material contribution of President Osorio. National power in El Salvador had been supplied, since 1890, by the Compañia de Alumbrado Eléctrico, one of the oldest power companies in Central America. Its first power station, Agua Caliente, was set up near San Salvador, with 70 horsepower. It was increased through the years and, by the close of World War II, was equipped with four diesel electric units with a capacity of 2,000 kilowatts. Nonetheless, this was inadequate for postwar El Salvador; electrical needs increasingly out-stripped production of the old system.

In 1950, faced with this crisis of electric energy, the government initiated the construction of a new power plant on the unnavigable Lempa River, the main Salvadoran water artery. Some thirty-five miles northeast of San Salvador, a two-hundred-foot dam was erected, flooding nearby lands to create an artificial lake of twenty square kilometers, with a capacity of four hundred million cubic meters of water. The volume of lake water thus would permit a reasonable and controllable level in the Lempa River. This project was drawn up and administered by the Comisión Ejecutiva Hidroeléctrica del Río Lempa (CEL), an autonomous organ. The contract was let to the U. S. construction firm of J. A. Jones. This plant, "La Chorrero del Guayabo," was wisely planned so that it could be put into operation as soon as possible—the end of 1953—with a capacity of 30,000 kilowatts. This would later be increased to 45,000, and eventually 75,000 kilowatts. With the total cost estimated at twenty million dollars, the government promptly went to the International Bank for Reconstruction and Development, of which El Salvador is a member. It was granted a loan of $12,545,000. This was supplemented by a bond issue as well as a new government internal loan of two million dollars.

The expected 1953 opening was delayed, and the main turbine and generator were not in service until the summer of 1954. On June 19, 1954, President Osorio inaugurated the plant amid sirens, whistles, horns, and the cheers of a large crowd. Additional generators and another turbine were being completed in Switzerland and, in 1956, three more generators were added, increasing the capacity to 45,000 kilowatts.

At the same time, the CEL extended its plans. Sub-stations were constructed in San Miguel and San Rafael Carlos. An irrigation project was initiated with the use of waters in the lower Lempa, with vast coastal extensions continually increasing its production. And outside the CEL, the Compañia de Alumbrado Eléctrica developed its own construction program. In the fall of 1955, a new distribution circuit of 22,000 volts was completed around San Salvador. It was based on four modern automatic sub-stations, one of which, with 10,000 kilovolt-amperes, is the largest of its kind in Central America. In eastern El Salvador, the Compañia Eléctrica de Oriente also expanded its services, on a smaller scale. The result of these prolonged efforts for increased power and electrification has been the most thorough power system in Central America; with the plant at La Chorrero del Guayabo soon to reach its 75,000 kilowatt capacity, the national power problem is a thing of the past. With no serious power shortage, extensive electrical service is possible, and irrigation and flood projects are progressing.

The sum total of these economic plans is reflected, at least in part, by the national financial status. This gives additional testimony to the inherent soundness of the Osorio economic policies. Assisted by bumper coffee crops, exports in recent years have exceeded imports, assuring a flow of capital into the country. At the same time, the various measures of economic policy contributed to an upward trend in the value of international trade. In 1948, with the country badly battered economically and spiritually from a series of political upheavals, imports were valued at $41,496,731, with exports at $43,605,876. Six years later, figures showed increases of over 100 percent. Imports had reached $86,720,000; exports shot to $104,920,000. The external and internal debts, both of which had been on the rise, were checked and held steady. At the start of 1955, the external debt was $7,522,000, redeemed at $800,000 annually. The internal debt was $3,837,000. Added revenue from exports permitted the government to increase its expenditures each year, devoting more and more money to national improvements. The revenue and expenditures almost tripled from 1948 to 1955, with very little disparity between the two. During most years expenditures slightly exceeded revenue, but never enough to create a serious financial situation. The budget was fully balanced in 1954, and the 1955 estimate revealed only a minor discrepancy: revenues $62,212,774, expenditures $65,100,000.

A corollary to recent financial soundness is the impressive growth of the money supply. The last twenty years have shown an eight-fold increase, and much of this has come in the last decade, despite international trade uncertainties. Considering the end of December, 1949, as par of 100, the supply had risen to 172 by 1953, and today is some 35 to 40 points higher. In 1945, it was barely 45. On the basis of such data, Dr. Enrique A. Porras, Minister of the Treasury, announced on October 31, 1955, that the Salvadoran financial situation was in excellent condition: commercial balance healthy, revenue up, trade increasing, and money supply growing.

COMMUNISM THREATENS

In the midst of this expansion and development, El Salvador found itself confronted by a communist problem of serious proportions. Due to the successful Red infiltration of neighboring Guatemala, Osorio himself spent valuable time fighting the Communists. His success is ample testimony to his anti-communist orientation.

Many people forget that El Salvador and not Guatemala was the first Central American victim of attempted Red revolution. In 1932, the Salvadoran communist party, then the strongest in Central America, tried to organize the peasant revolt mentioned earlier and use it for their own ends. Dictator Martínez suppressed it ruthlessly, but the first overt Red action in the region had been made, and suggested future possibilities. Captured documents referred to a "Revolutionary Military Committee," calling for the formation of workers' and farmers' cells. In January, 1932, an order from the "General Headquarters of the Red Army of El Salvador" was issued urging peasants, workers, and soldiers to revolt and seize power. Bolshevik in operation, the Red attempt was a dismal failure, and literally thousands were shot down or executed, including many innocent victims of reprisals. But the lesson of this failure was the inapplicability of bolshevik patterns in a Latin framework, and this they were careful to remember in the subsequent Guatemalan interlude.

When the Red-tinged Arbenz government took power in Guatemala, in 1951, many former Salvadoran Communists established a Guatemalan base while creating the nucleus of a new organization in El Salvador.

Agents, propaganda, and money crossed the border illegally. In Guatemala City, the pro-government press continually attacked the Osorio administration, maintaining a steady barrage in support of growing subversive elements in El Salvador. By September, 1952, relations were so bad that President Osorio met Arbenz at the border. Arriving shortly before noon, the impeccably clad Arbenz was accompanied by the President of Congress, the U. S. Ambassador, and minor officials. Osorio, in a plain, tieless military uniform, included in his party the Ambassador to Guatemala, Lieutenant Colonel Funes, and the U. S. Ambassador to El Salvador. The two presidents exchanged a hearty *abrazo* and the short meeting was generally friendly. In both capitals, wide attention was given to the supposedly symbolic gesture of friendship, the *abrazo*. Newspapers published pictures of the scene and editorialized that relations were again on an even keel. Yet Ambassador Funes pointed out, on returning to Guatemala City, that his president had gone to the meeting for one reason, "to make it perfectly clear to Arbenz that El Salvador intends to use every weapon available to combat communist infiltration."[2]

Less than a week later, Osorio uncovered a communist plot in El Salvador. On September 26, 1952, he placed the republic under a thirty-day state of siege. Justifying the declaration as necessary to control the communist movement, he took painstaking precautions to check Red activities. In his decree to the National Assembly, he stated his purpose was "to counteract the infiltration of the Communists and other activities to the left." The border to Guatemala was sealed. On the twenty-seventh, the government announced the capture of Captain José Napoleon Ortiz, lawyer Armando Calderón, and two cadets, charging them with leadership of a revolutionary plot. Osorio explained that the plot had been discovered a week earlier, before the meeting with Arbenz. Whether or not this was discussed is unknown. In any event, the Osorio government continued the anti-communist crackdown. The police located several different caches of arms, most of which had been smuggled across the border from Guatemala. Osorio accused local Reds of building homemade bombs "with the object of terrorizing the people and endangering the future of the country." Written plans were uncovered revealing a communist created disorder to be led by local terrorists. Once there was lack of confidence in the government, the Reds hoped to lead a "popular" uprising. All in all, some twelve hundred Communists and assorted unsavory persons were rounded up.

Relations continued to be strained. In October, the communist-dominated Workers' Syndicate in Guatemala presumptiously announced that the entire Guatemalan working class was united against the Osorio government. It condemned Osorio for his Fascist treatment of the workers of El Salvador, treatment initiated with the object of destroying the democratic labor movement in that country. In January, the Communists plotted the assassination of Foreign Minister Roberto E. Canessa, an ardent Central American unionist and bitter anti-Communist. There was never any official comment on the attempt, but on Wednesday, January 28, the San Salvadoran daily *La Nación* headlined the plot, revealing that it had been discovered by the police, who jailed several conspirators. The paper reproduced a statement of the chief criminal investigator saying that the plot was a result of Canessa's anti-communist activities. The government never contradicted the investigator's statement. It was later revealed that three Guatemalans, a Costa Rican, and a Czechoslovak adventurer had entered the country illegally to ambush Canessa, but were apprehended before the attempt.

At the same time, the government initiated anti-communist legislation to restrict subversive activities. On November 27, 1952, the National Assembly promulgated a law, effective December 13, declaring any person propagating "totalitarian or communist doctrines" punishable by imprisonment. Supplementary offenses, such as actions "contrary to democratic principles," were also punishable by prison terms, ranging from three to seven years.

As the communist designs became more evident in Guatemala, her neighbor became increasingly embroiled in the situation. On April 22, 1953, the Salvadoran government submitted a message to the Secretary-General of the Organization of American States (OAS), Colombia's distinguished Alberto Lleras Camargo. They asked him to put before the Council of the OAS a recent exchange of notes. Guatemala, said Carlos A. Siri, the Salvadoran representative,

has complained of a campaign of defamation and calumny against it from El Salvador. El Salvador denies the charges and demands an investigation of Communist activities in Central America by the OAS. My Government hopes that the Government of Guatemala, after examining calmly and un-excitedly the refutation of its charge on the part of El Salvador, and of the other Republics affected, will reconsider and will rectify its attitude. Nevertheless, before the controversy before us can become one of international concern, acquiring a graver aspect . . . my Government believes the possibility exists, in the future, of invoking the pertinent parts of the charter of the OAS. . . .[3]

The charges were laid before the Council in its session of April 29, but it recommended bilateral action between the two governments, and then, if no satisfaction was forthcoming, a return to the OAS for reconsideration. As it developed, tension continued, in varying degrees, until the fall of the Guatemalan regime in June, 1954. Osorio remained on guard against subversion from Guatemalan communist agents.

Testimony to Osorio's militant anti-communism came from Angier Biddle Duke in June, 1954. Duke, returning to the United States after serving as ambassador in San Salvador, cited the nation as one taking "positive action" against the blandishments of communism. In describing the Osorio course of action, he said that it "is based on a frank program of true social progress and already [is] well along the road to making itself a small nation's example of democracy in action."[4] President Osorio remained quick to purge questionable elements from his own government as well. December 29, 1953, *Impacto* released the news that Salvadoran Chief of Staff Colonel Oscar Adan Bolanos, a long-time leader of PRUD, was dismissed due to a friendly attitude toward the Arbenz government and prolonged flirtation with the Guatemalan communist party. In such cases, Osorio responded with prompt if somewhat peremptory action.

Policy toward Guatemala remained unchanged until the downfall of Arbenz in 1954. Despite his scorn for their system of government, plus repeated provocations from Guatemala-directed conspiracies, Osorio pursued a course of scrupulous neutrality and non-intervention. We have seen elsewhere that both the Nicaraguan and Honduran governments cooperated openly with the rebels of Colonel Castillo, before the revolutionary invasion of Guatemala. Yet Osorio refused to play a part. He repeatedly rejected overtures from Castillo and suggestions from Nicaragua's Somoza to let Castillo launch his revolt from Salvadoran territory. There were good reasons for this. In the first place, El Salvador's well-trained army was and is small, composed of three thousand men. The air force consists of a bare handful of obsolete, prop-driven planes. Unlike Nicaragua and Honduras, it had not signed a treaty of military cooperation and assistance with the United States. As Osorio commented, this would have put a severe strain on the budget, which was oriented toward public works, the dam on the Lempa, and other construction projects. Osorio preferred to rely upon the good offices of the Organization of American States should the Guatemalans launch an attack.

At the same time, Osorio was convinced that the proper role of El Salvador was to remain aloof from the internal affairs of Guatemala. Obviously, this was legalistically correct under tenets of international law. And, as Osorio privately commented, he was convinced of the inherent instability of the Arbenz regime, preferring to disassociate his own government from its difficulties. This was in keeping with the traditional Salvadoran role of Central American mediator and advocate of regional union.

On May 27, 1954, barely two weeks before the end of the Arbenz government, Osorio told the Associated Press that the slightest spark could start a wave of violence engulfing the entire isthmus, although no Central American country wanted war. He related with quiet pride that Salvadoran relations with Guatemala were unchanged. Communists were not infiltrating, and there was no cause for alarm. He significantly declined to say that Guatemalan-based communism was no longer agitating in other American republics. After Castillo came to power in Guatemala, relations were correct but noticeably frigid. Castillo remembered Osorio's denial of Salvadoran territory to prepare his invasion. However, with the passing of time, he came to appreciate Osorio's position and reasonably cordial relations developed. Castillo and Osorio held several personal interviews. As late as November 5, 1955, the two issued a joint bulletin reviving the idea of a meeting of Central American presidents within the framework of the Central American Union (ODECA). While no such meeting was forthcoming, it was added evidence of the good relations between Guatemala and El Salvador.

Since the downfall of the Red government in Guatemala, communism has not disturbed the Salvadoran pattern of affairs. At present there is no evidence of a resurgence. The orientation of Osorio's successor, Colonel José María Lemus, seems strongly anti-communist. However, El Salvador presents a possible field for future Red exploitation. The Guatemalan case history shows how workers' organizations and national unions provide the Communists with an opportunity to entrench within society. This can scarcely be overemphasized.

Again and again it must be repeated that the underdeveloped, ignorant, poorly-organized ranks of laborers and rural workers in Central America are an excellent field for subversive organization and operation. The population density of El Salvador makes it an especially inviting target for Red agitation. In the 1940's, directors of the Rerum Novarum, then the leading Costa Rican labor organization, tried to direct and control Salvadoran labor. Their efforts went unrewarded. In 1948, a representative of the Confederación Internacional de Trabajadores (CIT) visited El Salvador and, at the end of his visit, reported, "the future danger lies in the fact that the working class, inexperienced in politics and confused as it is today, might believe in the communist leaders."

Labor organization was never constitutionally recognized until the ruling junta in 1949-50 drew up a new constitution. A supplementary decree in August of 1950 permitted formation of trade unions, with the exception of agricultural workers and those in seasonal labor such as sugar refining and coffee milling. The elective trade union posts could not be filled by foreigners. In October, 1951, the first labor convention in the history of the republic was convened in the capital. It announced that "El Salvador must adopt a position consonant with the [UN] Declaration of the Rights of Man. . . . Both totalitarian systems of the extreme left and those of the extreme right must be eschewed. . . . And as a patriotic ideal the hope of a Central American Union must be maintained. . . ."[5] Salvadoran unionism and labor organization is still in its infancy. The government has not devoted itself with much interest to the problem, and thus far there has been little cause. The agricultural workers remain generally independent of organization, and play no role in political affairs. Yet, as the succeeding years bring advancement of labor, the existing authorities will need to bear in mind the tragic consequences of ignoring the workers. Guatemala provides a vivid reminder.

POLITICS WITH PRUD

After his electoral victory in 1950, Oscar Osorio devoted his administration increasingly to matters beyond internal politics. However, he never forgot the fact that he was head of PRUD, the Partido Revolucionario de Unificación Demócrata. The former revolutionary movement, now engaged in running the government, was confronted only by ineffective opposition during the Osorio administration. When the 1956 presidential elections were held, as we shall see, all the candidates were or at one time had been influential members both of the government and of PRUD. In the earliest years of the Osorio presidency, the memory of recent revolution was fresh, and opposition was negligible. The new constitution, promulgated by Osorio when inaugurated in September, 1950, mentioned no restrictions on political opposition. And for the time being, there was almost none.

The first elections after Osorio's administration were the congressional contests of 1952. The dominant note was apathy. This was to become the pattern of subsequent elections. On May 12, the three-day balloting began, supervised by the Consejo Central de Elecciones which, true to tradition, was controlled by the government. The night before, the opposition parties withdrew their candidates en masse, accusing Osorio of having rigged the elections in the interests of retaining total legislative command. Amidst complete calm, some 280,000 of a possible 700,000 voted. (Women had received complete suffrage for the first time.) All fifty-four deputies of the National Assembly were members of PRUD or friendly toward it. The opposition promptly hailed the results as proof of their claims.

Two years later, the congressional elections followed an identical pattern. No candidates were entered in opposition to the fifty-four-man PRUD slate. The director of the Acción Renovada published a manifesto on March 22, 1954, explaining his party's non-participation. "The electoral laws and those in defense of the democratic and constitutional order now in effect, for the free and honest electoral exercises . . . will not be present at this election. . . . The right to respect determination and to adjust the public and private conduct to the postulates of decency and the exercise of civic duties is . . . ignored." He concluded with the hope that "the Salvadoran people before too long will have the opportunity of going to the electoral urns to select from among the popular candidates the officials they deserve."[6] With this widely published abstention a contributing factor, the public again reacted with apathy. On May 5, 1954, San Salvador's *Diario de Hoy* wrote that the elections, completed without disturbances, had only 631,390 of a possible 1,047,358 voting. By Latin standards, less than 70 percent participation is an indication of strong voter apathy, whether or not voting is compulsory.

Preparations for the presidential elections of March, 1956, began a year before the actual voting. Roberto E. Canessa, Osorio's foreign minister for almost five years, had resigned after a series of differences with the president. Early in 1955 he unofficially launched his campaign, although no public announcement was made. On March 10, 1955, PRUD held its national convention with several thousand delegates present. After a day-long discussion and a series of speeches, Minister of the Interior José María Lemus was selected as official candidate. A month later, at an all-night meeting of party leaders, with Osorio presiding, the candidacy of Lemus was accepted, after Osorio and others overrode objections of a small minority.

Almost at once the papers began to trumpet Lemus' candidacy. Even before his July resignation, the Minister of the Interior was enthusiastically discussed by several San Salvador dailies and, in two instances, received prompt endorsement. Canessa raised a cry of press censorship and of a paid press. Two other candidates entered the race in June—ex-ambassador to Guatemala Colonel José Alberto Funes, and army Inspector-General Colonel Rafael Carranza. Both joined the attack on press partisanship.

On June 7, speaking appropriately enough on Freedom of the Press Day, Osorio declared, "Freedom of the press means the development of one of the first constitutional maxims that we defend. With satisfaction I declare that while my government, in different situations, may be alleged to curtail personal liberties . . . it never curbs freedom of expression. We have maintained and will continue to maintain freedom of the press in spite of its activities, hoping that it will improve with maturity and experience."[7] Most impartial observers felt that the government was not actively pressuring the press into support of Lemus' candidacy. At the same time, several of the newspaper directors may have felt it more prudent to back the government choice. In any event, the fact that Lemus was the PRUD candidate undoubtedly seems to have been an important factor.

Attention was temporarily diverted from the campaign activities with the unexpected return to the capital of ex-dictator Martínez, who, after his fall in 1944, had spent succeeding years in Honduran exile. Now ailing, he had reportedly been advised to seek special medical treatment in Boston. Instead, he grandiloquently announced his intention of returning home: "I want to die in El Salvador." After arriving in San Salvador on July 8, he found his return had initiated formal charges in the National Assembly accusing him of executing twelve military leaders and various civilians during his last days of power. The populace was more aroused over Martínez' return than any aspect of the election campaign. The great majority, remembering only too well his thirteen years of despotism, demanded punishment for past misdeeds. As the

Assembly was completing its charges against him, the seventy-three-year-old ex-dictator flew to the United States. In New Orleans, he announced that his departure was for medical treatment. Granting that few would believe him, he insisted nonetheless that he would return home after treatment for ulcers. He did not.

The rest of 1955 brought sporadic and coldly received campaigning on the part of the candidates—Lemus, Canessa, Funes, and Carranza. In July, Dr. José María Peralta Salazar, PRUD President of the National Assembly, asked for a commission to study the electoral law, with a view to reforming it in response to constant criticism. The only positive result was a proposal, eventually, accepted, that the presidential and vice-presidential elections be verified the same day. Previously, verification of the Central Election Council had been a two-day task.

El Salvador grew increasingly jittery as the election approached. In mid-January 1956, *Time* reported that the presidential press secretary had issued a bulletin denying a revolution, a rumor resulting from army target practice in San Salvador one morning. Imperturbable Osorio was troubled to the point of clamping censorship on outgoing press reports. Rumors flew about San Salvador, and the capital gossiped of possible revolution, government graft, personal dishonesty, and the morals of the candidates.

As Osorio's handpicked candidate, forty-five-year-old Lemus had the undivided support of PRUD finances and its well-greased political apparatus. Opponents charged him with spending upwards of $100,000 a month, largely from government funds. "My supporters cheer me everywhere," he said. "Peasants want to touch me and hug me, and some even spit on me for good luck. A presidential candidate here can't be squeamish."[8] The author, traveling through El Salvador at the time, saw countless slogans, "Vota Lemus," painted on the paved highways. Large billboards advertised "Hoy Osorio, Mañana Lemus"—today Osorio, tomorrow Lemus. But not a single poster, billboard, sign, or notice for other candidates was observed.

The Canessa candidacy, in early 1956, seemed to have a reasonable chance of success. Running for the Acción Nacionalista, the handsome ex-foreign minister, respected throughout Central America as a polished diplomat and ardent supporter of regional union, financed his campaign from personal funds. A wealthy coffee grower, he could afford reasonable expenses, although his outlay was far outstripped by Lemus'. Attacking high prices, government corruption, and the lack of a land reform program, he said little about his own policies. Canessa hoped to win support on the strength of an attractive personality and a "throw the rascals out" approach.

The two other army candidates, Colonels Funes and Carranza, agreed on January 12 to unite forces. Recognizing Lemus as the man to beat, they settled upon a joint slate of congressional candidates and tentatively decided for Carranza to withdraw in favor of Funes. At 38 the youngest candidate, Funes campaigned vigorously through the countryside, hoping to draw the bulk of his support from rural areas. In a local adaptation of the "chicken in every pot" slogan, he offered landless tenant farmers four acres and a yoke of oxen.

The race was unexpectedly turned topsy-turvy on February 26, 1956, when the government controlled Central Election Council invalidated the candidacies of Canessa and Funes. Canessa's birth certificate, submitted months before with his petition for candidacy, was ruled inaccurate. Colonel Funes was accused of a fantastic plot to smuggle secret treasure out of Guatemala while serving there as ambassador from 1951 to 1955. Both men protested bitterly. Canessa noted bitingly that his parents were both living, as well as the doctor in attendance at his birth. Their testimony could clarify any birth certificate inaccuracies. And Funes grumbled that the story of secret treasure, an old charge, had been denied by the government a year earlier when, as ambassador, he was still a member in good standing of PRUD. Predictably, the election board gave the protests no notice.

In a final effort to salvage something from the wreckage, Canessa and Funes met with a minor candidate, José Alvaro Díaz. The three agreed to coordinate their efforts through a Comité Coordinador del Frente Unido, backing Carranza as a desperate gesture of defiance against Lemus, the Central Election Council, and official hostility. The next night Canessa was arrested for "promoting public scandal," as the government termed a bitter speech he had delivered attacking election officials. The radio station, La Voz del Trópico, was closed down for seventy-two hours. The opposition announced, "If we are living today in an atmosphere of unrest, it is due to the words spoken by the President of the Republic, Oscar Osorio, before the people and the armed forces offering to guarantee electoral liberty. . . . The official party flourished the banner of demagoguery, lie, and illegality. . . . The machinery of the government has inaugurated a system of electoral fraud. . . . The National Guard and the police oppose terror to the exercise of rights of citizenship."[9]

On March 1, 1956, three days before the election, Carranza also withdrew, leaving the field completely free for Lemus: "We withdraw from the elections because we do not want to justify with our presence the electoral fraud of the government. Salvadorans: we must not go to the polls in order to show some sign of protest over the illegality of a fraudulent election which is impending."[10] The disqualified Canessa and Funes, as well as Díaz, joined Carranza in signing the statement. In an electrifying conclusion that suggested impending violence, they wrote, "The people of El Salvador will leave the results of its civic struggle in the hands of the armed forces. . . . Together, the military and the citizens will undertake a struggle to regain possession of our country and re-establish constitutional government."[11] In the face of this near ultimatum President Osorio manned the dikes in anticipation of a flood of demonstration. He placed army units loyal to Funes under jurisdiction of the National Guard, which had been headed by Lemus for six years as minister of interior. He also commanded the ranking officer at Zapote Fort, in the capital city, to resign his post. The commander studiously ignored the order, remaining at the Fort. Many felt this was a tip-off to imminent violence.

On election eve, two days later, San Salvador was enveloped in a cloak of foreboding. Few people walked the streets after dark. Movie houses were without audiences. Salvadorans waited apprehensively for election day. They were fearful, prepared for almost any eventuality, and hopeful of surviving the storm as safely as possible. Yet a series of last minute developments climaxed what Paul Kennedy described in the *New York Times* as "by all odds the most rancorous and confused campaign in El Salvador's recent history."

The morning of March 3 the opposition filed suit against Lemus, charging him with falsifying his birth certificate to prove constitutional qualifications for candidacy. At the same time, Roberto Canessa attacked the police, crying that they were hunting the editor of his newspaper, *Patria Nueva,* after having broken into his home the night before. The government made no reply. In the meantime, a special election committee, appointed by Osorio to assist the election board, sanctioned the withdrawal, weeks before, of the major parties. At the same time it refused to permit the withdrawal of two minor parties, including that

supporting Carranza, who had retired from the race on the first of
March. Ruling that the two could not quit since ballots had already been
printed, they ordered party leaders to urge members to vote. In an act
of defiance, the leaders bought newspaper advertisements instructing
members not to vote or even go near the polls.

Many observers feared army intervention, for Carranza had been well
thought of as Inspector-General prior to his pre-election resignation.
Strong army elements openly favored his election. In an interview, he
announced that he would not leave his house during election day. In a
further attempt to avoid disorder, he instructed supporters to avoid all
demonstrations. Observing that the army had not intervened, he nonetheless did not reject the possibility of future interference. Funes, on the
other hand, feared outbreaks of violence. The ex-candidate of the Independent Democrats told interviewers that the probability of increased
confusion was great. Less sanguine than Carranza, Funes claimed the
government was anxious to seize upon the smallest possible incident in
order to attack the opposition and, in the event of a Lemus defeat, annul
the results. Alert to all possible dangers, President Osorio restricted the
army to barracks, calling on the National Guard to maintain order on
election day. All leaves were cancelled. Bars were shut down, and liquor
was not available in stores and markets. While there was no curfew in
San Salvador, people stayed off the streets the night before elections.

On March 5, enough returns had been tabulated to determine two
facts: Lemus had been elected easily, and the 1956 vote registered the
most apathetic turnout in history. Newspapers in the capital claimed that
the vote was very low, although the constitution makes voting compulsory
for those eligible to participate. Many people immediately assumed that
Lemus, scheduled to take office in September, would be able to do so only
after putting down a revolution. The opposition was reportedly preparing
a military blow. Policemen ringed the home of Carranza, hoping to keep
him from contact with followers. *Prensa Gráfica,* noting indications of
an extremely small vote for Carranza, claimed his withdrawal was a last
minute maneuver when he realized victory impossible. Unification of
the opposition forces should have come much earlier. There is little
question that the anti-government leaders damaged their cause by
squabbling among themselves almost until the polls opened. At the
same time, considering all the forces operating in favor of Lemus, it is
unlikely that the final verdict would have been different.

President Osorio, interviewed as returns recorded the Lemus victory, said he felt no steps were necessary against the opposition, although he did attack their "illegal" withdrawal. He denied any possible need of restricting civil liberties. Discussing the outcome, the swarthy face of the usually phlegmatic Osorio lit up with satisfaction. He lamented the withdrawal of other candidates, repeatedly characterizing the other parties as mere personal groups without ideas. He openly admitted restricting minor civil guarantees on March 3 and 4, but claimed it had been necessary due to widespread uncertainty. He warned that any forthcoming turmoil would severely damage Salvadoran economy.

The final results, tabulated several days later, awarded Lemus 677,748 votes, almost double the total won by Osorio in 1950. A record number of 718,000 votes was reported, the figure swollen by the addition of women voters. Opposition parties received 40,000 votes. With the announcement of the results, the opposition claimed totals had been falsified, with government figures inflated some three times. In the capital, most guesses ranged from 150,000 to 200,000 votes cast. In San Salvador itself, most observers insisted that no more than 10,000 voted. Yet the government claimed that the forty-six polling places handled 75,000. A projection of this percentage through the countryside, where apathy was supposedly even greater than in San Salvador, would mean a vote of 150,000 at best. Whatever the total, there is no question that voter disinterest resulted in the lowest participation in history.

President-elect Lemus held a series of press conferences in the days following his election. He told interviewers he intended to continue PRUD policies. Expressing complete confidence that nothing would impede his assumption of office in September, he extended the olive branch to his opponents, refusing to criticize their withdrawal. Lemus said he disagreed with the action, but the opposition leaders must know how best to follow their needs. He hoped all the ex-presidential candidates would become members of the new National Assembly. Certainly, he said, they were among the most capable people in Salvador, and he intended to have the most able men in his government, regardless of party.

Despite this quiet approach, the opposition scorned his peace offering. Two days after the election, opposition forces issued a manifesto rejecting the legality of the elections and stating that the people did not support the government-selected candidate. Instead, "Salvadorans gave on the occasion a great example of civic spirit in refusing to justify its fraudulence by abstaining from the vote. . . . The parties that form the united front repeat . . . their unbroken decision to continue struggling against the dictatorship of the official party."[12]

On March 8, 1956, interviewed by the Costa Rican paper *La Nación,* Carranza declared the election a total farce. He attacked Lemus as a foreigner, claiming his true nationality in doubt. The electoral law of the government dominated Assembly, he stated, made free expression of choice difficult. That was the main reason for his withdrawal. The elections constituted a clear repudiation of the government through omission of voting. Such was the great moral victory of the people against indifferent leaders.

Despite an aura of uncertainty in the capital, the passing of time brought no military movements, subversion, or strike protests. It seemed increasingly apparent that too many Salvadorans didn't care one way or the other. Whether or not they were pleased with election results, none were about to throw the country into violent reaction to redress the decision.

José María Lemus

Lemus himself was a familiar and not unpopular figure in Salvadoran politics. Born the son of a professor in July, 1912, in Puerto Oriental de la Unión,* he had to fend for himself after his father died. During a youth of poverty he peddled candies in the streets, helped deliver mail, and took any chore which paid. Entering the elementary military academy as a teenager, he later attended the Military Academy of El Salvador, graduating at the top of his class in 1933. After study in the United States, he returned to his republic and began advancing through National Guard ranks, gradually progressing to lieutenant colonel. He was appointed Undersecretary of Defense in 1948, although not an active conspirator in the revolution that brought the PRUD to power. Briefly serving as military attaché in Washington, he returned in 1950 as Minister of Interior under Oscar Osorio.

Lemus also became active in other circles. A member of the Ateneo de El Salvador, he helped found the Sociedad Bolivariana in El Salvador in December, 1949, and was elected its first president. He also published a

---

* Due to the early death of his parents and vague birth documents, opponents have accused him of not being native born. No evidence sustains this.

number of slender volumes, including *The Military Ethic, For Country and For Freedom, Eulogy for Venustiano Carranza,* and *Art and Trades with the Social Problems of Youth.* He has been awarded citations from the governments of Colombia, Venezuela, Mexico, Panama, and the Dominican Republic, among others.

A well-dressed, husky six-footer, Lemus succeeded in building up considerable personal popularity. A genial individual, his moderate post-election comments only underlined the potential popularity his character might bring. George Weller wrote that

> José María Lemus, the genial handshaker who has just become Salvador's president . . . [has his] door open to the unwashed public . . . to reach him I had to penetrate through seven antechambers of patiently waiting people, all eager to wring his hand and whisper in his ear. . . . His favorite way of talking to men—I watched him handling dozens—is to place his left hand on their shoulder, hold their right hand tightly clamped in his, and listen to every word they say while staring into their eyes with the solicitude of a psychiatrist.
>
> When he breaks out of this double grip, the suppliant instinctively knows the interview is over.[13]

Before his 1955 nomination he had said "The plan of the present government is the plan of the party [PRUD] and therefore I consider it to be the platform of PRUD now. I will accept it and will continue similar policies, which in this case can have direct connection to the political situation."[14]

Just what, in specific terms, did Lemus hope to do? He soon made this more obvious than it had been during the campaign itself. The composition of his government, he hoped, would be national, not partisan. He wanted the cooperation of capable, patriotic elements of the citizenry during his six-year administration (1956-62). He declared himself satisfied with small farmers' credit and housing for city poor. He praised the stabilization of wages and increased economic compensation for the productive efforts of the worker, noting that the value of the colon had remained much the same for many years. He also expected to continue taxation of the wealthy families who control Salvador economically. He promised to push the drive for electrification begun by Oscar Osorio. Nearly one million persons—half the population—still lived where electric plants were lacking. Until they were serviced, the power program was unfinished. As for capital, Lemus said that his country needed medium industries financed by foreign capital, and hence foreign capital was invited.

In foreign affairs, the President-elect announced continued non-interference in internal affairs of neighboring republics. He reiterated, as he had during the campaign, his fervent belief in Central American union. He called on the area to adopt total amity, a common customs system, and to repudiate plots and intra-country subversion. Central America, with a common population destiny and common problems, had no valid reason for existing in six separate subdivisions. Union was slowly, but much too slowly, being approached. Work and sacrifice had to be dedicated to the cause. "The formation of the ODECA has obeyed the desire to make Central America realize it must become a power entity . . . [to] authentically interpret their destiny." No nation, he repeated, was more devoted to regional union than El Salvador. If Lemus was speaking from patriotic motivations, he nonetheless was quite accurate.

Through 1957, the Lemus administration devoted itself to fiscal and trade policies. Special commissions met with the United States to take up the problem of double taxation, which had been recently negotiated in Honduras removing articles from taxation in both that country and the U. S. As his officials began to study the Honduran agreement, the President announced interest "in bilateral negotiations with the United States. We want to reach an accord on this matter." Long months lay ahead for the group. Business dealings with West Germany and Japan also increased. West Germany offered technical assistance, sending Germans to Salvador as well as training nationals in German universities. Costs were to be split between the governments. Satisfactory negotiations were eventually completed.

The capital was briefly stirred up by other measures designed to stabilize wages and prices. A new rate of municipal taxes was approved for San Salvador, eventually passed into law over Lemus' veto. Monthly water and property charges were raised. Taking effect in May, 1957, the new scale was designed to affect only the rich. Those of more modest means soon joined in the protest against it. In time the rate was accepted, and found to contribute only in part to a gradual wage-price increase. Long overdue legislation was passed later in 1957 against the common practice of usury. Funds were authorized the Rural Credit Cooperatives to protect civil employees against outrageous interest rates and credit grants. Due to the organization's large scale loans to small businessmen and farmers where collateral was lacking, the national level of interest rates was reduced.

The impressive achievements of the Osorio government increasing electric power nationally were added to by Lemus. The Lempa River Hydroelectric Commission announced projected construction of two new generating plants, one with 30,000 and the other with 15,000 kilowatts, equalling the capacity of the Lempa hydroelectric station. The first phase, costing over two million dollars, would include a dam for regulation of the waters of Lake Guija. Control of Guija, which belongs equally to Guatemala, would guarantee year-round water supply for the Lempa station. Development was given priority over final expansion of the "Cinco de Noviembre" dam to its maximum 75,000 kilowatts. The total project at Guija was estimated as a $9,200,000 investment. Guatemala gave approval to the plan with the proviso that Guatemalan users would be furnished power at the same rate as Salvadorans.

Lemus' over-all efforts were favorable in the first half of his term. By espousing national non-partisanship he lured into his government capable men who had shunned politics previously. His idea envisaged the distribution of wealth through legislative and social experiment. In Salvador, where the wealth has for generations been controlled by a remarkably small number of families, the thought was almost revolutionary. It gradually caught on, aided by large projects, such as low-cost housing, aimed at raising living standards. Those with great wealth began to invest their funds in the country, not sending them abroad as before. With the growth of investment possibilities, a more stable political and economic system developed which, at this writing, has meant the only Central American government with a sturdily reliable national atmosphere.

The budget for 1958 was among the highest in history, some seventy-two million dollars. President Lemus announced in September, 1957, that Salvadoran industrial products were annually exceeding forty million dollars in export value, with raw materials bringing in an additional twenty million. Foreign investment was up, agricultural commodities steady. The exportable crop of coffee was the greatest in history. But, 1958 also meant a time for reappraisal. The coffee harvest dropped from the previous record nearly 20 percent. Restricted export volume and lowered prices brought a concomitant reduction in revenues.

An international agreement to support coffee prices held out hope for greater stability in future years. El Salvador met with six other coffee-producing nations in Mexico City to negotiate the agreement under which she was allotted 552,484 sacks as her export quota during the early 1958 period. The hope was to apply partial control to the international coffee market, adjust to demand, and maintain equitable price controls. Only Brazil and Colombia were granted larger allocations. Lemus had rushed legislation through Congress in November, 1957, to meet the agreement, establishing a National Coffee Department to operate the program. Salvadoran exporters received quotas of 40 percent of the previous year's export totals. The agency bought up coffee withheld from trade.

Mild but necessary belt-tightening was engendered by coffee restrictions. The budget was not reduced, however, and by the close of the 1958 fiscal year there was a small treasury surplus from 1957. With small industry being emphasized, the Department of Economic Promotion continued to invest capital in development projects. And the highway system was pushed along with additional appropriations. The coastal highway along the entire Pacific coast was cut through previously underdeveloped areas. Although the scheduled September, 1958, completion date could not be met, the road was already bringing new areas into national economic planning for the first time. While the economic picture continued to improve, El Salvador remained, on the international front, the moving force behind the drive for regional unity. For the last decade no other nation has devoted itself to this project with such determination. When the other republics have quarrelled over matters of hypersensitive nationalism, El Salvador has stepped in and pacified the disputants.

Spring of 1954 was such a time of regional crisis. Seldom has the isthmus been more sorely beset. To the south, Nicaraguan President Somoza, narrowly escaping assassination, laid the blame on the doorstep of Costa Rican President Figueres, and the two countries were at one another's throats. A flurry of diplomatic notes only created greater rancor. In Honduras, the Gálvez government was laboring to end a disastrous strike by banana workers which was crippling the national economy. Meanwhile, communist Guatemala was spreading subversion far and wide. Abortive incidents against the Honduran government led to eventual severance of diplomatic relations. And the raggle-taggle band of revolutionaries under Castillo was preparing to launch its invasion of

Guatemala from Honduran soil with the unofficial sanction of that government. Finally, Panama was immersed in vital negotiations with the United States over terms of the Canal Zone contract of 1936.

In the midst of all this, El Salvador herself was hard pressed to maintain impartiality. We have seen earlier how she refrained from meddling in the Guatemalan case. President Osorio, although opposed to the Arbenz government, felt obliged to stay aloof from what proved to be that regime's death throes. He also rejected overtures from Castillo, refusing to permit his invasion of Guatemala from El Salvador. A personal plea from Somoza left him unmoved.

Despite this welter of bitterness and anxiety, El Salvador was a model of calm propriety and disinterested assistance. Following the downfall of Arbenz, the Guatemalan revolutionaries were divided in allegiance between Castillo and Monzón, the latter a friend of Osorio. The eventual agreement between the two was reached at a long interview in San Salvador, watched over by U. S. Ambassador Peurifoy and Osorio. And after the mutual pacification of the rival groups, Osorio promptly extended diplomatic recognition. On September 29, the two nations signed a treaty of friendship and cooperation, further cementing relations.

The enmity between Costa Rica and Nicaragua belongs in another chapter. However, in this context, we must record Osorio's April, 1954, offer to mediate the dispute between the two, which had brought them to the verge of war. Costa Rican Foreign Minister Mario Esquivel immediately accepted the offer. But Nicaraguan policy, in keeping with the outraged indignation of Somoza at escaping assassination so narrowly, refused to sit down at the same table to negotiate with Costa Rica. However, a series of little-publicized talks and discussions were held in San Salvador, with Osorio continually cautioning a more rational approach. In mid-August, the Salvadoran Ambassador to Guatemala, Félix Osegueda, made President Figueres quite angry while attempting to reduce friction. Figueres' outburst was ignored by Osorio who quickly sent Osegueda to Managua and transferred Roberto Castillo from there to Costa Rica.

Almost simultaneously, on August 17, Carranza went to Managua for private talks with President Somoza. Four days later, Osorio announced from San Salvador that Somoza had agreed to mediation on the grounds that the agenda be drawn up beforehand. Foreign Minister Canessa flew to San José for a new series of talks with officials there, also stopping briefly in Nicaragua. The eventual pacification was a result of many factors which are detailed in Chapters Five and Six. None was more important than the continual counseling by unexcitable Salvadoran officials against further inflammatory exchanges.

At the same time El Salvador was sympathetically conscious of Honduran difficulties. External problems lessened with the overthrow of Guatemala's Red government. And there was little to be done regarding the strike, which was a purely internal matter. However, throughout 1954, Osorio was in close personal contact with President Gálvez, offering him moral support and reiterating the friendship of his government. They met several times for informal talks at the Goascorán River boundary.

Panama also received Salvadoran backing in negotiations with the U. S. over a canal contract. While the transaction was negotiated in an atmosphere of friendship, this made the matter no less critical to Panama. Foreign Minister Canessa declared, on July 23, 1953, that he was "sure that the government of the United States, giving a new demonstration of sympathy for the aspiration of the hispanic people, also is interested in revising relations with Panama in the light of modern international law. . . ."[15]

Such has been the role of El Salvador in recent Central American diplomacy. Repeatedly, this small republic has served as the catalytic agent turning neighbors' bellicose arguments into resolvable differences of opinion. In this respect every nation of the area is in its debt. The story of the movement for Central American union has often been the tale of Salvadoran initiative, leadership, and sacrifice in the face of studied neglect by others. So intimately is the Salvadoran role intertwined with the development of the ODECA, its contributions must be credited to Salvadoran leaders of different political leanings. With the initial success of the Lemus administration, new impetus was anticipated in the campaign for Central American union.

Recent Salvadoran problems have been faced by Lemus with aplomb and confidence. Over and over he has reiterated his faith in the spirit of Central American unity and the part his nation must play. No one has denied that El Salvador is home, hearth, and heart of regional amity. If the long sought unity movement is ever consummated, the years of labor by Salvadorans, both public and private, will bring fitting tribute.

The future promises a more advanced El Salvador, better equipped to fulfill its destiny. Problems still abound: light industry is not yet a significant force, and national economics must be oriented away from reliance on coffee. Land reform is needed, distribution of income is still inadequate. But there is promise that these obstacles may be hurdled. The Osorio administration unquestionably contributed worthwhile works to national progress. The only serious black mark is the absurd electoral fiasco of 1956 that brought Lemus to power. Today it does not seem too visionary to hope that he will continue to follow Osorio on the path of national economic development and modernization. Perhaps the most important factor of all is the continuing influence El Salvador will assert in the movement for Central American unity. This, after all, is in the long run the best hope for progress throughout the isthmus.

Chapter Four

HONDURAS

OF ALL THE Central American republics, none is more ruggedly mountainous and geographically isolated than Honduras, located in the very heartland of the isthmus. It is the pivotal area of the landbridge between Mexico and South America. Bordering Guatemala and El Salvador to the northwest and Nicaragua on the southeast, Honduras has been geographically and politically in the center of regional life since it shed Spanish colonial garb in 1821.

Yet the predominant factor in Honduras today, as it has been for over a century, is the very fact of its geographic separation from its neighbors. The rough-hewn Honduran geographical factors are direct barriers to participation in regional politics. The visitor to Honduras need not be reminded of the imposing contour of the Honduras terrain. Physiographic diagrams of Central America clearly represent the obstacles to national participation in regional affairs. Yet, as Honduran scholar William Stokes has observed, the central position of the republic has made it "a willing participant . . . or unwilling victim of . . . machinations of Central American power politics."[1] Invasions of bordering countries have been launched from Honduran soil as recently as 1954. Political exiles have flocked there through the years, sometimes remaining years before directing a counterrevolution in their own countries, or perhaps passing into that obscure political twilight from which even Latin caudillos never return. Uncertain boundaries have created continual friction. Honduras and Nicaragua are still wrangling petulantly over a disputed slice of land that lies unproductive and largely uninhabited.

The bulk of the population is located in the provinces of Francisco Morazán and Comayagua, in north central Honduras. This region is one of highland mountains and valleys. Much of the area is heavily timbered, but the mountains are conducive to village isolation and intense local feeling. Transportation has been improved at an insignificant pace; most Hondurans living outside the capital have never traveled more than a few miles from home. There are no roads, or else they are impassable much of the year. Towns develop and grow their own food staples and trade with one another. There is little knowledge of or interest in people living only a few miles away.

However, the past decade has brought a gradual swing away from these geographic facts. The population has gradually been shifting toward the northern coast, gathering in the Caribbean ports of Puerto Cortes, Tela, and La Ceiba. This is directly attributable to the banana plantations of the United Fruit Company. Most of the migrating Hondurans have gone to work in the fields or at the company's wharves and loading facilities. It will be some years yet before the dominant Honduran population has left central Honduras, however. In the meantime, the facts of geography necessitate severe curtailment of political and economic developments. Greater shifting in population is needed before Honduras can correct the isolation and localism that are incontestably characteristic.

Many Central American travelers, especially motorists, leave Honduras bearing stories of a barren, empty, utterly obscure little nation. This impression is easily come by. Motorists, entering the country from El Salvador at the Goascorán Bridge, follow a dusty, washboard-surface road toward Nicaragua. There is little scenery; the area is lowlying and hot, not tropical, but oppressive nonetheless. The few, distant mountains seem relatively small. There is little vegetation and few people. Only seldom are peasants seen trudging along the road. Few places give a more overwhelming impression of barren isolation, agricultural poverty, and scenic monotony. This, however, is a small part of Honduras. The regions around Tegucigalpa, the capital, and the banana coast to the north, are the two important areas, and upon them has been erected the national economy, oligarchic and backward though it may be.

No Central American republic coincides more closely than Honduras with the popular, un-informed idea of a banana republic. To begin with, it is the only nation that is, literally, a banana republic. Bananas are the primary export and main staple of the national economy, although the percentage of banana exports has dropped in recent years from 65 percent to barely 50 percent. Still, this is a much higher percentage than its neighbors, to whom coffee is the more important.

Honduras is 71 percent rural. The capital has a population of 72,385, excluding neighboring Comayaguela, which in recent years has been considered part of Tegucigalpa. No other population center compares with it. The rural population is 86 percent mestizo.

Political preconceptions of Central American republics are appropriate to Honduras. The country's history has been dotted with revolutions, invasions, palace intrigues, and civil wars. A recent estimate in *Time* (December 12, 1954) credited Honduras with an average revolution a year for its 138 years of independence—and this even though the past quarter century has been, by Honduran standards, politically stable. The heritage of Honduras is one of colonial centralism, absence of representative institutions, and three centuries of subservience to autocratic Spanish rule.

Perhaps the foremost preconception in the minds of most is of a caudillo, the dictatorial, paternalistic, authoritarian leader who runs the country high-handedly and disregards the usual tenents of democratic practice. Honduras met this requirement under the sixteen-year presidency of one man, General Tiburcio Carías, a figure who has been prominent in national politics for the astonishing span of sixty years. He is neither the most controversial nor impenetrable figure of regional contemporary affairs. Yet few can approach his former ascendency or rival the fascination of his career. Even today the political life of the country is close to that of Carías.

General Tiburcio Carías

Recently, two North Americans were touring the hilly streets of Tegucigalpa. One of them noticed a figure on the other side of the street. Followed by several others, the man walked slowly along the road, occasionally nodding to a passerby. Obviously aged, he was of huge stature for a Honduran—probably six feet, four inches, and easily 260 pounds. His stern countenance was delineated by a deeply lined face. His mustache was white, but a full head of hair was dark despite his age. "Look at that man over there," said one. "He looks just the way you'd picture a dictator down here, doesn't he?" His companion smiled and added, "That is Carías. He was president for years." This story is apocryphal and unsubstantiated, but it is illustrative of the impressive appearance of Carías. Even today the General has a dignified, somewhat grim, and notably commanding appearance. He gives the impression of authority, of self control, and control of others. For many years he exercised unchallenged political power in Honduras. To some, he was a ruthless tyrant. Others feel less harshly and have interpreted his years of power as ones of national progress, advanced by one-party rule in the absence of adequate democratic institutions. The difference is one of degree. Perhaps Carías' unquestioned dominance meant dictatorship. But conceding this, there are marks on his record which are uncharacteristic of dictatorship. This makes him less easy to classify. To do so, it is first necessary to understand the background of the two Honduran national parties, as well as political events transpiring long before the last decade, with which we are primarily concerned.

One of the rare qualities of Honduran politics has been the durability of its two political parties. Few Central American—or Latin American—parties have been more than a personal vehicle. Once the star of the leader has fallen from the political heavens, the party disintegrates and reforms in other groups. But not so in Honduras. The Liberal party was first called into being at the close of the nineteenth century. For perhaps twenty years it existed tenuously as a personal machine for its founder, Céleo Arias. However, with the death of Arias in 1890, the party reformed under Policarpo Bonilla, who proceeded to create a political organization. The Liberals became a permanent organization with a predetermined hierarchy and policies. However, its policies have coincided, basically, with those of the second political affiliation—the National party.

The National party also was created before the turn of the century, although initially weaker than the Liberals. It was organized on a hierarchic basis in 1911 and, from 1920 on, exercised considerable influence at elections. It drafted a program in 1919 under the leadership of Carías and Dr. Paulino Valladares, adopting the name Democratic National party. Since the national elections of 1923, it has been known as the National party. In 1923, its program was revised, and policies outlined then have continued virtually unchanged to the present, thirty-five years later. The Nationals advocated "strict observance of the constitution, establishment of a Central American Union when feasible, less politics and more administration in government, financial reform, free elections, harmony among the Honduran people, and protection of capital and labor."[2]

Honduras has no conservative group as such but there are conservative elements in both the National and Liberal parties. Many of the National leaders began as supporters of the Liberals. For example, Carías was one of the youngest participants in the revolution of 1894, a Liberal uprising. He also served as Fiscal General of Production in 1908 under Liberal President Dávila. The two parties have followed and even today pursue remarkably similar principles.

One fundamental difference exists between the two parties, and this is important in any evaluation of Carías. The National party has repeatedly attacked revolution and armed uprising as incompatible with the principles of democracy and therefore unjustifiable. Stokes has written that the party has demanded permanent peace within the country. While agreeing with the Liberal party on basic democratic ideals and the theoretic relationship of state and individual, the Nationals have insisted upon the immutable evil of anti-government revolt. The Liberals have never felt so constrained and, as recently as 1954, were narrowly prevented from staging a full-blown revolution. Their opponents have stubbornly maintained the principle regardless of circumstances. The election of 1923 provides concrete proof.

The National party supported Carías for president in 1923. At forty-seven, a veteran of years of political activity, General Carías, an experienced farmer, mathematics professor, and part-time military leader, was opposed by Liberal Policarpo Bonilla. Carías, a robust and popular candidate, won with a clear plurality, but due to the participation of minor candidates, failed to win 50 percent of the total vote. The final count gave him 49,453 to Bonilla's 35,474. Needing an absolute majority of 53,134, Carías was therefore 3,681 short of the necessary total. The Liberals refused to attend congressional meetings, blocking the quorum necessary to take action. In such a situation the only recourse was revolution. Carías was the obvious choice of the people and enjoyed wide army support. Remaining faithful to his campaign promises, however, he refused to seize power.

For several months the republic was in chaos, until the United States stepped in to conduct a meeting of disputing elements. In the meantime, Carías, as a result of the complete governmental disorganization, had led his forces into military action, and by April 28, 1924, he was in control of the capital and most of the outlying regions. Under the U. S.-sponsored negotiations, however, the General's vice-presidential running mate, Dr. Miguel Paz Baraona, was chosen chief of state. Carías relinquished command to the new president and withdrew to await the next elections. In recent years, his critics have conveniently forgotten these long past elections. Yet the fact remains that Carías not only won the election freely, and a military campaign as well, yet he handed over power to the person ultimately selected as President of Honduras. He formally gave Paz Baraona his support, and thus was instrumental in reducing national tension.

In the elections of 1928, Carías was again the National candidate and, to the surprise of everyone, lost a close but clearcut decision to Liberal Mejía Colindres. Votes were re-tabulated, verifying Carías' defeat. The General sent personal representatives to meet Mejía Colindres; accepting the results, he promised to back the new government fully. Still in control of the bulk of Honduras' military force, he might have seized power. Again he was faithful to the National party principle of peaceful succession to office.

So surprising was the General's action in these two elections—1924 and 1928—that his support was much greater in 1932, and he won a decisive victory over Liberal Angel Zúñiga Huete. Following his victory, Carías met with outgoing President Mejía Colindres, exchanged pleasantries at the Casa Presidencial, and began to outline his plans. Just as he took office, a group of dissident Liberals rebelled and were suppressed after a series of bloody encounters. It had been the Liberals who resorted to revolution, not the Nationals.

None can deny the fact, as we shall learn, that Tiburcio Carías was a dictator of the first order. However, one need not be an apologist to point out facts that are often overlooked. Carías scrupulously turned his back on obvious opportunities to seize power by force, when his opposition would have been slight. He refused to do so despite the urging of many advisers. In 1924, he not only won a free election but temporary military control of Honduras, yet he turned over the reins of government to the eventual presidential designate. And his election in 1932 was overwhelmingly accomplished in a vote controlled by the government of another political party. Criticisms that he was placed in office by foreign interests, contrary to the wishes of the people, are without the slightest foundation in fact.

Carías was elected in 1932 to a four-year term, forbidden constitutionally to win re-election without a gap of at least one term. As 1936 approached, members of the National party began to talk of Carías' continuation in office. It was decided to draw up a new constitution extending the presidential term. In January, 1936, a constituent assembly was elected, and two months later it promulgated the Constitution of 1936. Article 202 permitted the President and Vice-President to remain in office until January of 1943. There was no change of the previous executive tenure sections, except to provide that the existing chief executive continue until 1943. Thus was born the principle of continuismo.

This was obviously a device whereby Carías might remain in power. The action was carefully legalized. Congress had authority to call a constituent assembly, which in turn had authority to draw up a new constitution as it saw fit. There was nothing illegal about the constitution itself. But none can deny that it was a carefully contrived plan to continue the General's administration. Carías at that time may have been able to win new elections, for he remained reasonably popular. Nonetheless, he perpetuated his power through the doctrine of continuismo. Referring once more to Stokes, we read that continuismo "is difficult to justify, for it interrupts progress toward political objectives . . . charted by the people. It resulted in one-party government . . . produced fear that the fundamental freedoms would no longer be protected . . . reconciled the opposition to the use of the old and unsatisfactory method of revolution as a means of changing political power."[3]

Three years later continuismo was again invoked. On December 12, 1939, the presidential tenure was extended until January of 1949. As revised, Article 202 of the Honduran Constitution read that "The constitutional presidency and vice-presidency of the republic exercised, respectively, by the citizens Don Tiburcio Carías Andino, doctor and general, and Don Abraham Williams Calderón, engineer and general, shall terminate January 1st, 1949; and for this purpose the effects of Article 117 of this constitution shall be suspended until January 1st, 1949. . . ."[4] Article 117 declared simply that "The presidential term shall be 6 years and shall begin January 1st."[5] Nationals will still argue with determination, as they did then, that continuismo was in reality democratic, because the people favored the doctrine. When pressed as to how they knew the people's will in the absence of elections, they say it was "commonly known" that the policy would be popular. That may have been so, but no recourse through the ballot box was offered. Hondurans could express no acceptance or rejection of continuismo. Only in the fall of 1948 were the people finally permitted the right of voting for a president, and at that time Carías appeared to be naming a sycophantic follower to the position.

During his sixteen-year administration, Carías put through a number of important measures. When he first entered office, he was pressed by internal dissension—stirred up by willful Liberals—and a near-bankrupt treasury. Refusing to launch any reprisals against the opposition, the General set about pacifying the country by a series of conciliatory moves. Eventually he was successful in stabilizing the internal political situation. All political "enemies" of the regime were permitted to participate actively; the only restriction was an agreement by such to abstain from revolution, conspiracy, or clandestine anti-government activities. Despite government control of the military forces, there were rarely any repressive measures exercised against the populace.

Financially, Carías adopted a belt-tightening economy program which soon alleviated the acute monetary difficulty. The budget was balanced for the first time in years, although at the expense of such unpopular measures as reduction of public servants' wages. Not until World War II were national finances again jeopardized. Honduran revenue accrues in large part from international trade, which was severely curtailed during wartime. Trade restrictions were serious enough to reduce total trade to its lowest figure in thirty-five years. Only after the Allied forces won their final victory was Honduras to right itself financially.

With Honduran geography so seriously handicapping economic development, improved communication was, as it is today, a grave problem. The very construction of highways is difficult; passes are tortuous and elevated, if not non-existent. The central mountains, although rugged, are heavily forested, and cleared only with difficulty. There is a hardrock base beneath much of the more passable territory. President Carías inaugurated a road-building program to improve communications. Year after year he budgeted 10 percent or better of the national expenditures for road construction. In 1942, the Export-Import Bank loaned Honduras one million dollars to complete construction of the Inter American Highway. While never paved, the road itself was soon completed, linking El Salvador and Nicaragua with Honduras. Over one thousand miles of roads were completed by 1945, and the impetus to improve the national road net has never been lost.

Internationally, Carías maintained good relations during his long regime. Abstaining from conspiratorial activities with other Central American republics, Carías thus contributed to regional stability. Or, to be more precise, his aloof position did not weaken the already-shaky foundations of regional peace. Honduras was twice involved in a boundary dispute with Nicaragua, a controversy which is with us today. In both cases eventual negotiation salved the nationalistic irritations of both countries and reduced regional disagreement.

Notable among Carías' "accomplishments" was the complete stifling of legislative initiative. From 1925 to 1933, the Congress for the first time began to exercise independent government action. Aided by querulous executive leadership, the legislative organ operated under its own motivation and developed sufficient strength to withstand and even challenge executive policy. Carías soon changed this. With fellow National party members dominating Congress, the General found it no hard task to reassert legislative subservience to the executive. It has never really recovered from sixteen years under his thumb. The General also kept a tight lid on the Honduran press. For nearly two decades it was restrained. Censorship of a sort always existed, even though negligible at times. However, no paper publishing serious or continual criticism of the regime was likely to remain in business for long. Only *La Epoca,* of all Tegucigalpa dailies, operated with government approval, and that because it was the Carías paper, directed by a close ally of the General, Fernando Zepeda Durón.

From this brief sketch of Carías' extended presidency, what conclusions may be drawn? What was he—dictator, devoted patriot, misguided politician, prophet of progress? How might his years in power be evaluated? In the first place, there are a number of charges made against him which should be dismissed. Many have been voiced by liberal educator Germán Arciniegas. In *The State of Latin America* he has written scathingly of the triple scourge of the Caribbean—the Three T's. This refers to Tiburcio Carías, Tacho Somoza of Nicaragua, and Rafael Trujillo of the Dominican Republic. In regard to Carías, Arciniegas criticizes the General for pioneering Latin American aerial bombardment in the 1924 fighting. He sarcastically credits Carías with a trail-blazing innovation in methods of blood-letting and points out that the same questionable tactics were repeated in 1933 when Carías assumed the presidency. To Arciniegas, this is but one example of his callousness.

The question of military weapons is really irrelevant. Few military leaders have ever been constrained in the use of different arms against a belligerant opponent. Carías cannot justifiably be attacked for using bombing in the conduct of military operations either in 1924 or 1933. Had his opponents possessed the means, they would have employed the same tactics, and without drawing legitimate criticism. What is important is the cause for which the General was fighting.

We have already noted that he was blameless in the fighting of 1924 and 1933. In 1924 he was the legally elected choice of the people. Repudiated by an irresponsible Congress, he refused to take power by force. Only when dissident politicos began to fight did the General take military action. After pacifying the country, he accepted a compromise agreement which delivered the presidency to his vice-presidential running mate. Eight years later the General was elected to office by a large majority. There can be no serious doubt that his election represented the will of the people. He took arms only when directly opposed by a segment of the defeated Liberal party. After he reduced the revolt to minor proportions, he declared a policy of pacification. Within two years political exiles were permitted to return to Honduras and work actively, as long as they refrained from conspiratorial activities. In each instance evidence strongly suggests that Carías was undeserving of any valid criticism. In fact, the incidents reflected credit on him, in his refusal to seize power in 1924, and in avoiding oppressive reprisals against his opponents in 1933. There are many valid criticisms of the General which cannot be excused. These are not among them.

Many have chided Carías for wiping out municipal autonomy. His supporters have countered that municipal autonomy in Honduras has always been a dubious proposition. Municipal governments have fallen under the control of the strongest government officials, and autonomy has been almost non-existent. This is basically true. However, Carías made no attempt to alter the situation, when he, better than any other president before or since, might have done so. Had he exerted his personal power, he might have reorganized municipal life, established the basis for democratic action, and conceivably eliminated the bitter local pride which has rebuffed continual efforts to unite the republic in spite of geographic handicaps. And in 1940, he further centralized municipal government by a reorganization plan substituting nationally appointed officers for local representatives. Responsible only to the executive, these men were imposed on communities by federal rule regardless of the appointee's brilliance or sheer incompetence. This measure simply strengthened the established custom of local subservience to central control.

Nepotism and government favoritism have also been charged against Carías. His government, as do most under dictatorial control, reflected his will completely. Many close friends received influential, well-paying government jobs. Two of his sons became ranking diplomatic representatives of Honduras abroad. Once again, Carías' defenders claim that this was typical of Latin American politics. Carías wanted important positions filled with men who agreed with him. After all, "a cabinet is seldom dismissed for incompetency, but rather for disagreement with the president."[6] But again, Carías cannot be excused on the grounds that his Latin contemporaries followed the same practices. No doubt he could have unloaded many more government posts on eager, ungifted friends. Nonetheless, he was guilty of surrounding himself with a large number of agreeable yes-men.

The staunchly conservative strain in Carías was evident in other policies which reflect no credit upon him. Despite his general lenience with political opponents and agitators, Carías felt an example should be made of serious lawbreakers as a deterrent to future criminals. As a result, some three hundred prisoners, including several political transgressors, were made to work in the capital while chained to heavy balls. Foreigners recall vividly the picture of these criminals slowy trudging through the streets under armed guard, dragging ball and chain by their ankles. Only within the last ten years has this practice been eliminated. His conservatism also led Carías to resist woman suffrage and labor organization, both integral parts of any developing democratic scene.

The Constitution of 1936, which was still in effect when Carías left office in 1949, specified that all Honduran citizens must vote, that it was an obligatory, unrenounceable public duty. Article 24 granted citizenship only to males. There was no provision for female citizenship, and Honduran women were refused suffrage. In the field of labor, Carías was equally reluctant to recognize accepted twentieth-century practices. Section XII of the Constitution, "Concerning Labor and the Family," consisted of eight different articles (191-198). None of these made any mention of labor organization, nor the slightest hint of such a move. The near-disastrous results of this became apparent in the 1954 banana strike.

All these, then, were negative results of the Carías administration. Final destruction of municipal autonomy, subjection of Congress to executive whim, nepotism and personalismo, harsh and ostentatious criminal punishment, non-recognition of woman suffrage, smothering of labor organization, suspension of national voting privileges from 1937 to 1949—these were part of the Carías heritage. Others have been considered dictators for less.

In any judgment of Carías, there are positive accomplishments which also belong on the record. From his earliest political activities Carías pursued a form of representative democracy. Over sixty years ago he fought as a youth in the 1894 Liberal revolution, a fight leading to recognition of presidential election by popular vote. He was the first presidential candidate in history to accept a defeat in open elections (in 1928) without starting a revolution. And earlier, in 1924, he had been the first Honduran to win both an election and revolution and yet accept the ironic course of events that awarded the presidency to his vice-presidential candidate.

It seems certain that when he was elected in 1933, Carías' personal integrity, honesty, and goodwill were impeccable. He was highly popular. Few Hondurans have been so truly national leaders. Today, ten years after leaving the presidency, Tiburcio Carías is slowly becoming a figure of the past, although the octogenerian is still the power of the National party. All this cannot mask the fact that his accomplishments often fell sadly short of what he might have done. While in power he created a strict, one-man government, prolonging it for sixteen years by the pseudo-doctrine of continuismo which rejected the idea of free, honest elections. Monopolistic control of the state strangled any serious manifestation of public opinion.

Carías may be considered in the context of Chapter One's discussion of the conflicting values of a Central American dictator. As the unchallenged chief of state, he was in a position to provide many material necessities for his people. This could partially justify and help explain his anti-democratic actions. However, considering the length of his rule, the inescapable fact remains that Carías' accomplishments were not consonant with the potentialities of his position. In short, he pursued actions that were often suspect and clearly contrary to democratic principles. His failure to achieve more for Honduras while exercising absolute authority is the worst condemnation of his methods.

In 1949, Hondurans were skeptical of Carías' intentions when he relinquished the presidency to a friend and National party member, Juan Manuel Gálvez. He removed himself more completely from the government than anyone expected, partly because of Gálvez' complete independence. Only in the last two years has Carías again stepped into the political limelight, but never again will he stand for public office. However, for sixty years, Carías has been a prominent political leader, and that he will probably remain until the day of his death. Above all else, he provides striking testimony to Honduran admiration of decisive, authoritarian leadership. Only in recent years has this diminished.

POLITICAL REDISCOVERY

The first presidential change in sixteen years took place on January 1, 1949, when Dr. Juan Manuel Gálvez took office in Tegucigalpa. A member of the National party, he had been a prominent lawyer for years and was relatively inactive politically. His selection by Carías—bypassing Abraham Williams, Carías' only vice-president—was considered an indication that the aging General had handpicked a pliable successor to follow his orders. Those who knew Gálvez were skeptical, and events were to prove him completely independent of his predecessor. Having won election in October, 1948, without opposition, Gálvez took office supported by a pro-National Congress. There was no serious political opposition elsewhere.

Dr. Gálvez synthesized his objectives into four categories—economic growth, education, health, and communication. Immediate efforts were initiated to advance road construction. Carías had insisted all funds appropriated for highways be channeled directly into construction and repair. None was used for land surveys. Gálvez ordered survey teams to begin work at once, laying out new routes and improving the course of hastily-planned or improvised backcountry paths. Some 15 percent of the budget was devoted to road construction, and the sum increased later in Gálvez' administration. The 1953 budget, for example, of $20,740,388, allotted over 25 percent to road construction. At the same time, small bridges were built on major arteries. Previously, most roads had dipped down into creekbeds and climbed up the other side. During the dry season this was adequate, but when the rains came, the streams could rise three or four feet in a period of minutes, leaving travelers marooned.

The effect of this was to facilitate the movement of agricultural goods and products, as well as reduce the powerful forces of isolation and village localism. People were able to travel more easily from village to village, learning more of their neighbors and of Honduras. Fewer sections were left completely cut off from the outside, and small communities became less self-supporting. Instead, they could trade with neighboring vicinities. Much work remains to be done today—the only paved highway in the country leads south from Tegucigalpa to the junction of the Inter American Highway at Jicaro Galán. Many areas remain basically isolated; the increasingly important economic activities of the north coast are inadequately connected with the central mountain areas. The best transportation is a railroad operated by the banana interests. However, President Gálvez gave new impetus to the problem. As the President himself said, "My administration has tried to develop the following communications: to improve the interoceanic and inter-American route; construction of the highway to the west—from San Pedro Sula to Santa Rosa de Copán . . . other branches of importance in other areas are being built also."[7] Transportation was also improved by continued expansion of air service by Tranvías Aereas de Centro America (TACA) which flies to some sixty different fields in Honduras.

A healthy Honduran economy depended on much more than improved transportation and communication. President Gálvez was well aware of the importance of economic development. Both in matters of finance and economic technical improvement, positive measures were required. National finances had been operating securely under Carías, but after the 1945 recovery from wartime curtailments less attention was paid to the situation. Foreign investments were negligible, except for the banana business; government revenues were not increasing, and the foreign debt began to mount. The need for additional expenditures could not be met without added income.

In July, 1950, after a year's study by a group of Honduran and foreign experts, the Gálvez government created two state banks, both autonomous organs, designed to protect and strengthen national finance. The Banco Nacional de Fomento offered low interest, long-term assistance to peasants. Money was also funneled into development projects designed to improve agricultural methods. Its sister bank, the Banco Central de

Honduras, was endowed with $250,000 capital and the power to adopt whatever measures necessary to control the worst vicissitudes of international finances and to reduce the perils of sudden price fluctuations and financial dislocation. Promptly restoring complete freedom in foreign exchange transactions, the Banco Central enabled Honduran currency to seek its own level, where it has stayed ever since at a rate of approximately two lempiras to the dollar. The external debt, most of which was owed Great Britain, was reduced by a series of payments. In 1952, three years after Gálvez took office it was down to only $361,937, and the sum was almost completely liquidated by the close of his administration in 1954.

Activities of these two state banks were instrumental in the improvement of Honduran finances. For the first time in several years the financial situation could be characterized as healthy and growing. Revenues were up ten million dollars in four years. A small boom brought a rise in national prosperity. Exports increased 60 percent in the first three years of Gálvez' presidency. Direct investments of the United States climbed to some seventy million dollars. The money supply grew from a value of 100 in 1949 to 142 in mid-1953, and economic and political disturbances in the next three years failed to reduce the total. After the first half of his six-year term, Gálvez told Congress in a constitutional message on December 5, 1952, that the large increase in revenue was due not only to matters of internal policy, but also to encouragement of foreign investment in Honduras. He announced that the foreign debt would be paid off completely within a year and praised the new income tax as a "beneficent innovation of your government."

Less instrumental in this financial resuscitation were two legislative measures which, nonetheless, were part of Gálvez' monetary policies. In 1950, Congress responded to his wishes by revising the income tax law. This increased taxes on individual businesses as well as commercial enterprises, and a new tax office was created to process tax collection. Like all Central Americans, the Hondurans had evaded payment of taxes and had falsified figures wherever possible. While they still avoid payment where possible, they are less able to do so; collections are still inefficient but improved over pre-1950 conditions.

A law passed in the spring of 1952 strengthened Honduran finances by authorizing a new issue of government bonds designed to equate the seasonal influx of government funds with expenses. This flux, due to the seasonal nature of the banana industry, was an annual occurrence. The bond issue was first approved only for the approaching fiscal year of 1953, but it was later extended after proving a mild success.

Agricultural methods also had to be improved if the economy was to thrive. The banana industry, thanks to the efforts of UFCO, returned a handsome profit to the enterprise and to the Honduran government as well. But economic dependence on bananas was obviously dangerous, as was apparent in years of floods, tropical storms, or Panama disease. Progress was slow, but the Gálvez years saw for the first time a slight reduction in the importance of bananas to the economy. For years contributing two-thirds of all Honduran exports, by 1955 bananas accounted for barely 50 percent. The work of foreign experts, including North Americans working through Point Four, helped the farmers improve their methods. Coffee, never very important, was given particular attention. Midway through his term in 1952, Gálvez could report an annual increase in revenue of roughly three million dollars as a result of improved technology and the new lands opened up by loans of the Banco Nacional de Fomento.

Cattle herds increased as well, and cattle remained the second most important agricultural item. With expansion of the road net, it became possible to market meat in neighboring villages, instead of consuming it at home. With this encouragement, cattlemen enlarged their herds. In July, 1953, a cattle committee began operations, intended by the government to orient cattlemen's technical activities and improve stock. The Committee was composed of five men, representatives of the Banco Nacional de Fomento, the Ministry of Agriculture, Honduran cattlemen, the Sanitation department, and North American assistance agencies. By 1955, figures revealed nearly one million head of cattle, the most of any Central American country.

The last of Gálvez' outstanding problems was education. Literacy in Honduras today is estimated at 35 percent; it was even lower in 1949 when Carías left office. Educational opportunities at all levels were essayed. At the University of Honduras, the School of Economic Sciences and the School of Orthodondistry (the first in Central America) were established. The educational system was revised, and new buildings were built, although the scarcity of teachers was too often overlooked. Education received a large share of the annual budget, usually near four million dollars, or some 20 percent of the total. On a more lofty plane, the Casa de Cultura was opened in hopes of stimulating cultural interest. The

Ministry of Public Education, hoping to advance national culture, sponsored various concerts, plays, and lectures, as additional Casa de Cultura activities. President Gálvez conceded that the effects might be small, particularly at the start. Still, it was hoped that such efforts would in time become more important.

Surpassing perhaps all Gálvez' material policies was his desire to breathe life into democratic ideals, to rejuvenate the long-dormant popular desire for individual freedom. Gálvez bent to this task unceasingly, and won his greatest popularity and success as a result. At the start of his administration he set out to break the time-honored precedent of governing the state and ordering its affairs from the Presidential Palace after a few quiet talks with trusted intimates. Rejecting this atmosphere of political machination and undemocratic government, Gálvez converted the building into an open forum of sorts. Working daily at his desk from 8 to 12 and 2 to 5, like any government employee, his door was always open to give citizens a hearing, to listen to their complaints and receive comments. His closest collaborators were also available to discuss business with any visitor, in fact, they were obliged to do so.

On Saturdays, the President would take his private plane and fly to some part of Honduras, dedicating a new school building, visiting a hospital, riding muleback through the mountains to examine a suggested roadbed. Almost fanatically devoted to honest government, he felt it desirable to examine personally the expenditure of government funds if possible; for Gálvez, it usually was possible. All his predecessors, including Carías, traveled very little, spending most of their time in Tegucigalpa. Instead of living withdrawn from the people, the President went among them at every opportunity. This was apparently entirely spontaneous. Believing passionately in the doctrine that only the people are sovereign, he tried to mingle as much as possible, being receptive to complaints, problems, and public opinion in general. From town to town and valley to valley he flew in his little plane, studying the needs of the people. On any weekend he might suddenly appear in a small, cloud-shrouded mountain village; he would often land at a tiny airport and ride by jeep or muleback to the nearest village, entering homes and shops unannounced. More than anything else, this explained his immense popularity. The people saw in Gálvez a president of the republic who would come walking into their thatched hut, squat on his heels before the fire, and talk to them about family problems, their cow, or their ten acres of land. As one partisan journalist wrote somewhat too enthusiastically, the Gálvez administration meant "here a new road, there a new acqueduct, elsewhere a schoolhouse where children need not sit on the ground."[8] Foreign reporters were only a little less enthusiastic.

A Salvadoran daily wrote that he was accomplishing for Honduras in one administration more than anyone had thought possible, and all the while operating within the narrowest limits of his office. Costa Rican journalist Alfredo Martinez wrote of Gálvez as comparable to Costa Rica's president at the time, popular Otilio Ulate. Gálvez ran a government of associates and collaborators, not sycophants. He was providing, wrote Martínez, an era of probity and administrative honesty. When he strolled through Tegucigalpa streets, sitting down in a cantina to have a drink, he did more for the advance of democracy than any dozen speeches.

One of Gálvez' few critics has been a young Argentine journalist named Abel Alexis Latendorf. In a recent publication Latendorf attacked the Carías dictatorship, revealed to his readers the backwardness of Honduras, and ridiculed the de facto president in 1956, Lozano Díaz. In these comments he was basically correct. But in a feverish attempt to criticize North American imperialism even where it did not exist, he also called Gálvez an ex-United Fruit lawyer who protected UFCO interests at the expense of the people. Gálvez, he claimed, was also guilty of the deaths of many revolutionaries during the latter years of the Carías regime. In fact, he triumphantly summarized Gálvez' government as using "persecutions and jail as favorite expedients."[9]

Such irresponsible criticism is an insult to the integrity and patriotism of the Honduran people, as well as Gálvez. Gálvez was indeed at one time a UFCO lawyer. It would be difficult to find many competent Honduran lawyers who have not served at one time as UFCO lawyers. The other charge is without foundation, since Gálvez simply had no connection with the events to which Latendorf referred. Normally, the Argentine's attack would not deserve any comment at all. Owing to the wide circulation of his writing, however, his gross misinterpretation must be mentioned. Latendorf, imbued with the need to find fault with U. S. intervention and interference, proceeded to splatter Gálvez with the same brush used against Carías. This is an outright injustice to one of the most democratic Central American presidents of recent years—one of the very, very few.

Central American observers, not so far removed from the subject as

Latendorf, have only the highest praise for Gálvez. On June 19, 1952, *Diario de Costa Rica* praised him for directing the most active and progressive government in Honduran history. He had raised investments by nine million dollars his first year in office, with succeeding years higher. Public freedoms were more fully developed than under any predecessor. Citizens had political and individual rights which were not abrogated at a minor provocation, and the Honduran people under his leadership were dedicating themselves to national, material, and even spiritual development. Gálvez himself continued to live a modest, unassuming life, ignoring the urging of friends to build up a political party founded on his evident popularity. He insisted he could only live by dedicating himself to a continuous defense of the national interests.

All this is correct in essence. However, Gálvez was not able to establish political maturity on a solid base. As Chapter One pointed out, many years of stability and democratic practice are necessary in Central America before responsible citizenship and mature political leadership may become an expectation, not a surprise. And in a little less than six years, certainly, Gálvez could not do more than light the way toward the democratic ideals Honduras must learn to embrace. However, two major events occurred during his last year in office which indicated the continuing irresponsibility that had lain dormant for five years. One of these concerned the national elections scheduled for November, 1954. The other culminated in the strike of the banana workers, which in time threatened the government with bankruptcy, the country with civil war, and the people with communism.

Yankees, Bananas, and Communists

Acreage of UFCO and its various subsidiaries extends throughout the Central American states. In Honduras, the company owns 39,253 acres of banana lands. This far exceeds the acreage in Guatemala, over which so much disturbance was created by the Communists. Only in Costa Rica, of all the Central America states, does UFCO have more acres of banana plantations than in Honduras. For years, the company had plied the banana trade at great profit, enjoying a privileged position in the national economic situation. At the time, it scrupulously paid the government a percentage of its profits each year, money which came to be the bulk of the government's annual revenue.

Through these years the workers were unorganized. Carías never saw fit to smile upon labor organization. As a result, there was none. The workers lived in backwardness and ignorance. Their wages, it is true, were by Honduran standards reasonably good. As in Guatemala, native laborers drew better pay from yankee employers than from Honduran management. It was only a matter of time, however, before the combined forces of poverty, illiteracy, disorganization, and exploitation would unite, demanding better working and living conditions, formal organization, and adequate land reform. That time came in May, 1954, with the first general labor strike in Honduran history.

The crisis that was to endanger the very economic and political life of Honduras began on April 10, 1954. Dock workers at the UFCO wharves in Tela refused to load a ship about to embark for the United States. They demanded double-time pay for working on Sunday. At once the situation was brought before a labor court, where the judge said there was no legal provision for double-time. The men returned to the wharves. Few realized what was augured by this initial action.

The same thing took place the following weekend, and again the workers were refused double-time pay. Labor relations worsened and, on April 28, President Gálvez dispatched a detachment of troops to the major Caribbean port, Puerto Cortes, as a precautionary measure. By May 3, the strike had spread like wildfire through the different UFCO land divisions. All four—Puerto Cortes, La Lima, Tela, and El Progreso —were on strike. Thousands of workers were idle. They demanded immediate wage hikes and better working conditions. Company officials conceded that nearly twenty thousand men were on strike but declined to comment on the workers' requests.

La Epoca, long the Carías paper in Tegucigalpa, blamed communist agents for instigating the action. Truthfully, the strike had begun without much prior planning. Quite naturally, communist elements were prompt to capitalize as best they might on the situation. However, they did not initiate it. The government, hearing reports of violence, sent additional troops on May 6, flying them to San Pedro Sula, from which they drove by jeep and truck to La Lima, a few miles from the coast. North Americans, threatened by thousands of strikers, were virtual prisoners in their homes. Servants joined the strikers' cause, making it more difficult for UFCO officials and families living in the area. Communications were cut, and armed bands roamed the streets of Progreso crying, "we are the law."

Government radio station TGWA, in communist Guatemala, urged strikers to accept nothing less than a 50 percent wage increase. Honduras promptly sent a protest to Guatemala, demanding the end of such broadcasts, as well as an explanation. At the same time the government prepared to expel known non-Honduran Communists accused of agitating among the workers. Two consuls at the Guatemalan embassy were declared persona non grata and sent home. The government announced that any others found to be creating disturbances or inciting opposition to public order would follow. From UFCO, which had been presented with an ultimatum demanding a reply within forty-eight hours, there was no word.

Saturday, May 8, the strikes extended to parts of the Tela Railroad Company, a subsidiary of UFCO which owned most of the Honduran railroads. In the coastal departments of Atlantida and Yoro, rail workers had quit. At the same time, laborers at La Ceiba, a port to the east of Puerto Cortes and Tela, also went on strike, and another port was completely paralyzed. The government, remaining non-committal on the merits of the dispute, insisted on maintenance of public order. Observers were a little surprised when the national political groups, already organized and preparing for November elections, promptly offered the Gálvez government wholehearted support. The National party offered Gálvez its help in maintaining order, and the newly formed Reformistas announced an agreement with the President to support him in whatever measures were taken to end the strike and resolve the difficulties. The Honduran press, hailing these agreements, refused to take sides in the argument. As *La Crónica* said, "we hope the dispute will end with the best solution for national well-being."

Basically, the banana workers wanted an across-the-board 50 percent increase, and a forty-four-hour work week, instead of forty-eight. They also asked for additional health and educational facilities, as well as added housing and annual vacations. As Daniel James wrote, it was implicit that they receive recognition of labor's right to organize. "Demands expressed the crying need for an enlightened social attitude on the part of Honduran leaders, and in UFCO's case seemed to indicate that the Company had learned little from its experience in Guatemala. . . ."[10] UFCO stubbornly refused to give an answer in less than thirty days, insisting that a month was necessary to study demands. The government, recognizing the impossibility of rendering judgment in only forty-eight hours, suggested fifteen days as a compromise. However, officials insisted that thirty days were necessary, and no reply would be forthcoming before that time. J. Felix Aycook, general manager of the Tela Railroad Company, reiterated the company position on May 8, saying that discussion of terms could not begin for thirty days, and not even then, if the strike continued. There could be no negotiation until the strike was ended. He also reported that the Tela Hospital operated by UFCO was about to run short of food for its three hundred patients as a result of the strike. He appealed personally to some two thousand workers camping on the Tela baseball field, but they were adamant.

Three days later, Minister of Interior Juan Antonio Inestroza tried to end the strike during a personal visit to the northern zones. By this time the workers for the Standard Fruit Company had joined the strike, raising the number of strikers to some twenty-two thousand. In Tela he sat down with leaders to discuss the situation, but there was no agreement. Inestroza declared later that reports of coercion were exaggerated, that at the very most only 10 percent of the workers were on strike against their will. Tela remained completely shut down, as did Puerto Cortes, the largest port. The government reported the general situation worse, particularly when General Inestroza's efforts were rebuffed. In Tela, even the schools were closed. There, and elsewhere, strikers had closed UFCO commissaries, and North American families began to view with alarm their diminishing food supply.

In Tegucigalpa, there was complete order, but activity was growing. University students and typographic workers organized to raise money to send strikers. The communist organization in Honduras, the Partido Democrática Revolucionario Hondureño came into the open after months of inactivity, distributing leaflets encouraging the workers and urging solidarity in the face of government pleas. The Honduran teachers' association added its official sanction to the strike. People were listening to Radio Guatemala City, which continued to encourage the movement despite protests of the Honduran government. Government officials themselves grew uneasy. At no time had they taken the action lightly, but UFCO and Standard Fruit officials warned them that bananas ready for harvest would soon begin to deteriorate. Damage to the harvest meant a commensurate dent in the national treasury, and much money might be lost. Already the Banco Central had lost almost a million dollars in foreign exchange as a result of Tela Railroad inactivity. *El Día* reported that the strikers appeared increasingly well supported financially, and might be able to hold out indefinitely. No end was in sight.

The next phase of the strike began on May 13, and by the close of the week was in full swing. Only banana company employees had participated, but now the laborers in other industries joined the movement. Workers for the Honduran Brewery, British-American Tobacco Company, New York Rosario Mining Company, several shirt-making factories, and a forest and timber company all went on strike. By May 18, nearly fifty thousand workers were on strike, out of a national population of 1,608,000. The government stepped up official efforts to end the strike, sending a team of mediators by plane to La Ceiba to speak with Standard Fruit Company workers. Reconciliation at this point was impossible. Elsewhere along the coast, essentials were becoming scarce. With commissaries shut, the ports closed, and railroads motionless, no new foodstuffs were arriving. Both employers and employees began to feel the pinch.

Partial agreement was reached for the first time on May 19, when Standard Fruit workers agreed to return to work after talking with government mediators. They also recommenced operations on the railroad from Tela through La Ceiba to Olanchito, a few miles inland. Details were unannounced, but as it turned out, the company had agreed, in principle, to accept the strikers' demands pending final arrangements. On the same day, UFCO began to negotiate with the strikers, with government mediators presiding. Before considering other matters, workers indicated that general superintendent Girdner and La Lima Hospital administrator Dr. Ramírez must be removed. There was no immediate announcement.

Elsewhere, the strike was expanding. Workers at Santiago Balan y Compañía, a Cuban firm, walked out after continual threats. Mediation at several of the minor firms was suspended. Only Standard Fruit could show substantial progress. At UFCO, where all the trouble began, workers' representatives presented petitions asking for wage increases of from 30 to 72 cents per hour, depending on salary. Common banana laborers got approximately 20 cents an hour; they wanted 72 cents per hour. The men receiving 39 cents per hour asked for a 30 cent raise. Other requests for which they petitioned included time and a half for extra work, and the usual demands for better living conditions, medical attention, and educational facilities.

By this time, increasing attention was directed to the communist hand in proceedings, both internally and through Guatemalan meddling. Guatemala, severely pressed by its own internal problems, was nearing the end of its rope; in five weeks the government would be overthrown by Castillo. However, for the present, it was openly encouraging the strikers through radio and press, as well as by lending aid and agents to the strikers. By May 20 the situation was tense, and Guatemalan sources were claiming that Honduras had broken diplomatic relations. Four days later the *Chicago Tribune,* for years one of the best U. S. papers on Latin affairs, reported that war between Guatemala and Honduras was near. Honduran frontier guards had captured five Guatemalans crossing the border without papers, apparently on their way to assist strikers. President Gálvez was constrained to ask the United States to invoke the newly signed Pact of Mutual Assistance. Lincoln White of the U. S. Department of State announced that Honduras was being sent arms under terms of the new treaty. A shipment of small arms, jeeps, and trucks left from Mobile, Alabama.

From Guatemala came reports that troops were seen moving around Chiquimula, only some sixty kilometers from Santa Rosa de Copán, in Honduras. Honduran patrol planes also saw Guatemalan military forces much nearer the border and, a week before, troops had been spotted at Puerto Barrios, a Guatemalan port near the border. On May 25, Ambassador Jacinto Octavio Duran was called home from Guatemala City for a conference and did not return. Guatemalan Foreign Minister Toriello, desperately grasping at straws to halt the deterioration of his country's position, sent a telegram to Tegucigalpa on May 27 proposing a non-aggression pact. After study, Honduras rejected the offer. Foreign Minister J. Edgardo Valenzuela said his government felt it unnecessary in view of other existing treaties guaranteeing the same friendship.

While this was transpiring, it was still not clear just how large a role communism was playing in the strike. It had begun without Red agitation and, only as the weeks passed, did communist participation become more prominent. Eight Tegucigalpa newsmen had flown to La Lima to interview Professor Manuel Valencia, who was beginning to emerge as leader of the strikers. Calling himself secretary-general of the strikers, Valencia claimed to represent the sincere elements of the workers. Attacking the committee in Progreso as riddled with Communists, he accused them of harming the workers' plans. He also had rather unflattering comments for UFCO officials and repeated to the journalists the strikers' basic demands. In response, UFCO's William L. Taillon replied to the same newsmen that UFCO was delaying further negotiations until the arrival of an expected government commission. Even then, he did not expect immediate talks, for he questioned the identity of the strikers' representatives. He expected to wait until internal organizational difficulties were resolved.

Tela Railroad Company officials explained, a few days later, that negotiations with its workers had also been halted. In a letter to the government mediation commission, they noted that the central committee of strikers had suspended negotiations on the last day of May, 1954. The company wanted to open commissaries to supply food both to strikers and isolated officials and their families, but plans were cancelled when the strikers refused to operate the trains necessary to carry food to the company's commissaries. The government mediation commission charged that the suspension resulted when the central committee of strikers refused to stand by an agreement they had accepted only two days before. For the first time, the government itself was angered by the laborers' actions. After such apparent bad faith on the part of the workers, the government doubted they could deal with the strikers as a responsible body.

On June 1, the strikers began to struggle among themselves for representation on the central committee of strikers. This effort lasted several weeks, during which time both employers and government mediators marked time impatiently. It was immediately apparent that a large number of strikers were angered by the bad faith of their leaders in negotiation with UFCO officials. The majority considered these men guilty of breaking off relations unnecessarily. Conditions which were accepted on one day were rejected by the strike committee the following day when they were to sign the agreement. Several members demanded the resignation of Agusto Coto, who was instrumental in deceiving UFCO negotiators.

While the strikers were feuding with one another, Foreign Minister Valenzuela warned that the government would be forced to adopt "certain measures" if the paralyzing action were not soon ended. He explained in a press conference that the government was losing hundreds of thousands of dollars. Yet with talks broken off, there was no likelihood of immediate settlement. In addition, the minister said public order would be maintained. Regardless of the strike conditions, national peace was not to be jeopardized. The government was sympathetic to the strikers, but insisted upon retention of total public security. If necessary, emergency measures would be applied.

By this time, Communists had succeeded in stirring up a great deal of trouble, hoping to establish their supremacy in labor. Honduran Reds appeared as strike leaders and influential members of local strike committees. In Progreso, they soon seized complete command of the area strikers. One of the "legal advisers" was the secretary general of the Partido Democrática Revolucionario Hondureño, José Piñeda Gomez. The party was recognized as the Honduran communist organ, but without much effect, at this point. Pamphlets were distributed clandestinely, falsely claiming the authority of the united strike committees. A radio was established, although never very important. Efforts to stir up the Liberal party, which had now been out of power for over two decades, were unsuccessful.

Authorities of the government arrested four strike leaders at San Pedro Sula on June 2, after gaining reliable information that they were known Communists. The government gave proof that the efforts of the four were wholly communist-inspired, with no intention of helping Honduras. They were headed by Agusto Coto, who claimed the secretary-generalship of the strikers; it was he who had broken his word in UFCO negotiations. The others were Manuel A. Sierra, connected with the Guatemalan CGTG, Rubén Portillo, and Modesto Rubio. On receiving news of the arrest, leaders of other strike committees attached to Coto all responsibility for the recent failure of negotiations. Professor Valencia in La Lima said that his strikers recognized the economic danger they were creating. Expressing complete confidence in President Gálvez, Valencia also announced the formation of the Unión Sindical de Trabajadores Hondureños (USTH), with himself holding the post of secretary-general. Miguel A. Ruiz was secretary of organization and Arturo Rivera Santamaría the secretary of relations.

The next day, Valencia emphasized in the San Pedro Sula daily paper, *Orientación,* that his new organization in La Lima was completely removed from the strike committee of Progreso. He repeated accusations of extreme leftist orientation on the part of its leaders and attacked Agusto Coto, in particular, for conducting the negotiations that had brought the strikers to the present impasse. He further conceded the grave effects of the strike on the national economy. On June 3, one member of the government commission told newsmen at La Lima that he anticipated new negotiations in a matter of days. Roberto Arellano Bonilla declared that his hope, and that of all concerned, was a new negotiating commission completely free of communist influence. In the same vein, Valencia said that "when we began the strike we didn't know that we had Communists among us. But we have had some communist infiltration by Hondurans and therefore we have been slow in the matter of negotiations. We are now trying to eliminate the Communists and solve the strike as soon as possible."[11] Asked about Coto, he simply said that "we didn't want him to represent us." Workers told reporters the same thing the next day. They wanted to return to work as soon as possible.

With employers still biding their time, strike delegates from Puerto Cortes, Tela, La Lima and Batáan met on June 5, without Progreso representation, in an effort to accredit an official delegation to meet with fruit functionaries the following week. Valencia was the moving spirit behind the conference. On the heels of this meeting came news of a settlement between the Tela Railroad Company and its workers. The railroad strikers were granted a substantial pay increase plus other benefits. Both parties, reportedly pleased, returned to work on the lines. The picture seemed brighter.

The day that railway workers agreed to terms, however, UFCO set back chances of an agreement by a move of extraordinary foolishness. With the strike now entering its fifth week on a wide scale, they distributed by air twenty-three thousand leaflets stating a new company proposal on one side and a message from Gálvez and his ministers on the other. UFCO offered workers a 19 percent increase for those receiving $1.18 a day. Those earning from $2.00 to $2.80 were conceded a 10 percent raise, while those earning from $2.80 to $4.00 a day would receive a 5 percent increase. UFCO also offered free medical aid for families of employees paid less than $75 per month. Two-week vacations each year were guaranteed to all workers receiving $75 a month and up.

Strikers were highly incensed by this move. Raúl Edgardo Estrado, a high official of the reorganized strike committee, wrote an angry letter to Tela Railroad manager Aycook, accusing UFCO officials of bad faith in making a direct offer to the workers over the head of negotiators. Hinting that bloodshed might become unavoidable, he declared that the central committee of strikers was prepared to meet company negotiators at any time, any place. The new committee had total authorization to deal as representatives of the workers. However, the offer of higher wages and accompanying privileges expressed in the leaflets had to be withdrawn first, so that negotiations might again commence "before it is too late." The UFCO leaflet bombardment was termed an underhanded UFCO maneuver to divide strike leaders. Certainly the move could scarcely have been more ill-conceived.

U. S. Ambassador Willauer, in Tegucigalpa, expressed the general opinion when he said he hoped the company and strikers could reach an agreement in "an equitable form," the sooner the better. He believed a strike solution "would be facilitated if both the Company and the workers realize that their common interests are greater than their differences."[12] Notwithstanding his words, there was no apparent end to the work stoppage. The plight of those living in the paralyzed areas became worse. Tela Railroad manager J. Aycook telegrammed President Gálvez that the Tela Hospital was in dire need of personal supplies. He blamed this directly on the strikers. Following government communication to the strikers, the situation was alleviated, although the hospital was still sorely pressed, as were families of North Americans living in the area.

Finally, on June 12, came rumors that discussions would be reopened shortly in the six-week-old strike. Before the end of the day the government mediation commission officially announced that talks would begin the next day, which they did, at San Pedro Sula. Two weeks after the doublecross by communist Coto, the two sides were prepared to deal with one another again. The commission assured UFCO that the existing strikers' committee was truly representative. However, UFCO negotiators were understandably wary. One of them admitted that "the company has little confidence that tomorrow's meeting will bring any concrete result. There is still doubt that the new committee is authorized to represent all the strikers."[13]

Thus discussions between banana strikers and UFCO were reopened. The strikers' demands were the same as outlined before, providing from a 30 to 72 percent wage increase plus different fringe benefits. In all, a list of thirty "official" demands were presented to UFCO. More than a week passed, and the representatives continued to wrangle over terms. No apparent progress was being made. Outside Honduras, other labor organizations prepared to offer a hand. Arthur Juaregui flew to Honduras as representative of the anti-communist Confederación Internacional de Sindicatos Libres and was joined on June 28 by members of the United States' American Federation of Labor. The Organización Regional Interamericana de Trabajo (ORIT) also sent negotiators, who arrived after considerable delay on July 20. All these groups were concerned that communist subversion might become serious in the absence of agreement.

The government announced hopefully several times that an agreement was at hand. However, the days dragged by without solution. On July 11, the banana strike passed its seventy-first day. Anti-yankee feeling was finally beginning to build up; speeches denouncing imperialism became common, even in Tegucigalpa. Insults were tossed back and forth freely by the elements involved in the dispute and tempers were reaching the breaking point. A few days later, the negotiators suddenly came to terms. Strikers won notable concessions from UFCO, although not all that was demanded. Wage boosts were only a little lower than the percentage increases they had demanded since May. Paid vacations, hospital facilities for families, and a moderate program of newly constructed homes were granted.

Irreparable financial damage resulted from the strike. UFCO and Standard Fruit lost nearly fifteen million dollars. Bananas had ripened and perished on the stalk, unpicked. And in Honduras there are an estimated 14,500,000 stalks of bananas. Both UFCO and Standard Fruit through the years have survived various troubles. As long as bananas can be picked and exported, they are reasonably happy. In this instance, of course, bananas were not picked, and the loss was severe. Workers themselves lost over two million dollars in wages. Perhaps the worst loser was the Honduran government, one million dollars poorer as a result of losses on export-import duties. This was a great part of the annual revenue, and the budget was thrown severely out of joint. A hasty recalculation of expenditures was forced upon them. Faced by such a loss only a few months before the first presidential election in six years, the government had reason to be distressed.

In the long run, the most important result of the strike was the new position of Honduran labor. It was inevitable that they would in time demand and be permitted some form of organization. Carías had forbidden it for sixteen years, and the enlightened Gálvez fell down in this respect, also. Of the concessions won by the Honduran workers, probably none was as important as the knowledge that together they formed a potent force in national affairs. "Nothing, henceforth, can obliterate that knowledge from their minds or prevent them from making new efforts at new organization. The question is whether Honduran labor will be encouraged to develop a native, anti-Communist leadership or be driven, as Guatemalan labor was, into the arms of the Communists."[14]

The government, once the strike was settled, requested the visiting foreign labor experts to help formulate effective organizations. In July, 1954, President Gálvez said that his government had asked for help from these groups, and was subscribing to the ORIT. "We need central scientific advisers from the ORIT to succeed in Honduras . . . [we need] elements capable of speaking technically for the Instituto de Seguridad Social in problems of labor and other social aspects conforming with the legislative program that the National Congress will likely issue."[15] The afore-mentioned Juaregui, a labor leader from Mexico, worked on future union organization. He followed several weeks of study and conferences by presenting to the government a series of suggested labor laws. He pointed out that the union organization should be neither religious nor political. Among other things, a substantial number of workers would be sent to labor schools in Puerto Rico and Mexico to undergo instruction in the rudiments of labor unionism. After all, he declared, "Honduras is fully capable of having union organizations." And after a round of discussions and meetings, most of his suggestions were adopted.

Despite the 1954 near disaster, Honduran labor has been generally quiet since that time. Before its new leaders were able to form even the basic nucleus of a longterm organization, let alone add flesh to the skeleton, Honduras was embroiled in one of the most rancorous political situations of recent years. This was the second serious blow for President Gálvez' attempt to establish basic democratic tenets once and for all. Today, more than four years later, the political scene is still unpredictable and fluctuating. Where the present political leaders may take the country, how seriously they may divide the people and set them against one another, is still unknown.

POLITICAL MUSICAL CHAIRS

The presidential campaign and elections of 1954 were acrimonious and hardfought. The results were in doubt for some time; once they became known, a variety of occurrences prevented any candidate from taking office. An untimely heart attack and an obscure vice-president became decisive factors. Honduras continued two years after these elections without a constitution or a de jure head of state, and was governed by decree. These regrettable circumstances can be understood by an explanation of the antecedents of the 1954 electoral campaign.

Early behind-the-scenes maneuvering prepared the way for a bitter, angry campaign. By the end of the year Honduras was on the brink of revolution. For the first time in the century, more than two political parties were to participate significantly, as a result of the National party's decision to run for president none other than Tiburcio Carías. After six years on the sidelines, the doughty old man chose at the age of seventy-eight to move back into the Casa Presidencial. Once the General made known his desires, there was no question of his candidacy. His years in office had built up a powerful following within the party which would never be overcome. And no one forgot that he had been the party leader, both in and out of power, since 1919. He was officially nominated on February 20 at the Palace Theatre. Gregorio Zelaya Reyes was nominated for vice-president.

Not everyone in the National party was satisfied with the decision, however. A small but determined minority had disapproved not only of the continuismo of Carías, but felt that the General's day was over and the party should turn to younger men. A number of these, ardent admirers of President Gálvez, waited for some indication of his preference. Gálvez never made any such choice publicly. Rather, he maintained an impartial attitude during the campaign and elections. In retrospect, many think he had further presidential ambitions. Be that as it may, he could not legally return to the presidency at once and insisted that no efforts be made on his behalf. He quickly squelched a movement to change the constitution that he might run to succeed himself.

Motivated by many factors, then—dislike of Carías, rejection by Gálvez, opposition to the National party old guard—a number of dissidents broke away from the party to establish the Partido Reformista. Looking ahead to the presidential race, their sights were set on Carías, they wanted to block his return to power almost as much as to boost their own cause. For a time they considered supporting the yet unannounced candidate of the Liberal party. A union with the Liberals, they felt, would have almost certain success in defeating the General. On March 3, 1954, a leading Liberal presidential hopeful proposed to Durato Díaz Medina, the Reformista chief, a pact in which the two parties might agree not to join any other political group—*i.e.,* the Nationals—for the October elections. The Reformistas discussed the proposal but decided to let it die unanswered.

The Reformistas were further strengthened after the official nomination of Carías. Another group of Nationals, led by Carías' longtime vice-president, Abraham Williams, walked out of the National party. This completed the break between Williams and Carías which had begun in 1948 when Carías chose Gálvez over Williams as his successor. On his sixtieth birthday on March 16, in Tegucigalpa's stylish Belair Restaurant, Williams made a speech that was a barely veiled threat against National party regulars who had attacked his defection bitterly. "If they [party loyalists] want blood, they will have blood. I see reunited around me the youth of Honduras . . . [who] must be ready when I have to call them."[16] The Reformistas, heartened by this further split in National ranks, prepared for their own convention. Meeting on Sunday, March 21, they chose Abraham Williams for presidential candidate and Filiberto Díaz Zelaya as his running mate. They advocated constitutional reform permitting a presidential incumbent to succeed himself. By this stratagem they hoped to attract galvistas who were staying aloof from the campaign.

Watching from the sidelines, with evident satisfaction, was the Liberal party. Relishing the damaging intra-party battle and the emergence of the Reformistas, the Liberals were encouraged in their own prospects. Early hopes that the Reformistas might support their candidate proved groundless; nonetheless, they considered Carías a formidable foe, and he seemed to have lost at least a part of his former support. The Liberal candidate was not known. Their longtime leader, Angel Zúñiga Huete, defeated by Carías in 1932 and an unsuccessful opponent to Gálvez in 1949, had recently died. There was no heir apparent. Possibilities included Celeo Dávila, Ramón Villeda Morales, and Santiago Mexa Calix. Dávila appeared the likely choice. Yet, after years of law practice in Costa Rica, where the Costa Rican branch of UFCO was among his clients, he was somewhat out of touch with necessary political contacts.

Meeting on Sunday, April 26, the Liberal party happily enjoyed its first open, unhampered convention in years, thanks to the non-interference of President Gálvez. After a day long meeting, Ramón Villeda Morales was nominated for the presidency, with Enrique Ortiz the vice-presidential candidate. There were and are many Liberals who maintain Villeda steamrollered his way to the nomination on the strength of deals and suspicious arrangements. These are the same Liberals who criticized Villeda for remaining in Tegucigalpa, attending government social fetes, and pursuing his medical practice while most prominent Liberals were in exile, patiently waiting their return to Honduras. In any event, Villeda won the nomination with at least the support of the majority. After twenty-one years out of power, the Liberals were not about to throw away their chances because of a personal squabble.

Honduran election laws provided that campaigning be restricted to the one-hundred-day period immediately preceding election day. Designed to shorten the period of angry campaigning and name-calling, this limitation has never succeeded in reducing friction to other than moderate proportions. In 1954, with the government keeping hands off, campaigning was unrestrained, and it grew quite rough as election day approached. More people than ever before were approached, harangued, and appealed to for votes.

For the Liberals, forty-five-year-old Villeda, in active terms a relative newcomer to politics, proved an adept campaigner. Brushing aside charges of leftist leanings, he campaigned, traveled, and spoke incessantly. His campaign was vigorous and confident; he fully expected to win. His first official declaration in July revealed the attitude with which he approached elections.

Opposite our internal and international panorama, Honduras must form its soul on the molds of a liberal philosophy. Neither for the right nor the left: to the center. . . .

The Liberal party of Honduras will fight for the international defense of democracy as a fundamental concept of American right that determines the very existence of the hemispheric community.

The Liberal party is not a political group in systematic opposition to the government of the Republic. . . . The Liberal party has offered its backing to the government of Honduras, as a guarantee of democratic institutions and of national sovereignty. The Liberal party trusts that President Gálvez will know how to guarantee the electoral right of a climate of free liberty with the exercise of democracy.[17]

Despite Villeda's optimism, many of the Liberals were worried about possible government interference. After all, they reasoned, wasn't President Gálvez a National? And wasn't he put in power by Carías? Surely the government would intervene from time to time. Such an outlook made the Liberals rather touchy. At the slightest provocation they magnified the grievance into direct insult or electoral intervention.

When the government refused them a train to send supporters to a political rally, they reacted indignantly. On August 20, their newspaper, *El Pueblo,* shot back that the government had sabotaged a rally at San Pedro Sula by refusing to make available adequate trains. Yet the government had taken the same stand a few weeks before when the Reformistas requested trains for the same purpose.

For the Nationals, Carías did a minimum of active campaigning. While Villeda concentrated on traveling the countryside to reach outlying rural areas, Carías limited his appearances to a few of the population centers. Convinced of his forthcoming victory and slowed by age, he made no effort to match the campaigns of his two rivals. The National party shared his confidence and offered little more than a promise to return Honduras to strong, centralized government. There was little reason, Nationals felt, not to expect a victory. Many Hondurans still held Carías in awe, as before. And under his nominal leadership the party had won 76 percent of the total vote in 1952 municipal elections. And in 1953, despite a strong campaign by the Liberals, they polled 44,334 votes. Liberals and Reformistas together polled some 10,000 less.

The Reformista campaign never really got off the ground. Abraham Williams campaigned actively, and attacked his opponents with anger and frequent bitterness. Yet he drew small crowds, and rarely did his turnouts match those of his opponents. He had served as vice-president under Carías, and so was well-known, but the strong man had completely dominated political life. Many people felt that Williams would follow the same poicies as those of Carías; if this was what they wanted, they were more likely to favor him than Williams.

The political climate became cloudy in August when a crime wave gripped the nation for nearly two weeks. Night after night, stores, shops, and saloons were broken into. Bands of men, numbering from five to forty, roamed darkened streets as vandalism ran rampant. The government ordered a general disarmament, and only a very few citizens in special circumstances were permitted to carry weapons until after the election. At the same time, political meetings became nearly uncontrollable. A crowd of twenty-five thousand assembled from across the countryside in Progreso one Sunday at a rally featuring a speech by Villeda. By the time it was finished, the Liberal candidate was hardpressed to restrain the crowd from mob action and a breach of public order. Other manifestations disquieted the country. On August 7, reacting to growing uneasiness, the Archbishop of Tegucigalpa instructed all parishes to exhort the people to solve political disagreements peaceably.

The three parties agreed to end their campaigns on September 26, two weeks before elections, in order to help insure tranquillity. Perhaps indicative of a public trend was the attendance at the closing speeches of the candidates. Villeda drew a cheering throng at Puerto Cortes. Carías spoke to a modest, less enthusiastic audience in Nuevo Ocotepeque. A small but noisy crowd heard Abraham Williams' final appeal for votes at Amapala, on the Pacific coast.

The two weeks preceding election day were not placid. Police announced the thwarting of an attempt on the life of Carías. An official of the Central Penitentiary was arrested for complicity in the plot. Political arguments were frequent, and encounters often ended in brawls, especially in the more frequented bars. Reliable sources in El Salvador were quoted by the Associated Press as expecting an outbreak of violence at any time. Members of the diplomatic corps in Tegucigalpa had attempted to arrange a non-violence pact among the three candidates. This attempt failed when Carías' spokesman refused on the grounds that there was no reason to trust the word of his rivals.

Attention was diverted from the election by a series of floods brought on by heavy rains at the end of the wet season. Former capital Comayagua was nearly inundated. Landslides buried people alive and small rivers overflowed their banks at La Lima, Progreso, and Chamelecón. Railroad contact with the north coast was snapped. President Gálvez flew to San Pedro Sula to direct rescue work. Reformistas organized a comité de socorro to help flood victims. General Carías contributed one hundred quintales of flour for distribution among the homeless. The Dirección de Sanidad Pública sent supplies and equipment to hard-hit areas, and the Red Cross provided medicine from its Panama headquarters. By October 7, with waters receding and most of the damage accounted for, a haggard President Gálvez announced grimly that over one thousand had perished in the inundations, with another four thousand left homeless. A few areas remained isolated pending further recession of the flood waters.

Members of all three parties requested a delay in the October 10 elections, pleading that disastrous rains had made forthcoming elections inappropriate. The government countered with the argument that the democratic process should not be interrupted, regardless of circumstances.

Elections were not things to be tampered with, and had to be held as scheduled. There was also increased danger of violence if elections were postponed. As it was, the Minister of War ordered the army to be sure that no voter was intimidated, while the Minister of Interior warned civil municipal authorities to take whatever measures necessary to guarantee civil rights.

On election eve all three parties claimed victory on the morrow. The Nationals accepted the victory of Carías as a foregone conclusion. They saw no way for him to lose. Liberals, almost as certain, had misgivings about government interference. After the long years of inactivity, they could scarcely grasp the thought of returning to power. The Reformistas, most militant of the three, announced defiantly that they were going to be armed in order to insure their ascendency after the inevitable triumph.

With 411,354 voters eligible, most estimates anticipated a total of perhaps 275,000 votes. The constitution made voting compulsory for eligible citizens. This was never enforced, however, and no one took it seriously. Many people worried about the possibility of a virtual three-way split in the voting. Thus no candidate would win an absolute majority. Unless one of the parties won close to 150,000 votes, the decision might well be forced into the National Congress. Under the constitution, a complicated process might follow. The ninth section of Article 101 read that

> In case an absolute majority is not obtained, [Congress is] to elect a president and vice-president from the two citizens who obtained the greatest number of popular votes for each office. If the Congress does not make the declaration of the election of president and vice-president within 20 days counted from their installation, the Supreme Court of Justice shall do so within the 7 days preceding the date fixed for taking possession of these offices, said court being authorized in this case to receive the oath of office of those elected. . . .[18]

The effect of this clause was to throw elections into Congress, where the political complexion might render it unable to make a choice. By the time a decision could be handed down by the Supreme Court of Justice, peace might have been shattered and revolution broken out. Later events were to follow this pattern closely—to a point.

Early election returns gave Villeda a clear lead, but nearly a week passed before the final tally was announced. Villeda received 121,213 votes, far ahead of Carías with 77,041. The General failed to score as heavily as expected in the population centers, and Villeda drew a large total in rural areas. Abraham Williams ran far behind with 53,041. The Liberal party itself appeared to have won a narrow majority in the Congress, although several seats were disputed. Villeda, however, lacked by 8,869 votes his required majority; the 121,321 count gave him 48 percent of the total. In such circumstances, the National Congress was to choose the president. The first legislative session was not due until October 29. In the meantime politicos began to jostle for position.

Villeda gave a victory statement followed by an interview with *El Mundo*. A bookish-looking man wearing horn rimmed glasses, Villeda again belied his appearance with a number of outspoken comments. Declaring himself a man of firm democratic convictions, he exulted that "The triumph stamps the battle as that of Honduran Liberation. . . . I was opposed by communism, official influence . . . and other equally grave factors. . . . If a small band of willful people try to keep me out of office, rivers of blood will flow in Honduras."[19] Claiming an absolute majority of congressmen, he expected to be declared president despite doubts in other quarters. He said he was aware of rumors that Carías and Williams might reconcile their interests to select the former as president, but scoffed at the report.

The preliminary meeting of Congress on October 29 dealt with jurisdictional matters and set the date to name the president as December 5. At first, the Liberals were credited with twenty-six seats in the fifty-six-seat chamber. Thus, with a total of three more, they would have the necessary majority to choose Villeda as president. There were several disputed seats, however, and the Liberals challenged them in hopes of winning the necessary three. The maneuver backfired, and after the realignment was completed, they had lost three more instead. This left the Liberals with twenty-three seats, the Nationals with twenty-two, and the Reformistas with eleven. The situation was clearly dangerous. If the Nationals won the support of only a few Reformistas, Carías would be named president despite Villeda's victory at the polls. If the decision were carried to the Court, Carías also had a good chance. The Supreme Court magistrates had been appointed to their six-year terms when Gálvez took office, and were elected by the pro-Carías Congress of 1949. Thus the General was likely to be named if the decision was carried to the Supreme Court of Justice.

On November 10, Villeda issued an appeal in hopes of being selected by Congress when it convened.

General Carías can look with pride on the final defeat of his political life . . . if he does not interfere in the just and legal solution of the presidential succession of 1954. . . . Decidedly the triumph cannot be taken away from the Liberals because we have arrived at it by an honest process and what has happened cannot be reversed.

The Honduran who lived [through] the past violent dictatorship has new sentiments, new ideas, new purposes, and, in a word, new life. He cannot return to terror because he already knows it. He does not withdraw from his free condition because it has cost him much to achieve that liberty.[20]

Five days later the vital barrier preventing political chaos was removed when President Gálvez was stricken by serious illness. Physically exhausted by his efforts to battle recent floods, overextended by the rancorous political events of past weeks, the strain had taken its toll. On November 16 it was announced that he had suffered a heart attack. It was later learned that his illness was a grave internal difficulty made worse by his tired condition. Convening the cabinet at once, Gálvez requested a leave of absence for medical treatment. He was granted permission, and Vice-President Lozano assumed executive powers during Gálvez' absence. The President also gave general orders to all army garrisons to be alert, and asked public employees for complete loyalty to his temporary successor. Ironically, the President was stricken while taking part in the funeral procession of an old friend.

Gálvez flew to Panama on November 16 and was admitted to Gorgas Hospital in the Canal Zone. His own doctors and members of the hospital staff examined him at once. After a week, he was again flown away, this time to Miami, accompanied by two doctors and a son. He was to convalesce in a Miami hospital over a month before returning to Honduras, by which time the political situation had taken another unexpected turn. Of Gálvez' heart attack, it must be observed in passing that his sudden departure was not, as some suggested, an excuse to shed the executive robes at a difficult moment. This is scarcely fair. The President sustained a grave physical attack and left the country to receive the best possible medical treatment only after doing everything possible to assure political tranquility. In the capital, Lozano announced that he would try to continue the policies of "my old friend," and the cabinet remained intact. There were no upsets, although the country was dismayed at the delicate health of Gálvez. No one gave particular attention to Lozano, a colorless political workhorse. They assumed he would continue, though perhaps weakly, the President's impartiality in the forthcoming political procedures, and everyone was intimately involved in the continuing machinations of electoral politics.

Deputies of the Liberal party elected provisional functionaries for the new Congress in a preliminary session on December 1. In the absence of National and Reformista deputies, the Liberals elected General Santiago Meza Calix provisional president and Modesto Rodas Alvarado provisional secretary. Liberals were confident that Villeda would be named president, for it was increasingly plain that the National and Reformista forces would not unite. The personal antagonism of Carías and Williams was too strong for that.

Two days later Liberal hopes plummeted sharply. The regularly convened session of Congress found the chamber more than half empty. Unable to agree among themselves, National and Reformista deputies boycotted the meeting, leaving the Liberals unable to take any action whatever since two-thirds of the members were necessary to form a quorum. Until Congress was formally convened, no action could be taken on the presidency. As a result, the stalemate could last, in accord with the constitution, for twenty days; then the Supreme Court of Justice would make a choice, within seven days. The Liberals, reluctant to risk a Court decision that might well name Carías, pondered their next move. A revolution seemed the only alternative since constitutional means appeared exhausted. Before the possibility developed, Lozano took action.

Gálvez' vice-president had never been an important man politically, although gaining moderate prominence as part-time minister and cabinet member. A sixty-nine-year-old businessman and one-time bookkeeper, he had been overshadowed completely by energetic Juan Gálvez, and was quietly closing a twenty-five-year political career. A man of violent temper and poor health, Lozano was pushed into the job of maintaining order until an election winner was named. It soon became apparent that no winner was to be named. No one was altogether sure of the Honduran Supreme Court of Justice, consequently no party was willing to risk its candidates on the unknown quantities who were to choose a chief executive. In the end, no one took the case to the Court, and no decision was made. Lozano, faced by this lack of decision and the danger of revolution, took the decisive measure. On December 6, 1954, Lozano declared himself "chief of state" and assumed complete dictatorial powers.

Taking command of all three government branches, he declared himself the absolute state authority for an indefinite period. He suggested that it would probably last two years. "My government will act like a magnificent sun which illuminates everything and burns no one."[21] The same day Lozano called on the military authorities to avoid trouble, be politically impartial, and work for reconciliation of the Honduran family. In a radio message to the nation from the Blue Room of the Presidential Palace, he called his steps necessary in view of constitutional imperfections. Qualifying his government as de facto and referring to himself again as "chief of state," he told Hondurans the government would not be a dictatorship for such would be "too much work for one man." A Consejo de Estado would be formed to advise and assist him in operating the government while a new constitution was prepared by a constituent assembly. He announced that the membership of the Consejo de Estado would be announced the next day. It was nearly two weeks however, until the composition was completed.

Lozano pledged himself to maintain individual rights and freedom of the press. He warned, however, against improvident criticism or "possible subversive propaganda." Noting that Honduras, with limited resources, was passing through a critical economic period, he said that his government would guard democratic principles jealously. Questioned by newsmen, he assured them that he was fully supported by the National party, and was confident that Liberals would also cooperate in his efforts to protect Honduras until constitutional order was re-established.

The next day Chief of State Lozano granted political amnesty to all those jailed for political purposes in the past three years. He proclaimed it a sign in favor of complete re-establishment of civil rights. By implication, he was condemning the policies of his friend and former chief, Juan Gálvez, suggesting that civil rights had not been properly protected. He decreed that the move must bring a return of absolute harmony among all Hondurans. In time, references to harmony under Lozano were to become farcical.

The Experiment Breaks Down

Lozano's action was welcomed at first. Villeda expressed relief that resort to violence might be avoided. Carías visited Lozano for ninety minutes on December 9 to offer National party support. At the end of the conference the two embraced cordially. The fledgling labor movement greeted the emergency measures with approval. Their spokesman, Gustavo Adolfo Zavala, told the press he was organizing syndicates on the basis of democratic ideals. The Standard Fruit Company workers in Tela had formed a thirty thousand member union. Several others were organizing with a membership of at least ten thousand. He said that "We hope that the government stabilizes itself and then we will demand union agreements that are not unilateral, only for the good of the employers, but true agreements reached through bilateral negotiations, and we want to have a labor code, written not only by Honduran lawyers but edited with the aid of the OIT, CIO, AFL, and of course the Organización Regional Interamericana del Trabajo. If we obtain a code written only by lawyers of our country, it will have little value."[22]

The year 1955 in Honduras was at first a struggle for Lozano to establish some sort of political calm. His most energetic activities were dedicated to this goal. On January 15, 1955, he requested the directors of the three political parties to close their Tegucigalpa offices for the month, opening them only one hour in the morning and another in the afternoon. A month later, with considerable behind-the-scenes agitation, Lozano issued a call to all parties for abstention from activities encouraging a climate of political unrest. Charging them with a "certain atmosphere of obstruction," he expressed disappointment that after two months, he still had to issue such reprimands.

In March, after several weeks of apparent quiet, the police uncovered communist plans for intense anti-government maneuvers. A projected congress of young Communists in Tegucigalpa was forbidden. News that Red-tinged ex-President Arévalo of Guatemala was encouraging the meeting no doubt influenced Lozano's decree. Shortly after, he also proclaimed a thirty day ban on political meetings. No reunions or concentrations of a political nature were permitted. Public order would not be disturbed while he could prevent it, the chief of state testily repeated. Simultaneously he announced an arbitrary price increase in aguardiente, a cheap brandy-like liquor. He hoped to cut down national consumption. A general tax increase on beer and cigarettes was also decreed. He hoped to increase national income nearly 50 percent by these measures to build up the financial reserves depleted by the 1954 strike. Tax on income was hiked from 15 to 30 percent.

By May 20, 1955, Lozano was able to announce that inscription of voters would begin in June. The five-month process would try to establish the eligibility or non-eligibility of every citizen to vote for a national constituent assembly. The chief of state expressed the hope that once an assembly was elected, a new constitution could be drawn up, and by 1956, new national elections might choose president and congress.

Lozano's "national conciliation" was beginning to fray at the edges. The Liberal party organ, *El Pueblo*, trumpeted a declaration that Villeda was the actual Honduran president despite delays to his assumption. Furthermore, electoral liberty was being undemocratically restricted by government decree. Lozano, responding to the charge, announced that

> I must declare that to fulfill my promises to the Honduran people of giving free elections, it is necessary to proceed to base the matter on a clean electoral census, that doesn't permit adulteration of any sort. . . . It must be remembered that this election census will be permanent, and already constitutes a public document in which rests the effectiveness of a completely free vote. I am intimately interested because the census must also include the greatest possible protection for the individual's voting rights, and I will not stop providing protection . . . regardless of the number of editorials that the press publishes by way of criticism. . . .[23]

In a direct warning to the Liberals, he added that "It seems that the moment has come to declare publicly that my spirit of tolerance, of broadmindedness with every class of political element . . . is being taken as a sign of weakness by my Government. I will . . . maintain the public order and carry out my purpose of national conciliation . . . I will use all measures at my disposal through the government, even though my government is only de facto. It is essentially democratic."[24]

Lozano's efforts to bring about a new, legally constituted government proceeded at a snail's pace. When the five-month inscription period ended in October, the task was unfinished. The chief of state granted a two-month extension. January and February of 1956 were devoted to revision, and only by March, 1956, was the electoral count completed. Lozano then sent a projected electoral statute to his Consejo de Estado for study. Eventually, they approved the project after making minor changes, and Lozano issued it as another decree. Approval of the electoral statute meant that elections might be held for deputies to the national constituent assembly that was to vote a new constitution and, subsequently, choose a constitutional president. Elections were tentatively scheduled for late June.

Opposition to Lozano had steadily mounted with the passing months. The Liberal party, having assumed a position of primacy nationally, became increasingly irritated by his slow progress. Inevitably they began to attack him without reservation. On December 12, 1955, just a year after he took power, they were charged with trying to destroy the interim government. Liberals retorted angrily that even though Villeda was the true president, they were planning no uprising. From that time forward, the two maintained a running exchange of castigation and criticism. Liberal attacks were joined by those of the Nationals, particularly Gonzalo Carías, son of the octogenarian ex-dictator. On May 18, the government Office of Intellectual Cooperation denounced the opposition of villedistas and backers of Gonzalo Carías and said they were about to "try to promote an armed movement . . . with the goal of overthrowing the government." Villeda called the charge absurd and sarcastically commented that "It would be totally inane to try to tumble from power a government that can fall from power without any help."[25]

By the summer of 1956, twenty months of government by decree had left Honduras at sea. Lozano's difficulties continued to increase as political attacks grew increasingly sharp. Most of the turmoil came from Liberal carping. In turn, he fought back roughly, if not wisely. He also proceeded to organize politically, something paradoxical for a person running a provisional government.

Lozano succeeded in creating a group favorable to his retention of power. This included government bureaucrats whose jobs lay in his hands, as well as important army elements. With this nucleus Lozano formed the Partido Unión Nacional (PUN), hoping to create personal electoral power. Although still a minority group, the PUN became a recognized political force when joined by the Reformistas. Finally admitting their weakness, the Reformistas chose Lozano rather than the other two parties they had opposed so bitterly. Williams, Reformista standard bearer in 1954, agreed to the coalition. Presumably his ambitions were superceded by those of Lozano.

In June, the Liberals gathered in Tegucigalpa for their national convention. Sincerely fearful that Lozano would insure himself extensive tenure by manipulating the Supreme Electoral Tribunal in elections for the constituent assembly, the Liberals prepared for the election, hoping to prevent Lozano from winning an assembly majority. Their meeting was harrassed by Lozano. National police were instructed to put the capital "off-limits" to all non-Tegucigalpa Liberals. Any political demonstrations were to be handled forcefully. In an effort to secure his position, he finally named the date for elections to the constituent assembly—October 7, 1956.

Honduras was stunned when, on July 9, Villeda was arrested, taken to an airfield, and flown into Guatemalan exile. He was accompanied by two other leading Liberals—party chairman Francisco Milla Bermúdez and *El Pueblo* editor Oscar Flores. None was given any notice whatever. Lozano went on the air almost at once to explain the banishment. Speaking over a technically defective national network, he called the move unavoidable. He announced that Villeda had tried to organize a general strike of banana workers, thus obstructing the work of his government. "Honduras simply cannot afford a general strike at this time . . . there was no other choice. . . ."[26] Villeda fired back from Guatemala that his expulsion was "inexplicable." The action could only be attributed as a "sign of insecurity and weakness of the de facto government of Julio Lozano." He denied complicity in any plot and characterized his apprehension as being "in a tumultuous manner, without any means of explanation."

Nothing could have stirred up more trouble in Tegucigalpa. University students led week long attacks on the police, both verbal and otherwise. The new Legislative Palace was stoned by a crowd on one occasion. Police broke up several demonstrations with tear gas, and on one occasion fired into the crowd to break up a student gathering at a Tegucigalpa high school. A half dozen demonstrators were wounded by week's end and many others jailed. For the next few days, police stood at intersections searching passersby for weapons. Business was reduced to a minimum, the National University padlocked, and extra police called to duty. An uprising was expected at any time. Lozano gave a detailed account of the supposed labor strike planned by Villeda. Presumably it was first set for June 20 but then postponed until July, by which time Villeda had been expelled. Liberals repeated previous denials.

Trouble was not limited to Tegucigalpa. On July 17, the police shot down two brothers in La Ceiba, leaders of the youth branch of the Liberal party. Other Liberal journalists, including the editors of *La*

Voz Liberal and the weekly *Basta,* were jailed for subversion. At the same time, Lozano, trying to still foreign criticism, rationalized his action in a letter to James G. Stahlman of the Inter American Press Association. He claimed to possess "extensive documentary background showing links of the three expulsees with Communists residing in Mexico and in Honduras itself . . . they . . . were in association with recognized Communist agents infiltrated into Honduras, [and] were trying to persuade organized labor on the north coast to enter into a planned uprising."[27] Most observers felt Lozano, like Castillo in Guatemala, was finding "communist" interference in every manifestation of opposition to the regime.

After two weeks, Honduras began to calm down. Villeda had continued from Guatemala to Costa Rica. His exile there was unpopular, but criticism slackened. Just when the situation appeared under control, a barracks revolt tried to overthrow the regime by force. At 1:30 A.M. on August 1, the San Francisco infantry barracks, commanded by Major Santos Sorto Paz, sent troops out through the city to seize strategic points. The First Infantry Battalion was called out against the rebels and by 6:00 A.M. the four hundred rebels had been repulsed and driven back inside the barracks, across a forty yard wide park from the United States Embassy in downtown Tegucigalpa. Loyalists brought up machine guns, only to find their shots bouncing off the walls of the barracks.

Four mortars were taken to the nearby Prado Hotel, carried through the lobby and up four flights of stairs to the roof. Thus situated on one of the highest vantage points in town, government troops began to lob round after round on San Francisco. Accuracy was surprisingly good, and by 9:10 the rebels ran up a white flag. Loyalists picked up their mortars, carried them back downstairs and out the lobby of the Prado, nodding to the desk clerks as they left. The battle claimed more than one hundred dead or wounded. Again Lozano cracked down and 130 suspects were rounded up. Extra troops patrolled the city. Liberals were predictably blamed. In Costa Rica, Villeda suggested that the government would seize on the opportunity to postpose elections. In the capital Lozano commented, "I will have to think this over." In the meantime, he declared a twenty-day state of emergency in the Francisco Morazán department, prohibiting public meetings and political gatherings. Newspapers were censored; outgoing commercial cables were examined by the government. Courts-martial were ordered for those involved in the revolt, and suspects were continually picked up on the streets by steel-helmeted soldiers.

On August 2, the day after the uprising, Lozano set up a three-man junta to deal with "subversive" elements. It was to coordinate the defense of Tegucigalpa in case of further disturbances. Alarm was raised on the eleventh when Lozano collapsed from overwork and was ordered to rest for fifteen days. The junta was assigned the task of maintaining public order nationally, and many interpreted this as an indication that Lozano had resigned and turned power over to the military. Rumors suggested a heart attack. Actually, the unbending Lozano had lost his temper during a conference, as he often did, and collapsed in the middle of the floor. Mexican cardiologist Ignacio Chavez announced after medical examination that Lozano was suffering from fatigue complicated by a bad cold. Ordered to bed for two weeks, Lozano empowered the junta with peace maintenance. Within a matter of days he was meeting officials in his bedroom, and soon lifted the state of emergency and disbanded the junta.

Although seventy-one-year-old Lozano remained in harness, he still suffered from arteriosclerosis, overwork, and temper tantrums. On September 13, he was finally forced to fly to Miami for a short rest. In a reversal of the process followed in 1954, he turned over his position to Chief Justice and ex-President Juan Gálvez. The latter had recovered from his illness and returned to Honduras in early 1955. Although nominally supporting Lozano, he had not been active politically. While approving Lozano's announced goal of restoring democratic government, Gálvez privately deplored many of his methods. Nonetheless, he resumed power temporarily while Lozano recuperated on Florida shores.

Hondurans welcomed the change. Many openly wished "Don Julio" a nice trip, enjoyable vacation, and non-return. The author, staying in Tegucigalpa at the time, was told repeatedly that if only Gálvez remained interim president, elections for the constituent assembly would assuredly be free and honest. However, Lozano returned to Honduras three days before elections, dourly commenting that elections would be free and democratic no matter what measures might be necessary. The police were called out in large number. Each corner in downtown Tegucigalpa had at least one, and usually two policemen leaning casually on a rifle.

Most observers predicted a victory at the urns for Lozano and his PUN. The Liberal leadership was almost all in exile; Reformistas continued to support Lozano as a matter of expediency; and Carías announced that when Lozano returned the National party would abstain from the election rather than be a party to inevitable fraud. Abraham Williams predicted that the assembly would support the regime, designate Lozano as president pending adoption of a new constitution, and choose at least two vice-presidents as well.

Elections of the seventh bore out his predictions. Official results released a week later showed the PUN to have won all fifty-six seats. Not one anti-government candidate won. Lozano unctuously said that he would be pleased to serve the will of the people. Williams scoffed at opposition attacks, saying "they are just bad losers. Losers always claim fraud in politics everywhere." However, Hondurans remembered election day. At 3:15 P.M. a large group of Liberals in the main square of Tegucigalpa were suddenly fired upon pointblank by police, without provocation. Before the eyes of foreign newsmen several were wounded, including three who died the next day. Things were even nastier in outlying regions. Many cast ballots under gunpoint. Others were sent home without voting. Ballot boxes were switched with pre-stuffed ones. The opposition fought back at places; four policemen were dragged from their car and slain by machetes near Villanueva. In all, over two dozen perished. Even ardent Lozano supporters were appalled. Such events were outrageous, and sealed Lozano's fall beyond any doubt. Lozano, probably well-intentioned when he took power, had gotten a taste of executive prerogatives and decided to stay in power at all costs. He kept his position only by dictatorial rule founded on fear and suspicion. Initial efforts to achieve a new, popularly elected government based upon suffrage and democratic exercise of choice had broken down completely.

Unexpectedly, and without the anticipated bloodbath, Lozano was pushed out of office later the same month. On Saturday, October 20, a delegation of officers visited Lozano to request his resignation. He agreed in principle but asked for a brief delay. Overnight the officers completed their plans. At 8:00 A.M. on the twenty-first, armed forces took up positions around Tegucigalpa. Planes swooped over the city, nearly scraping rooftops. The military insurgents called on Lozano at the Presidential Palace and repeated their demands. He yielded, and in mid-afternoon officially turned over power to the junta. In a ceremony before the assembled diplomatic corps, the revolutionaries gave their word not to prosecute lozanistas. With this, the sour old chief of state retreated to his hilltop residence, soon to leave Honduras.

It was a group of young, democratically inclined officers who engineered the coup. As Lozano had increasingly ignored all but the trappings of democracy, they had decided to make their move at last. The three-man junta directing the operations was composed of Colonel Hector Caraccioli, thirty-four-year-old Air Force commander, Major Roberto Gálvez, thirty-one-year-old son of ex-President Gálvez, and General Roque Rodriguez, commander of the military academy and, at fifty-five, the dean of the trio. In a "Proclamation of the Armed Forces of Honduras" they guaranteed "a return to the rights of the people, authentic constitutionality, and respect for the institutions of the Republic. On our military honor we promise to return the government to a civilian element that has authentic popular support. We will remain in command only during the time democratic criteria and national interest necessitate. We intend to govern democratically with the collaboration of all Hondurans of good faith."[28] *New York Times* correspondent Paul Kennedy was told that "The decision [to revolt] was made when it became apparent that the election of the National Union party was opposed by the great majority of the people. The armed forces did not want to be placed in a position whereby they had to enforce the laws of a Government that did not represent the will of the people."[29] Thus Julio Lozano went the way of all would-be dictators.

RETURN TO CONSTITUTIONALITY

The junta showed immediate signs of true reformers. The youthful leaders—Rodriguez merely lent them prestige—declared political amnesty, opened cell doors to political prisoners, consulted with Villeda, and won his support aong with that of the National party. A new cabinet was formed representative of different political groupings. Its dominantly youthful note was sounded with the membership of several young supporters of Caraccioli and Gálvez. A new Supreme Court was named shortly, also including members of the major political parties. As expected and hoped, the October 7 election of a constituent assembly was annulled, a move that brought enthusiastic national response.

The junta's problem was the installation of an assembly capable of drawing up a constitution upon which a permanent government might be based. They were anxious to do away with such procrastination as

Lozano had followed. The junta insisted on establishing a constitutional basis for whatever government followed, and in that direction lay their goal. There was temporary confusion early in 1957 when Foreign Minister Esteban Mendoza resigned and rumors suggested the departure of Major Gálvez from the junta. However, the junta proceeded calmly to draw up electoral plans, and a timetable was soon set up. It called for the proclamation of an election for a constituent assembly on September 21, with its first meeting convening on October 21, anniversary of Lozano's overthrow.

Further plans were outlined in mid-July, after the dismissal of General Rodriguez from the junta. In the final days of June the ministers of defense and interior wrote open letters to the newspapers accusing Rodriguez of having played politics. He was asked to resign on July 5, and when he refused, was dismissed the following day. He called his dismissal a matter of personality, but would not dispute the action although accusations were without basis. "The important thing is unity of the armed forces and . . . compliance with the promise to hold free elections."

The junta announced the same month that the October meeting of the assembly gave it the option to adopt a constitution, elect a new president, or provide for general elections. The first elections, those of September, would be held for the first time under provisions of proportional representation. Thus all parties would seat deputies in proportion to their national strength. All parties concurred, including the Liberals, who might have won 80 percent of the seats or more under the traditional plurality arrangement. But Liberal leaders, after momentary hesitation, apparently felt that under a plurality representation their sweep would be so complete as to threaten the assembly before it could convene.

By September, all parties were campaigning nationally amid an atmosphere of freedom and moderation. The junta was carefully fulfilling its promises of an honest election. The Liberals, in particular, campaigned vigorously, led by Villeda, who had returned from a brief tour in Washington as ambassador to the United States. Often accused of being a dangerous left-winger, if not a communist sympathizer, Villeda took particular efforts to belie the accusation. He reiterated opposition on all terms to communism, as well as his friendship for the U. S.

When elections were held, over a half million went to the polls. Violence was held to a minimum, although four were killed and nine wounded in incidents to the southeast of Tegucigalpa. The Liberals piled up a large majority, reflected in their capture of thirty-six of the fifty-eight seats in the assembly. Although Villeda had expressed a preference for presidential elections, the November meetings of the constituent assembly felt otherwise, and Villeda was not reluctant to accept their mandate as chief executive. On the sixteenth, after nine hours of rancorous discussion, he was named to begin a six-year term on January 1, 1958. The final vote was thirty-seven to twenty. The provisional junta accepted the decision without comment. Villeda was inaugurated as scheduled, giving Honduras its first legally elected chief executive in nearly four years.

Ramón Villeda, previous winner in the 1954 election, had never been popular with certain elements of his party. "Little Bird," as he is sometimes called, had been a shrewd opportunist ready to accept help wherever it might be found. However, this propensity does not establish a connection with communism. For this reason he is a doubly powerful man. Recent events indicate that the responsibilities of office have brought to him a new awareness of the problems confronting Honduras. He is a powerful man of strong character and not one to be dealt with lightly. If he maintains the vigilance over Honduran affairs that has typified his political career, there may be a change in the nation's nineteenth-century existence.

In November, 1957, the president-elect studied a report of the Honduran Economic Council. It was far from comforting. The economy had been growing worse for two years. Thanks to the laborers' strike, 1954 was disastrous, and 1955 agricultural crops were hit by severe floods. The Office of Internal Taxes estimated a loss of two million dollars to the government. The 1954 budget had reached thirty million dollars, the highest in history. Business activities for many months were curtailed pending developments of political turmoil. UFCO and Standard Fruit tabled plans for extensive programs worth hundreds of thousands of dollars to the government, and activities today are only returning to normal after the long period of acrimonious politics.

Villeda learned of the 1957 budgetary deficit of $5,000,000, as well as the drop of net reserves from $11,400,000 to $11,000,000 in less than one year's time. Banana shipments would be well below the 1956 level of $7,000,000. Added to these business ills were the labor situation and general communist activities. Labor, finally organized after years without representation, had proceeded rather slowly. Following the 1954 strike, UFCO had to lay off thirty-five hundred of its twenty-one thousand employees. With so many bananas rotted on the stalk, the harvest was smaller. Elsewhere in the economy, organization of labor came about more slowly, with the absence of trained leaders creating a gap into which the Communists were trying to step. This had been part of their formula in Guatemala. As labor leader Gustavo Zavala had admitted himself, the communist problem in labor was a genuine one.

Daniel James wrote in 1954 that Honduras was second only to Panama on the communist Central American priority list. Until modern labor legislation and land reform come to Honduras, the danger remains. Political circumstances still seem to preclude the adoption of any such laws. On March 21, 1956, Foreign Minister Esteban Mendoza candidly admitted as much while addressing the Overseas Press Club in New York City:

> The continued infiltration of communism on the north coast of Honduras represents a threat to the security of the countries of Central America and the Caribbean area. The Communists have never lost hope of recovering power in Guatemala. . . . In connection with various elements in Honduras, extremist followers of Lenin and Stalin have tried several times to start a revolt on the north coast of Honduras, which would serve as a springboard for an attack on Guatemala. . . .
>
> Thousands of workers [9,000] are found without work on the plantations of UFCO today as a consequence of the extensive strike and destruction of banana plantations by the floods occurring in the fall of 1954.
>
> In spite of the interest and the efforts of the government to solve that afflicting situation, which extends over a wide area, the Honduran exchequer is not in economic condition to take additional steps. . . . The recent facts of infiltration, carried forth by individuals suspected of being communist agents, have obliged us to increase our vigilance.[30]

As Villeda's government got under way, he took steps to alleviate economic problems. A request was made to the International Monetary Fund to increase the Honduran quota from $2,500,000 to $7,500,000 as a means of protecting the currency. Money was poured into an agricultural development program. Road construction was also pushed. In December, 1955, the Lozano government had received over four million dollars from the World Bank for road construction. In May, 1958, Villeda's administration received an increase from the Bank by signing a $5,500,000 highway loan, devoted to the cost of a new paved highway linking Puerto Cortes on the Caribbean with the national highway network and Tegucigalpa. The loan was for repayment in twenty years with annual interest of 5⅜ percent. While social services were studied, they received less emphasis, the attraction of foreign capital for roads and agriculture being considered more important.

After a year in office, Villeda's government showed promise of an improved and more enlightened approach to Honduran problems. The return of constitutional government was the first step in a long path toward more progressively sound government. But the future remained rather gloomy. The tragedy stems from the fact that this need not be so. A prominent Honduran educator, Jorge Fidel Durón, rector of the University of Honduras, said as much a few years ago at the Fifth (1954) Conference of the Caribbean in Gainesville, Florida:

If it were well-governed, Honduras could easily be converted into a model. Nevertheless we have chosen to live in continual political agitation in which the best intentions are rendered helpless and where a cabal of professional politicians have taken advantages of the situation and have prospered. We have been prisoners . . . of strong political, economic, and commercial forces, principally in the hands of better organized neighbors. But Honduras goes surging valiantly against all dangers, and according to what I believe, nothing will be able to stop it now from reaching our goal of pacific prosperous existence based on international cooperation.[31]

His analysis of Honduras' existing situation is acute. But the peroration of the last sentence is sadly inaccurate. Honduras has rarely been "surging valiantly against all dangers," but instead, plunging blindly into every endeavor with a common obedience to the forces of elemental folly and immature, irresponsible, political thievery.

Chapter Five

NICARAGUA

LARGEST AND LEAST DENSELY populated of the Central American states is Nicaragua, bordered on the north by Honduras and on the south by Costa Rica. With two coastlines, each over two hundred miles long, Nicaragua is a country of geographic contrast. The mountainous Central American cordillera rises to a modest height in the western third of the country, running northwest and southeast. In the east, the country slopes toward the Caribbean, ending in the once notorious Mosquito Coast, an aptly named jungle area that provided refuge for Caribbean buccaneers. Nicaragua's 57,143 square miles support a population at the low density of 21.0 per square mile. The two largest lakes south of Texas—Nicaragua and Managua—are linked by the Tipitapa River, forming part of an undeveloped transport system.

Nicaragua has been endowed with a moderately varied economic heritage superior to that of its neighbors. Eighty percent of the population deals in agriculture, the leading industry. At the same time, agriculture utilizes only 10 percent of the area of this Wisconsin-size republic. More than half the country is covered with valuable forests, only a small portion of which would be difficult to convert from timber to marketable lumber. Soil is fertile and mineral deposits, especially gold ore, are potentially significant, though largely undeveloped. Cattle growers raise the best beef in Central America, and the broad tropical plains of the east are ideal for bananas and sugar cane, which do not thrive on the milder climate of the higher elevations.

Until recent years, probably no Central American state was wasting its natural potential as shamelessly as Nicaragua. Following its independence from Spain in 1821, nothing happened. Occasional internal strife and dissolute government only helped contribute to general stagnation. The state of affairs was deplorable. Citizens lived uncertainly, and only the poorest illiterate peasants escaped political insecurity. They were presented, at the same time, with an oppressive and sometimes losing battle for minimal subsistence and survival.

Only in the past two decades has Nicaragua begun to pull itself out of the century-old quagmire. These years have been a time of material accomplishment far exceeding any previous efforts. And they have been directed by Anastasio Somoza, a dictator in every sense of the word. Because Somoza has been master of Nicaragua for years, the country today reflects the imprint of his administration. His recent assassination does not change this circumstance. All Nicaragua's achievements and shortcomings as well are attributable to its longtime leader. To understand Nicaragua, we must go back more than twenty years to find the first strands from which today's pattern has been woven. These reveal the fateful events bringing Anastasio Somoza to power.

The Coming of Somoza

For the United States the twentieth century brought many things, including a new foreign policy sparked by a man of continual activity, Theodore Roosevelt. With the country swept by a fierce passion for nationalism, foreign policy became, in less developed areas, that of outright imperialism. This was outlined in the so-called Roosevelt Corollary and subsequent commercial interference that is even today attacked by critics of the United States as "dollar diplomacy." Several of the smaller Caribbean nations were subjected to United States imprudence; among these was Nicaragua.

In the midst of one of its internal eruptions in 1909, Nicaragua executed two soldiers of fortune who claimed U. S. citizenship. A naval force quickly intervened, and from 1912 to 1925, a body of U. S. marines was stationed in Managua, maintaining a modicum of peace in the face of bandit raids and smouldering public resentment. Thus plunged into Nicaraguan affairs, the United States did not withdraw until the days of Franklin Roosevelt and the Good Neighbor Policy. Influence was asserted in energetic terms. As early as 1924 the United States took steps to withdraw from Nicaragua, pending results of the 1925 presidential elections. Prepared to convert its marine headquarters into a legation recognizing Nicaraguan sovereignty, hopes proved premature. Weeks after the election was completed the defeated forces rebelled and took control of the government. The U. S. again stepped in to restore peace, designating an interim government pending new elections. Three years of patient negotiation by Henry L. Stimson led to new elections in 1928; an open, democratic vote named General Moncada president. With U. S. support he took power.

Hoping to withdraw from Nicaragua permanently, the United States went to great lengths to insure continued stable government. The marines remained in the country, organizing and training a national constabulary as an effective governmental instrument capable of buttressing the legitimate government. By 1931, the marines reduced their force, and a few years more saw the last of the unpopular "gringos" leave the country. National pacification was completed, except for the activities of an irresponsible insurrectionist named Augusto Sandino. Refusing to come to terms with the government, this semi-bandit harrassed the peasants by small forays into the villages for food, money, loot, and women. As the U. S. commanders prepared to depart, they searched for a man capable of pursuing the elusive Sandino. The found him in vigorous young Anastasio Somoza. This discovery changed the course of Nicaraguan history.

Son of a San Marcos coffee planter, Anastasio Somoza was born in 1896. Growing up on the plantation, he was educated first in Managua, later at the National Institute in Granada, and briefly in Spain. He traveled to the United States to learn bookkeeping and business administration at the Pearce School in Philadelphia, also taking a job as bookkeeper for an automobile agency where he learned some of the choice four-letter words that spiced his English conversation. During his seven years in Philadelphia the young Somoza developed an enduring respect for the United States, became an ardent follower of the Philadelphia Phillies baseball team, and married the daughter of an outstanding Nicaraguan surgeon.

Returning to his revolt-riddled homeland, Somoza worked variously as an accountant, sanitary inspector, sports promoter, and automobile agency manager. Combining these activities with that of tax collector of León after 1925, Somoza soon was deeply involved in the swirling political waters. A firm supporter of President Moncada when the latter was inaugurated, he was rewarded with the post of Governor of León. Soon afterward named secretary to the army chief of staff, Somoza was shrewd enough to build personal strength. President Moncada, growing apprehensive of his growing influence, dispatched him to Costa Rica as Nicaraguan minister. Before long, the ebullient Somoza had to be recalled and, although barely in his thirties, promoted to foreign minister.

In the 1932 arrangement withdrawing the last U. S. troops, Somoza was named director of the army, in which he had become active, and from that day until his death in 1956 he controlled the Nicaraguan military. His first job was final pacification of the rebel Sandino, and Somoza personally directed the military campaign against him. In 1934, Sandino agreed to make peace and came to Managua under a truce preparatory to disbanding his guerrillas. Following a banquet at the Presidential Palace in his honor, Sandino left with a handful of his assistants and in a matter of hours had been cut down by a volley of machine-gun bullets.

Somoza has been blamed by his opponents for the dastardly killing. In response, he later published a short account of the affair absolving himself of guilt. The incident was so shrouded in secrecy that to this day few people know the truth, and they have never told. Whether Somoza was personally responsible cannot be established, although he is highly suspect. As commander of the military, he was responsible for their participation in any such action, and it was established that Nicaraguan soldiers participated. The result was to make a martyr of the lawless Sandino. To this day he is referred to with reverence by many chafing under the Somoza regime.

In a short time, Anastasio Somoza was the most powerful man in Nicaragua; it but remained for him to enter the next elections to assume the presidency in name. Aided by palace intrigue, he was easily elected. On January 1, 1937, Anastasio Somoza took office as Nicaraguan president. Until late 1956, Nicaragua was his. Some of the many critics of Somoza have reached back a quarter of a century to attack U. S. Minister Matthew Hanna for promoting Somoza's appointment as army chief in 1932. One writer has charged Hanna with falling prey to the colorful vocabulary, outgoing personality, and adept dancing of Somoza. This assumption contends that a serpentine Somoza seduced gullible United States officials by the sheer force of his social graces. But the point of view of Minister Hanna is easily appreciated. The future of an independent Nicaragua depended in large part upon strong military support for civil government.

This implied a sound, stable commander of the Guardia Nacional. Few of Somoza's critics have impugned his administrative capacity or strength of character. To the U. S. officials, the man seemed most likely to hold together and strengthen the Guardia Nacional. It was four years after the departure of the U. S. forces that Somoza reached the top. His social charms and North American naïveté were scarcely the decisive factors.

It was by a combination of historical circumstance, administrative ability, inherent shrewdness, and not a small quantity of luck, that Somoza moved into the presidency twenty years ago. Nicaragua today is a reflection of the Somoza policies and practices. One of these is the question of democracy and free government, or the lack of it. Of equal importance, however, were the Somoza measures to advance national wellbeing.

Internal Developments

Any examination of internal progress must deal in comparative terms, contrasting conditions in 1937 with those existing today. This can be categorized under finance, agriculture, economic development, transportation, and health. Whatever may or may not have been achieved lies at the door of Somoza.

In 1937, Nicaragua was harried by a pressing economic crisis, one which had prevailed with varying severity for years. Coffee producers were being outstripped by their neighbors. National economy rested upon the unpredictableness of international prices. Known mineral deposits were totally undeveloped. Taxes oppressed large segments of the population unable to bear the burden. Fiscal deficits plagued the governments. Lack of highways prevented the transporting of rural products to the larger commercial centers. President Somoza ordered liberalization of foreign investment laws. Anxious to alleviate the tax burden, he planned to attract foreign capital as a means of meeting government expenditures without drawing upon national sources. As the durability of the Somoza government became apparent, foreign businessmen were increasingly willing to invest. This was curtailed during World War II, but after the Axis powers surrendered investment became greater than ever before.

A series of laws provided appropriate safeguards for foreign capital, probably the most liberal and rigidly enforced in Central America. On February 26, 1955, the present law was enacted by the National Congress, reflecting the substance if not the practice of an earlier code.

Article 1. Foreign capital may come into and leave the country without restrictions, in accordance with the provisions of this law. By foreign capital it will be understood . . . capital existing and originating outside Nicaragua, belonging to foreigners or to Nicaraguans who have permanently resided abroad. . . .

Article 9. The foreign capital registered will enjoy the following rights:

a) Total or partial withdrawal . . . at any time;

b) Unrestricted remittance of net earnings from the capital registered; this applies also to interest earned where loans are concerned;

c) Re-exportation or alienation of machinery or physical equipment covered by foreign investments, and free remittance of proceeds from their sale. . . .

Article 15. Foreign capital enterprises may contract the services of technical administrators, accountants, auditors, and other specialized personnel in accordance with the laws on the subject.[1]

This bill granted foreign enterprises equal treatment in Nicaraguan courts. Labor laws were not to discriminate against foreign capital, and those applicable to Nicaraguans would be equally valid for non-nationals.

No one was more aware of the importance of this legislation than Somoza. Long a friend of the United States, he was emphatic in encouraging U. S. business interests. On April 17, 1955, addressing the National Congress concerning the new Foreign Investments Law, he declared that "Readjustment of development plans, expansion of the national economy, a climate of peace and security, and the high credit standing of the country, all these factors have combined to create extremely favorable conditions for investment of foreign capital. In order to provide such investments with adequate safeguards, on February 26, 1955, a law was enacted which fundamentally provides for foreign capital to come into and go out of Nicaragua with no restrictions whatever."[2]

His regime devoted itself equally to the growth of private enterprise. There was no expectation that increased foreign investment alone would shore up a sagging fiscal structure. The government established the National Bank of Nicaragua to propel the drive for additional national enterprise and individual investment. Each year additional credits promoted such activity. By 1954 the figure had climbed to $104,123,143, some $37,000,000 higher than 1953. Continued though less marked advance was shown in 1955. Roughly 39 percent of the total bank credits were issued by the National Bank of Nicaragua; the loans were channeled primarily toward agricultural development with industry receiving a much smaller sum. In the absence of later figures—owing to deplorable slowness in compiling such data—1954 shows:

Farming and agricultural improvement	$25,035,607.73
Industry	3,359,750.43
Commerce (imports)	11,194,545.60
Miscellaneous	2,541,361.24
Total	$42,131,265.00

Of the credits distributed to agricultural improvement alone, they were spread over:

Cotton and cereals	$15,599,076.57
Coffee	4,524,428.83
Cattle	2,535,622.63
Tractors, farming implements	2,376,479.70
Total	$25,035,607.73

These renewed administrative efforts to further national economy appear more impressive when contrasted to figures of but a few years earlier. Again, 1954 data is the most recent:

	1950	1954
Cotton, cereals	$3,009,716.72	$15,599,076.57
Coffee	2,224,033.15	4,524,428.83
Cattle	1,432,806.23	2,535,622.63
Tractors, farming implements	991,567.41*	2,376,479.70
Total	$7,658,123.51	$25,035,607.73

* 1951 figures here; 1950 data unavailable.

From a financial standpoint, this growth of investment, besides aiding economic development, helped the government regain its fiscal integrity. Taxes, long the most oppressive of the entire isthmus, were cut drastically and collected with a minimum of graft and inefficiency. Income tax, while low, was firmly established, with foreign tax experts guiding Nicaraguan judgment. The sounder the government finances, the more favorable the conditions for investment. At the same time the government was careful to use its financial health to develop trade, increase imports, and promote economic progress.

Imports rose slowly at first, but since 1950 there has been a sharp increase. Exports have raced forward at even a greater pace, so much so that there is an uncorrected inbalance between the two. Imports in 1954 were 70 percent greater than in 1949. Exports tripled during the same era.

YEAR	EXPORTS	IMPORTS
1949	$21,300,000	$25,600,000
1950	34,642,000	24,701,000
1951	46,184,000	29,967,000
1952	51,332,000	39,709,000
1953	54,506,000	43,550,000
1954	66,200,000	43,560,000

Of particular note was the new role played by Europe as a buyer of Nicaraguan products. Figures showed that the U. S. continued to be the largest buyer of Nicaraguan products. However, Europe increased its imports almost fourfold. Nicaraguan exports to Europe in 1949 were valued at four million dollars. By 1952 they had risen to fifteen million, and by 1953 to seventeen million. The United States continued to spend from twenty-four to twenty-eight million dollars annually. Thus Nicaragua retained commercial ties with the United States while expanding European trade operations.

At the same time, the budget granted increased economic and capital aid in keeping with its policy of economic development. Expenditures have been planned each year with scrupulous regard for estimated revenue, and the discrepancy remained small.

YEAR	REVENUES	EXPENDITURES
1950-51	$14,111,000	$14,111,000
1951-52	19,487,000	19,758,000
1952-53	26,440,000	25,320,000
1953-54	30,515,000	30,323,000
1954-55	32,068,000	32,066,000

The figures above show a sharp upward climb during the past five years. This has been due in some part to favorable international prices of coffee and cotton. In a 1955 message, President Somoza warned the citizens that circumstances could change, swinging quickly away from the conditions abetting national prosperity:

The high prices of coffee and cotton on the international market are transitory factors in our present boom. But largely we depend on them to get the things we must import. To be able to meet a decline in prices on our export commodities we must adopt in the economic field a strategic position and be prepared for defense should the occasion arise. To avoid inflation and the upsetting of our international balance of payments we must adhere to a policy of caution. Government expenditures on public works and imports of luxury goods should now be carefully watched.[3]

Choosing his 1950 political platform as his sounding board, President Somoza announced his intention of adopting long-term government action to further economic development. The following years, just as opponents were talking of Somoza reneging on his promises, he requested the International Bank to send to Nicaragua a survey mission, as had already been done elsewhere. He asked assistance in forming a complete economic plan. In response, a mission from the International Bank studied and conferred from July, 1951, to May, 1952. During that time the mission traveled an estimated ten thousand miles within the country, covering principal agricultural and timber regions as well as the few industrial installations. Visiting all departments and most towns of a thousand or more, the mission spared few pains in its recommendation.

According to the agreement, the official mission was threefold: "(a) to assist the government in the preparation of an over-all, long range development program; (b) to advise the government on current economic policies as well as improvements in the existing administrative and financial structure to prepare the groundwork for such a development program; (c) to coordinate the work of specialized experts from the Bank and other international agencies and to assist the government in carrying out their recommendations."[4] Nicaragua gave the examining experts full cooperation. The minister of economy chaired the National Economic Council, which in Nicaragua includes ministers of finance, agriculture, public works, and the manager of the National Bank. United States Point Four officials were also consulted by the visitors, particularly in matters concerning agriculture, education, and public health. The personnel of the mission itself represented the different relevant economic fields. Experts came from the Federal Reserve Bank of New York for public finance, the United Nations Food and Agriculture Organization for agriculture, the International Monetary Fund for banking and credit, and the Corporación de Fomento de Chile to plan a development institute. Nicaraguan officials, from President Somoza down, were hopeful that the mission could lend positive assistance in the formulation of a progressive economic development program and a broad strengthening of the national economic base.

In May, 1952, the mission announced its findings in "The Economic Development of Nicaragua" (see note 4), a report outlining existing conditions and suggesting specific objectives. Noting that Nicaragua is the largest Central American country and possesses unlimited land for development, the mission concluded that potentialities were great. The country was already progressing; that progress was attributable to both permanent and temporary causes.

Underlying economic changes were such non-transitory causes as the maintenance of peace and security, credit policies of the National Bank, and coordination of government activity. The two decades of Somoza's rule had brought unprecedented political stability. External disputes with Costa Rica never did more than jar the peace briefly. As for the National Bank, we have already seen its increasing contribution to private enterprise, particularly in agriculture, as a means of advancing national prosperity. The upward trend of Bank credits also proved a psychological encouragement to local businessmen to expand activities and extend personal commitments. Coordination of government activities came about from a series of measures—mostly executive declarations—eliminating duplication of effort and divided responsibility. While this mechanical revision is too detailed to describe here, its core was a number of high level committees, such as the National Economic Council.

In recent years the government has relied increasingly on expert technical advice from United Nations agencies, including the International Bank, and from the U. S. Point Four program. Loans have also been negotiated to back projects the government itself could not finance. By April 30, 1953, the International Bank for Reconstruction and Development had completed several loans, the original principal totalling $5,300,000. In June, 1955, the Bank in Washington granted a new loan of $7,500,000 for power expansion. The loan was transacted to help finance construction of a thirty thousand kilowatt thermal power plant in Managua, the second most powerful in Central America.* Transmission lines are to be laid to outlying communities as well. Also in 1955 agreement came from the United States to provide two-thirds of the money necessary to complete additional construction and repair work on the Inter American Highway.

Prices on the international market were cited as a transitory reason for Nicaraguan development. The boom of the 1950's in coffee and cotton was particularly large, with Nicaragua a grateful recipient of the resulting benefits. President Somoza himself warned that the very nature of the international market left no room for complacency. "Prices and conditions in the international market are likely to change. We

* Second to that on the Rio Lempa in El Salvador.

must strengthen basic parts of our economy in order to be prepared for any contingency that might arise in the future."[5] He pursued the same theme in his annual message to the National Congress in April, 1955, and suggested that the emphasis might even be shifted to expanded food crops, in order to avoid inflation and "not run the risk of upsetting the international balance of payments." Despite this warning, the fact remained that the temporary condition of cotton and coffee prices was a major factor in economic progress.

"The Economic Development of Nicaragua" outlined ten specific objectives. The only fiscal measure was furtherance and development of a long-term credit system and technical assistance for industries and agriculture. The other recommendations ranged over the entire national economy. Objectives were found in the fields of agriculture, transportation, communications, illiteracy, public health, industry, and power. The government, before tackling specific tasks described in the report, chose to establish an all-embracing plan entirely responsible for national advancement. The result was the Over-All Development Program, a five-year plan covering the 1952-57 period. Created soon after departure of the mission, the program provided for financial allocations of support to various phases of economic development for five years.

The Over-All Development Program channeled funds into six different categories: agriculture, transportation and communications, education, public health, industries, and power. Foreign exchange and local currency costs were totalled, and the goals divided into those of first priority and others which would be carried out "to attain a minimum rate of development for the country."

MINIMUM DEVELOPMENT PROGRAM

Agriculture	LOCAL COST	FOREIGN COST	TOTAL
Institute for Development	$ 6,675,000	$10,325,000	$17,000,000
Ministry of Agriculture	450,000	2,550,000	3,000,000
Transportation, Communications	14,610,000	7,365,000	21,975,000
Education (added to existing expenditure levels)	850,000	2,275,000	3,125,000
Public Health (added to existing expenditure levels)	2,850,000	3,950,000	6,800,000
Industries	1,310,000	490,000	1,800,000
Power	3,500,000	1,000,000	4,500,000
Total Minimum Program	$31,345,000	$27,955,000	$59,300,000

ADDITIONAL OPTIMUM PROGRAM

	FOREIGN COST	LOCAL COST	TOTAL
Agriculture	$ 1,000,000	$ 6,000,000	$ 7,000,000
Transportation, Communications			
Feeder roads	750,000	250,000	1,000,000
Tele-communications	1,265,000	425,000	1,690,000
Education	250,000	500,000	750,000
Public Health	2,125,000	2,125,000	4,250,000
Industries	1,500,000	500,000	2,000,000
Total Additional Program	$ 6,890,000	$ 9,800,000	$16,690,000

Agricultural plans included a 25 percent increase in the number of coffee trees, in an effort to match the coffee production of rival countries. There was no desire to increase the percentage of exports represented by coffee, already the major export commodity. Nicaragua was never as reliant on one crop as other American countries. Rarely did coffee comprise more than 50 percent of the total exports. By 1953 the figure was reduced to 39 percent, and it went even lower in 1954 and 1955. At the same time, the number of coffee trees was increased. This was reflected in 1954 when the net value of coffee exportations passed the twenty million dollar mark for the first time. Two years earlier, coffee exports were valued at $18,456,494. Additional impetus came from non-government sources in 1956 when an association of private Nicaraguan coffee growers was organized. Meeting in Managua on March 17, 1956, they formed the Federatión de Beneficiadores del Pacífico de Nicaragua. Limited to west coast growers, the organization included leading beneficiadores from Managua, Masaya, Las Sierras, León, and Jinotepe, as well as outlying regions. Created with capital of one million córdobas, the organization had two goals: reduction of fluctuations of supply and demand, and elimination of speculators in coffee.

In interests of agricultural diversification, the report urged further development of cotton, a new crop in Nicaragua. Acreage was increasing, and given the additional impetus of the development program, it continued to flourish. Of the six Central American countries, only Panama and Costa Rica have no cotton production to speak of. Nicaragua has far surpassed the others. In 1953, one hundred thousand acreas under cultivation yielded nearly that many bales. One year later, with cotton acreage nearly doubled, over two hundred thousand bales were produced. So profitable was this 1954 crop that planting for 1955 was increased by 25 percent. Despite warnings from experts that cotton was expanding too rapidly and carrying an untoward proportion of the economy with it, planters hastened to increase their acreage. In a rush to profit on the sure money-maker, planters and exporters alike urged further commitment to the cotton crop. It soon passed coffee as Nicaragua's leading export.

Within a period of months, this upsurge was threatened by a slump in production. Nearly 360,000 acres had been planted with cotton for the 1955 crop. Heavy, unseasonal rains damaged the crop severely and, despite the increased acreage, 1955 cotton production dropped to 175,000 bales, almost 30,000 less than in 1954. By the end of 1955, planters were concerned about probable international price reductions as a result of surplus dumping by the United States in mid-fall. The Nicaraguan government offset this fear in December by the drastic measure of offering to buy cotton at $29 a hundredweight and refund the difference between that and the eventual export price. However, the price remained near $31 a hundred, three dollars less than the 1954 average price. As a result, the economic shock was less than originally feared. At the same time, the natural reaction was future caution—probably a wise thing under the circumstances. The *New York Times* reported that of the seventeen hundred cotton planters in Nicaragua, nearly 20 percent refrained from planting any cotton in 1956.

Obscured by the meteoric climb of cotton and the continued prominence of coffee, other products have been developing on a smaller scale, with expansion and reorganization coming as a result of the development program. Nicaragua now exports both rice and corn, two products which it once raised only for domestic consumption. Banana and sugar production is small, but adds to the list of exports. Lumber production from Nicaragua's rich forests has been planned, with almost no results yet. Timber has dropped in recent years, providing only 8 percent of the country's exports. Beef cattle have long provided Nicaragua with high grade beef, the best in the region. Nine hundred thousand acres of land are devoted to livestock grazing, and for some years President Somoza was among the cattle owners who profited by running cattle over the Costa Rican border without paying the usual imposts.

On January 8, 1954, the government took additional steps to advance agriculture by opening the newly created Nicaraguan Institute of National Production. President Somoza, after making the main address, presented the Institute with a government check for five million córdobas. The government promised a total of fifty million córdobas by 1961, stretching the payments over an eight-year period. The Institute was designed to complement the development program in agricultural matters, and its first efforts were directed toward the coffee industry and growing industrial production.

Highways were virtually non-existent in Nicaragua when Somoza was inaugurated. Little was done at first to improve the situation. In 1943 Nicaragua had thirty kilometers of roads, with ten—less than two miles—paved. Recognizing the necessity of roads if markets were to receive rural products, Somoza began to encourage an extended highway system. Today, only El Salvador has highways rivaling those of Nicaragua. In 1955, the government published figures showing 3,693 kilometers of highways and roads, or about 2,290 miles. Paved highways, including the Inter American and Pacific-Atlantic connections, totalled 673 miles. Four hundred and ninety-eight miles of all-weather roads crossed the countryside, and there were 1,110 miles of dry season roads, some of which were passable during the eight-month rainy season.

Following U. S. Vice-President Richard M. Nixon's 1955 trip through Central America, the United States agreed to provide two-thirds of the remaining funds needed to complete the Inter American Highway all the way to Panama City. This agreement included Nicaragua, and the U. S. Congress, in due time, provided adequate appropriations. Nicaragua and the United States also signed a bilateral agreement by which the U. S. would lend an additional three million dollars in 1956 to complete the Pacific-Atlantic highway. President Somoza had signed an executive agreement with Franklin D. Roosevelt for an ocean-to-ocean highway designed for World War II defense purposes. The 162 mile road was begun in 1943, but at war's end construction was far from complete, and for some years no work was done. What had been built crumbled into disrepair. In April, 1955, the Department of State agreed to the three million dollar loan to hurry construction of the highway, which would be a major advance in the Nicaraguan road net. Later, the U. S. Bureau of Public Roads made a contract for the construction of 19.5 kilometers of the highway for $1,281,381. The highway, by the end of 1956, was completed past Santo Tomás, the midway point. The Nello Teer Company of Durham, North Carolina, was paid $2,600,000 to continue some thirty-seven miles. By the close of 1958, the highway, popularly called the

Rama Road, was nearing completion. Then the Pacific side of the country will be linked for the first time with Rama, the river port.*

Data emphasize the increase in highway transportation by a comparison of vehicles registered in 1940 and 1954. In 1940 there was a grand total of 234 passenger cars and trucks and six tractors in all Nicaragua. Fifteen years later there were eight thousand cars and trucks and some twenty-five hundred tractors. In the decade from 1943 to 1953, consumption of gasoline and diesel fuel rose from five million to twenty million gallons, a 300 percent increase. Such has been the progress in transportation. The accelerated program in recent years reflects in large part the report of the International Bank mission. Among specific objectives, it urged "completion of a major highway network linking the capital city of Managua with the cities of Granada, León, Chinandega, Jinotega, San Juan del Sur, the Tuma Valley, and with the east coast. . . ."[6] as well as a "complete network of farm-to-market roads."

In addition to road transportation, the report pointed out the inadequacy of port conditions and inland water transportation, suggesting "rehabilitation of the major ocean ports and improvement of lake transportation." Little was done to further lake transportation which had been thriving a century before, patronized by those impatient to get to the Pacific coast of the United States to pan for gold. The present-day transportation on Lakes Managua and Nicaragua, as well as the connective Tipitapa River, is almost non-existent. President Somoza has taken measures to "rehabilitate" the ocean ports, however. Tiny Corinto, which for years had struggled to bear the brunt of Pacific ocean trade, suddenly had its facilities expanded. Loading and unloading machinery was replaced, improved, and modernized. Docking facilities were also increased.

On December 19, 1955, President Somoza initiated construction of a new Pacific seaport, immodestly called Puerto Somoza. Designed to alleviate the shortage of adequate port facilities, Puerto Somoza is located at the Pacific point closest to Managua, where there was almost nothing before. Critics are quick to comment that cattlegrower Somoza owned a large livestock ranch nearby, and that steamship operator Somoza needed a new port to berth his ships. All this is perfectly true. At the same time, a new port on the Pacific was urgently needed, and now it is in

---

* The navigable Escondido River winds from the Caribbean port of Bluefields up to the river town of Rama, at the end of the Rama Road.

construction, already in partial use. Upon completion it will handle three ships loading and unloading simultaneously.

Two years before this Somoza became principal stockholder in the Mamenic steamship line. This private merchant marine, now being built in German shipyards, numbers fourteen vessels, all of more than one hundred thousand tons. Plans call for an increase within a few years. In the meantime, Somoza's Tamarindo ranch, connected to Managua by a modern paved highway, continues to send its beef elsewhere pending completion of Puerto Somoza. A highway extension is also being constructed to provide good roads from Managua and Masaya to Puerto Somoza—and the Tamarindo ranch.

The International Bank report also demanded a campaign to deal with illiteracy. There was to be a "reduction in the rate of illiteracy and a raise in vocational technical education and training." The Nicaraguan literacy rate of 40 percent was only third among the Central American states, but this was an improvement over the past. Pupils in 1938 had numbered 41,267. By 1955, they had tripled to 112,303. This is particularly surprising in view of the slow over-all population growth. Schools have been built at a rate roughly commensurate with the increasing attendance of children. In the three years preceding 1955, 552 new schools were built. As for teachers, enrollment in the educational courses of the national university increased, although not nearly enough. By 1954, the country published the news that it had more teachers than soldiers—4,991 to 4,052—a boast neighboring Costa Rica had been flaunting for years.

The school-building program included a national institute for technical and vocational training. A number of small vocational schools were established under the guiding hand of United States vocational education officials lent through Point Four auspices. At the national institute, workshops were equipped with modern machinery and tools. Visitors are proudly showed through the installation today. Institute officials point out dormitories, a gymnasium, and expansive grounds for athletics. They also tell visitors of the extension courses at night for students unable to attend regular daytime classes.

Nicaraguan educational facilities still remain wholly inadequate. Education is both free and obligatory from the age of seven to thirteen, but large numbers never attend. Despite the new schools, figures are deceiving, for many of the older ones are sagging, ramshackle buildings scarcely safe to enter. The author saw two such schools in south Nicaragua, near Rivas, on the Inter American Highway. This is a more populous part of Nicaragua. When such schools are of necessity shut down, they must be replaced by new ones. Thus the government continues, under the pressure of time and conflicting financial needs, to struggle against ignorance and illiteracy.

Public health is another crucial problem. The International Bank mission suggested both expanded hospital and health facilities, and "establishment of pure water and sanitation facilities in the main towns and many of the smaller communities." Outpatient clinics, mobile sections, and laboratories have been set up under the Ministry of Health to care for more than a thousand patients daily. Throughout the country, twenty-five health centers have been built to service scattered areas. The 1950-51 budget provided $412,000 for health facilities; in 1954-55 this had risen to $1,153,000.

Hospitals have been built at a growing rate. In the ten years from 1943 to 1953, the number grew from sixteen to thirty-seven. All but two of the sixteen Nicaraguan departments are serviced by at least one hospital. In the capital city, a modern hospital is being erected, the largest in Nicaragua. Reaching completion in 1958, its electrical, laundry, sterilizing, water, and sewage installations are the best in the country. In addition, the General Hospital of Managua continues to service the capital and has been reconditioned and expanded to one hundred beds at an expenditure of more than one million dollars.

For Nicaragua, then, the years under President Somoza brought a number of notable internal improvements: healthy finance, trade, and agriculture; improved transportation, health, and education; in short, a general development incomparably superior to conditions before 1937. Gross national products grew from $170,000,000 in 1951 to $310,000,000 in 1956. At the same time, many inadequacies remain. The economy is still over-reliant on international prices. Highway construction must go forward at a more rapid pace, reaching isolated interior regions. Education should raise the literacy rate to twice the present 40 percent. And health facilities are much inferior to those, for example, of Costa Rica and El Salvador.

In evaluating these Somoza measures, it must be remembered that many of these advances were very slow in coming. President Somoza made a belated start in highway construction, agricultural development, and public health. A check of the preceding data reveals that the greatest progress has come in the 1950's. Yet Somoza was elected more than a dozen years before. The record, then, is deceptive. In many instances the administration was clearly lax in developing necessary projects, ignoring situations as long as possible. Even so, Nicaragua progressed under Somoza's rule, and in this context his works are considerable. What will come in the period following his death is another question.

SOMOZA AND THE WORLD AROUND HIM

Nicaraguan external relations are much better known than internal problems. Intermittent disputes have made hemispheric headlines. Somoza always maintained a keen interest in world events, while in the Central American sphere he had been dominant for years. Probably no other figure was in the forefront of regional relations so often as Somoza, and his unusually long period in office, just recently ended, is but one reason. For the sake of convenience, Nicaraguan foreign policy can be divided into two classifications: Central American politics and U. S. relations.

Relations with neighboring Costa Rica have been particularly acrimonious for the past decade, and may continue so despite the death of Somoza. Much of the turbulence is directly attributable to the deep personal enmity of Somoza and Costa Rica's José Figueres. In the beginning, Somoza prompted the friction by illegal activities at the Nicaragua-Costa Rica frontier. Long the leading businessman of his country, Somoza had been active in the cattle business ever since taking power. During the early years of his presidency he arranged the illegal transportation of Nicaraguan cattle into Costa Rica. Herds were driven across the border into Guanacaste, the northern Costa Rican province, where the high-quality beef commanded a handsome price. Costa Rican beef, inferior to that of Nicaragua, could not rival the competition.

Rafael Calderón was elected to the Costa Rican presidency in 1940, and he struck up a friendship with Somoza. As the friendship matured, the presidents decided to do a little business on the side. Calderón agreed to receive Somoza's smuggled cattle and sell it for their mutual profit. Documentary evidence of this arrangement has never come to light, but it is a widely known fact that no one disputes. Costa Rican opposition to President Calderón seized upon the issue, subjecting the government to continual criticism. These men cogently argued that the ailing Costa

Rican cattle business had no chance while foreign beef of a higher quality entered the country illegally. Among the leaders of this opposition, who called their group the Civic Betterment Committee, was José Figueres.

In 1944, unable to succeed himself, Calderón named the unreliable Teodoro Picado as official candidate, backing his successful campaign. With Picado in office, Somoza and Calderón continued their profitable enterprise. They hoped to continue following a Calderón re-election in 1948. However, opposition had built up to the eight-year rule of Calderón and Picado, and newspaperman Otilio Ulate defeated Calderón by a ten thousand vote margin. After a week of political machinations the Picado government succeeded in annulling the election results, but at this point a pre-armed band of revolutionaries led by José Figueres rebelled to the south of the Costa Rican capital. On March 12, 1948, Costa Rica was thrown into a state of civil war.

The story of the revolution is complicated, and is detailed in Chapter Six. From the Nicaraguan standpoint, however, it was an illegal uprising against the government by a group of dissident young people led by an intense, doctrinaire left-winger (Figueres) who could be expected to turn his country upside-down with socialist reforms if given half a chance. For Somoza, both personal friendship and profitable business were threatened. He was quick to aid the beleaguered government forces. The exact extent of this help has never been made clear. Somoza was always careful of involvements outside Nicaragua. He was prepared to withdraw from any adventure if it seemed advisable. Certainly his assistance in this case was limited to small arms and ammunition.

José Figueres and others in Costa Rica insist to this day that a large force of the Nicaraguan National Guard marched across the border to fight alongside government forces. The story goes that two hundred guardsmen were somehow ambushed by revolutionaries in Guanacaste and annihilated. Somoza immediately withdrew other forces rather than risk everything on intervention. To Costa Ricans, even enemies of President Figueres, this is a familiar story, and they speak of it proudly. Nonetheless, there is no evidence that such a massacre did take place. Several prominent political figures have told the writer that they honestly do not know whether or not the story has any foundation in fact.

President Somoza admitted having sent aid to Calderón forces. As he put it, the legitimate government was faced with a challenge from insurgents, and in the interests of legitimacy and regional peace he felt obliged to contribute support. Just what proportions this aid took, he never said. Somoza did state flatly that he sent several planeloads of National Guard troops—about four hundred—to Villa Quesada in northern Costa Rica. In Somoza's version, he received a personal message from U. S. Secretary of State George C. Marshall, at the time heading the United States delegation to the Inter-American Conference at Bogotá. Marshall cabled Somoza to withdraw his troops in the interests of peace. President Somoza then recounted with pride the speed with which his planeloads of men swept back to Nicaraguan soil.

Elements of this story seem unlikely. In the spring of 1948 General Marshall was hardpressed by a multitude of problems, including the Berlin blockade and other cold war issues. He was barely able to leave Washington long enough to lead the U. S. delegation in Bogotá. That he could learn of a few hundred Nicaraguan troops in a tiny village in northern Costa Rica a few hours after their arrival seems dubious. One can speculate that Somoza actually did lose a body of troops in Costa Rica and quickly withdrew the rest, concocting the story of a telegram from Marshall. On the other hand, there may be no connection. Most of the actual fighting in Costa Rica was south of San José, far from Guanacaste or the village of Villeda Quesada. Be this as it may, there is no question that Somoza supported Calderón forces both morally and financially. He had no qualms about Nicaraguan participation in the Costa Rican civil war. This was but the first of a series of Nicaraguan interventions in the affairs of Costa Rica.

Early in December, 1948, while the Costa Rican revolutionary government was trying to get squared away, a counter-movement by Calderón was launched from Nicaraguan territory. In Managua he told the press, "the revolution was illegitimate and ill-conceived . . . my aim is to restore the state of things destroyed by a group of insensate men led by José Figueres, a legal and spiritual adventurer."[7] Following this statement, he left Managua for the border where he awaited word to proceed to Liberia, forty miles from the border. In Costa Rica the country quickly re-mobilized Figueres' army of liberation, and Figueres announced that participation of the Nicaraguan National Guard would mean a "real war" with Nicaragua. From Managua came immediate denials of complicity. Costa Rica was placed under martial law and press censorship as the government announced an all out effort to repulse the invaders. Archbishop

Sanabria, who had been instrumental in arranging a truce during the first revolution, also condemned the invasion.

Early reports were typically contradictory. Estimates of invading forces ranged from eight hundred to five thousand. Within a day the number was placed at three hundred. Fighting was sporadic and battle communiques referred to casualties by name rather than number. Two days after the invasion, the forces met at La Cruz, a few kilometers south of the frontier. Thirty-eight rebels surrendered, including their leader. This man, Ordones, admitted receiving arms from Luis Somoza, son of the President and himself president of the Nicaraguan Congress. Two days later he was questioned further when Figueres and Otilio Ulate went to the front. Ordones reportedly declared that Somoza had promised the revolutionaries full support. Once again Somoza issued a denial.

It was soon apparent that rebel forces were making little progress. They had hoped that calderonista elements in San José might rise there, but these hopes never materialized. As soon as the invasion began, Costa Rica had appealed to the Organization of American States. Accusing Nicaragua of overt interference, it demanded action under the Rio Pact (Inter-American Treaty of Reciprocal Assistance) which had become law but nine days before. Article 3 of the Pact declares that "The High Contracting Parties agree than an armed attack by any State against an American State shall be considered as an attack against all the American States . . . and . . . each . . . undertakes to assist in meeting the attack in the exercise of the inherent right of individual or collective self-defense. . . ." After referring to these passages, Costa Rica invoked Article 6, which reads, "If the inviolability or the integrity of the territory or the sovereignty or political independence of any American State should be affected by an aggression which is not an armed attack or by an extra-continental or intra-continental conflict . . . the Organ of Consultation shall meet immediately in order to agree on the measures which must be taken . . . to assist the victim . . . [and] for the common defense and for the maintenance of the peace and security of the Continent."[8]

The Organization ruled that the Costa Rican request was legitimate and called for an emergency meeting of the foreign ministers. At the same time a board of inquiry was sent to the area, headed by Dr. Bautista de Lavalle of Peru. The five-man commission went first to San José and then to Managua. Arriving on December 14, it was momentarily disrupted when Dr. de Lavalle suddenly withdrew from the commission on orders of his government.* Mexico's Luis Quintanilla was named acting chief of the commission. After two days in conference with Costa Rican officials in the Casa Amarilla, they continued to Managua on December 20, and two days later returned to Washington. At the airport they issued a short statement praising the cooperation of the two governments.

One day before Christmas, the OAS met to consider the commission report, passing a resolution calling upon Nicaragua and Costa Rica to refrain from hostile actions. Nicaragua was asked to keep a close rein on revolutionary groups forming in its territory. Costa Rica was requested to remove lingering elements of the Caribbean Legion, the latter dedicated to the overthrow of authoritarian regimes in Nicaragua, the Dominican Republic, and Honduras. Both nations were to observe the principles of non-intervention and solidarity, with the commission continuing consultation until assured of this by both governments. The report revealed beyond doubt that the invasion was prepared in Nicaragua. There was no clear evidence of official connivance, however, and after the first day of fighting, Nicaragua was reported to have taken all essential steps to keep the rebels from getting further supplies or aid from Nicaragua. Another five-man commission was assigned the job of observing the compliance with the request for the cessation of hostilities.

As a result of OAS action, Nicaragua and Costa Rica agreed in February to reach a peaceful settlement of their dispute. On February 21, 1949, Foreign Ministers Sevilla of Nicaragua and Esquivel of Costa Rica signed an amity pact. With this, the first phase of Nicaraguan-Costa Rican disagreement was effectively closed. Subsequent episodes were to dwarf the first in gravity. In Costa Rica, president-elect Otilio Ulate took office in late 1949 after an eighteen-month provisional government under José Figueres; relations immediately improved. Ulate had been highly critical of President Somoza in his newspaper, but during his administration was most circumspect in his relations with the Nicaraguan executive. In November, 1953, José Figueres was returned to office for a full term and, in a matter of months, he and Somoza were embroiled once more in vituperative exchange. Central America, already upset over the tottering Red regime in Guatemala, held its breath in hope that

---

* Costa Rica had not extended diplomatic recognition to the month-old revolutionary Peruvian government of General Manuel Odría, and so in pique Dr. de Lavalle was withdrawn.

Somoza and Figueres would maintain proper relations. In April, however, the storm broke.

On April 5, 1954, the Nicaraguan government announced the discovery of a plot to assassinate Somoza. The President announced that the revolutionaries came from Costa Rica. The border was immediately closed and a state of seige decreed in Nicaragua. In the government paper, *Novedades,* Somoza announced that three were already dead from a fusillade of shots following the attack.

The attempt directed against my life was perfectly planned, and the assassins had chosen the place [for the attack] shortly after I left the United States Embassy Saturday night where I attended a reception by the Ambassador [Thomas E. Whelan] for [Brigadier] General [Lesley J.] Whitlock. Nevertheless, their plan failed, for I had taken the precaution of sending a patrol out of the Embassy a few minutes before my departure. On seeing the patrol, they fell apart and some fled for Batahola while the rest of the group ran in the opposite direction. . . . We are investigating all details relating to this criminal attempt, and the Nicaraguan people must be convinced that the army and the powers of the state are alert, assuring the peace and the tranquility of the republic and its national institutions.[9]

The next day the Nicaraguan minister of foreign relations told newsmen that the Caribbean Legion was believed responsible. The assassins reportedly included Adolfo Báez Bone, Jorge Rivas Montes, and Amado Baena, all known members of the Legion. The Nicaraguan ambassador in San José delivered to the foreign minister a request for compliance with the 1949 amity treaty. The next day foreign newsmen in Managua saw a large number of troops ringed around the Presidential Palace. Somoza reported that

I am a spectator of what is to come. I am watching for the attitude that the Costa Rican government is going to take. I hope that it will proceed as it should and with the speed that is vital. . . . When things get so bad that an attempt is made on the life of the President of the Republic, things have gone far indeed, especially when friendly nations are involved. . . . The plot that has threatened the peace of Nicaragua and the lives of its inhabitants is supported by Carlos Prio Socorras,* Romulo Betancourt,† and another Central American government. . . . If the criminal attack had succeeded, Nicaragua would have served as a base of operations against Cuba, Venezuela, and the Dominican Republic.[10]

* Exiled Cuban ex-president.
† Exiled Venezuelan ex-president, and confidante and mentor of Figueres.

The following day, April 8, Nicaraguan Foreign Minister Oscar Sevilla spoke in a more conciliatory vein, declaring that Nicaragua would not take the case to the OAS. At the same time, President Somoza agreed that "the good people of Costa Rica are not in accord with bloodshed." Nonetheless, the Costa Rican consulate in Managua was shut, and a number of Costa Ricans in the country were imprisoned or put under temporary arrest. In San José, Romulo Betancourt categorically denied Somoza's charges of complicity.

The National Guard continued to pursue the assassins. The apparent chief of the plot, Pablo Leal, had been killed in the first clash between conspirators and government forces. Adolfo Báez Bone was also dead. Continuing the search, National Guardsmen pointed suspicion at Nicaraguan General and ex-President Emiliano Chamorro, a senator and aging critic of the Somoza regime. Somoza announced that the Guard had uncovered documents implicating Chamorro, and that Costa Ricans were also involved. It promised publication of the documents within a few days. On April 10, the government accused the owner of Managua's anti-Somoza *La Flecha,* Hernán Robleto. His whereabouts were unknown, although the newspaper continued to publish daily editions. On April 12, interviewed by NBC's Marshall Bannell and a *Time* correspondent, Somoza said that José Figueres had clearly been informed of the plot beforehand and did nothing to stop it. He gave full authorization to be quoted directly. At the same time he added that some of the revolutionaries' captured arms were labelled "Government of Costa Rica," and Managua newspapers ran photographs of the weapons.

The reaction in Costa Rica was unhurried. From President Figueres down, government officials disclaimed any complicity in the attempt. After several days, Foreign Minister Mario Esquivel asked Nicaragua for an explanation of the grave charges made by Somoza. He demanded withdrawal of Nicaraguan troops from the border, requesting that the frontier be re-opened. Esquivel told newsmen that Costa Rica would go to the OAS again if given no satisfaction. Nicaragua did not answer at once. The next day—Pan American Day, ironically enough—Ambassador to the U. S. Guillermo Sevilla (brother of the foreign minister) told the press in Washington that his government had most of the arms used by the would-be assassins, and that they were clearly Costa Rican. At the same time his government had full documentation of any and all charges made by President Somoza. Also in Washington, Alberto Martén and

Fernando Volio Sanchez, Costa Rican delegates to the OAS, denied all accusations.

Finally, Costa Rica agreed to negotiate directly on April 21. The OAS would not be called, except to arrange bilateral talks. Costa Rica's Volio Sanchez announced in Washington that Nicaraguan demands for face-to-face negotiations were satisfactory. Managuan newspapers immediately claimed a diplomatic victory. At the same time, Volio Sanchez had several points to clarify. In the first place, Nicaragua had lowered border restrictions affecting Costa Rican citizens. Furthermore, troops surrounded the consulate in Managua and refused to grant safe conduct to refugees claiming diplomatic asylum there. Nicaragua refused to bring the OAS into the affair directly, and a number of troops were stationed at the frontier to enforce its closure.

By this time, all Central America was in an uproar. The Somoza-Figueres feud was already well known, and there had been apprehension ever since Figueres returned to office in late 1953. General feeling was that Somoza had indeed been unduly provoked. At the same time, it was hoped that he might wield his considerable power as a stabilizing influence, rather than picking more trouble with Costa Rica. An editorial in San Salvador's *Diario Latino* asked Somoza to step down for the sake of avoiding all-out war. It felt he was the spark that might start a fire carrying to all other Central American countries. Admitting that the assassination attempt was unjustified, *Diario Latino* insisted that "in a gesture of true Central Americanism, Somoza should abandon power." On April 22, ex-President of Costa Rica, Otilio Ulate, traveling through El Salvador, called the crisis the gravest in regional history. He saw the immediate objective to be a lessening of general tension and asked that regional peace be restored.

Despite attempts to arrange bilateral negotiations, efforts seemed stymied. Mario Esquivel told newsmen on April 24 that the situation remained grave: "We have called a group of prominent Costa Ricans, learned in foreign affairs, to consider the situation . . . and [to elicit] their opinion and advice on the most certain solution of the dispute with Nicaragua."[11] This group included ex-President Julio Acosta, ex-Foreign Minister Fernando Lara, future cabinet minister Alberto Cañas, and Raul Gurdían. President Figueres delivered a speech declaring his confidence that normal relations would be re-established. In Nicaragua, recriminations still reverberated, and there was little inclination to lessen the tension. *Novedades* published a story that accused Figueres of direct aid to the revolutionaries, a charge not levelled before. In short, Somoza was outraged over the plot, and in no humor to forget it. He told one interviewer angrily that "Hell, it's no crime to overthrow a government in a fair fight, but murder is something else."[12]

After a period of inactivity, Anastasio Somoza, Jr., chief of staff of the National Guard, stirred up the dust with another blast at Figueres: "There is an individual in the south who lives envious of the peace, liberty, work, and progress of Nicaragua: José Figueres. . . . I can say it openly. . . . The people who came here were not going to fight a battle; they only brought enough munitions to liquidate General Somoza. But we will maintain the peace. . . ."[13] The next day, May 6, 1954, President Somoza broke several days of silence in another interview. He announced that weapons were found on Nicaragua's Pacific coast, including small arms, rifles, grenades, machine-guns, and ammunition. If these were communist-delivered arms, he warned ominously, Nicaragua would soon become another Korea, and would be for the free world equally important.

Inside Nicaragua, the pursuit still continued to apprehend all the conspirators. The government had captured and quickly brought to trial Jorge Ribas, supposedly the chief of operations for the revolutionary Caribbean Legion. Ribas, a Honduran citizen and career adventurer who had a wife in San José, smilingly admitted to the assassination of Colonel Francisco Arana some years before (see Chapter Two). During his trial, he admitted talking in Mexico with Cuba's Prío Socorrás, but he refused to testify against Figueres. On the other hand, he issued no denials when asked about Figueres' involvement.

On the diplomatic front, Nicaragua belatedly replied to Costa Rica's demand for explanation of its charges against Figueres. On May 14, Oscar Sevilla sent a forty-three-page document, with appendices, including the trial testimony of Ribas and other assorted bits of information. Photostats of relevant documents were presented. Supposedly, all three Somozas—the President and his two sons, Luis and Anastasio—were to be killed followed by widespread anarchy, chaos and terror. In San José, Nicaraguan Ambassador Guerrero delivered the official document along with a private note from Sevilla. After delivery of the note, several more weeks passed without action. Costa Rica, after acknowledging receipt of the document and promising to study it, had nothing more to say.

On June 4, the Nicaraguan embassy was forced to deny a story in San José's *Prensa Libre* that relations were about to be severed formally. "The Government of Nicaragua has not even considered the possibility of such a withdrawal, but does hope at a prudent time for the reply of the Costa Rican government. . . ."[14] Two days later Ambassador Guerrero corrected himself to admit that he was prepared to go home at any moment, while the *Miami Herald* repeated the story. The *Herald's* Edwin Lahey reported that President Somoza considered Costa Rica, like Guatemala, a "nest of communist conspirators," and anticipated breaking diplomatic connections shortly. Finally, on June 10, 1954, sixty-six days after the attempt on Somoza's life, Nicaragua announced the withdrawal of its ambassador from Costa Rica.

The action was still incomplete. Before Guerrero could leave San José, El Salvador requested Somoza to reverse his decision, to give Costa Rica one last chance to reply. Costa Rica had reportedly been surprised by Nicaraguan action and asked El Salvador to delay the action if possible. Nicaragua announced that relations would be maintained until June 27. If no satisfaction had come by then, Guerrero would be recalled once again. A day before the deadline, Sub-director of Protocol Arnaldo Ortez flew to Managua with a voluminous reply to the Nicaraguan demands. Oscar Sevilla said only that the note would be studied before Nicaragua made any further statement.

Days passed and June turned to July. Nicaragua was reportedly preparing another diplomatic paper, but details were unknown. President Somoza mentioned offhand one day that he would be willing to meet Figueres at the border if it might contribute to a return of normal relations. Figueres quickly fired back that Somoza "wants to meet me at the border to have a picture taken with me to show to his people." Actually, as Edwin Lahey wrote later, President Somoza had in mind a meeting with .45s. As their reply was further delayed, it became known that Nicaragua considered the Costa Rican communication wholly inadequate and was once again considering the recall of its ambassador. On July 16, now more than three months after the attempt that triggered the whole dispute, *Novedades* wrote that the events had inflamed Nicaraguans and that war was surely near. President Somoza was quoted to the effect that Figueres had no respect for Nicaraguans and was ambitious to get up a puppet government. He claimed that two hundred armed Costa Ricans had arrived at the border, shouting across to Nicaraguan guards that they would soon be eating in the Nicaraguan Presidential Palace. Not to be outdone, José Figueres told the Associated Press that he feared imminent invasion. Airports were watched, and in San José all lights were extinguished from 2:00 to 5:00 A.M. for nearly a week.

Actual fighting broke out on July 25 when a band of calderonistas, apparently hoping to help finance a new, Guatemala-type revolution, swarmed into the small town of Sarapiqui and robbed a bank. Nearby Costa Rican forces rushed to the scene and the following day surrounded and captured most of the rebels. The rest headed toward the San Juan River and safety in Nicaragua. In the process, a Nicaraguan air force plane was fired upon and damaged. Nicaragua promptly sent two more notes of protest to San José. Foreign Minister Sevilla said that "if President Figueres wants war, he will have it. The patience of our government is not unlimited." Costa Rica denied the charges, but there was no question about their having fired upon the Nicaraguan craft. Its port engine electrical control was damaged by rifle shots, although it managed to limp back to a Nicaraguan airfield. Whether or not the plane had been covering for the retreating calderonista rebels is a moot point. President Somoza angrily dispatched a mile-long convoy of tanks and troop-carrying vehicles to the border "to defend Nicaragua's territory." After reviewing the armored units at the Presidential Palace, he rode at the head of the column to the Managua outskirts before sending them to the border. With troops thus stationed at the border, it seemed that events were a clear prelude to war.

The United States, a vexed spectator through this series of events, rushed six air force planes to Costa Rica on the first of August. The planes, C-47 transports, carried neither passengers nor freight, and stopped at San José's La Sabana airport for only three days. The gesture was quickly understood, however. It was an obvious warning to Somoza and dissident Costa Ricans against precipitating more fighting. The planes not only provided reassurance to Costa Rica, but suggested to all Central America that one serious revolution—that in Guatemala two months before—was quite enough for the time. Nicaraguan forces were soon withdrawn from the border and the crisis passed. As *Time* wrote, "Nicaragua's Tacho is the kind of man who understands such gestures."[15]

With the retirement of Nicaraguan troops from the border, the second dispute was ended. Unlike the first, Costa Rica was far from blameless. The attempted assassination of General Somoza, which quite rightfully enraged him, was clearly engineered from Costa Rica. Elements of the Caribbean Legion* had been quartered in a nineteenth-century fortress overlooking east San José, and some of these men, many of whom were Somoza-hating Nicaraguan exiles, had lived, eaten, slept, and trained at President Figueres' plantation, *Lucha Sin Fin*. It was learned later that a Mexican bus had been driven across the border into Costa Rica with a cargo of arms hidden under a false bottom. Some twenty-five rebels took the arms and sneaked into Nicaragua, traveling north on Lake Nicaragua and up the Tipitapa River to Lake Managua, where they were to meet 175 others. They took weapons to arm these other men.

For some reason these men never showed up, and the twenty-five rebels immediately panicked. A few fled at once. The others hesitantly proceeded with their plans. Since they had obtained President Somoza's personal schedule of trips and appearances for a period of two weeks, they had a good chance of success. And, as one Nicaraguan later related to the author, "they came damned near getting the old man." By failing, however, they signed their own death warrants, and the National Guard rounded up eighteen, lined them against a wall, and summarily executed them without trial.

It is remotely possible that President Figueres did not know of the attempt personally, although this is quite unlikely. There is no question that members of his government and many high-ranking figueristas were well aware of the plot. Members of the Caribbean Legion themselves boasted in San José cantinas of plans to kill Somoza. Even today, there are figueristas who refuse to deny previous knowledge of the attempt on Somoza's life. When asked about it, they smile meaningfully and, after appropriate hesitation, change the subject. Perhaps José Figueres himself did not know of the plot. Certainly members of his government did.

In Nicaragua, Anastasio Somoza sincerely believed, until the day he died, that Figueres was behind the conspiracy, and that others would follow unless Calderón was returned to power in Costa Rica. Since the attack on him was so treacherous, Somoza felt no qualms about using all means at his disposal to topple the Figueres regime. And this idea was behind all his actions in the frenetic summer of 1954. Certainly his actions cannot be condoned. He clearly meddled in the affairs of a neighboring state in hopes of overthrowing its legally elected government. At the same time, the conspiracy against him was powerful provocation, and his

* Details of the Legion and Figueres' relation to it will be found in Chapter Six.

actions are understandable. Even in Latin America there are certain ethical norms of conduct. Assassination is not one of them.

The next outburst culminated in the January, 1955, invasion of Costa Rica. Agitation had begun the previous November, however, and fires of resentment were smouldering. In mid-November President Somoza negotiated a deal for twenty-five North American F-51 Mustangs from Sweden. The prop-driven Mustangs were among the best warplanes of World War II, and by this purchase Tacho quickly obtained the most dangerous air force in Central America. On November 27, President Figueres announced that Costa Rica faced a grave situation in the coming days. A rebel force of Calderón's was preparing to invade Costa Rica. Two hundred and fifty soldiers were already at the border, poised for the attack. In New York City, Figueres' confidante and ambassador-at-large, Daniel Oduber, admitted that the identity of the rebels was undetermined. He insisted that they must be supporters of Calderón. Nicaragua's ambassador in Washington, Guillermo Sevilla, said Figueres showed alarming nervousness and lack of serenity. Professing friendship between the two countries, he observed that tensions had been reduced during the administration of Otilio Ulate. However, "it is serious that Señor Figueres now discovers phantom invasions so easily and has not been able to discover the invasion that Caribbean Legionnaires in Costa Rica launched against Nicaragua at the beginning of this year with the aid of his government, developing a sinister plan to assassinate President Somoza and start a civil war in Nicaragua. . . ."16

Anxious to avoid war, the United States once more took measures designed to pacify the belligerents. The Air Force sent six jet fighters to the Panama Canal Zone. The obvious idea was to discourage private adventurers willing to fly one of Somoza's new planes in support of invading calderonistas. It was learned that planes would be sent to strafe and bomb San José. Agitators in the capital would arouse the crowds, inciting a march on the residence of President Figueres and forcing his resignation. As long as planes could be kept from the air, invaders would have less chance of success. Danger was momentarily allayed and, in the first week of December, Figueres announced laconically that "no invasion is expected this weekend."

The bitterness between Somoza and Figueres soon broke out again. On January 9, 1955, Costa Rica appealed to the Organization of American

States that an American government had sent "a fleet of 10 military transport planes, fully manned, into Nicaragua . . . [suggesting] that the hour for launching an attack has arrived."[17] Unofficially, they claimed that Venezuelan planes had been dispatched to Managua. The OAS Council was called into extraordinary session at 10:30 A.M., Sunday morning, to hear Costa Rican representatives Fernando Fournier and Antonio Facio present the case. They charged that an "army of adventurers" was about to launch an attack; Nicaragua was termed a "flagrant and repeated disturber of the peace." Guillermo Sevilla rushed back from Mexico City where his brother Alberto was seriously ill. The Council, after a three-hour debate, ruled that there was no immediate action required. They proposed postponement of action until a second emergency session the following Wednesday. This would give the twenty-one member nations time to consult their governments.

A few hours after Costa Rica called upon the OAS for help, a band of Costa Rican exiles flew into the airport at Villa Quesada and took possession of the small town. Simultaneously, several hundred others crossed the border to the north, while a third group came in small boats from the Nicaraguan Pacific shores. Communications at Villa Quesada were immediately cut, and only after receiving a telegram from the mayor of neighboring Zarcero did the Costa Rican government learn that the town was in rebel hands. President Figueres announced that "I consider this a Nicaraguan act of aggression." He gave as his interpretation the thought that "Somoza had released the mercenaries in his country and sent them into action earlier than planned." He added that the invasion was initiated from Nicaragua and, while rebel trucks were of Costa Rican origin, the planes and troops themselves had come from Nicaragua. Somoza's claims that the affair was purely internal were efforts "to fool the Organization of American States by spreading propaganda."

Reaction in Managua was quick and typical. Somoza said that Figueres' accusation of Nicaraguan and Venezuelan complicity against the government was "the worst thing I've ever heard. Nobody ever called me what that man called me. The least was that I had a family of gangsters." Figueres, moreover, was "a damn liar." He refused to issue an official reply. "Why should I?" he asked, "I wouldn't go that low." His suggestion which met with snide amusement outside Central America was a sincere request that Figueres meet him at the border with revolver in hand! "If he has so much personal hate for me, let's put it on a man-to-man basis. There is no reason for bloodshed between our two countries. If he hates me, as was evident when he tried to assassinate me, then why not settle it this way?"[18] Informed of the challenge, Figueres contributed to the exchange of theatrics by replying, "he's crazier than a goat in the midsummer sun."[19] Perhaps Somoza, a crack pistol shot, was not crazy. He often took pleasure galloping along on a horse shooting lizards on one of his ranches.

The fighting was chaotic, erratically reported, but real. Costa Rica rushed forces north at once, and the enemy was engaged at different points. The rebels sustained losses at several points, but instead of folding up, merely withdrew, regrouped, and returned to the attack elsewhere. For several days it seemed possible that insurgents might press forward toward the capital, although government forces were generally holding their own. The rebels had the advantage of air superiority. The day after the invasion began, as an added fillip, they even strafed San José from a twin-engined fighter, succeeding only in arousing the josefinos and chipping several sidewalks. The loyalist "air force" consisted of a commercial DC-3 transport with machine guns mounted at the open cargo door.

In the meantime, the Organization of American States once more prepared for action. On Wednesday, January 2, the Council of the OAS named a five-man commission to investigate the invasion, including the ablest of the OAS delegates. Two days later, while the commission was investigating conditions in Costa Rica and interviewing officials in San José, the Council adopted a resolution condemning the attack of "foreign forces," at the same time requesting Nicaragua to stop the flow of equipment to the rebels. In one of several unprecedented OAS actions, they accepted the offer of U. S. observation planes by Latin American affairs chief Henry Holland of the Department of State. Navy planes were sent from the Canal Zone, and commission members and aides flew over the battle scenes and the border in particular, on the lookout for evidence of Nicaraguan collusion. They reported that supplies were clearly being introduced over the border, although Nicaragua itself could not be charged with complicity.

Details of the fighting and the eventual surrender of the rebels is not important in this context. That part of the story will be related elsewhere. Our interest for the moment is the Nicaraguan participation and involvement in the affairs. With the appearance of the OAS on the scene,

President Somoza was fully cooperative with officials and complied with their requests, including temporary establishment of a buffer zone along the border. He also interned the remnants of rebel forces when they fled across the border in defeat. The final report of the OAS, replying not only to Costa Rican charges, also dealt with Nicaraguan accusations concerning the earlier attempt on Somoza's life. In an apparent effort to ruffle as few feelings as possible, the commission report was only mildly critical of the disputants, to the dissatisfaction of both. An evaluation of Nicaragua's role, unfortunately, cannot be based on the published findings of the commission.

According to information from the U. S. Embassy in San José, the original invaders numbered four hundred, of whom perhaps 10 percent, at best, were members of the Nicaraguan National Guard, all fighting out of uniform. The troops were commanded by Teodoro Picado, Jr., son of the former Costa Rican president put in power by Calderón. Educated at West Point, young Teodoro was unquestioned field commander. Calderón, living in Nicaraguan exile, admitted having planned the invasion from Nicaragua, although he never implicated Somoza. At the same time, it is generally accepted that the troops were trained for some weeks before the attack on the spacious lands of different Somoza *fincas*. An additional connection is the fact that ex-President Teodoro Picado served as personal secretary to Somoza in Managua, at least to the extent of drawing a salary. Certainly, Somoza knew about invasion plans, just as Figueres must have known about the 1954 plot against Somoza. The hatred between the two was so great that neither would stop at anything. Somoza told *New York Times* correspondent Sydney Gruson, in the midst of the fighting, that he was sorely tempted to throw the full power of his military forces against Costa Rica and held back only because of the "innocent blood" that would be shed.

A militant anti-communist who used all his influence against the Arbenz government of Guatemala when it was in power, Somoza was never convinced that Costa Rica's Figueres was not implicated in communist designs against him. Although often calling the Figueres government "communist coddlers," Somoza admitted that Figueres himself was no Red. At the same time, he believed until his death that Figueres was in concealed privity with Central American Communists for his own ambitious purposes. It is for this reason that Somoza believed that the 1954 attempt on his life was planned, or at least abetted,

by communist conspirators. This was but another personal reason for
his deep hatred for communism.

"Benevolent Dictator"

For years President Somoza was referred to by outsiders—as well as
some Nicaraguans—as a dictator, a despotic strongman in the worst
tradition of Latin American politics. As a general statement, it was
probably true. At the same time it implied a number of things not
necessarily true. Somoza's character was an exceptional blend of personality, charm, intelligence, and acumen.

Somoza was president from 1937 until his death, with the exception
of a very short time. After nearly a decade in office he placed Leonardo
Arguello in office in 1946. Arguello surprised all by acting independently,
soon ordering a change among ranking officers of the National Guard,
still Somoza's private domain. When Somoza objected, Arguello gave
him twenty-four hours to gather his effects and leave Nicaragua. Somoza
asked for three days and his request was granted. Thus, given the time
to rally his forces, he ousted Arguello and, a few months later, put his
uncle Victor Remón y Reyes in office. When the old man died in 1950,
Congress returned Somoza to the presidency. He served out the rest of
the term, and was himself re-elected in 1951 for a six-year term.

Leader of the National Liberal party, Somoza was ineffectively opposed
by the Conservatives for many years. He pacified them by an agreement
with Conservative leader Emiliano Chamorro signed April 3, 1950. A
new constitution was adopted permitting the minority party a fixed
proportional representation in the two congressional houses—the Senate
and Chamber of Deputies.* Conservatives thus came to hold a third of
the legislative seats, as well as a quota of diplomatic missions and Supreme
Court seats.

In his sixty-first year, Somoza occasionally spoke to friends wistfully
about stepping down. Until his sudden departure from the scene in late
1956, however, there was no heir apparent. His two elder sons were
slated to take over eventually. However, Anastasio Jr. had spent his
career in the National Guard while Luis, the politician, did not appear
to have the requisite popularity or force of character. It was in view of
these factors that in February, 1956, Somoza agreed to stand for re-election.
Just a day before he was assassinated, Somoza was officially nominated

---

* Nicaragua is the only Central American republic with a bicameral legislature.

by the National Liberal party convention. The expectation was for his re-election and extension of his power through 1963, over twenty-five years after first taking power.

For years, Somoza was the target of continual attacks by the Sociedad Interamericana Prensa (SIP). They maintained that he was a tyrant intent, among other things, upon complete press suppression. Through the years this dispute was waged without satisfaction to either party. In recent years, the SIP has worked diligently to dissipate what it considers press censorship. Ronald Hilton, Director of Stanford University's Hispanic-American studies, has written that the Nicaraguan press has been made aware of Somoza's authority even since 1937. A detailed report in 1953 called the existing press law vicious and tyrannical. Nicaraguan law condemned articles prejudicial to the good name of the republic. This permitted the government to interpret the news and to suppress any articles to which it took a dislike. Somoza referred his critics to a recent statement in defense of news and public information. "Public opinion in my country is constantly kept informed about public matters. In 1954 I delivered three political public messages on Nicaragua's economic development, one [exclusively] on the political situation. I often hold press conferences with both local newsmen and foreign correspondents. Reports, bulletins, and magazines are issued from the various government agencies. I listen to the people and I am listened to by them. We carry on a dialogue."[20]

A disagreement cropped up on May 4, 1956, when President Somoza invited the SIP to help him prepare a new press law. He wrote SIP president James G. Stahlman of his intention to abolish the present press law criticized by the SIP. Promising to advance a new code at the next legislative session, he wrote of a desire for the "intervention of a technician or specialist designated by your organization." Somoza obviously hoped to placate the SIP and bring to an end the years of bickering between the two. President Stahlman promptly declined. He maintained that when a constitution guaranteed freedom of expression and press—as does the 1951 Constitution of Nicaragua—no further legislation was necessary. He cabled Somoza that "We believe that the press ought not to be submitted to any law that does not apply to the general citizenry. . . . Your Excellency will see that we do not look for special privileges for journalists or papers, because the press that accepts the condition of privilege, renounces a part of its independence."[21]

Critics of the Somoza regime have also attacked the United States bitterly through the years. Arguments that the United States supports military dictatorships in Latin America are understandable, and in many cases valid. However, Nicaragua was somewhat different. From the U. S. point of view, Somoza was indeed a good friend. He always co-operated fully with the United States, before and during World War II, then into the cold war years. Ambassador Guillermo Sevilla in Washington called home for instructions more than fifty times in recent years preceding various international conferences. His instructions always read the same: "cooperate fully with the delegation of the United States of America." More than once, Nicaraguan persuasion has been instrumental in helping align other Latin nations behind an unpopular policy of the United States. The Department of State has rarely made a request of the government that was rejected. Until his death Somoza was anxious to attract as much foreign and U. S. capital as possible, another reason his country enjoys the best credit internationally of all Central American republics.

Yet for such loyal support, Somoza was rewarded poorly. Despite a mutual security pact, he was frequently frustrated in attempts to buy arms. This was understandable when he wanted to turn them against Costa Rica. At other times, his requests were summarily rejected, often without official explanation. Somoza once said, "The United States may rest assured of the loyalty of Nicaragua's friendship which, as an official and as a private citizen, I always have promoted. In the hour of danger it will find us alongside the Stars and Stripes."[22] Economic aid has also been negligible. Only for the Inter American and Atlantic-Pacific Highways has the United States contributed a sizeable amount for improvement. The U. S. apparently has little realization of the small sums necessary to help modernize a country such as Nicaragua. Somoza himself summarized the matter succinctly. "What advantage do we get from being friendly? You treat us like an old wife. We would rather be treated like a young mistress."[23]

As the reader has gathered, Anastasio Somoza was a gregarious, affable man of high good humor. An old picture hanging in the Nicaraguan consulate in New York City reveals Somoza as a handsome youth during his pre-presidency days with the National Guard. By 1956, although weighing two hundred pounds and showing progressive baldness, Somoza was still an impressive man. Few people, even in a short interview, failed to enjoy his candor and effusive good humor, regardless of their political opinions. To English-speaking visitors he spoke in colorful, often unprintable terms. Despite his age, Somoza was still an energetic dancer and crack shot. He was always aware of charges of being a dictator, and contradicted them with apparent humor. In 1952, while visiting Washington, he said, "I resent being called a dictator. If I'm a dictator, I wouldn't be able to afford to leave my country."[24] On the other hand, in 1948, also traveling in the United States, he told a San Francisco consul that there was no danger in leaving Nicaragua. "They're all fools. There's no one there who could do it [lead a revolution]."[25]

More than once Nicaragua was referred to waggishly as Somozaland. Somoza admitted to owning nearly 10 percent of the arable land in his country. His interests included distilleries, sugar mills, cotton gins, lumber, cattle, cement, soap, textiles, ice-making, and even a barbershop. He was principal stockholder of the Mamenic Line for overseas shipping, and the Nica Airlines was operated by his son José. His personal wealth was estimated at sixty million dollars, one of the greatest fortunes in the Western hemisphere. Nicaragua's road system almost always seemed to lead to or go past one of his ranches or coffee fincas. A new road to his Tamarindo Ranch, forty miles from Managua, has almost no houses or people along it. There are towns in Nicaragua with the names of Puerto Somoza and Somoto. Standing by the National Stadium is a large statue of Somoza. Many have considered Nicaragua a large ranch; certainly he operated it as one. Almost any serious decision had to go to Somoza for resolution. Ministers were glorified clerks.

There is no disputing the fact that Somoza ruled Nicaragua single-handed for many years. At the same time, no one can rationally assert that Nicaragua did not progress under his regime. Somoza came to power in a chaotic, undisciplined, revolution-haunted, backward little country. He brought unprecedented peace to heal many of the fissures which had divided Nicaraguans for years. In 1955 Somoza could say, with accuracy, "All the progress the country has made during the last eighteen years would not have been possible unless peace prevailed. The government has successfully tried to maintain peace as a fundamental basis of its constructive work."[26] Once peace was achieved, Somoza turned toward economic and material problems, and results through the years were generally gratifying. Much of the increased Nicaraguan wealth rubbed off on Somoza, to be sure. Nonetheless, the economic condition of the people grew better than ever before. Even in more remote areas, the peasants are generally assured of growing enough crops on which to live. This seems meager, yet is an improvement over earlier conditions.

None of this denies the suppression of democratic opposition, prohibition of trade unionism, occasional outbursts against freedom of the press, and continued undemocratic government. Drew Pearson has written that years ago, in a moment of revelation, Somoza told Franklin D. Roosevelt that "I want to treat everybody good. Democracy in Central America is like a baby—and noboby gives a baby everything to eat right away. I am giving the people liberty, but in my style. If you give a baby a hot tamale, you will kill him." What Anastasio Somoza accomplished in Nicaragua perhaps no one else could have done. Today the "baby" is more than twenty years old, and certainly ready for more democracy, far more than that afforded by "liberty, but in my style."

On September 21, 1956, at 11:00 P.M., Somoza and his wife were guests of honor at a reception in the Workers' House in León. One day before, he had been nominated by the National Liberty party as their 1957 presidential candidate. Happy with his renomination, Somoza was in rare form, regaling friends with ebullient stories and dancing an energetic cha cha cha. Suddenly a young man darted from among the crowd of dancers, pulled out a Smith and Wesson .38 revolver, and fired five shots pointblank at the President. As he fired the last shot he was pulled down from behind by Arnaldo Ramirez Eva, chief of Nicaragua's national building program, and a moment later riddled with bullets by presidential bodyguards. He was struck by more than twenty bullets. Somoza, wounded four times, sat conscious in his chair awaiting medical aid. Told that the assassin was killed on the spot, he said, "he should have been captured alive." One bullet had missed the President and wounded a woman.

News reached Managua almost at once, where U. S. Ambassador Thomas Whelan, a close personal friend, sent a helicopter to return the President to Managua. At the same time he called Washington and, without Nicaraguan request, asked for immediate medical aid. President Eisenhower ordered a medical team from Gorgas Hospital in the Canal Zone to fly to Managua. Two surgeons, a bone specialist, and an anesthetist answered the call. A few hours later, informed of the gravity of Somoza's condition, Eisenhower ordered Major General Leonard D.

Heaton, commander of Walter Reed Army Hospital, to join the other U. S. doctors in Managua.

On Sunday, September 23, the decision was made to fly Somoza to Gorgas General Hospital in Panama, where facilities were superior to those available in Managua. Once in Panama, Somoza was immediately operated on to remove the bullets. One had passed through his right forearm, breaking the bone. Another lodged in his right shoulder, a third in the right thigh, and the fourth, the most serious, had stopped at the base of the spine. A four-hour neurosurgical operation succeeded in removing all but one bullet which was considered unimportant. Panamanian neurosurgeon Dr. Antonio Gonzalez Revilla removed the missile from the base of the spine, severing two or three nerve roots to do so. The post-operation statement said that Somoza's lower right leg was paralyzed because of the bullet near the spinal column. Otherwise his condition was called satisfactory and his chances of recovery good.

On Monday the President took a sudden turn for the worse. Surgeons opened a hole in his windpipe to aid breathing. At the same time he developed paralysis of the entire left side of his body. Removal of the bullet at the spine apparently caused the paralysis. Although at the same time the right leg paralysis was lessening, the new development was called "an unexpected postoperative complication which has not yet been fully evaluated." Colonel Charles Bruce, health director for the Panama Canal Zone, would not amplify his statement except to note that the President's blood pressure and temperature were good, his heart action strong. Through the week Somoza began to improve slowly, and there was hope for his recovery, although he had never been fully conscious since reaching Panama. At 4:40 A.M. Friday morning, Panamanian President Ricardo Arias and Canal Zone Governor William R. Potter learned that Somoza's condition was grave. They joined Señora Somoza and the President's daughter, Lillian Somoza de Sevilla, at the President's bedside. At 5:05 A.M. on September 29, Somoza was dead.

In Nicaragua, Somoza's sons had moved into complete authority immediately after the shooting. Luis, thirty-four-year-old president of Congress and first in line to the presidency, took charge of the government with the support of Tachito, at thirty-two the commander of the National Guard. Luis, meeting with the cabinet Friday night, declared a state of seige, suspending constitutional guarantees of free speech, free assembly, and habeas corpus. A curfew was set in Managua from 10:00 P.M. to 5:00

A.M. There was complete calm in Managua and business opened as usual on Saturday. The two Somozas immediately began an investigation. On Saturday over two hundred opposition leaders were taken into custody, including eighty-four-year-old Emiliano Chamorro and the equally aged Enoc Aguado, leader of a group of liberals who had opposed Somoza's renomination. Pedro Joaquin Chamorro, publisher of *La Prensa*, was also arrested. His newspaper had been opposing Somoza's re-election.

The assassin had been identified as Rigoberto López Pérez, a Nicaraguan who had been working for several years as a phonograph record salesman in El Salvador. He had only returned to Nicaragua recently. In fact, he was first thought to be a Salvadoran, not a Nicaraguan citizen. There was no evidence of motive beyond a possible dream of martyrdom and apparent hatred for Somoza. In a literary contribution to the León *Cronista* a few days before the shooting, he wrote that "immortality is the aim of life and of glorious death." He also claimed that the "devil is the greatest poet who is not recognized by humanity." The Somoza brothers asked Salvador's President Lemus for aid in the investigation, since the killer had recently come from El Salvador.

On September 26, Nicaragua dispatched messages to all the Central American republics notifying them that Nicaraguan exiles and others were planning a revolution. Nicaragua requested that subversive activities be curbed, stating that subversives abroad hoped to take advantage of the situation. The notes invoked a resolution dealing with subversive activities of political exiles, a measure adopted by the meeting of Central American foreign ministers in August, 1955. The messages requested that "necessary measures be taken to exercise the most effective and strict control over the subversive activities of all persons who propose to endanger the peace and security of Nicaragua."

The next day Foreign Minister Sevilla claimed that exiles were forming a united front. He listed nine exiles as leaders of the group. The so-called united front included Nicaraguans in Guatemala, Honduras, Cuba, Costa Rica, El Salvador, and the Dominican Republic. Costa Rican exiles included Adolfo Díaz, Nicaraguan President in 1911, and his nephew, Ernesto Solorzano Thompson. The sole survivor of the 1954 plot against Somoza, Manuel Gomez Flores, lived in Mexico. Hernán Robleto, publisher of *La Flecha*, also lived in Mexico. Against all these men, Sevilla said, he had asked their countries of asylum to take "preventive measures." It was a few days later that Nicaraguan exiles in Mexico, celebrating the death of Somoza, predicted the organization of an "army of liberation" that would free Nicaragua from the Somoza family. Alberto Gámez Reyes said in Mexico that Somoza's sons would not be allowed to continue his tyranny. He optimistically pointed out that there were sixty thousand exiles in Costa Rica alone. Actually, there were nearly that many Nicaraguans working in Costa Rica, but a relatively small number of them were exiles from their land.

In Managua, the number of persons held for questioning soon reached three hundred. In a week's time, however, virtually all were released, having revealed nothing new. Opposition newspapers began to republish several days before Somoza's death. Señora Margarita Cardenal de Chamorro flew from Chicago to publish *La Prensa* while her son Pedro was in custody. *La Noticia* and *La Flecha* also returned to the streets the next day. All three, however, were under instructions to limit their political reports to government accounts.

There was no further excitement during Somoza's week-long struggle for survival. Somoza, who had received an apostolic benediction from Pope Pius XII during the week, lay in state at Sacred Heart Catholic Chapel in Panama, where a requiem high mass was held. After the mass his body was escorted with an honor guard to the Albrook Field air base and flown back to Managua. Tens of thousands of Nicaraguans were either at the airport or lining the route from La Merced Airport to downtown Managua. In the first of eight days of national mourning, the body lay in state in the National Palace. Nicaraguans filed past the casket all night long at the rate of fifty a minute, many moved to tears of grief. The body had been met by two sons—Luis and José—at the airport. Tachito had not attended, in order not to provide joint targets for assassination. After a night in the palace, the casket was moved to the Cathedral of Managua for a pontifical funeral mass, then transported in turn to city hall, the Presidential Palace, the Army Enlisted Men's Club, and back to the National Palace. On October 2, 1956, Anastasio Somoza was laid to rest in the Pantheon of Officers of the National Guard Cemetery.

Reaction varied widely. Citizens in El Salvador were overjoyed. Costa Rican President Figueres, traveling in Europe, hoped that Nicaragua would establish a democratic government. The Uruguayan parliament passed a resolution honoring the murderer, Rigoberto López Pérez. At the same time Cuba declared a three-day period of national mourning. Mexican President Ruiz Cortines sent deep personal sympathy. Panama expressed condolences. President Eisenhower stirred up ill feeling in many quarters when he expressed his sympathy and called the attack "dastardly."

Editorial comment was also in disagreement. Many dailies lamented his death as the passing of one of the great Latin American leaders. Others hailed it as a great event in democratic life. *El Mundo* of Buenos Aires attacked President Eisenhower for his telegram to Nicaraguans. "In an emphatic document . . . Eisenhower brands as 'a dastardly attack' the gesture of Rigoberto López Pérez and points out the great friendship of the defunct dictator toward the United States . . . it would seem that the passing . . . [is as if] one of the stars which adorn the North American flag had been extinguished."[27] One of the few rational and dispassionate comments came from the *Washington Post and Times Herald* on October 1: "Nicaragua has been freed of dictatorship by assassination and her free neighbors in the Americas now will hope that she can leave both institutions behind her in the next phases of her political life.

"Anastasio Somoza was personally admirable to those who could tolerate his self-serving, anti-democratic regime. Some could not, including his assassin, whose foul deed cannot be excused. Now that his bullet has ended President Somoza's life, however, Nicaraguans can seize the opportunity to liberalize their political machinery."[28]

A DYNASTY SOMOZA?

Death set the stage for possible revolution in Nicaragua. The uncertainty following the shooting and eventual death of Somoza was great, and many expected outbreaks at any moment. No one was sure of the sons. However, they were given one final push from their dying father. His stubborn fight for life gave them time to consolidate their positions. Had the old dictator died at once, all Nicaragua would have gone up in anarchy. As it was, the sons had a full week to consolidate their position. Opponents, still respectfully fearing the father, refrained from open troublemaking in the event he should recover and turn vindictively on those unloyal to him.

Luis was sworn in as Acting President on October 3, taking office at once. The eighteen-man Nicaraguan cabinet submitted resignations as a matter of formality. Luis refused them, and the ministers continued in their posts. Five days later he traveled to León, site of his father's assassination, to receive the nomination of the National Liberal party for the 1957-63 presidential term. In accepting the nomination he surprised no one by promising to follow his father's policies. Scheduled elections took place in February, 1957, with Luis standing for his father's office. The old Conservative party chose to abstain from the voting, claiming government interference made participation impossible and without value. A group of dissident Conservatives, however, formed the Partido Conservador Nicaraguense some three months before the voting. They entered fifty-six-year-old Edmundo Amador as their candidate. Amador himself admitted the futility of opposing the government. He added that "our struggle is not for today but for tomorrow." Referring to the refusal by most Conservatives to take part, he added that the withdrawal "would not have affected Somoza but the Conservative party itself." Although initially pressed to obtain the necessary twenty thousand signatures to get on the ballot, this conservative splinter group firmly rejected all suggestions to leave the race.

On February 2, Luis Somoza told newsmen that "I enter the elections tomorrow absolutely sure of the triumph of the Liberal party, because the entire Nicaraguan population has been showing it with manifestations of affection. . . ."[29] In an election granting women exercise of the vote for the first time, some half million voters were inscribed. Somoza announced his hope of winning 85 percent of the vote. That hope was realized. Following his election, Luis was expected to continue his father's policies without change. Luis had studied nearly ten years in the United States, graduating from the University of California as an agricultural engineer. Later he studied agriculture at Louisiana State University and the University of Maryland. Elected a deputy to Congress in 1951, he had served alternate months as president of the Senate and the Chamber of Deputies, proving himself conciliatory, self-effacing, soft-spoken. Some critics preferred "weak."

The survival of Luis and his brothers depended initially on economic matters. They hoped for and were to see banner 1956-57 crops distracting attention while their rule was secured. Much of their father's former opposition had been among well-to-do merchants and exporters, to whom personal prosperity was the overriding criterion. The old dictator had worked hard to make their—and his—cotton production as profitable as possible. At the same time, production costs had gone exceedingly high.

There was little real danger to the old man as dissatisfaction among these people was more a nuisance than anything else. With his sons, the situation was different.

Cotton production looked optimistic as 1956 drew to a close. The crop was estimated to bring in thirty-five to forty million dollars based on a harvest of 650,000 quintales of cotton. Sales were to drop well below these figures, but not until the brothers had further secured their power. In October, 1957, the United States granted a credit of five million dollars to help a foreign trade dollar shortage. Earlier in the month, a similar measure was negotiated with the International Monetary Fund, by which Nicaragua could draw up to $7,500,000. This credit was limited to six months. By the close of 1957, however, economic dangers threatened. Additional loans brought the total to nearly fourteen million dollars, and $1,500,000 in gold was sold to balance 1956 trade deficits. In November, the government was forced to freeze all but essential imports, all others required an advance deposit in the National Bank of the necessary sum before an import permit would be issued—and that only after thirty days. New economic demands required an increase from sixty-five to one hundred million dollars annually to balance obligations. By mid-1958, however, the latter figure was still out of reach. Despite the corner-cutting involved in restraining the budget, the administration began a modest, low-cost housing project, at the same time borrowing more money to cover increased agricultural production. By the close of 1957, the balance of trade was adverse. A shift in the final quarter balance pushed imports over exports by nearly $1,500,000. With cotton giving way once more to coffee as the leading export in dollar value, the export outlook for 1958 was not good. The 1958 coffee crop brought nearly 15 percent less revenue, and coffee also dropped, due to an international price reduction, although volume shipments changed very little.

On the political front, developments strongly suggested an attempted change from the way of life under Somoza. Luis announced the initiation of a liberalizing approach soon after his inauguration. He praised his father's efforts, and insisted he would have liberalized political practices had he lived. "You analyze what he did for Nicaragua and you will find he brought it distinct advantages. There are times in a country's life when only one man can save it and that was the case with my father and Nicaragua."[30] Luis announced the "continuation" of press freedom. "About 90 percent of our editors are behaving like good newspapermen, but the remaining 10 percent are too passionate . . . they must . . . give all sides of a story."³¹ He brought attention, with justifiable pride, to the establishment of bi-weekly presidential news conferences at which he answered questions about all phases of national affairs. Observers noted that newspapers indeed seemed free to criticize the government, although they still leaned a bit in the direction of caution. Luis brought others into governmental operation by delegating responsibility as his father never did. Ministers were instructed to appear before Congress to justify their policies, and the first such appearance was a rare and widely heralded day in Nicaragua. Luis found himself opposed on different occasions to businessmen whose support for his father was almost traditional. Economic troubles could not convince him of the necessity to devalue the córdoba, and by mid-1958 his wisdom was clear. He also pushed a greatly expanded social security program in the face of opponents who, on this issue, included his brother Anastasio.

The completely unexpected impetus given liberalization was underlined in April, 1958, when Luis sent a new law of presidential succession to Congress. He requested the adoption of a constitutional amendment forbidding the president to succeed himself. This would include anyone in his family—something significant when Anastasio is kept in mind. Skeptics at first disbelieved, then concluded that the Somozas would not be included in the measure. They were confounded when Congress approved the action and did include the Somozas in its provisions. The danger of eventual retribution at the hands of his enemies after leaving office in 1963 apparently could not sway the President from his course.

As events moved through 1958 there was great interest and curiosity about the success and background of such movements. When the two brothers took over the reins of government from the strongman, it was felt that their efforts would be even more restrictive, and certainly less successful. Neither son has the personal characteristics of the father, who in the end ruled by personality as much as anything else. Young Anastasio probably has his father's ruthlessenss and native shrewdness, but he is a brusque man, quick to anger and slow to forget. He had experienced certain unpopularity with old cronies of his father who were forced to serve under him in the National Guard. With his father dead, he needed much more than the West Point training he had undergone. Luis, as has long been known, is not as conservative as his brother but, in spite of his first eighteen months in power, has shown limited qualities of leadership and strength. It is a bit surprising that his disagreements with Anastasio have generally indicated the latter's willingness to defer, if a bit reluctantly. Between the two of them, Luis and Anastasio still do not equal their father, except in the palest fashion. Should either one slip, or—a provocative possibility—turn on the other, Nicaragua is destined for another period of turbulence.

In an interview with *Latin American Report* published in May, 1958, Luis Somoza plumped firmly for closer relations with Honduras and Costa Rica as well as for the advance of economic measures leading to a federation of Central America. He insisted on the necessity of the constitutional reform prohibiting presidential re-election: "I submit . . . that the person who has held the Presidency of the Republic in the previous term may not be elected President in the following term, nor any of his relatives within the fourth degree of consanguinity or affinity.

". . . I personally believe that although the principle of rotation in power restricts in a certain way the free manifestation of popular opinion on the person of its preference for President of the Republic, it is healthful for the normal exercise of democracy in countries such as ours."[32]

Certainly Nicaragua is ready for and deserving of a more liberal regime than that of Somoza. Whether or not it can win this in the near future, no one can answer. Hope exists, at least. Perhaps Luis will succeed in bringing to the country its first free political life. But whatever his intentions, execution is the tricky thing. He recently told the *New York Times* that "I am going ahead with my experiment in democracy in Nicaragua and we are making progress." But coupled with these words was a sentence that was an ominous reminder of bygone days. "But we are still too close to violence; if my political enemies show violence, [then] the Government must counter with violence."[33]

Chapter Six

COSTA RICA

"Central American Switzerland," "Land of Eternal Spring," "Heart of the Americas"—these are some of the expressions frequently and misleadingly applied to the second smallest country of Central America. Costa Rica is a land of paradoxes and contradictions. It has managed through the years to create the superficial impression of being singularly distinct from its neighbors. But Central America is not homogenous, and Costa Rica differs but little from the supposed norm. The idea of being totally removed is but one of the widely disseminated contradictions.

The republic rests compactly between Panama and Nicaragua. Surrounded on the other sides by oceans, Costa Rica is divided in the center by the Meseta Central—the mountain range extending through Central America from Mexico to Panama. Again, terrain gradually falls from the Meseta Central to rolling lowlands that in time change to steamy coastlands. The mountains include active volcanoes, notably Poás, with reputedly the world's largest crater. Situated in the center of the Meseta, nearly equidistant from the two oceans, conveniently placed in a natural amphitheatre, is the capital and heart of the nation, San José.

To understand Costa Rica more fully is to understand first what it is not; in this case a negative approach has advantages. In the first place, the climate is not that of "eternal spring," enthusiastic travel blurbs to the contrary. Tropical lowlands are hot, and seasonal rains fall eight months of each year in the mountains, often reaching a maximum of 160 inches annually. "Heart of the Americas" is a title claimed by several Latin American states, none of whom has credentials to support the claim. The phrase "Central American Switzerland" is more understandable, though nonetheless inaccurate. Costa Rica speaks of its peaceful, democratic existence. Yet a major revolution within the last decade was bloodier than the colonial battles of earlier centuries. At least three times in the last fifteen years the government has been undemocratic and unrepresentative to the point of dictatorship. Another contradiction is the widely circulated boast that Costa Rica has no army, and fewer soldiers than school teachers. While the army was abolished in 1950, there is a police force of some 1,250 plus 700 coast guardsmen. Panama also has no army, but its police force more than serves the purpose. Nicaragua and Honduras can also boast of having more school teachers than soldiers. Whether or not their educational systems equal that of Costa Rica is entirely beside the point. Contrary to declarations of bucolically peaceful, constructive living, marauding bands roamed the northern province of Guanacaste at will until very recently. Robberies are still high in the area. Only eight years ago a family of foreigners was assaulted, killed, and robbed of all their possessions while passing. Only a small child survived.

Such facts are basic to our understanding, for so many heralded national traits are no more than imaginative myths. Costa Rica is in some ways more advanced than its neighboring countries, but democracy is young and insecure. Elections are only partially honest, and the results are not always observed. Educationally, although in need of much expansion and modernization, the Costa Rican system is the best on the isthmus. Perhaps because of this no recent Costa Rican leader has been a military careerist; the military has been uncommonly inactive in political affairs—a lesson neighboring countries have yet to learn. In point of fact, then, Costa Rica is well ahead of its sister republics in many fields, notably political maturity and liberty. Nonetheless, it is far from the well-seasoned government of democratic practice prevalent among the more advanced members of the Western world. Costa Rica today is in a position to slip back just as its neighbors show signs of awakening to the more advanced precepts of democratic government. Whether or not Costa Rica can withstand the retrogressive forces acting against her is the critical question. If not, the work of many years will be needlessly sacrificed. This is yet another reason to recall Costa Rica in paradoxical terms.

RECOURSE TO REVOLUTION

To understand Costa Rica today we must go back a dozen years to the revolution of 1948 and the events preceding it. Only today are there signs that the republic may be turning ever so slightly away from a heavy preoccupation with political affairs. It has not been thus for many years. In 1940, a prominent San José doctor, Rafael Calderón, was elected president with the support of conservative forces. Constitutionally prohibited from succeeding himself, Calderón arranged for the election of the brilliant but hesitant lawyer Teodoro Picado, who took office in 1944 after defeating ex-president León Cortés in what were basically dishonest elections. In 1947, the government announced it was supporting Calderón's intention to return to office in the 1948 elections. By this time, however, opposition to calderonismo had assumed imposing proportions; the eventual result was Costa Rica's first resort to violence in years.

After eight years of calderonismo it had lost its appeal for Costa Ricans. Policies were increasingly unpopular and conducted with disregard for public opinion. As opposition began to mount, Costa Rica skidded toward revolution. Indications of dissatisfaction came from almost daily eruptions, inflammatory editorials, and illegal police action. Newspaperman Otilio Ulate, the opposition leader, wrote in February, 1947, "The country is in a dilemma; either it must abandon the suffrage or have a civil war to restore honor and integrity to the public."[1] Incidents mounted with a fistfight at the entrance of the Legislative Assembly in March and the bombing of military headquarters in San José a few weeks later. Anti-government feeling burst forth in July with the "Huelga de los Brazos Caídos,"—Strike of the Fallen Arms.

On Sunday, July 20, 1947, government forces precipitated a clash in Cartago, the ancient national capital some fourteen miles outside San José. As two theatres disgorged their crowds simultaneously from the afternoon movie, police launched an attack with tear gas, stones, and clubs. Moments later machine guns were fired into the crowd. Two were killed and several wounded. The government disclaimed knowledge of the attack, although high ranking army officers were seen at Cartago during the fight. Crowds gathered outside the San José offices of *Diario de Costa Rica,* the newspaper of Otilio Ulate. Ulate wrote the government that "No code in the world authorizes any government to turn machine guns and rifles on an unarmed city because of its political opinions . . . I leave to your own conscience what you must do as chief of state. . . ."² For several days there were repeated clashes between police and citizens. On Wednesday, the twenty-third, opposition leaders called a halt to these outbursts and asked for a national strike. An opposition bulletin announced that "The Committee of the National Strike informs its partisans that this decreed strike has the character of pacific resistance and does not authorize any act of violence against persons or properties."³

Those in sympathy with government brutality were asked to continue work. Others were to close shops, stores, theatres. At once, transportation and communication were at a standstill. The government was confronted with a paralyzed capital. Shops were boarded up; bank doors closed; barbershops, grocery stores, dry cleaners, pharmacies, even the bars were closed. President Picado nervously announced that the government would keep order at all costs. But there were no incidents of violence. The public simply remained inactive. The extent of the dissatisfaction is clear in view of the great amount of money lost through the shutdown. On Thursday, the strike committee circulated a mimeographed bulletin announcing that "The Strike continues throughout the territory of the Republic . . . the most significant fact is that of the presence in the streets of San José of communist groups armed with carbines and Mausers. . . . Pay no attention to rumors. The strike continues to prosper." At the bottom of the bulletin were the words, "circulate this leaflet."

The government blamed three factors for the strike and tried to neutralize activities where possible. First, opposition politicians were kept under close surveillance and warned against inciting the citizenry. Secondly, bank managers were instructed to reopen their doors. However, as they replied, there were no employees to man the offices. In desperation, the administration named civil authorities to control the banks. In a few hours this failed as the strikers ingeniously appeared en masse to make large withdrawals. Business was too great to handle; the government gave in. With businesses remaining shut, Picado tried to deal with the third factor. Taking to the air, he appealed for a return to normalcy. "Of course I cannot tolerate the existence of two governments: one in the streets, by the violent imposition of political parties or groups, and another in the Presidential House, where the constituted powers of the republic reside. . . . Everything will be solved by legal and peaceful means, as the majority of Costa Ricans may wish . . . [I] will not let violence guide my steps."[5]

After a week of failure the government decided to arm a force of mariachis* to fight for the government. They were fully armed, as were members of the Vanguardia Popular (the front for Costa Rican Communists), whose leader was a compatriot of Calderón. Mobs of mariachis roamed San José under orders to force the opening of as many stores as possible. Few proprietors were present, so the mobs proceeded to break down barricaded doors, smash windows, destroy and loot store goods, and create havoc wherever they went. Time and again nearby policemen pointedly looked the other way while mobs went about their task of destruction. They punctuated the sacking with cries of "Viva Calderón," or "Viva Vanguardia Popular." The government represented these attacks as desperate efforts of poor starving loyalists to get subsistence rations.

Picado hoped to provoke outright revolution. Violence would have been easier to deal with than a passive strike. The opposition was farsighted enough to avoid just that danger. Otilio Ulate repeated demands that the government disavow the Cartago violence and offer guarantees of electoral impartiality in forthcoming elections. Ulate also offered free food and provisions to those who might be in need. Then he addressed military forces:

> This call is directed to the armed forces of the country, to the soldiers of Costa Rica . . . to warn them that they must refuse to continue lending their services to a Government that orders them to machine gun their compariots in cold blood and without provocation. The national movement of civil resistance . . . has as its object equal benefits for all honorable Costa Ricans, regardless of the political party to which they belong, because it originated on the refusal of the Government to grant to the people effective guarantees for the free exercise of the right to vote.[6]

On August 1, the strike was finally ended by one of the most extraordinary occurrences in contemporary Costa Rican history. A group of feminists in San José, Cartago, and Alajuela issued a manifesto calling for the end of dissension. They sent a message to President Picado asking for the restoration of all liberties. On the morning of the second, some eight thousand strong, they marched on the doors of the presidential home singing the national hymn and waving white flags. "We have a guarantee

* Unemployed lower-class vagrants willing to fight if armed and bribed.

of complete security that our manifestation will not be interfered with. To the gentlemen who have insisted on protecting us, we ask them vehemently to abstain from doing so, that it may not be said there is any political provocation in our movement. We are absolutely sure that there will be no Costa Rican capable of disturbing such a parade, respectful of mothers and Costa Rican girls who only ask for liberties for our people."[7]

President Picado was significantly absent, and the women prepared to pass the night in the park next to the presidential home. A number of soldiers gathered, hurling choice epithets at the women. At 11:30 the park was thrown into pitch darkness and soldiers began firing into the air. The women scattered, either leaving or taking refuge in nearby homes. Although they were dispersed, the government finally conceded the impossibility of its task, and agreed to terms of the general strike committee. The next day, August 3, 1947, a nine-point agreement was drawn up. Key sections stated that the government would

. . . create a Committee of Investigation formed by three full members and three alternates. They will be named by the National Election Tribunal. . . .

The Executive Power will present to the Constitutional Congress immediately a projected law granting just and due reparations to all persons wounded by the disputes. . . .

The President of the Republic guarantees all employees that the Executive Power will give absolute liberty . . . to affiliate with any Political Party with which they have sympathy without any reprisals or dismissals for such a motive. . . .

The President of the Republic, the two leading Political Parties, and the Deputies of said parties, agree to give all their support and to maintain in their posts the present members of the National Election Tribunal . . . [and] to recommend to the citizenry that they observe a complete truce in political activities for eight days. . . .[8]

An epilogue was signed by the President, the Unión Nacional, and the Partido Republicano Nacional. In a further guarantee of free and honest elections, they would support the decision of the newly established three-man electoral board: "The Committee of Investigation will be formed by three full members and three alternates. . . . Those selected will be persons of recognized independence, of political impartiality, and of unquestioned moral rectitude. . . . The resolutions of the Committee will be taken by a majority of votes. The decision of the members of the Committee of Investigation will be obligatory and binding on all Costa

Rican citizens. . . ."[9] The investigation committee was to play an important role in the coming presidential elections.

Campaigning for the February, 1948, elections grew in fervor as the time neared. There was no apparent interference in the opposition fight, and Otilio Ulate was not prevented from advertising his candidacy, despite government preference for Calderón. At the end of January, the heavily financed Calderón campaign concluded with a demonstration in the capital before an estimated crowd of twelve thousand. At the same time, what was to have been the climax of Ulate's campaign was cancelled at the last moment for lack of funds. During the one week political moratorium before election day, speculation ran high as to the outcome. Calderón's chances seemed bright in view of his support by government funds and army leaders. The inauguration of several badly needed social reforms during his 1940-44 administration was remembered by many. However, the fifty-two-year-old Otilio Ulate was widely popular. A respected journalist of many years' standing, he was strong with the lower classes, among whom he had associated freely. Handicapped by financial limitations, however, his campaigning was curtailed. All things considered, a close race seemed in the offing—barring government intervention.

During the week prior to election day, the President's brother Rene, minister of government and commander of the military, declared his intention of using troops if necessary to keep order. Announcing formation of a special mobile unit that would deal with possible disturbances, he insisted that there would be no interference in the voting itself. "I am determined that no Costa Rican will be able to say that the police or army interfered with his free ability to vote. But if anyone disputes the result and menaces my forces, the real shooting will start. . . ."[10] There were still doubts as to whether President Picado would permit a Calderón defeat. After eight years in power, the Calderón-Picado duo seemed unlikely to relinquish control of the profitable business of government. Some felt that there would be no armed opposition even in the face of obvious ballot-box fraud. Otilio Ulate, questioned on the point, said "I am a friend of peace and an enemy of civil war, but I prefer civil war to enslavement of the people."[11]

On election day, early returns showed Ulate leading in San José and the Meseta Central, but trailing the ex-President in the provinces. Ulate's margin was small. Early on February 10, the lead widened and Calderón called a press conference. He issued two conflicting statements. First he conceded defeat. In the next breath he charged fraud, an astonishing claim in view of government control of the ballot boxes. Official newspaper *Ultima Hora* reiterated the charges. Rene Picado added that ". . . this has been a crooked election and does not represent the will of the people."[12] Ulate answered claims of fraud with the caustic statement that no one was more adept than his opponent in the matter of fraudulent elections. Ulate's headquarters were deserted and he awaited developments at a private home. The same day *New York Times* correspondent C. H. Calhoun cabled that several thousand uncounted ballots had burned in a fire which completely destroyed a schoolhouse. Although the origin of the blaze was unknown, it had gutted the building. Calhoun reported the floor covered with the ashes of burned ballots. These had been moved to the school for added security after Calderón's charges of fraud. All were completely consumed. Even without these votes, Ulate's lead was up to ten thousand votes, and victory was assured. In the congressional race his Unión Nacional won twenty-four seats, Calderón's Republicano Nacional twenty-three, and the communist Vanguardia seven.

Final computations gave Ulate 54,931 votes; Calderón trailed with 44,438. The special three-man election jury, formed after the strike-ending agreement the previous August, adjourned to a room in the Hotel Costa Rica to examine the results and decide the outcome. The three-member jury was considered honorable and fully qualified for the delicate task. After extended hours of consultation the men emerged with the announcement on February 28, 1949, that Otilio Ulate had indeed won the election. Accusations of fraud were not borne out by the facts, it was decided. Only two of the three signed the statement however. Koberg did not agree with the findings and refused to concur.

Reaction was mixed. Ulatistas were elated; to them the final step in the certification of victory was complete. However, Koberg's refusal to sign the document led government forces to reject the decision. *Tribuna* editorialized that the final decision would come from Congress. President Picado said that without Koberg's vote the decision of the committee of investigation was invalid. The legislature would have to decide the winner. The Legislative Assembly was packed with calderonistas, who certainly would not certify an Ulate victory. The situation was further aggravated when Rene Picado refused to turn over control of the military to the president-elect within twenty-four hours of the announcement by the committee as was demanded by law.

On March 1, 1948, the Assembly met in special session. After an acrimonious meeting in which debate was long and stormy, the Assembly voted twenty-seven to nineteen to annul the results. Rejecting Ulate, they declared that new elections would have to be conducted in April, if the atmosphere were "appropriate." Cries of outrage rose in chorus. The decision was such a gross violation of the law that even some calderonistas were shocked. The agreement signed by all major political parties, including that of Calderón, had sworn to accept the decision of the committee. A key clause, already quoted (see page 215) said that ". . . resolutions of the Committee will be taken by a majority of votes. The decision of the members of the Committee of Investigation will be obligatory and binding on all Costa Rican citizens. . . ." This was the sworn agreement the government proposed to flaunt in contradiction of a clear expression of public opinion.

Hoping to check possible excesses, the government decided to place Ulate under arrest. Before jailing him, unidentified uniformed men fired into a house in the suburbs where Ulate was staying. The president-elect was unharmed, but his host was mortally wounded. It later developed that the attack was a half-hearted attempt by minor officials to assassinate Ulate. He was arrested in the presence of an amazed diplomatic corps, attesting to an offer of safe conduct from the regime. Ulatistas immediately appealed to the diplomats for intercession; Rene Picado left the country after escorting Ulate to the penitentiary, announcing his work completed; the city was quiet, but businesses closed and Pan-American Airways cancelled incoming flights.

Once again the population was outraged, and one day after being jailed, Ulate was freed by a fearful government. He announced that "my message to my people is, 'have faith in our victory.'" Amid rumors that a military force was forming south of the capital, the Archbishop of San José interposed to win a truce. Ulate promised to delay by twelve hours a radio broadcast calling for another general strike. All radio stations agreed to make no political comment during that time. On March 7, the Archbishop negotiated a forty-eight hour truce during which time the disputants might discuss the situation. Business interests represented by the bankers pleaded desperately for some settlement. One of their spokesmen said that "Only a peaceful settlement of the political dispute can save the nation's economy. Banks are now closed, for the Government could not stop a run on them."[13] The truce held, but Archbishop Sanabria was unable to bring about even a temporary agreement. He finally withdrew his offer of mediation. The country was apprehensive, and no one seemed to know what would come next. On March 12, the answer came from the mountains south of San José.

THE FIGHT FOR DEMOCRACY

Fighting broke out some forty-five miles from the capital between tiny units of a rebel force and official troops stationed in small towns nearby. After initial confusion, it was apparent that fighting was led by the insurgent José Figueres, a young agriculturist who was the political action chief of the Ulate forces. A mobile unit of government forces drove to Figueres' plantation, *Lucha Sin Fin,* but found his *finca* a small fortress and withdrew after two were killed and four wounded. Figueres, one of the younger political figures and a relative newcomer to the political scene, had not been particularly close to Ulate. However, his efforts against the regime had been unstinting. Shortly before the election he had begun gathering and training a motley band of revolutionaries on his plantation. Figueres claims today that he formed the rebel band to prevent annulment of elections. However, since purchase of arms started before the campaign closed, this is not entirely true. What he would have done had Ulate legitimately lost or not been denied his rightful office, no one can say. In any event, he had a small force armed with a variety of old, obsolete, and even rusty weapons. With these he opposed the army of some two thousand well-equipped men. President Picado, ordering a thirty day period of martial law, expected to quell the rebels easily.

In the first few days, there was very little fighting. The government was slow in dispatching troops to the area, and there were only infrequent contacts. Part of Figueres' strategy was to continue his revolution long enough for the citizenry in San José to rise up against the government there or, at the very least, to pressure the government into negotiation. As a result, he was in no hurry to force the fighting, outnumbered and outgunned as he was. The terrain in the area of fighting is among the most mountainous in all Central America, rising to ten thousand feet in places. With only one acceptable highway and a few small side roads, transportation was also poor, making warfare more difficult, particularly for attacking government troops.

For nearly two weeks fighting was spasmodic. Figueres conducted a defensive battle. Using guerrilla tactics, his forces struck at small isolated garrisons or important bridges and buildings, accomplished their objective and withdrew to the mountains before casualties were sustained. Fighting near the southern extension of the Inter American Highway, they were able to swarm down on small convoys or groups of government troops, wreaking havoc on the unsuspecting foe and escaping prolonged battle, in which they were bound to be at a disadvantage.

As Figueres anticipated, the situation in San José grew chaotic. President Picado in effect turned over complete control of the fighting to brother Rene; he was President in name only. Calderón himself was relatively inactive, other than trying to persuade his good friend Somoza of Nicaragua to send forces in support of Picado. More important than the others was Manuel Mora, chief of the Vanguardia Popular, the Costa Rican communist party. Mora had in different ways been politically related to Calderón. In the uncertain days of 1946, and 1947 especially, the government had come to rely heavily upon Mora. As opposition mounted, the regime was willing to sell its soul to the devil in exchange for support. Hoping to buttress its position, the regime was increasingly friendly with the Communists. Subsequent political analysts have charged Calderón and Picado with being potential Communists themselves. This is not so. However, they had no great reluctance in associating with Manuel Mora in order to retain power. When the government position began to crumble after the February elections, the well organized Mora supporters were increasingly important and soon became the real pillar of support.

Mora's followers, armed and uniformed, contributed to the military forces in the capital. These included not only communist party faithful, but "irregulars," mariachis who were offered the chance to earn drinking money and act important at the same time. Encouraged by the confident participation of the Vanguardia, President Picado took heart. On March 23, he announced that the rebellion was contained and would soon be totally extinguished. On the same day, hundreds of leaflets were circulated in the Meseta Central. Titled "Liberación Nacional: Primera Proclama," they were addressed to non-combatants.

Costa Ricans, are you doing what you can for the triumph of liberty? The army of national liberation is fighting brilliantly in the theatre of war. You can help the patriotic effort greatly by blocking roads with wood and rocks, cutting telegraph and telephone lines . . . in trying by all means to disorganize and dismember the usurping government.

Are you doing what you can? . . .

Do what you can, be it little or much, to support the army now, and be ready and prepared for our triumphal entrance into all the towns of the country. We will come; soon, very soon, we will arrive.

Help us from afar and repeat this promise that must be passed from breast to breast like a divine conflagration:

WE WILL FOUND THE SECOND REPUBLIC![14]

The proclamation was signed, "José Figueres, Commander in Chief of the Army of National Liberation."

Leading an attack of several hundred men, Figueres soon won outright control of San Isidro del General, the last town on the Inter American Highway. In the meantime, small landings at the tiny Pacific ports of Dominical and Potrero Grande harrassed loyalist troops, although not in themselves a serious threat. Warfare in the San Isidro valley spread throughout neighboring sectors. To the south, several hundred people left their homes and went to the Panamanian border, rather than continue to live in fear of raids by one side or the other. Toward the Pacific, the United Fruit Company evacuated several of its smaller installations in anticipation of possible fighting there. A temporary truce finally halted the fighting at the end of March, in observance of Holy Week. Except for this respite, fighting continued on an increasing scale as the rebels built up confidence by occasional victories and apparent lasting power.

The boldest stroke of Figueres' campaign came on the last day of March when San José was attacked from the air for the first time in history. One of three TACA Airline transports, seized on the first day of revolution, flew over the capital at a dangerously low altitude and dropped a bomb on the presidential residence. It fell to the courtyard below and only slightly damaged the building. The psychological effect was great, however. The government was shaken by the attack, while the citizenry was impressed by the daring, as well as the scrupulous care taken in attacking only the government building rather than launching indiscriminate city bombing.

With the coming of April, Liberación Nacional began to take the offensive for the first time. Troops slowly advanced toward the capital, seizing the village of Tajar, near the important city of Cartago, after a pitched battle. Small parties also landed on both coasts, tying down scattered government troops and distracting frustrated officers from organizing a serious plan of action. Appeals to the people were stepped up, and the tone was one of increasing confidence. Figueres went on the clandestine radio repeatedly. Introduced by the introductory strains of Beethoven's Fifth Symphony, he explained again and again that only a "second republic" could free Costa Rica from impoverishment at the hands of special interests and the privileged government class. At the same time, despite censorship, propaganda sheets were circulated. On April 1, 1949, the second proclamation from the army of liberation was published. It promised to restore order and good government and to end poverty and was signed by Figueres.

In many of the smaller villages, terrorism was rampant. In some of the Pacific coast settlements, in particular, armed bands looted and killed. Order was maintained only with difficulty in some of the more populous areas, and only the largest cities were free of opportunistic vandalism. By April 12, the rebels had succeeded in establishing a base at San Ramón, forty-five miles northwest of San José. With this position secured, they were able to ring the capital geographically and advance from all sides.

The next day at five o'clock, a ceasefire was called. Settlement was in the air. A meeting was held along the Inter American Highway at which both the government and Figueres were represented. Members of the diplomatic corps lent their presence in hopes of hurrying a final agreement. Father Benjamin Nuñez presented Figueres' demands at the meeting. Following an armistice, the government was to be turned over quickly to the Liberación Nacional, which was prepared to operate on an emergency basis until the constitutionally elected authorities could take charge.

Government representatives did not receive the proposals with enthusiasm. President Picado was willing, but his influence by this time was negligible. Armed forces in San José were in control of the capital, and they were under the thumb of Manuel Mora. Determined to keep Figueres out of the city, Mora still entertained hopes of hanging on until aid might come from Nicaragua. Negotiations continued. On April 16, President Picado agreed to Figueres' terms and signed the final agreement. Manuel Mora stubbornly refused. With personal control of San José barracks, weapons, and manpower, he forbade Picado or Calderón to leave the country, announcing simultaneously that he would continue the loyalist fight as long as necessary. At this point the negotiated truce seemed meaningless. On April 17, hostilities reopened. José Figueres warned that "if the Communists keep blocking the settlement, we will march on San José ... willing to make concessions ... we will not accept any international commitments, and above all nothing that would conflict with the policies of the United States against communism."[15] While Figueres' forces girded themselves for one final assault, communist irregulars surged through the streets of the capital looting, stealing, and burning indiscriminately. Wholesale arrests were made of many protesting, innocent citizens. The diplomatic corps continued to urge Mora to surrender. U. S. Ambassador Davis, in particular, directed pleas to the Communist to give up what was obviously a losing struggle. On April 19, he finally relented, faced with no alternative to a street fight ending in annihilation.

The longest and bloodiest civil war in Costa Rican history was concluded. A poorly trained, loosely organized band of revolutionaries, outnumbered two to one and armed with inferior weapons, had defeated the government in the six-week uprising. It had fought with determination, courage, and intelligence that belied its lack of military experience. After weeks of slashing guerrilla raids, it came out into the open and continued with a succession of victories. When the army of national liberation paraded down San José's Avenida Central on April 24, it was indeed a glorious moment. None of this had been necessary. President Picado and Calderón apparently had never considered the probability of serious revolution when they directed the annulment of elections. Knowing that their military advantage was seemingly unchallengeable, they were completely unprepared for the resulting armed opposition. With the army inexplicably undisciplined and unready, the government replied only feebly to the revolutionaries. Small cliques took orders only from Calderón, President Picado, Rene Picado, or Manuel Mora. Only the supporters of Mora gave a respectable military account of themselves. The army itself was from the beginning uninterested in the struggle, and this was the important factor in its humiliating string of setbacks.

Figueres' army of national liberation occupied the military barracks as government armed forces surrendered en masse. There were occasional clashes with some of Mora's men, but these soon ended. Teodoro Picado fled to Nicaragua, Rafael Calderón to Mexico, and Manuel Mora to Cuba. When doubts about the new government were expressed, Figueres explained that his troops were supporting the provisional government of Herrera which would in turn be replaced on May 8 by a junta.* "The same organization that gained victory will shortly assume the total direction of the country and will guarantee rapid reorganization and the restoration of normal conditions. . . . Then we shall begin to execute the grand constructive plans of the second republic."[16] As the new government was received with enthusiasm, President-elect Ulate added his approval: "The country must feel intensely proud of Señor Figueres and his brave boys."

With the provisional government under Herrera, a tremendous task of reorganization and accumulated work was faced. In the last weeks of the Picado regime, office work had collapsed, and widespread chaos faced the revolutionists when they took office. Figueres, refusing to set up a military dictatorship, pleaded for patience on the part of the people: "We must establish order throughout the country in the shortest possible time before taking measures of a civil and political character."[17] In the short time before the junta took power on May 8, the provisional government groped for an answer to its problems. Costa Rica was not only politically disorganized but nearly bankrupt. The revolutionists had expended every possible source of money in launching and conducting their battle and could do nothing personally. In the meantime, a less temporary government had to be formed to take office on the eighth.

Searching for someone other than himself to head the junta, Figueres asked Ulate to become junta president. However, while agreeing that a period of emergency government should precede his own constitutional term, Ulate refused to participate actively in the temporary organization. He believed that as emergency chief he would be forced to rule with an especially firm hand, at least occasionally taking action for which, as president-elect, he could not be responsible. Figueres finally decided to take the presidency himself. He announced that he would call a constituent assembly on the eighth when the new government took power. It would draw up a new constitution after which congressional elections would be held. Three months would be allotted to form the constituent assembly, with three more to debate and draft a new constitution. Once elections constituted a new assembly, the Ulate administration would

---

* A San José businessman, Jorge Herrera, was chosen to head the provisional government during its first weeks. He retired from politics soon thereafter.

take office, with the junta resigning all emergency powers. At the same time, its maximum duration would be eighteen months. On May 8, 1948, the final phase of the revolution opened when the junta government under José Figueres took power.

The first task of the junta was to ferret out all elements that might stage a counterrevolution. On May 30 the new government arrested 220 alleged Communists, seizing at the same time a large cache of submachine guns. Apparently the group was awaiting a propitious moment for their counter-coup. The government uncovered their whereabouts before the movement began. Slightly unnerved by the magnitude of this threat, the government doubled its guard on the northern border, and patrols scouted the San Juan River looking for revolutionaries who might sneak across the frontier from Nicaragua. The atmosphere began to relax when once again danger flickered. On June 19, Figueres announced that a major military attack had been planned for the twenty-eighth. As forces invaded from Nicaragua, San José and the two major ports, Puntareuas and Puerto Limón, would be put under aerial attack. At the same time communist and pro-Calderón elements would rise up in the capital and smash the new government. The elaborate plans included the assassination of Figueres and Ulate. The government response was a thirty day suspension of civil rights and the arrest of thirty-five suspected Communists. On July 17, full constitutional guarantees and civil rights were restored. Continuing its war against subversion, the government banned the communist Vanguardia Popular on July 18. It also outlawed secret political parties and the use of violence for political purposes.

Satisfied that its regime was in safer waters, the junta turned to financial and economic problems, intent on shoring up the nation's deteriorated financial state. Several different means were employed. One was that of outright loan. First the government negotiated for a twenty million dollar loan from the Export-Import Bank to pay outstanding accounts and finance a large public works program. Then it went to the International Monetary Fund for additional financing that might pay for the machinery and clothing imports Costa Rica needed. At the same time, a few months' business activity and government operation reduced the gravity of the situation. On September 25, the economic council refused a five million dollar loan from the National City Bank of New York, citing the "inconvenience" of using gold reserves of the Bank of Costa

Rica deposited in the United States. The loan had been offered at 3 percent, with yearly payments of one million dollars on the principal after the sixth year.

Internal measures to increase revenue were more unusual. Tax facilities were speedily reorganized to render the collection of income tax less ineffective. It had been traditionally avoided in one way or another. In the face of the Latin heritage of non-payment of taxes, the government's position was surprising. Even more startling was the proclamation of a 10 percent capital levy, something unprecedented in Central American political history. Designed to pay off debts of former governments and help finance a reconstruction and development program, the levy was directed to the wealthiest sector of the population. For less prosperous citizens or small businessmen with a yearly income of less than ten thousand dollars, the levy meant nothing. The wealthy were hit hard by the law, however, for the 10 percent levy took a sizeable chunk from even the most affluent businessmen. The tax went into effect in November, 1948. A month before another junta decree had announced drastic import restrictions. "Private" importations were forbidden, with future imports to be made through junta control. A 50 percent tax was declared on the c.i.f. value of luxury merchandise, and 30 percent on semi-luxury goods. Near panic broke loose in business circles. Importers were dazed and said that the importation of luxury and semi-luxury articles was prohibitive. In reply, government spokesmen explained that it was necessary to reduce imports, since they more than doubled the value of exports. Thus capital might be introduced into official channels from the private market, helping alleviate government financial worries.

While re-establishing order and shoring up the treasury, the junta was dealing simultaneously with a third problem—national political reorganization. The first stage was the election of representatives to the constituent assembly. The three-month period for registration and recognition of parties had to be extended in September since only Ulate's Unión Nacional had complied in time. By October, seven different parties had presented a slate of candidates for the forty-five-member constituent assembly. The major parties were the Unión Nacional, the extreme right-wing Partido Constitucional, and Figueres' Partido Democrática Socialist.

A general holiday was declared for the December 8 voting, and election officials urged neutrality away from the ballot box. Two days after the voting, results showed that Ulate had won an overwhelming victory, his Unión Nacional having won nearly 80 percent of the total vote and, with it, thirty-three of the forty-five seats. The constitucionalistas captured six, and Figueres' belated effort to organize his own supporters brought him only four seats. The following month the constituent assembly met for the first time and began to frame a constitution under which Ulate would finally become president. Three days after the election, however, a calderonista counterrevolution was launched with an invasion from Nicaragua. Many of the details have already been accounted in Chapter Five. However, at the risk of some repetition, certain aspects must be mentioned here. The invasion was formed by calderonistas determined to overthrow the junta, exile Ulate, and take the presidency for Calderón. The ex-President was aided substantially by Nicaraguan dictator Somoza. Many of his supporters had fled to Nicaragua after Figueres' victory, and under Calderón's leadership and Somoza's eye had passed the intervening months planning their return.

The thrust was first planned for early 1949, but Costa Rican internal affairs caused a last minute change of plans. On December 1, Figueres had disbanded the army of liberation, calling for a return to the tradition of schoolteachers, not soldiers. Minister of War Cardona warned that this was not to be taken as a sign of weakness. Costa Rica would fight if necessary. At the same time he announced that the national police force would be maintained at one thousand men and the coast guard at seven hundred. To Calderón this seemed the time to strike. He allowed a few days to pass in order for the army of liberation to be effectively dispersed. Then, with elections on December 8, he reasoned that there might be at least a little excitement and perhaps irregular activity which would aid his attack. The ace in the hole, if he had one, was the hope that josefinos would rise up in the capital to overthrow the junta. There were still substantial numbers of communist supporters willing to help, and Calderón was not totally unpopular in San José. It was with such thoughts in mind that he ordered the attack for December 12, 1948. In Managua he called a press conference, that there might be no doubt of the counterrevolutionary leader. "The revolution was illegitimate and ill-conceived . . . my aim is to restore the state of things destroyed by a group of insensate men led by José Figueres, a legal and spiritual adventurer."[18] At the border there were conflicting reports. After initial disagreement, it became apparent that the invaders numbered no more than three hundred. The first pitched battle was December 14, two days after the first attack.

At La Cruz, a few kilometers south of the frontier, a band of rebels was surrounded and thirty-eight men captured. Elsewhere fighting was light and inconclusive. On one occasion several Costa Rican loyalists were wounded as two groups of government forces fired upon one another, failing to establish identity.

The junta government had reacted immediately in San José, mobilizing the army of liberation and re-establishing its former organization and command. The country was placed under martial law and press censorship. A national effort was decreed to repulse the invaders. In the midst of the confusion, Figueres took time to accuse the Nicaraguan National Guard of participation. This, he said ominously, could mean nothing but outright war. Somoza denied the accusation sharply. He wheeled to the counterattack with a statement that "the forces he led [the army of liberation] were made up almost entirely of foreigners in the Caribbean Legion . . . this . . . is Nicaragua's enemy and has openly threatened us with the overthrow of our Government some day. . . ."[19]

Fighting slackened in the next few days, and the invaders were obviously making little progress. The Costa Rican people were standing firmly behind the junta, belying its short existence; there was no sign of trouble in the capital. The government turned to the Organization of American States for assistance, appealing for intervention on the grounds that Nicaragua was impinging upon sovereign rights. The Costa Rican delegate in Washington officially invoked Article 6, which says in part that "If the inviolability or the integrity of the territory or the sovereignty or political independence of any American State should be so affected by an aggression which is not an armed attack . . . the Organ of Consultation shall meet immediately in order to agree on the measures which must be taken . . . to assist the victim. . . ."[20] A board of inquiry was sent to the area. The five-man commission spent nearly a week in San José, then continued to Managua. They encountered official cordiality in both cities. Returning to Washington one day before Christmas, the commission presented its report to the council of the OAS, which in turn approved a resolution calling upon both countries to refrain from hostile actions. Nicaragua was held guilty for permitting the formation of a revolutionary group on its soil. Costa Rica was enjoined to remove the presence of the Caribbean Legion and offer no further encouragement to its members. Both parties to the dispute were to observe the principles of non-intervention and solidarity. The commission report stated unequivocally that the invasion came from Nicaraguan territory. However, there was no evidence of direct Nicaraguan collusion. It had, in fact, prevented the rebels from getting supplies across the border after the first day of fighting. The counterrevolution was broken, and the junta returned to the task of reconstituting a representative Costa Rican government.

RETURN TO CONSTITUTIONAL GOVERNMENT

Following the December turmoil, the junta returned to the preparations for the delivery of office to Ulate. Most of the events of the next months were dedicated to the consummation of this goal. The constituent assembly opened on January 14, 1949, approving on the following day the election of Otilio Ulate from the preceding March. It was agreed that he would take the presidency after elections for the regular Legislative Assembly. Originally it was understood that the junta would relinquish power after eighteen months, on November 8, 1949. However, in early 1949 the Figueres government proposed that its tenure be extended six months, in order to assure completion of the national tranquilization that was to precede Ulate's inauguration. The president-to-be agreed to the proposal, stating that problems left by the Picado government were grave enough to warrant six months' extension of the junta's life. The constituent assembly concurred in the decision by a vote of 26-19. Thus the junta was to be prolonged until May 8, 1950. There were those who thought this was but a step in Figueres' establishment of a military dictatorship. They were convinced that Ulate had been persuaded or bribed to go along with the provisional government that its power might be more firmly established. As it developed, the junta later decided there was no need to extend its tenure, and Ulate was able to take the presidency in November as originally planned.

The last open threat to Ulate's inauguration came on April 2, when Colonel Edgar Cardona, minister of public security, tried to engineer a coup against the provisional government to which he belonged. With a small group of followers he seized the Artillery barracks and the Bellavista barracks, the latter on a hill overlooking the San José business district. Colonel Cardona had little support; his hope was to draw support from other military elements, particularly dissatisfied members of the liberation army who opposed the impending disbanding of that force. If the military came to his side, Cardona reasoned, there would be little to stop him. He soon learned that even hotheaded young army irregulars had had their fill of revolution, however, and no one joined him. The Artillery barracks surrendered early the next morning, and Colonel Cardona was taken prisoner. On the other side of town, Bellavista barracks, under Fernando Figueroa, refused to yield. After a full scale two-hour bombardment, he changed his mind. The following day Cardona's chief co-conspirator, Claudio Cortés, brother of former president León Cortés, was also jailed. Total casualties on both sides were seven killed and twenty wounded. Although crowds shouted "death to Cardona," the junta chose to be lenient. Today he lives in Costa Rica a free man, although not active in politics or the military.

Figueres' popularity increased after refusing to prosecute Cardona harshly. Cardona, apparently angered by Figueres' refusal to appoint a man of his choice as director of the police, had little standing as a national political figure, and his defeat merely boosted government prestige. Figueres declared that "the disloyal . . . elements have been defeated. The dark legend that force is able to rule . . . has perished today."[21] The people cheered enthusiastically. Two days later the army was once again disbanded, the second time in five months. It only remained for the constitution to be completed and a new Congress to be elected, and the junta's task would be complete. In mid-August, the new document was finished and approved, giving the country another measure of stability. It was, of course, different from its predecessors, but there was little in it to change the operating procedures of previous governments. The executive powers had been slightly restricted, but the president still was in fact the dominant force. Roman Apostolic Catholicism was endorsed as the state religion, although Title VI also was careful to state that the religion would not "impede the free exercise in the Republic of other religions not opposed to universal morality nor proper customs."[22]

On October 2, elections were conducted for deputies of the Legislative Assembly as well as for municipal officers. Again, as in earlier elections for the constituent assembly, there were only three parties with more than negligible support: Unión Nacional, Partido Constitucional, and Demócratas Socialistas. The government, intensely concerned in bringing out all voters, cashiered a fleet of cars to comb the roads and byways, offering to drive voters to the polls that they not fail to cast ballots. When returns were complete, Unión Nacional had polled fifty-one thousand of the seventy-two thousand votes cast, winning thirty-three of the forty-five Assembly seats. Both of the two vice-presidents, who under the constitution had become elective officials, were ulatistas. It was a smashing affirmation of Ulate's great popularity. The Social Democrats and Constitutionalists were left far in arrears.

Just as the final step seemed complete, Ulate's accession was jeopardized by precipitate action on the part of Figueres. After several months of rather rough going, Figueres and the entire cabinet resigned on October 26, barely two weeks before the scheduled inauguration. Figueres' political troubles began shortly after his July announcement that he was willing to accept nomination as vice-presidential candidate. He would be "honored to collaborate with the next Government." Thus he showed himself willing to play a role secondary to that of Ulate. At the same time, he blocked efforts of followers to drive a wedge between him and the president-elect. Figueres planned to resign from the junta, head a national party in the congressional contest, and campaign nationally. The relationship to Ulate's party would be one of "cooperative opposition." One month after his initial statement, Figueres withdrew his candidacy. Speaking over the radio, he expressed his approval of Ulate's vice-presidential choices. He preferred to continue his work as head of the junta, he announced. This statement killed off his party for the present. Its list of Assembly delegates was withdrawn. It was October 26 when Figueres and the provisional government resigned. The constituent assembly passed a bill putting the jobs of all ten thousand government employees on a temporary basis. The measure permitted the discharge of all civil servants, regardless of grade, without warning or compensation. This meant a complete sweep of all government officials was possible. Low grade workers receiving under six hundred colones a month could be fired without notice and without receiving any terminal pay.

Figueres was seething. Pointing out the injustice of the law, he refused to continue in power, and the cabinet backed him fully. He wrote Ulate to be ready to take charge of the government within twenty-four hours. He was determined not to continue as junta leader. Ulate was equally insistent that, after the various difficulties in re-establishing constitutional government, it was foolish to permit a break, particularly with the inauguration only two weeks away. Figueres angrily asserted that the bill must be revoked, but this would have been exceedingly difficult. Ulate finally promised not to exercise the power of dismissal he had been voted. With this assurance, Figueres stayed on for the remaining two weeks. Otilio Ulate was duly sworn in as President of the Republic on

November 8, 1949, exactly nineteen months, twenty-eight days, and three presidents after having won election. With the inauguration of Ulate, the nation was hopeful of an administration of peace and progress. Prospects suggested a "new day" in Costa Rica. Ulate, immensely popular when he took office, had started years before as a newsboy in Alajuela. Moving to San José as a youth, he became a reporter and, by the age of twenty-six, publisher of *Diario de Costa Rica,* one of the better newspapers. A widely traveled journalist, he was always independent, and his paper followed the same path. His only previous political office had been that of national congressman, to which he was elected in 1916 at the age of twenty-one. After a month he was jailed for opposing the regime, and a budding political career was apparently cut short.

A large, ugly, but not unimpressive man, Ulate was and is today respected for his lack of pretense and sincere concern with the problems of even the lowly street begger. Combining his popularity with a new constitution, a new Legislative Assembly, and only weak minority opposition, it was entirely reasonable to anticipate an administration of peace and progress—certainly that was what strife-ridden Costa Rica needed while the wounds of the revolution healed. The first two years of his administration were devoted to the stabilization of shaky finances, improvement of foreign credit, and a less sickly internal loan situation. There was a dollar shortage to be dealt with, and the fluctuating exchange rate of the colon also demanded stabilization. While Ulate was interested in development of agricultural and industrial potental, he realized the only basis for an effective program would be a sturdy financial structure. This was lacking, and he was forced to work for the alleviation of such fiscal and economic ills. The development program was postponed.

When Ulate took office, Costa Rica's unredeemed overseas trade commitment was $20,500,000. By June, 1951, this was completely liquidated and the Central Bank had a $6,500,000 reserve for letters of credit. In 1950, the Central Bank, Costa Rica's currency-controlling and money-issuing authority, began to release a sum in excess of three million dollars to liquidate the overseas debt as quickly as possible. Debts of previous administrations were soon wiped out, and the credits incurred by Figueres and early Ulate commitments were gradually cancelled. In place of the 1949 disparity of 3.5 between the official dollar rate and that obtained on the open market, the money changers soon were paying less for dollars than the government. The public external debt remained in default, but shrank in two years from $58,500,000 to $30,000,000.

Aside from a generally sound financial policy, the administration benefited from marked business improvement and foreign trade expansion. A coffee export tax was introduced, charging three dollars on each hundred pounds of coffee. Two private banks were established to reinforce the nationalized banking system. Revised civil service regulations cut expenses and eliminated duplication. Figueres' pet scheme, the 10 percent capital levy, was ignored. Trade with the United States increased. Exports for 1950 were $34,700,000, and the next year rose to $38,000,000. Imports also grew, increasing over a million dollars after Ulate's second year. The coffee and banana harvests were also larger than in other years. UFCO expanded both its banana trade and its African palm oil plantation in 1951. With all this, President Ulate could claim after two years in office, "No small part of my Government's strength is due to the spirit in which all the ministers have carried out their duties. . . . We can now turn . . . to material reconstruction."[23]

President Ulate announced on November 1, 1951, a two year development program. Satisfied that national finances were on a sounder basis, he proposed to increase agricultural and industrial production while developing the republic's undeveloped latent resources. Pivot of the switch to material reconstruction was a four million dollar loan from the International Bank for Reconstruction and Development. Much of the loan was to be channelled into construction of a large international airport, El Coco, a few miles outside the capital. More was directed to a hydroelectric project and the purchase of industrial and agricultural equipment, largely from the United States. Financing the hydroelectric project was delayed, but in October, 1952, Foreign Minister Alfredo Hernandez Volio flew to Washington seeking further financing of this program by the International Bank. Plans had been made involving a dam and power plant on the Raventazon River on the Caribbean, a plant which would have a 75,000 kilowatt potential. Expense was calculated at some thirteen million dollars.

During this same visit to the U. S., the foreign minister negotiated one of the major fiscal accomplishments of the Ulate years by arranging a settlement of the remaining foreign debt. He concluded a deal with the United States Foreign Bondholders' Council to liquidate an accumulated United States interest of some five million dollars. He also arranged to clear up a default in the U. S.-owned Pacific Electric Railway. This general settlement was probably the most important part of the administration efforts to rehabilitate national finances. On October 31, 1952, the Foreign Bondholders' Council said it had reached an understanding with Volio regarding assumption of service of Costa Rica's defaulted dollar bonds on an adjusted basis. Volio appeared before the Assembly on his return to explain the previously unannounced terms of the agreement. As he enumerated individual phases of the agreement, the government would float a new twenty year bond issue in New York City with 1½ percent interest increasing gradually to 3½ percent by 1956. The bonds would be exchanged at a nominal value for issues in default in 1952. The 7 percent Costa Rican bonds and 7½ percent Pacific Railway bonds had each increased in principal from a thousand to eleven hundred dollars in consideration of the fact that national interest payment was in arrears. The two issues of 5 percent refunding bonds were to be exchangeable for new bonds at par. All new bonds were extended twenty years. He added by way of footnote, that 75 percent of the bonds were owned in the U. S., 20 percent in Great Britain, and the remainder in France and Germany.

The 1952 business expansion continued into Ulate's final year in office, despite the excitement of presidential elections in early 1953. In his final state of the nation speech, President Ulate summarized the accomplishments. An unpaid commercial debt of $20,500,000 had been converted to a dollar reserve of similar quantity in the Central Bank. An international airport was being financed and constructed near the capital, replacing the inadequate La Sabana airfield. The Inter American Highway was nearly completed through northern Costa Rica to the Nicaraguan border. Almost all of the twenty-year-old foreign debt of $26,500,000 was liquidated, largely due to the agreement with the U. S. Foreign Bondholders' Council. Thirty-five percent of the total foreign debt would be paid when Ulate left office in November, 1953. The internal debt, while still sizeable ($27,000,000), was reduced by $1,250,000. A budgetary surplus of one million dollars was left over from 1952, and supplementary appropriations in 1953 of three million dollars were available for public works and educational expansion.

Agricultural improvement was equally heartening. Production was more diversified that in any other Central American nation. All the basic food stuffs were raised in Costa Rica, in quantities generally sufficient to make their importation unnecessary. Only wheat and lard had to be imported. The exportation of coffee continued to climb, with the 1952 crop valued at twenty-nine million dollars. Ten years before, a crop of the same volume had brought only eight million dollars. Bananas continued to bring in revenue second only to coffee. The 1952 harvest was valued at fifteen million dollars, breaking all previous records with 10,500,000 stems, an increase of a million over 1951. Once-abandoned plantations on the Caribbean, susceptible to Panama disease, were taken over by the Standard Fruit Company. They proceeded to develop a different type banana, somewhat less marketable but still in demand and, more important, not susceptible to Panama disease. Exports skyrocketed more than ten million dollars to sixty million in 1952, and imports rose five million to $55,700,000.

For Costa Rica, much of the credit for the expanding and diversification of agriculture was due the Point Four mission from the United States. It got a jump on missions elsewhere in the region, finding the task easier because of the sizeable number of small landowning farmers. The main base of U. S. assistance through Central America was set up in Turrialba some thirty miles east of San José. At this center, new plant species were developed, other seeds were improved and studied, hybridization experiments were conducted, and select young men were trained in scientific methods, these to be taken back to their native lands. The institute, today a powerful force in Central American agricultural development, devoted its early efforts, in particular, to Costa Rican problems, much to the advantage of the republic. A new extension service was established in 1952, operated exclusively by trained Costa Ricans.

For all these reasons, then, the administration of Otilio Ulate was notably successful. Probably no Costa Rican president in recent years has made such a valuable contribution. Ulate's procedure was the operation of an honest, disinterested government adhering to conservative fiscal policies at a time when the country was tottering on the brink of financial disaster. Through a combination of hard-headed policy making and sturdy monetary economics, the administration led the country back to its favored position among Central American economies.

Otilio Ulate faced communist activity during the first years of his administration and conscientiously fought them at every turn. Shortly after his inauguration, a large communist meeting was raided in a San José suburb, resulting in the arrest of seven Red leaders and the eventual exile of several. The communist Vanguardia Popular, although outlawed by the junta, still conducted meetings under a different guise, and only by police activity could they be curbed. In April, 1950, another gathering, billed as a student meeting, was visited by members of the Civil Guard, who found over two hundred Communists, fellow travelers and interested observers reading documents attacking "yankee imperialism." Twelve Reds were sentenced to prison terms of varying duration. Thus under government attack, the Reds tried to form a successor to the illegal Confederación de Trabajadores Costarricenses (CTC), which had once been influential in the labor movement. Communists filed the documents necessary for legal recognition of the San José Federación de Trabajadores in opposition to the Roman Catholic Rerum Novarum. This was squelched when President Ulate warned on November 13, 1950, that the government considered it illegal and would withhold the protection of the law. Pointing out that many of its leaders and affiliations were similar to those of the CTC, he refused legal recognition. The group soon faded away.

Revolutionary plots were of a minor nature during the Ulate years. In early spring of 1951 a series of bomb explosions in San José ruffled public order temporarily. Beginning in mid-March, bombings occurred sporadically throughout the capital, including the market place and one of the larger movie houses. Eight separate explosions were carried out before the government brought them to an end. On April 4, a large cache of bombs, automatic rifles, and other explosives were discovered in private homes, apparently in readiness for a possible coup. Damning lists of names were found, headed by the uncle of ex-President Calderón, Prospero Guardia. Communist elements were also involved in the terrorist plans. Presumably Calderón was directing the movement from Mexican exile. Forty-eight were arrested by the Civil Guard, completely breaking the back of the abortive plot.

Less violent but more startling was the one serious political crisis under Ulate, one precipitated by his own peculiar actions. In September, 1952, with campaigning already underway for presidential elections the following July, Deputy Ramon Arroyo brought up in the Assembly a charge presented by the Unión Cívica Revolucionaria, a party styling itself the champion of civil rights. Two members of the party had allegedly been attacked and beaten on order of police commandants. Congressman Arroyo demanded investigations. The protest was legally a matter for the military, and the Assembly had no obligation to investigate. However, by a vote of twenty-three to twenty it was decided to appoint a special committee of inquiry. Five of the six top-ranking police officers immediately resigned, calling the verdict a deprivation of their authority. Parenthetically, they also demanded satisfaction by challenging Arroyo to meet them on "personal terms." Colonel Manuel Ventura did not resign and was pressed to reorganize the security forces in the highest echelons. At this point President Ulate grew angry, declared that the congressional vote amounted to a show of no confidence, resigned the presidency, and angrily stalked out of the capital to his *finca*. First Vice-President Alberto Oreamuno Flores assumed the presidential duties.

Ulate's action was indeed extraordinary. Certainly the vote in the Assembly was unwise in view of military legal jurisdiction. However, it was scarcely sufficient provocation for Ulate to resign. As it was, a serious situation became instead a critical one. Despite the continuation of the administration under Oreamuno, there was the genuine possibility of a military *golpe*. Ulate certainly need not have retired to his country home. However, having let his pride override his judgment, there was nothing left to do but await the findings of the committee of inquiry. After the initial shock, Costa Ricans responded in a wave of sympathy for Ulate. He was pictured as a martyr to his office and the "street corner agitators" who signed the declaration of the Civic Union. The President stirred the people by blaming the crisis on political enemies. He never made any admission and, indeed, probably never recognized the fact that his resignation itself was the major cause of the crisis he blamed on political opponents. Fortunately, Ulate was able to return to office after sixteen days when the investigators gave his administration and the insulted police officials a clean bill of health. On October 13, 1952, the President returned to his post from self-imposed exile, and the administration settled down to the routine of government business once more.

Ulate's successor was to be chosen in July of 1953; in Costa Rica this meant that campaigning necessarily would begin many months earlier. There was never any serious doubt that José Figueres would declare himself, and in time he did. A new group called the Partido Liberación Nacional (PLN) began campaigning in the fall of 1952, although the convention did not officially nominate Figueres until April. Raul Blanco Cervantes and Fernando Esquivel Bonilla were named as vice-presidential candidates, and a full slate of congressional candidates was also selected. Working in favor of Liberación Nacional was the apparent popularity of its candidate. Figueres was naturally remembered for his leadership of the 1948 revolution, and his popularity had been increased by his handing over the government to Ulate just as opponents were accusing him of perpetuating military rule by decree. A man of forty-six, Figueres drew the fervent adherence of many young Costa Ricans, especially a group of self-styled "young intellectuals" who, despite fatuous pretensions, had a certain influence.

Figueres was first opposed by two men: Mario Echandi and Fernando Castro. Both men faced disadvantages in running. Echandi, a former member of the Ulate cabinet, was a brilliant and somewhat impetuous young politician distrusted in urban circles. He had generated considerable enthusiasm in the countryside, however. He was rumored to be President Ulate's preferred successor, although this was repeatedly denied by different members of the government, as well as by Echandi himself. Only after considerable maneuvering did Echandi win nomination by the Unión Nacional. The other candidate, sixty-eight-year-old Castro, was a millionaire coffee planter who had not been active in political affairs. Running as the candidate of the Partido Democrático, Castro was not particularly effective as a campaigner, due in some part to his age. However, he was known and respected by conservative business and agricultural interests, obviously a "safe" man for the continuation of previous traditions—in short, a true conservative.

As the campaign gained momentum in early 1953, all three candidates devoted themselves to the accumulation of "adhesions." In Costa Rica, a chief means of political propaganda is this system of recording support. Throughout the country representatives of the various candidates travel with posters and buckets of glue. They stop at house after house asking permission to put a poster on the most conspicuous wall. At the same time, all townspeople are asked to sign a document declaring their adherence to the candidacy of a particular candidate. There is nothing binding in this through either law or practice. At the same time, it is generally hoped that most people will vote for the candidate to whom they "adhered." Full-page newspaper advertisements, for example, would show Figueres or Castro delivering an address in some town. Then would follow a list of "adherers," running well into the hundreds. This form of campaigning continues almost until election night.

The 1953 Costa Rican contest soon became a two man race when Mario Echandi withdrew for various reasons, some of them obscure. Among these reasons were different political pressures and negotiations. His withdrawal after many had committed themselves to his candidacy made it difficult for these supporters to work actively for another candidate and undermined some of the support for Castro, who had competed directly with Echandi for the support of many of the same political figures. The entire campaign was completely dominated by José Figueres. He went tirelessly from town to town, making hundreds of appearances and talks in different parts of the country. In general his activity was not unlike that of United States candidates during the grueling rigors of primaries. Figueres appeared often in the major cities, but his appeal was clearly pitched to the ears of the lower classes. Figuerismo became a popular byword of the poorer classes, although many were baffled by some of his promises. He spoke of socialism adapted to the "reality of the present Costa Rican needs and possibilities," meaning a program of social and economic reform.

Figueres had long advocated a series of measures to shore up agriculture and make the national economy less dependent upon variations of international prices and buyer demand in foreign lands. These economic ideas, discussed at length in subsequent sections, were enthusiastically received by the less prosperous. To them, Figueres' plans were not fully understandable. However, he claimed to be interested in raising the standard of living, and that was something they wanted fiercely. The warnings of businessmen and economists that Figueres' plans might not work went unheeded. Another facet of Figueres' campaign was his reiterated determination to do everything possible to strengthen democracy in Latin America and oppose the regimes of Somoza in Nicaragua, Trujillo in the Dominican Republic, Pérez Jimènez in Venezuela, and others he accused of being despotic and undemocratic. He declared again and again that Latin America had passed the point at which democratic government was not only a desire but a crying necessity. He was pledged to exercise official influence in pursuit of this belief.

Liberación Nacional even presented a formal program, something rare in Latin politics. This "ideological program," appropriately enough, had something for almost everyone. In fact, there was very little it didn't promise. To attack it would be like slurring God, the Costa Rican flag, *fútbol*,* or the weekly lottery. For Castro there was no such program. Until the final weeks of the campaign, the Democratic candidate offered very little except a promise to continue the "traditions" of Costa Rica. In his later speeches he spoke of agricultural development. Himself a cattle breeder as well as coffee grower, he made a point of his experience with agriculture and the necessity of a level head in the presidency. This appeal, belated as it was, aroused little enthusiasm. It was left to Figueres to fire the popular imagination.

Determined to avoid the divisive rancor of such as the 1948 election, President Ulate took active measures to ensure a proper and free election. To avoid any show of violence, he prohibited the carrying of firearms. Anyone caught with a weapon would be imprisoned from six to twenty-four months. Expressing his determination to suppress disorders firmly, he warned members of the armed forces and government employees as well against any expression of favoritism. They did so at the risk of instantaneous dismissal. Further precautions included the appointment of a delegate to each of the seven national provinces with plenary powers to suppress any intimidation or violence. Delegates were members of the Civil Guard, holding complete authority in electoral violence.

As election day dawned the outcome was in doubt. Despite Figueres' domination of the campaign, the question was whether or not all the people crowding to his rallies had been captured to the extent of voting for him. As Sydney Gruson wrote in the *New York Times,* the vote was for or against figurismo. Castro himself had reminded listeners more than once that they might avoid figurismo by voting for him. Business interests were almost entirely behind Castro. They feared Figueres would launch a "soak the rich" program to finance his development plans, and his avowed interest in socialist doctrine was another source of concern. Assured that Castro would not be likely to rock the boat, they supported him instead. How many others might also fear figuerismo was the major imponderable confounding the experts.

Both candidates were predictably optimistic about their chances. Figueres declared expectantly that he hoped for 70 percent of the vote, the largest plurality in history. While many of his backers were willing to settle for the narrowest of victories, he was not. "A close vote, even in my favor, would be a great disappointment. It is unimportant whether

---

* Latin *fútbol* is the same as North American soccer.

or not I gain the presidency. The important thing is whether the majority of Costa Ricans have realized that the time has come for great changes in the country."[24] On July 26, 1953, the decision was reached. Figueres led from the start. Only four hours after the counting began, his daily *La República* claimed a two to one victory. At the same time the official count was low, and Castro said it was ridiculous to form conclusions so early. Final tabulations verified *República's* early claim, however. Figueres received 111,553 votes to 60,379 for Castro, a little short of 70 percent, but certainly a smashing affirmation of Figueres' campaign efforts. Four months later José Figueres was inaugurated as President of the Republic. On that day, 8 November 1953, the stormiest and most controversial figure in contemporary Central American politics assumed power.

FIGUERES: DEMOCRAT OR DEMAGOGUE?

In a region notable for its striking political figures, few are more extraordinary than José Figueres, one of the more unfathomable men of our times. Admirers have called him "the leading hope of the liberals in Latin America" (Arthur M. Schlesinger, Jr., Harvard historian), "the outstanding democratic leader of Spanish America" (Romulo Betancourt, ex-president of Venezuela), and "the leader of a new political movement and meaning in his part of the world" (*United Nations World,* November, 1953). To others Figueres is a "communist sympathizer" (Rafael Calderón), "a man trafficking in political intrigue and unease" (*Excelsior,* outstanding Mexico City newspaper), and even "a gutless ——— without the brains of a scarecrow" (Anastasio Somoza). Somewhere between these two extremes lies the enigma of José Figueres. Born of Catalan parents near San José in 1909, Figueres went to the United States in his youth, studying there several years. Returning to Costa Rica, he bought a coffee *finca* in the rugged mountains south of the capital and became an agriculturist at *Lucha Sin Fin,* as he called it. Like other coffee planters he had to import high-priced coffee bags, and after several years diverted acreage to fibrous sisal, from which coffee bags and hemp could be made. In a period of fifteen years he became a well-to-do planter, owning two farms as well as the bag manufacturing factory. In the operation of his *finca* Figueres applied ideas which were later to be reflected in his political activities. Interested in socialism, he established a small state of his own. Sharecroppers—over five hundred of them—

could sell products to him at average market prices or elsewhere if they could get a better offer. He helped build sanitary homes, set up a communal vegetable farm and a dairy to provide free milk for the children. Medical and recreational needs were also met.

Figueres was inactive politically until the 1940's when he became a member of the Civic Betterment Committee, a group of young men dissatisfied with the right-wing government of Rafael Calderón. By 1942 Figueres was completely wrapped up in politics, and he was soon exiled as a result. On July 4, 1942, a Nazi submarine sailed into the Caribbean port of Limón and calmly torpedoed a UFCO ship anchored at the dock. The ship sank and the U-boat slipped away. In San José feeling ran high as shops owned by Germans were attacked and looted. The government did little to suppress the violence, which eventually ran its course and subsided. Four days later Figueres made a radio broadcast in which he scored the government for laxness in permitting its defenses to admit a German submarine into the main harbor unmolested. Before the broadcast was finished, listeners heard scuffling, then a musical interlude. Police had been dispatched to the studio where they took Figueres into custody, cutting off the broadcast, then spirited him to a plane and out of the country. Such was his first brush with the authorities, but it was not the last. By the time of his return in late 1944, Figueres had decided to participate wholeheartedly in national politics.

Within a few years Figueres was reasonably well known in political circles. When trouble stirred in 1947 he was with Ulate in opposition to Calderón and Picado. We have already seen his leadership of the six-week revolution bringing a military junta to power. After handing power to Ulate, Figueres began to travel extensively in the hemisphere. Speaking at university forums and hispanic conferences, he voiced again and again his ideas on Latin American affairs and U. S.-Latin policy. With eyes on the 1953 campaign, bolstered by the prestige of leading a democratic revolution, he reiterated his ideas repeatedly. From these speeches he first gained prominence outside Central America. For our purposes, his statements are well worth examination. At the Assembly of the Americas in Miami, Figueres spoke, in January, 1952, on "Crusade of Moral Rearmament: The Just Man." As in most of his speeches, the emphasis was largely economic.

The notion that all business is "private" is an illusion. In practice we accept every kind of social regulation, from the moment at which a company is founded and organized, passing then to control of quality and characteristics of their products, until the moment at which the benefits are distributed. Then comes the direct tax to ring the final bell of social responsibility to free enterprise.

If we could educate ourselves and accept the principle of the social function of productive property and of economic activity, the majority of our problems would become simplified. . . .

The beneficial collaboration of the state, that we now tolerate unwillingly as "government interference in business," and that we condemn to a partial failure by our lack of vision, must be accepted more complacently. . . . All life in society implies the renunciation of certain liberties in exchange for certain guarantees.

Figueres' second main point, also economic, dealt with the relation of Latin economic systems to those of the United States and of other dominating economies: "We are going to admit that our economic system has promoted exploitation and colonialism, engendering greed. But we ask you to realize that our business concepts are only a part of our philosophy of life that is based on respect for human dignity and elevation of the individual. . . . Then you will discover that our civilization has much to offer outside the field of economy, and that your world will derive inestimable benefits from contact with us. . . ."[25]

Figueres was even more explicit on economic matters in an address at Grinnell College of Iowa. There his announced subject was "A Latin American Looks at Point Four." He first said, "Three things we do not want. . . . First of all, we do not want a new wave of colonialism, such as foreign ownership has sometimes implied in the past. . . . In the second place, we are not interested in private investment in public utilities. We hold that the public should own the installations. . . . As a third objection, we resent the presence of speculators who assert that their motive in investing money abroad is to foster the development of our countries." After stating these resentments, he proceeded to the positive side of the picture. There were, after all, certain things which would encourage Latin economic development.

We believe that the soundest way of strengthening, from the outset, the economy of the Latin American countries, consists in paying a fair price for our products. . . . It may not be untimely to repeat that during World War II the coffee market was fixed by the Office of Price Administration at a level that turned out to be one half of the market price when controls were released. This meant that coffee producing countries contributed to the war effort, during three or four years, fifty percent of the gross value of their main crop. We do not complain. . . . But we think the North American people should know about these things, especially since they are so frequently told of the inequities imposed upon them by the expense of their foreign aid programs. . . . The healthiest source of income for any nation, as for any man, is the fair compensation for its own efforts.

He concluded this section of the speech by outlining the needs of Latin countries, admitting he had Costa Rica particularly in mind. National income had to be increased by negotiation for fair prices on export products and by improving production efficiency. Pooling of resources and markets with other nations might also help. Productivity had to be encouraged by the accumulation of local capital, both in private hands and public. Finally, the state would welcome and respect foreign business. At the same time, it would grant no privileges. This would "attract the type of businessman who likes to work in an atmosphere of honesty and lawfulness, and will discourage the speculator who is after juicy contracts and venal concessions."

Figueres devoted the latter half of this speech to the last of his three favorite topics—economic development, economic relations with foreign nations, and democracy in Latin America. For Figueres, economic development was too often given precedence over the fundamental issue—the moral issue.

Many of our countries are afflicted with dictatorship, militarism, and dishonesty. Yet they are all theoretically organized under democratic constitutions, and they are all pledged to the charter of the Organization of American States, which is based on the principles of freedom, human dignity, and representative government. This dualism between the law of the land and the life of the people has a moral effect which is in some aspects worse than no law at all. . . .

Businessmen are too eager to ask the government of the United States to protect their interests abroad. "A favorable climate" should be created for North American investments, they say. What about North American principles? What about representative government, honest administration, the reign of law, the dignity of man? Does the United States stand for these ideas or not? Is it in the name of these principles that we are fighting wars, or what? . . .

The Soviets stand behind communism; the rightist totalitarians stand behind militarism; why should not the democracies stand behind the principles of honest administration and representative government? Surely if the United States would frown on illegitimate government and corruption in the same manner in which some companies expect this country to frown at any threats to their investments, the history of the small American republics would take a different course. . . .

As a Latin American looking at the Point Four Program, let me conclude that we welcome, and appreciate, technical assistance; but we question the beneficent effects of capital investments, unless they are accompanied by corresponding amounts of moral investments. In these moral investments, we ourselves, the Latin Americans, must subscribe a large proportion of the stock.[26]

These were Figueres' three major ideals. Economically, Costa Rica had to expand by means of increased productivity, foreign assistance, efficient production methodology, and expanded acreage. National income had to be raised that funds might be channelled into development programs. At the same time, prices of coffee and bananas had to be maintained at a high level internationally. Secondly, foreign investment was welcomed, and would receive equal treatment with national enterprise. However, no privileged status would be granted. Treatment to all firms, foreign or otherwise, would be equal. Finally, the United States should help the erratic progress of democracy in Latin America by ending assistance to and encouragement of dictatorial regimes, whether or not they might be the legally constituted governments.

José Figueres is a spare, small man of great energy. Intense, restless, almost humorless, he is not a person capable of generating the affectionate esteem enjoyed by Otilio Ulate. However, Figueres in the years preceding his election had drawn the impassioned support of many Costa Rican youths. Those who had traveled abroad and seen disparities between Costa Rican life and that of the United States and Europe were searching for a way toward national progress. This is the force that put the Communists in power in Guatemala. In Costa Rica the same sort of force supported Figueres. It was a powerful one. At the same time, Figueres had gained a measure of popularity with the common man. He had pitched his campaign toward the "have nots," and they well knew it. As a result, they were genuinely hopeful that he might improve their status. They called him "tacones," or "heels," referring to the elevator heels worn by the self-consciously short Figueres (5 ft. 4 in.). Yet it was more a nickname of intimacy than derision. So it was that on November 8, 1953, José Figueres was inaugurated amid general popularity and optimism. His campaign had left the impression that he and the members of the Liberación Nacional had mapped out their plans fully. Once in office, they would immediately begin to implement their campaign promises. Here was a party with a program, and the plan would be put into effect at once. Figueres reinforced this hope in his inaugural address.

There come again to the government of Costa Rica the group of men and the set of ideas that inspired the War of National Liberation in 1948, reorganized the administration under the Founding Junta of the Second Republic, and made the popular suffrage respected by depositing power in the constitutional term that ends today.

During the provisional government that we exercised for 18 months we endeavoured to fulfill two fundamental missions: first, to re-establish the civic virtues of the past: administrative honesty and effective suffrage; second, to give a new impulse to our national economy; to foster the production, with the work of all, of sufficient wealth for all to feed their bodies and to embellish their souls. . . . In accordance with these principles, and in accordance with those governmental concepts, we must now govern. We are further compelled, because during the electoral campaign we presented to the citizenry a program inspired by those same ideas, asking them to vote not only for men but for principles, for norms of government.

His address was divided into internal and international policy, of which the former was the more lengthy and of more interest to Costa Ricans. "Our economic planning is based on a combination of public institutions and private enterprises. We must increase the number of proprietors, not only for economic and social reasons but also to make democracy effective. The right of ownership confers authority over things and persons, and it is desirable that such authority be exercised by the greatest possible number of citizens."[27] He continued by announcing the formation of several autonomous state organs, including a national board of tourism, an urban housing commission, and a rural farm board. Furthermore, the state would provide for those indigent persons without normal income because of physical or mental disability. Also, the government would try to meet the problem of "the poor child who walks our streets as a beggar, exposed to all vices, constituting an intolerable spectacle in a civilized society." Indeed, Figueres was ready to attack pressing government problems at once.

One of Figueres' first actions was to renegotiate the government contract with UFCO. He had campaigned for new financial arrangements, and in April, 1954, formal negotiations with UFCO officials began. In the meantime he tried to reassure North Americans of his intentions. He was confident, he told one interviewer, "that relations with the company can be turned into an example of cooperation between U. S. capital and underdeveloped countries." He had no desire to make their operations unprofitable or drive out further investment. Three discriminatory practices demanded revision. To begin with, UFCO paid no customs duties on any of its imports, a privileged status not shared by other companies. This, the President maintained, should be changed. The nation deserved the added revenue, and it was only fair that UFCO pay the import duties required of other enterprises. Furthermore, importation of company merchandise should be conducted at the same rate of exchange as national importers. This again would pay more money to the government and at the same time end discrimination against other businesses. Finally, there should be tax changes or some other revision by which UFCO would pay the government a larger stipend for its concession. The existing contract called for a flat 15 percent of the profits to be paid the government in income tax. This, he claimed, should be hiked to a fifty-fifty split. UFCO officials privately shuddered but made no comment. The expectation was that Figueres would lower his demands once confronted at a bargaining table. In his inaugural address the President had said,

We have proposed that the banana business be considered in the same light as the oil business; that it should leave in our country half the profits here obtained. We ask, furthermore, that the Company abandon all discriminations. . . .

We have offered to assume the social services that the Company is rendering, such as schools, authorities, hospitals, airports. There may have been a justification in the past for the intervention of the Company in the public services; but Costa Rica has now adequate institutions to assume such responsibilities and should no longer leave them in the hands of a private entity.[28]

After several weeks of negotiation, preceded by extensive propagandizing, a new UFCO contract was signed in San José on June 4, 1954. The most important change, financially, was UFCO's agreement to more than double its income tax contribution. Instead of 15 percent, Costa Rica would be paid 35 percent of its net earnings. Together with other minor taxes, including land imposts, UFCO's contribution to the national treasury reached 42 percent of its profits. Another provision bound UFCO to pay customs duties on roughly half its imported material. The government conceded its right to import materials for railways, harbors, irrigation projects, drainage and disease control, and similar beneficial public works, free of duty. The company also accepted recent minimum wage decrees which it had been fighting. The terms of the decrees had based the difference in wages between the coastal area (where UFCO holdings were largest) and the Meseta Central on the relative cost of living in the two areas. The government was to determine the precise formula. Finally, the company agreed to turn over to the government, free of charge, its social services, including schools, hospitals, dispensaries, and recreational facilities. This affected 68 schools, 3653 students, 130 teachers, 3 hospitals, 45 dispensaries, and 157 doctors.

Signed by President Figueres and Costa Rican UFCO manager Walter Hamer, the contract was valid for thirty-four years. From Boston, UFCO president Kenneth H. Redmond wrote his approval. "I think it is significant that we are able to announce this agreement as an expression of our implicit faith in the stability and progress of Latin America at a time when American [i.e., U. S.] enterprise is under heavy attack by elements of international communism in some sections of the hemisphere." He added that modification of existing contracts in other countries was expected through negotiations on the Costa Rican pattern. President Figueres, not to be outdone, commented that the "historic agreement" once again placed Costa Rica among the pioneers of Latin American economic development. He was pleased that his government was the first to consummate such an agreement. The contract was unquestionably an important step in the history of U. S.-Latin economic relations. UFCO, at various times in recent years a villain in the drama of "yankee imperialism," had shown willingness to renegotiate what was unquestionably a beneficial agreement with a sovereign country. Its general amity and friendship while discussing and settling the final document was added testimony to its cooperative spirit. And for both parties there were positive benefits.

Costa Rica's financial gain was obvious. National revenue from bananas would increase to forty million colones, over seven million dollars in U. S. currency. National pride had been salved by interested cooperation in reaching final agreement. Its demands had been met within reason, and Costa Rican prestige rose as a result. For UFCO, its intentions of good will seemed obvious. Turning over the company services was no unhappy task, for financing and administering these services now fell to the government. And the additional tax rates themselves, while increased, were partially offset by compensatory tax regulations of the United States, whereby much of the additional money paid Costa Rica could be deducted from UFCO tax obligations to the U. S. government.

Contract renegotiation, then, was a positive accomplishment of the Figueres government. Unhappily, it was one of the few. Otherwise, Figueres economic policies have brought Costa Rica rising prices, scarcity of goods, increased cost of living, and almost motionless wage rates. President Figueres long before his election called for better prices from the United States on raw products. This was rationalized on the moral grounds that the rich should aid the poor. He disagreed with the actions of the U. S. Department of Justice against UFCO for alleged monopoly of the banana trade. To Figueres, UFCO did more good than harm by its very bigness. For coffee, he urged the formation of a single company comprising the major planters of all coffee exporting nations in the region. This corporation would presumably operate as a control on supply and demand, while stabilizing the international price of coffee. In general, Costa Rica hoped for increased importation of goods from the United States, but at low prices.

At the same time, Figueres raised tariffs in early 1954. He explained that this was necessary to protect and encourage small light industries in Costa Rica. However, 1950 data shows that only fifteen thousand workers in Costa Rica could be classified as industrial. While the figures are somewhat dated, they show that only a small part of the population of 932,000 is engaged in industry. Yet to protect this fractional group, the entire population must pay the higher prices resulting from high import duties. The possibility of a large increase in industry seems unlikely. Certainly there is neither a skilled labor force nor significant mineral deposits. And while Figueres has urged the development of light industry in Costa Rica, no one has announced specifically what industries might be developed for general economic betterment. Nonetheless, exponents of the idea insist upon its practicality in the near future. To some, the best plan would be to import raw materials, process them in Costa Rica, and then export for sale in competition with countries possessing so-called natural industries. Even the most amateurish economist can see the preposterous nature of such a policy. The result would be continuous financial loss. Nothing could be more inevitable.

While industrial development remained dormant, consistently high tariffs forced up consumer prices. As a result, Costa Ricans were forced to buy relatively cheap but much inferior locally produced clothing, food, and even textiles. In the summer of 1956 the government levied an automatic one hundred colon tax on every pair of imported shoes. This raised the prices of foreign shoes the same hundred colones, some fifteen dollars. The purpose was to protect the small shoe industry in Costa Rica, which employed at best a few thousand part-time workers. The leading shoe factory, perhaps coincidentally, belonged to Figueres' heir apparent in the Liberación Nacional, his good friend Francisco Orlich. This process sent prices rising, and indexes pointed out an unhealthy increase in prices during the years of Figueres' administration. Tariffs remained high, importers charged higher prices; foreign companies became reluctant to ship goods in any great volume. As a result, foreign products grew scarce and invariably high priced, and were undercut by inferior local products. Prices rose, wage rates held the same, and the people suffered. This unfortunate pattern was created solely by the government tariff policy which Figueres never altered.

While his economic record was bleak, Figueres' political activities were even worse. Early murmurs of government graft or dishonesty gradually swelled to serious proportions, and by 1958 the figueristas were beset by scandal after scandal, aided by angry opposition forces who took full advantage of Costa Rican freedom of the press, freedom often bordering on outright license.

Scandal broke out in March 1956 in what has been called "L'Affaire Berger." On the eleventh, with no warning, it was revealed that a minor official at the French Embassy, Paul Berger, had been expelled from Costa Rica for "insulting the honesty of the Figueres government." Government spokesmen, including Figueres' own La República, painted a black picture of Berger's vocal criticism and disrespect for the government. However, M. Berger had undiplomatically mailed an explanatory letter to Ulate's Diario de Costa Rica. Anxious to continue its attack on the government, Diario eagerly printed the letter the following day. Among the "villains" were several government officials, including Minister of Agriculture Bruce Masis. Masis, whose business holdings included the San José franchise for Renault taxis, was being pressed financially. In need of further business and perhaps of financial aid through a new contract, Masis was anxious to enter business relations with Inasa, the

French company involved in the sale of Renaults in Costa Rica. An Inasa representative, Mario Gutierrez, went to Berger at the French Embassy seeking a recommendation from the business attaché. Asked of his confidence in Masis' representative Daniel Ratton, Berger explained his acquaintance through various negotiations and described Ratton as a poor administrator. This naturally discouraged Gutierrez and appeared to jeopardize Masis' chances of winning financial help.

The following morning the acting French ambassador, M. Lecuyer, called Berger into his office to discuss the matter personally. Berger found himself confronted by the Minister of Agriculture himself. The Frenchman repeated his evaluation of Ratton, despite Masis' suggestions that he could be mistaken. Finally, a few nights later at 11:30 P.M., Berger was approached outside the pensión at which he was living by Daniel Ratton and Edmond Woodbridge, the latter a member of the Consejo de Administración. When Berger again refused entreaties to deliver a more favorable opinion, Woodbridge pulled out a gun and threatened him. The French diplomat hesitated momentarily and then broke away, running toward the corner shouting for help. Police appeared almost immediately and took the three men for questioning. In a matter of hours Berger was on a plane leaving Costa Rica.

When the scandal first broke, the government replied with an announcement from Foreign Minister Mario Esquivel. Berger was charged with trying to interfere in matters involving high members of the government. He supposedly had threatened government officials, and to Esquivel, such a threat was unacceptable. He was also criticized for stirring up trouble with his note to Diario, although the existence of the note was totally unknown to the government when he was expelled. No comment was made by the French embassy. On March 13, Edmond Woodbridge, accused of threatening Berger at gunpoint, wrote a letter of explanation which Diario de Costa Rica published in full. It was totally unsatisfactory. He went to great lengths to establish the fact that he had not attacked or beaten Berger. He quoted the reports of the police stating that Berger had been untouched, and no physical harm was apparent. This was a complete diversion. Berger never charged Woodbridge with beating him, but rather with threatening him with a pistol. Police reports naturally agreed that Berger had not been physically harmed, and there was never any such suggestion in Berger's note. Woodbridge also referred repeatedly to Berger as "not a high functionary."

This was quite true but totally irrelevant. Regardless of Berger's rank, he had been grossly mistreated. And even if the exile were appropriate, it did not explain the Berger charges of government interference in public business, nor attempted bribery. There was no mention nor denial of the accusation. Some weeks later, after the furor had quieted, the new French ambassador gained permission for Berger to return to the country. Foreign Minister Esquivel admitted hasty action, although never mentioning the Berger charges of bribery and interference. This was the most persuasive argument testifying to the truth of Berger's story.

Less scandalous but equally damning was a speech by ex-President Ulate dealing with public works. For several weeks the government placed a series of large advertisements in the newspapers. Two sets of figures were given for schools and public buildings constructed during the Figueres and Ulate governments. These showed the Figueres government had erected more new buildings in less than three years than had the Ulate administration in four. After several weeks, Ulate spoke over a radio network to refute the charges. The government had listed eighty-five public buildings constructed under its Minister of Public Works, Francisco Orlich. Ulate had built only seventy-three. However, these figures were soon disproved. Ulate's speech numbered thirty-eight of the Orlich buildings as prefabricated construction, which his government did not use. Of the remaining forty-seven, seventeen were begun and partially completed during the Ulate administration. The present regime took full credit for this construction. At the time, Ulate provided the names of some sixty-five additional public buildings constructed during his own administration, all conveniently overlooked by the government newspaper advertisement. As Ulate explained, he had spent ninety million colones in four years on public works. Figueres in less than three years had consumed 120,000,000 colones. This would have been fine had the result been increased construction. However, the government had less to show for its money than the Ulate administration. Ulate demanded that Figueres reject or deny his information if incorrect. The President said nothing.

Speaking on station "La Voz del Trópico," the former president also cited figures of government expenditure by way of further comparison. Under Ulate the total debt was reduced by 100,304,454 colones. Ulate thus reduced the public debt accumulated from 1871-1949 by 25 percent of the total. The trend was reversed by President Figueres. Ulate claimed, fully supported by the facts, to have followed a policy of order and economy. Agricultural production was stimulated, quotas were met for the Inter American Highway, and the Instituto Costarricense de Electricidad was supported. Under President Figueres, however, the debt had mounted once again, despite higher tariffs, UFCO renegotiation, high rents, and a bond issue.

The opposition of Ulate, who had at one time been friendly with his successor, was stated in part by the editorial of "Justus" printed in *Diario* in a pagewide, four-column editorial:

The governmental team of the Partido Liberación Nacional is a vast mercantile enterprise [which] administers the state without any interest in serving the Republic. . . .

The Figueristas—which is the same as saying government officials, because independent citizens have already abandoned the official posts—have attacked the opposition as negative because it follows the course of attacking government action without presenting constructive plans. All this would come in good time. First the people must learn of the iniquities of the government.[30]

Two months later, in May, 1956, a small scandal broke out in the national radio network. Although not affecting the populace greatly, it was indicative of increasing government disregard for private rights. The radio dial in San José is crowded with more than two dozen stations. Although regulation requires a minimum gap between frequencies, this is not complied with. Without warning, the government radio authority ordered the withdrawal from the air of one station due to improper frequency jamming. The Cámara Nacional de Radio carried out the action, somewhat surprised by the move. The next day the station was placed under the direction of Daniel Oduber, onetime roving ambassador to Europe, acting secretary-general of the Liberación Nacional, and a close personal friend of President Figueres. The other radio stations immediately rose up in arms. All broadcast a minute of silence in observance of the "death" of the station and its immediate rebroadcasting under virtual government management. Continual announcements interrupted all programs. Over the stirring strains of Finlandia came the melodramatic statement that "freedom of expression is in danger," and it continued in that vein. In the end, however, the protest was unsuccessful. The station continued operation under Daniel Oduber.

Of all the unsavory government affairs, however, the most fraudulent was uncovered in the Comptroller's office in mid-May. This dispute raged nearly two months before finally losing news value. On May 6, 1956, *Diario de Costa Rica* broke the story. The Comptroller's office had reported bribery of election officials by Figueres' Liberación Nacional in the 1953 elections. Only after more than two years had the fraud come to light. Under Costa Rican law, most of the election expenses, such as the printing of ballots, are incurred by the participating parties. During election time the political organizations contract a debt to the government for this amount, which is later to be paid back. Investigators of the Comptroller's office, compiling and itemizing the Liberación expenditure for the 1953 campaign, listed the total as 1,516,081.05 colones. This was higher by far than the total for Castro's Democrats. However, the important fact was the itemization of the expenditures, all government funds. The director of the Civil Registry, who supervises the registration of all eligible voters, was paid for "extraordinary work with detail." Pay had also been sent to the leaders of the labor organization, Rerum Novarum, which according to the Constitution was apolitical. PLN money had been sent to the federation without explanation. Other items included "corsages and flowers for social affairs, propaganda expenses in U. S. papers," and whisky, clothing, records, ice, and lunches for members of the Civil Guard serving as Figueres' bodyguards during the campaign. Figueres also rented a house for the campaign in addition to his *finca*. Comptroller-General Amadeo Quiros Blanco signed the report, which was duly presented before the Legislative Assembly.

On May 22, 1956, the Tribunal Supremo de Elecciones dismissed three officials as a result of the revelations: the chief official of the electoral registry, Mario Herrera Barrantes, the chief of resolutions of the registry, Victor Manuel Arias, and the chief of cedular department, Luis Rafael Mainieri. The vote of the tribunal was unanimous. The government was unable to answer the court decision of official collusion in the electoral processes. Just what difference the bribed officials made in the elections is speculative. It is obvious that the PLN paid them to help ensure its overwhelming victory. The election was certainly not completely free. In fact, a jeep wrecked on the road to Puntarenas a few days before the elections. Spilled in the crash was an already sealed ballot box containing five thousand ballots, almost all for Figueres. Such shenanigans indicate that the election was far from honest and above board. At the same time, so great was Figueres' margin that there seems little question he would have won the race in any event. What does remain in doubt is the size of his winning margin, which in 1953 was so triumphantly declared to be 66 percent.

In foreign affairs, the Figueres record, superficially superior, stands up very poorly under careful scrutiny. His long simmering feud with Nicaraguan President Somoza has been detailed in Chapter Five. In December, 1948, July, 1954, and January, 1955, there were invasions or threatened attacks from Nicaraguan soil. These were made largely by calderonistas intent on wresting power from the hands of Figueres. At the same time Nicaragua's Somoza was involved. There were no such incidents when Figueres was out of power.

After his successful 1948 uprising, Figueres maintained and trained members of the Caribbean Legion, a small group of idealist and professional adventurers dedicated to the overthrow of what it considered the dictatorial governments of the Caribbean. Members openly bragged in San José of their plans to overthrow the Honduran, Nicaraguan, and Venezuelan governments to install more democratic governments. In supporting and aiding this group, Figueres violated international law and the rights of sovereignty, refusing personally to recognize duly constituted authorities in these countries. It was a negation of his obligations to the Costa Rican people to become personally embroiled, especially in the series of intrigues against Nicaragua's Somoza.

Figueres was beholden to the Legion for help during the revolution of 1948 and found it hard to break loose—if indeed he ever tried. He had fought largely with Cuban arms sent through President Arévalo of Guatemala to Costa Rica. Figueres' long association with the Legion was established with convincing proof for the first time in early 1955. Ulate conducted a series of seven talks dealing with various phases of the Figueres government he had come to oppose so bitterly. Most of the charges were supported by legitimate photostatic documents, which were published in newspaper form. Later they appeared in entirety in a folder titled "Where Does Sr. Figueres Take Costa Rica?" The document was never available in bookstores and was difficult to come by except through well-placed friends, although it contained only statements already printed in the newspapers.

Ulate first revealed the connection between Figueres and Red-tinged Juan José Arévalo of Guatemala. The former president quoted the text of a U. S. congressional subcommittee investigation on Central American communism:

> In January of 1954, the men who were identified with the conspiracy to assassinate Somoza left Guatemala toward Costa Rica where president José Figueres was accused of being a friend of the Arbenz communist government and openly hostile to Somoza. . . .
> If the plot to assassinate President Somoza had succeeded, observers believe that a communist or pro-communist government would have blossomed in Nicaragua. In that case, a blow or revolution would have been tried in Honduras. This could have given the communists control of three of the Central American republics, and it would have been easy to apply strong pressure on El Salvador and Costa Rica, which at that time was showing its friendship toward Guatemala openly.

In December, 1947, three months before the Costa Rican revolution began, a secret agreement known as the Pact of Guatemala was signed between "representative groups of the Dominican, Costa Rican, and Nicaraguan Republics, to overthrow the dictatorships in their countries. . . ." This pact of alliance was suggested and supported by President Arévalo of Guatemala, and Figueres signed for Costa Rica.

Continuing his attack, Ulate charged that Figueres received arms in 1948 through Guatemala, a fact generally accepted by the public for some years. Here Ulate lacked positive documentation, although there is little real doubt of the veracity of the charge. At the same time, the charge was less authoritative than other parts of the report. In a passage subtitled "Heavenly Dreams and Implacable Realities," Ulate quoted freely from several different sources critical of the Figueres regime. One of these was Dr. Manuel Romero Hernández, Salvadoran ex-deputy and ex-delegate to the United Nations, who wrote, in January, 1955, in San Salvador's *Diario Latino*:

> The presence of Figueres is characterized by an addition from the Civil Guard, for the President of Costa Rica does not walk alone, but as any other Latin dictator does, with bodyguards; and—the worst thing—he violates the principle of non-intervention in the politics of fellow sovereign states. . . . I ask: do Figueres' acts respond to the traditional Costa Rican policy of peace and friendship?
> Let the people of Nicaragua as those of Costa Rica deliver to the Presidency persons who know how to respect the principle that the sovereignty of a country is not the attribute of one person, but of a government . . . never using it to satisfy caprices and personal enmities or to commit deeds before the eyes of the world that show they are no more than crazy. . . .

Ulate also had documented statements from former Caribbean Legion members praising the support and aid given by Figueres. After the 1948 decision of the OAS, he was forced to turn the Legionnaires away from their training grounds in Costa Rica. However, he never stopped intriguing with them against other governments. Ulate concluded his long critique with a final and telling declaration: "All the Presidents of Costa Rica procured and obtained pacific solutions of their difficulties with Nicaragua, which are frequent between the two. It is reserved for President Figueres the sad destiny of carrying the discord to the point of the spilling of blood of the Costa Rican people. . . . I am not the oracle of Delphos, but what I predicted ten months ago has happened . . . Sr. Figueres continues to pursue his obsession with international meddling."[31]

In all fairness, it must be granted that Figueres has been attacked by his enemies as have few men in Costa Rican history. To those who have not or are not now following his banner, no insult is too far-fetched. He is often called a foreigner due to the migration of his parents to Costa Rica two months before his birth. Many call him a coward because of the omnipresent bodyguards and his reluctance to stroll the streets of the capital as did his predecessor. Yet the writer has personally seen Figueres at least a dozen times when any one of a number of people might have assassinated him. Indeed, only complete seclusion can prevent the death of any president by violence, should his assassin be willing to trade his own life in the bargain. Figueres personally felt he ought not to spend time gladhanding his way through crowds of citizens, and so did not often make informal appearances. The President also was criticized for his two marriages with North American women, the first ending in divorce in 1953. People bitterly muttered about his apparent unwillingness to marry a Costa Rican.

Among Figueres' governmental policies was the creation of a number of autonomous state organs, which have been enumerated before. Some of these were little more than jobs manufactured for unemployed figueristas—an excellent example being the Instituto Nacional de Turismo, which may soon be shut down under Figueres' successor. The most ambitious of all these, the Instituto Nacional de Viviendas Urbanas (INVU), met with very limited success. INVU was the largest single effort of Figueres' government, hailed by its spokesmen as certain to develop the economy and public welfare. It was initially granted a 350 million colon budget, and subsequently received seventeen million colones annually. The result was the construction of a large number of small, low cost, low interest houses available to the less moneyed classes. In 1955, 421 were built and 829 in 1956. However, the majority were erected with brick-like blocks, composed of 97 percent earth and 3 percent cement! If this withstands years of eight-month rains, the cost will be reduced considerably. However, it is yet not known whether such a high content of earth will stand up in heavy rains. If so, the INVU program will be literally washed away in a few years.

Figueres' record also shows a number of minor incidents, unimportant individually, but which combine to form an indictment of him. For example, shortly before the 1948 revolution, Figueres put up his *finca* for sale. A San José buyer refused to pay eight hundred thousand colones. A few months later, while head of the victorious provisional junta, Figueres claimed reparations of two million colones for damage to his *finca* incurred during the revolution—more than twice its value a few months previously. Another incident tarnishes the record. It has been claimed that during his first visit to the U. S., Figueres enrolled at the Massachusetts Institute of Technology and received a degree in electrical engineering. There is definite proof that he was in the U. S. longer than the four necessary years. When first interviewing Figueres during the revolution of 1948, foreign newsmen wrote approvingly of his love for the U. S., his study there, and the M.I.T. degree. Figueristas often spoke of his intellectual prowess and cited the degree as testimony. Refutation of this comes from a letter to the author from the M.I.T. Office of the Registrar in April, 1956. It reads in part that ". . . continuing our investigation for the records of Mr. José María Figueres [Ferrer], we are still unable to find that anyone by that name was ever enrolled in the regular sessions of the Massachusetts Institute of Technology." As a previous letter from the author assured that there was no misunderstanding over the last name as used by Latin Americans, the only possible conclusion is that here again is a falsehood perpetrated on all those who would listen. It is, of course, possible that Figueres attended night classes or sat in on special sessions, of which M.I.T. keeps no record. However, he never received a degree from the institution.

One final circumstance shows the depths to which his administration would stoop. Severe floods and high winds struck Costa Rica in 1955, damaging many crops, including not only export products but food for home consumption as well. There was a temporary food scarcity of critical proportions. In response to the need the American Red Cross sent several loads of food—free, of course—to alleviate the distress. Only a part of the shipment was ever distributed. Instead, a few months later, non-perishables were being sold in the San José market with the government pocketing the money. In some cases there was no effort to conceal the sale. Some of the crates were still tagged "Red Cross, USA." The government had diverted a portion of the free food shipment from the needy, selling it months later for 100 percent profit. It can hardly be argued that food could not be given away, yet people would buy it on the open market. The incident itself might have been unknown to Figueres, but was perpetrated by his administration. And as he received credit for its accomplishments, thus must he be responsible for its faults.

A PROMISE OF BETTER THINGS

As Figueres' term drew to a close, members of Liberación Nacional began to consider a candidate for 1957. From the early days of Figueres, his party had spoken of its plans for twenty years' progress, inferring the continuation in national office of its candidates. Minister of Public Works Francisco Orlich, an old associate and personal friend of Figueres, was the president's unannounced choice, and Orlich gradually took command of the party apparatus to the extent a campaign might demand. At the same time, many figueristas distrusted him, preferring First Vice-President Raul Blanco Cervantes, a more conservative member of the party. Near the end of 1956, ex-Minister of the Treasury Jorge Rossi rejected the candidacy of Orlich and announced his own availability. He soon gathered his own supporters in a Partido Independiente and opened pre-election activities. By March, 1957, the monolithic front of the figueristas cracked open with the joint resignations of four cabinet members, the ministers of foreign affairs, public security, finance, and agriculture.

Opposition in the meantime had been mobilizing, and its strength seemed secure in the absence of factional disputes. In June, 1956, the Movimiento Democrático Oposicionista (MDO) was inscribed with the election registry. Organized primarily by followers of Otilio Ulate, who was ineligible to run again until 1962, it succeeded in winning the adherence of other elements—backers of the hopeful Mario Echandi, remaining calderonistas, and the handful of supporters for the aging Castro. Barring a disagreement, their party seemed to have the advantage over the strife-ridden government party. In February of 1957 the MDO held its convention in the San José *fútbol* stadium. Four men had announced their candidacy: Mario Echandi, Alberto Oreamuno, Fernando Lara, and Manuel Escalante. Echandi had led the fight against Figueres in the Assembly, and his supporters were vocal and determined. Oreamuno, the former vice-president of Otilio Ulate, was his mentor's obvious choice. Escalante, a moderate calderonista, was well thought of but lacked political organization. Lara, one-time foreign minister, had no prospects for success. Ulate's support for Oreamuno made the doctor a slight favorite. A few days before the convention, however, the exiled Calderón announced his support of Oreamuno. His switch from Escalante sent some of the calderonistas into open revolt. At the same time, a number of anti-Calderón delegates dropped their support of Oreamuno, who consequently was seriously hurt by the move. Perhaps Calderón wanted to put his money on the winning horse, as it were. The results were quite different.

Echandi came within fifty-eight votes of the required majority—out of forty-six hundred ballots cast—on the first ballot. He received twenty-two hundred votes, Oreamuno sixteen hundred, the other two men far in arrears. Escalante immediately announced his support of Echandi, Lara followed, and Echandi won on the second ballot. Escalante and Lara had both been ideologically closer to Oreamuno, and Escalante had voiced his distrust of Echandi both in public and private. However, Lara and Escalante could not have swung the vote to Oreamuno without holding every one of their delegates, and their control was not that strong. There was also a danger of Echandi's splitting off and running independently, should he lose a very close vote. These were all factors that must have influenced Escalante. There is no evidence whatever of a deal between the men.

So it was that Mario Echandi won nomination. In the moment of triumph, his words were surprisingly moderate. "I feel proud of being a Costa Rican to see the brilliant page of civic spirit written this morning. I share with the other candidates responsibility for the campaign. We need the ability of all, to form a government of Costa Ricans."[32] Oreamuno was magnanimous despite his loss. "The fact that I have lost . . . is an unimportant fact; men are transitory, ideals are eternal. Liberty, justice and lack of privileges . . . are the ideals consecrated in the grand Party of National Opposition. . . ."[33] He urged all Costa Ricans to work and campaign for Echandi.

With Mario Echandi set against Orlich and Rossi, the battle was joined. It raged for eight months. President Figueres, shaken by the MDO show of unity, angrily defended his record. The budgetary deficit of twelve million dollars? "A matter of little importance." He had promised a balanced budget six months earlier. Charges of intervention? "We have had a long fight to preserve our institutions, and we mean to keep on preserving them." This despite his complicity in region-wide intrigue. Socialistic government? "We work for the people, whatever they say." Apparently the people did not appreciate the efforts.

Liberación's Orlich found support in the outlying regions, but was received with universal coldness in population centers. Pledged to pursue the Figueres policies, Orlich promised further development of public health, transportation, and electric power. He drew on the support of Figueres, who urged his re-election although not campaigning publicly, as many had expected. In short, Orlich was reiterating the promises of Liberación issued in 1953. And despite successful campaign techniques, he suffered from the many broken pacts of the Figueres administration. Jorge Rossi was running an uphill battle from the beginning. In his early thirties, he bore the mark of youth before an electorate that wanted to follow a more mature man. And his organizational power was negligible. As a campaigner he proved a fair speaker, but crowds often took his appearances much less than seriously. The backing of four former Figueres cabinet ministers was not likely to bring much help at the polls. His position generally supported the party and program of Figueres, with the promised intention of reviewing budgetary policy and slowing the nation's headlong plunge into debt—a debt he refused, as former finance minister, to recognize openly.

Echandi ran probably the smoothest campaign of the three. He had formed with defeated opposition leaders a reasonably cooperative team. Escalante was the party treasurer, Oreamuno presided over the consultative committee, and Lara was party secretary-general. Echandi himself served as political action chief. There was surprisingly little acrimony among the recent rivals. They were united on a vigorous and deeply felt mistrust and personal dislike for President Figueres. Ulate stood in the background with his great prestige behind Echandi. Echandi opened a frontal attack on the government, calling for a complete reversal of its major trends. While foreigners characterized his position as conservative, it was less that than a responsible return from the extravagant excursions of José Figueres into fiscal insolvency and political adventurism.

Elections came in February, 1958, with UN observers invited by President Figueres to oversee the election as insurance of honest results. Forty percent of the vote was necessary for the victory; a strong Rossi showing would insure a two-man run-off in April. Rossi ran very poorly, however. The combination of youth and poor organizational support cost him dearly. Orlich ran reasonably well, but in urban areas he showed very poorly, and the victory was Echandi's. Final results gave Echandi some 102,000 votes, with Orlich 10,000 behind. Jorge Rossi limped in with only 25,000 votes. Echandi's percentage was forty-seven; Liberación Nacional had been repudiated.

One electoral surprise was the strength of calderonista candidates for the legislature. After many had called his movement dead, the long-absent Calderón still was a name to be reckoned with. Liberación led in legislative seats, with supporters of Echandi and Calderon following. Three rossistas also squeezed into the Assembly. There was a momentary respite following the election at a major social gathering in the capital, where all three candidates, President Figueres, and the newly elected Guatemalan president, Ydigoras, shared a convivial evening. But, the tacit truce was too unnatural to survive, and supporters of Orlich planned to control the legislature, while elected calderonistas agreed to support the president—when they decided to do so.

The election of Echandi brought a new outlook to the country's government. Echandi was born in San José forty-two years earlier, and his father had served as president years before. In 1947 he was secretary-general of Ulate's Unión Nacional, and he had served as foreign minister before his abortive candidacy for president in 1953 took him eventually to the Legislative Assembly. A large man more than six feet tall, Echandi had always been a political storm center. As a kind of maverick he had never been admired by the upper classes, and his final ascension to the presidency was primarily a triumph of his persuasive way with the middle and lower classes. A vigorous enemy of every government but that of Ulate, he was even indicted for treason in 1955 for sympathizing with the attempted Calderón revolution. The charge was later dropped.

Echandi tried hard to calm the nation, something needed badly. He named to his cabinet a widely representative group of men, including members of all factions, and he called for an end to destructive political irresponsibility. In pre-election trips to Washington and through Central America he established personal contacts with other heads of government, and everywhere reiterated his hope of uniting the Costa Rican family while maintaining smooth relations with its neighbors. The promise of further respite from politics was smashed abruptly in May, 1958, at the opening session of the legislature. The Liberación delegates ignored the sizeable number of non-party deputies by nominating and forcing through a slate of officials and chairmen representing only their group. At the same time, packed galleries had to be cleared after jeers and epithets drowned out the first words of José Figueres as he made his last official address. Echandi called for "the advance of the working class . . . [to give] stability to the democracy of Costa Rica and tranquillity to my spirit." But his hopes were dim. As the period of reckless political squabbling headed forward undeterred by a reasoned judgment of the republic's needs, there was only the prospect of executive and legislative organs responding to the call of bitterly antagonistic enemies. *La Nación* unhappily editorialized that "The hopes for the future are clouded still, by the probability of non-cooperation between elements of the government. Without some form of civic cooperation for the national well-being, Costa Rica faces continued trials in seeking mature and ordered political life."[34]

Chapter Seven

PANAMA

CONNECTING THE Central American isthmus and the gigantic land mass that is South America, bounded on north and south* by two oceans, is Panama. Crossroad of world trade, geographic center of the Western hemisphere, this small republic is a strange contrast between old and new. Modern office buildings in Panama City are but minutes away from century-old tourist attractions illustrative of the unique local folklore. An intensely tropical land only nine degrees north of the equator, Panama has for years been thought of as something synonymous with the Panama Canal. Others may knowingly observe that there is a Republic of Panama, but that in reality it is only a small backward colony where U. S. citizens live while keeping the Canal open.

There are some 910,000 people in Panama to dispute such a claim. Panamanians are proud of their independence, aware of their friendship and unavoidable intimacy with the United States, and anxious to protect possible encroachments upon national sovereignty. At the same time, towering over Panama's past and future is the Panama Canal, linking two great bodies of water while bisecting the Republic of Panama. It was because of the United States that Panama was able to establish and maintain its independence from Colombia in 1903. Income from lease of the Canal has in large part supported the national economy for years. One third of all Panamanian revenue derives from the Zone, through wages

* Contrary to popular concept, Panama lies east and west, the Canal running north and south.

paid Zone employees or expenditures by temporary U. S. personnel assigned to the Zone.

Internal politics have also revolved about the Canal. Impassioned
nationalists have harangued, attacked, argued, rioted, and more than once
revolted as a result of policies concerning the Zone and the U. S. citizens
living there. Communists have manipulated nationalistic zeal for their
own lurid purposes, continually agitating the political waters. Alternating
waves of nationalism and communism have swept the country periodically,
leaving behind the debris of political chaos, turbulent passions, and rotting
political institutions. The swift succession of presidents was best characterized a few years ago when the incumbent told a visiting journalist,
"I am, in a way, just a guest in this presidential palace for a little while."
Through all this, the Canal Zone has remained an omnipresent component
of Panamanian national life

There are those, including some Panamanians, who object to a geographic classification of Panama with the other Central American states.
To them, Panama is the joining of North and South, with the best
cultural and economic characteristics of both. The historic development
of Panama as part of Colombia permanently aligned them with South
American principles. Panama won its independence some eighty years
after the Central American states. Nonetheless, in the compelling facts
of life of contemporary Panama lie strong contradictions. In broad outline, the economic life of Panama is strikingly similar to that of its
Central American neighbors. Essentially a one-crop country, with a
population 65 percent mestizo and rural, it faces problems of illiteracy,
poverty, lack of housing, insufficient electric power, and unstable political
institutions. The overwhelming balance of trade is with the United States.
The country is quite small in area with resources somewhat limited. The
Indian element is as lacking in influence as in its neighbors, barring only
Guatemala. And, as is true of the others, its best chance for significant
and fully legitimate nationality seems to lie in regional unity.

The past decade in Panama has been one of crisis and chaos. Political
instability, revolutionary outbursts, and bloody riots have been common.
Petty political jealousies and personal squabbles have plagued a turbulently
unpredictable decade. Nowhere are politics more graft-ridden, more
corrupt, than in Panama. Periods of apparent peace and maturity have
alternated with the vicissitudes of dictatorship, both strong and efficient.
Even in the strife-filled Central American republics to the northwest, no

country has followed a more violent postwar course than Panama. The people themselves have not suffered the personal violence such as struck so many innocent bystanders in Guatemala. But the leadership of the republic has been beset with a chain of incendiary political outbursts un-equalled in this period of flux and transition. Recent events have been so chaotic that true leadership has long since abdicated. Not one of the last six presidents served a full term in office. The tale of contemporary Panama, then, is necessarily couched almost entirely in terms of political upheaval—and the overshadowing Canal Zone.

FROM REVOLUTION TO REMÓN

At the close of World War II, Panama was in a position to enjoy an unprecedented economic boom. Stringent wartime regulations were lifted. International trade, resuscitated and invigorated by the return to peacetime commerce, began pouring through the Canal. Tourism grew more profitable than ever before and business rose accordingly. The larger cities took a deep breath and expanded to service the growing hordes of sailors and merchantmen visiting the country for a night or a weekend before their ship continued. The United States loaned technical and agricultural experts for economic diversification. The government of Enrique A. Jiménez, firmly anti-Axis during the war, pursued its democratic course with inefficiency but sincerity, and the people were less politically unaware than before. A quick shuffling of presidents in 1948, first to Domingo Arosemena and then, in 1949, to Daniel Chiari, aroused little public disturbance. However, in 1949, former president (1940-41) Arnulfo Arias, who had shrugged aside the existence of German espionage and undercover maneuvering in the early war period, staged a comeback that returned him to the presidency on November 24, 1949. With limited public support, he rebuilt his power and immediately reverted to his former policies. Democratically inclined Panamanians, dismayed at his reappearance, remembered his first presidency too well.

A graduate of Harvard Medical School, Arias was an intelligent but unprincipled man, a spellbinding public orator. Having somewhere acquired fascist ideology, he pursued it with a keen shrewdness. Winning election fradulently in 1940, he had not only condoned Axis sabotage and espionage but developed an active anti-Negro policy. He deprived naturalized Jamaicans of their Panamanian citizenship and made second class citizens of them. An ardent supporter of white supremacy, Arias extended the presidential term to six years by changing the constitution, and he apparently hoped to wipe out representative government entirely. In 1949, after seven years in political limbo, the surgeon was ready to perpetuate the same warped policies on the populace. The flamboyant doctor, estranged even from his brother, Harmodio Arias, famous international lawyer and ex-president himself, was in a position to feed his lust for power.

Arias overthrew his predecessor with the support and planning of Chief of Police José Antonio Remón, the outstanding figure active in politics. Remón, who had personally led the police crackdown that effectively curbed Axis activity during the war, found himself in a position of considerable power. As head of the two thousand-man National Guard, he controlled the only military organization in Panama. The alliance of Arias and Remón was a strange one. Remón was not in agreement with the admitted beliefs of Arias, and he might just as easily have led a revolution himself. Especially in view of subsequent political actions, Remón seems to have been a most extraordinary bedfellow for Arias.

Once in power, Arias instituted the expected measures. He shut down *El País* after the paper ran a strong attack in its columns. A series of protest meetings brought no result. Even the combined statements of six ex-presidents left him unmoved. In another action, his minister of labor refused to grant labor unions legal status, despite their rights under statutory law. He practiced nepotism to the extent of installing four relatives in the cabinet. Opposition was repressed. Public employees had to make "voluntary" contributions to the administration. Arias also set up his own secret police, being unsure of Remón's continuing support. Nearly seventeen months of government followed the same pattern. Popular resentment became overwhelming. During his last weeks as president, Arias granted an interview to Victoria Bertrand for the *UN World*. Miss Bertrand, quickly charmed by the genial Arias, described in warm phrases the welcome she received, and the obvious culture and charm radiated by the President. He was quoted as telling her that "Panama is a democracy, that you can see readily. Once I was called a dictator . . . It was the fashion then. Now no one denies that I am giving full liberty—and the opposition takes plenty of advantage of it. . . . Yes, Panama is a full-fledged democracy. . . ."[1]

A few weeks later he attempted to strangle remaining democratic practices by dissolving the National Assembly, suspending the Supreme Court, and setting aside the constitution, revising it unilaterally by decree. On May 8, 1951, a general protest strike was called. Nearly fifteen thousand men and women congregated before the police headquarters demanding to see Remón. Rioting broke out. Other crowds gathered to demonstrate before the President's official residence. A small coterie of Arias troops fired on the crowd, and Chief of Police Remón turned in disgust against him. The beseiged President refused to wilt under pressure, however, and prepared to fight. Barricading himself in his study, he defied his attackers. Only after a prolonged effort did two officers of the National Guard break into the room. In the confusion that followed, both were shot, one apparently by Arias himself. When he finally surrendered, the scene showed the office a shambles, two men dead on the floor, and blood spattered on Arias' white linen suit. The President was led from the room and placed in jail under heavy guard. Two weeks later, after a quick trial before the National Assembly he had so recently disbanded, the ex-chief of state was condemned as having abrogated constitutional rights of the people and also deprived of the right to hold public office or participate in any way in political affairs. He also began an abbreviated prison term lasting nine months and twenty-seven days. Final accounting after his overthrow tallied fourteen dead and 192 wounded. With Arias thus ousted, Supreme Court Chief Alcibiades Arosemena assumed the provisional presidency, with elections scheduled for May, 1952. All Panama expected Remón to declare for the presidency, and before 1951 was out his candidacy was official. Arias cried that the Colonel would soon seize power by military *golpe*. Others felt that the elections would be rigged, that the apparatus would guarantee a Remón victory. But there was much ahead before a new president was named.

Both then and now, the Panamanian political spectrum is composed of small personalized parties of every tint and hue. Few retain any degree of permanency, and most are centered on an individual or particular issue. In a matter of weeks, there were several groups adhering to the Remón candidacy. He was supported by the Coalición Patriótica Nacional (CPN), composed of five separate organizations. These were the Partido Revolucionaria, Partido Liberal, Partido Renavador, Unión Popular, and Partido Nacional Revolucionaria. The early unification of these groups behind Colonel Remón and the coordinated campaign and financial arrangements gave him unusually cohesive support, despite friction and occasional disagreement.

While Remón began campaigning, others weighed the decision to run. One of the undecided was Rodolfo Herbruger, ex-ambassador to the United States. On January 19, 1952, he admitted to reporters the possibility of campaigning for the Partido Panameñista, promising to announce definite plans shortly. Two days later he told the press he would campaign for the office. Herbruger was at the time a political exile, having fled in May, 1951, after the overthrow of Arias, for whom he had been minister of the treasury. Questioned about his status, Herbruger said he would in time return to Panama. He insisted there was great support for his efforts. As to the Arias fall from power, he explained that the entire cabinet was involved in emergency measures solely to alleviate a financial crisis when the revolution occurred; Arias had been laboring purely for the welfare of all Panama, despite repeated interferences by Remón. Herbruger necessarily did not attack the opposition candidate Remón, perhaps in hopes of returning home legally. Asked of the May 10 revolution, he dodged the issue of constitutionality. "I couldn't say if it was done unconstitutionally: he [Remón] took emergency measures because he felt obliged to do so. . . . The emergency measures that he took were to convoke a plebiscite, at the same time declaring the Constitution of 1941, in effect, subject to the plebiscite." He also discussed the worsening financial system, blaming it on the maladministration of the Banco Fiduciario de Panamá. He said the bank made too many investments, ignoring the ceilings indicated by law. As a result, it had suspended operations and created a mild panic. "Thousands of small depositors ran the risk of losing their savings, and the economic structure of the country became gravely menaced."[2]

Two weeks later, following notices in Panama threatening him with detention upon his return, Herbruger hedged on his plans, delaying the trip indefinitely. Three members of the Partido Panameñista, supporters of Arias, espoused his candidacy and agitated for Arias' release from prison. Panameñistas worked actively as elections neared. In late January they held up traffic on the main street of Panama City for a full hour. Some forty sympathizers lay down in the street, protesting for an hour the jailing of their leader. Police coolly rerouted traffic, and the demonstrators left just as mounted police arrived to enforce movement. A week later an official directive circulated through government offices asking Arias' release. His backers charged Minister of Justice Erasmo de la Guardia of giving no sign of action. A prompt reply was urged. None was ever issued. Finally, on February 6, 1952, an extraordinary committee of the National Assembly announced the adoption of an amnesty law. Arias and other Panameñistas imprisoned after the revolution were to be freed; all exiles could return without reprisal. The next day, Arias was released. After nearly ten months in prison he appeared pale and thin. Set free at 5:00 P.M. from the Carcel Modelo, he rode through the center of Panama City in an open car. Followers joined the vehicle to form a miniature parade. Sra. Arias and Assembly Deputy Norberto Zurita shared the ride with Arias.

A few months before, such an amnesty would have appeared out of the question. Many Panamanians, however, disapproved of the jailing of the ex-president and his cohorts, regardless of past crimes. As feeling mounted, Arias gained a modicum of popularity. It seemed possible that other parties, opposed to Remón, would unite on the issue to force election of someone other than Remón. Passage of the amnesty and prompt signature by provisional president Arosemena set free Arias and other members of his regime. Two days later, Rodolfo Herbruger made one last announcement from Washington. Declaring his departure imminent, he said that "The passing of the amnesty law by the National Assembly last Wednesday confirms my faith in the moral reserves of the Panamanian people. . . . With the amnesty closed a painful chapter in Panamaniam history . . . this confirms the absolute necessity that the next election in Panama be an expression of principles inspired by democratic practice and the highest sentiments of the country."[3] His chances of election, he announced, looked bright. Two weeks later the same Herbruger was discussing the possibility of withdrawal in support of another anti-Remón candidate. On February 20, 1952, he announced his willingness to swing his support to a national unification candidate to oppose Remón. Apparently realizing the strong feeling running against all Arias cabinet ministers, he referred to recognition of the "abyss opening at my feet." "Thinking of the future of the Republic and of each Panamanian, I accept without hesitation the proposal of the Partido Panameñista that all the candidates to the presidency of the republic withdraw their candidacies, opening the way for a national candidate to whom we all can turn to support, for the good of Panama."[4]

In the meantime Roberto F. Chiari of the Partido Alianza Civilista (PAC) had also entered the race for his party. A prominent Panamanian politician, Chiari had actually been president for five days in late 1949 during a period of extreme unrest. Like Remón, his backing came from a coalition of small political organizations, which in sum comprised the Alianza. These four were the Partido Nacional Liberal, Frente Patriótica, Revolución Independiente, and the Partido Socialista. He presumably was also supported by Herbruger, who finally withdrew, ending his querulous quest for office. A Panama City lawyer named Moreno Correa was also entered in the race; but the contest was clearly between José Remón and Roberto Chiari.

While the two opponents canvassed the inhabited five-eighths of Panama, the temporary government of Arosemena labored at the impossible task of preventing riots, demonstrations, and disorders of any sort. Almost every day a new outburst confronted the government. The police force, well-trained through postwar years by Remón, nonetheless was compelled to restrict disturbances to the minimum. They themselves came in for criticism on the issue of partisanship. Chiari and his supporters charged the National Guard with favoritism, alleging police prejudice in favor of Remón. Events suggest that the police admittedly were not disinterested bystanders. However, they apparently did try to curtail erupting political passions.

On January 9, 1952, the government expedited an order to jail a radio broadcaster for commenting that the fall of provisional president Arosemena was imminent. Italo Zappi was accused of "propagating false information" and attempting to create lack of confidence in the temporary government. The order to Remón's successor, Bolívar Vallarino, was issued by the Minister of Government. Zappi was in charge of all radio broadcasting for the Partido Revolucionario Independiente, a member of Chiari's four-party coalition. Student activity disrupted the usual course of affairs the next day, in the first of a series of student political actions that harrassed the government. Police announced having blocked the advance of a small group of striking students in downtown Panama City, capturing two before the movement was broken up. The band of youths had tried to enter Liceo de Señoritas, a government school, to interrupt classes. One of those captured was a known communist youth leader.

Following days brought almost daily meetings of different sorts, although there was rarely any display of physical force. A prolonged two-month strike by University of Panama students protested government partiality in favor of Remón. Only in mid-January did the strike end, when the Unión de Maestros ordered them back to class after lengthy conferences with Minister of Education Rubén C. Carlos. Shortly after, with the calendar date indicating the approach of term-ending examinations, an executive decree refused to extend the period to compensate for lost time. Angered, the students initiated another strike in hopes of improving upon their status. Marching on the Presidential Palace on January 30, they insisted on presenting a formal complaint to the chief of state. A presidential secretary informed them that President Arosemena was receiving visitors in a small house. With this news some of the students were discouraged and drifted away. The hundred remaining, however, caused difficulties by refusing police orders to disband. They insisted on waiting in the street until Arosemena could speak to them. After a twenty-minute stalemate the police attacked, sabres and nightsticks in hand. Mounted police soon arrived to join the pitched battle. Students retaliated by raining rocks on the police, many of whom picked up the stones and threw them back. Shops in the area closed at once, boarding their windows where possible. Most remained shut the rest of the day. The worst of the violence lasted an hour, and it was a full two and a half hours before complete calm was restored. A few of the students were jailed; most were driven away or forced to quit the fight.

The government also had to deal with other problems. On the last day of January, Minister of Government Miguel Angel Ordóñez said that the wave of disorders was part of a "preconceived plan." He refused to elaborate, but issued a warning to the opposition that the students must abstain from initiating further outbursts. At the same time, the toll of the previous day's battle was announced as eighteen students wounded or requiring medical aid, with twenty-four taken into custody for questioning. An opposition deputy in the National Assembly, Jorge Illueca, noted in a January 31 radio address the rumors of a forthcoming suspension of individual guarantees until after the election. Cautioning against such measures, he announced that any suppression or government imposition of a state of seige would be a sign of tyranny that would be opposed. He declared that the police would have to oppose all pro-Remón attempts to terrorize the opposition, whether or not by force.

Professor Raul de Ronx succeeded Ordóñez as Minister of Government in mid-February when the latter resigned to run for the mayoralty of

Panama City. The government position was not altered. Wednesday, February 20, the police announced the arrest of three men reputedly involved in a plot to assassinate Remón. *La Nación,* a pro-Remón paper, announced the news in its morning edition, with an exclusive interview with the police chief verifying the story. The previous weekend, the conspirators had intended to strike down Remón as he left a meeting of his political backers in the suburb of Río Abajo. Unexpectedly Remón had left early and the assassins were unable to strike. They had been armed with small weapons and carried sticks of dynamite as well. No official connection was established with any of the various political organizations involved in the campaign.

Most Panamanians welcomed the elections of May 11, held just a year after Arnulfo Arias had been unseated. The government prohibited political demonstrations after midnight of May 6, refusing requests from both coalitions for last minute rallies. Each presidential candidate was permitted a final radio appeal for votes. And so on May 11, 1952, Panamanian voters went to the polls to elect their next president, two vice-presidents, and fifty-three deputies. Last minute pre-election estimates anticipated a turnout of some 180,000 to 190,000 voters. The Coalición Patriótica Nacional calculated that their candidate was sure of eighty-five thousand votes. This, supplemented by a majority of the forty thousand independent voters, would leave the opposition with perhaps sixty thousand votes at best. On the other hand, Chiari's managers predicted ninety-five thousand sure votes, increased, in turn, by half the independent vote. Both parties thus claimed victory by a large margin.

Many Panamanians believed that the winner would be the one to control the government and the Junta Nacional de Elecciones. Both, it seemed, were controlled by Remón. His years of association with the Guardia Nacional would be an assurance of election. Attacking Chiari as the captive of the old, landed Panamanian oligarchy. Remón suggested that a Chiari victory would impoverish the country financially and encourage pro-leftist organizations—a remarkably curious combination. Roberto Chiari, at fifty a vigorous campaigner, charged government intervention and electoral fraud. However, he appropriately claimed confidence at winning popular approval. A suave, cultured speaker, he was convinced that even the uneducated Indians of the interior would follow his banner. Deposed president Arias, attacking Remón at all times, announced that "force and fraud will triumph" over Chiari. Election returns straggled in Monday morning. Provincial counting was held in the capitals of the nine provinces, and tabulations were sent to Panama City and recounted. In the meantime, uncounted ballot boxes were locked up and guarded in the National Bank. Only by late Monday was Remón clearly winning in Colón, the Caribbean port and second most populous city. Chiari forces conceded the loss while hinting at foul play in Colón's Reserva India de San Blas, where a backward indigenous population was controlled by pro-government parties. But Chiari claimed victory in Panamá, Chiriqui, Veraguas, and Cocle, all provinces.

By Friday May 15, claims and counter claims filled the air. Both candidates demanded concession by the defeated foe. Chiari, backed by anti-Remón dailies *La Hora* and *Prensa Libre,* charged fraud in San Blas, Panamá, and Cocle. But official returns showed Remón in the lead by a four to three margin. On May 19, Chiari announced the dispatch of a petition to the Junta Nacional de Elecciones demanding annulment of the results. At a press conference he voiced lack of confidence in the Junta itself, explaining that his supporters were there outnumbered by seven to six. Cynical journalists scoffed at the charge. Chiari retorted that "it is absolutely certain I have won," yet the tally continued against him. By this time Remón led by 59,988 to 30,582. The result was clear. Chiari breathed continued defiance. "We need true peace in which to work and unfortunately we don't have it, because the country is ready to fight to impede the attempt to establish that worst type of dictatorship, a military dictatorship . . . we civilistas must save our country from dictatorship, from moral decomposition, frustration, and the extremes of chaos."[5] Three days later Remón replied. Ridiculing Chiari's statement in *Estrella de Panamá,* he declared himself ready to "oppose violence with violence, if necessary." He noted that the count had passed the halfway mark. Of the 699 districts 365 had been tallied, giving him an insurmountable lead of 82,615 to 45,064. "I am the President-elect of the Republic by the free and supreme will of the great majority of citizens. I will govern without hate or rancor toward any person." Contradicting Chiari's claims he explained the basis of his victory: "the popular desire for peace, order, and administrative activity [was a major factor]. . . . I trust that Chiari and his advisors will decide to accept the facts calmly . . . it would be very painful if the advice of the irresponsible prevailed, initiating violence to try to annul the result of the election. If that happens, violence would be met with violence, and in that way public order would be re-established immediately."[6] The protest to the Junta Nacional de Elecciones was disallowed, and final results gave Remón an emphatic margin of victory, 133,208 to 78,094. In mid-June, confident that there was no revolutionary threat, Remón embarked on a good will tour of Central America prior to his scheduled inauguration in October.

Remón: Strongman and Democrat

José Antonio Remón was no newcomer to Panamanian politics. Born in 1908, he studied as a cavalry officer at the Military College from 1928 to 1931, returning to Panama with a commission as captain in the National Guard. Rising in rank through the years—interrupted by attendance at the Fort Riley, Kansas, cavalry school—he became influential during the war years and was largely instrumental in curbing sabotage and subversive Axis activity during World War II. Promoted to Commanding Chief of the Guard on February 14, 1947, he soon emerged as the most powerful political figure in Panama. Involved at least indirectly in the selection of four different presidents, he was almost literally a king-maker. Remón showed great organizational ability in the Guard. Obtaining the top post when police morale and efficiency were low, he patiently reorganized it while improving its technical capabilities. Improving discipline and security, he fought for better pay and modernized equipment. Only after five years of turmoil did he decide to enter politics openly.

Remón was immensely popular. Aided by his dynamic wife Cecilia, soon a political figure in her own right, he assumed the presidency on a wave of popularity and affection. Despite such sentiment, few Panamanians had illusions about him. His election, most believed, would be the start of a military regime. After five years behind the throne, he seemed sure to be a strong man. No one knew much of his plans, but Panamanians were content to accept the badly needed tranquillity his administration promised, hopeful that his policies would not interrupt the normal conduct of business. They were willing for the moment to accept a strong man if political turbulence was curbed.

Vague throughout the campaign about his policies, Remón was more explicit in his pre-inaugural swing through Central America. In San José he told Costa Rican newsmen that "My plan of government is simple, as it consists of obtaining the greatest possible well being for my countrymen. . . . Not only is my desire [in international relations] to maintain good relations between the Republic of Panama and all the civilized countries of the world, but I will try to tighten the bonds of fraternity that have always existed among the peoples of our continent." In education, he said that "One of the objectives that my Government will pursue will be to diversify public education in such a way that it will be effectively within the reach of all citizens. . . . In my opinion, the education and instruction of a people constitutes its best defense and is the most solid base to perpetuate liberties across the centuries." Public health was also vital to him. "The health of the people is a matter that has worried me deeply all my life. I will try within our economic means to continue and to augment the campaign of health and social aid . . . preventive medicine must become widely used . . . as it is preferable to prevent illnesses rather than cure them." And in agriculture, he promised that "My Government will aid agricultural development on two fundamental points: the first, to distribute to the farm worker lands to till. Second, to create permanent and remunerative markets for agricultural production."[7] His hopes for Central America were summarized best in a press conference held in San Salvador later in his tour. "I will have an 'open-door' government. . . . I desire with all my heart that Panama take part in the organization of the Central American states, and I will make suggestions to accompany it. . . . My government will try democratically to advance regional principles. Only by means of consolidation of the entire isthmus can we continue to advance the economic and social progress of Central America."[8]

On October 30, 1952, before assembled members of the Supreme Court of Justice, the National Assembly, thirty-six foreign ministers, and twenty thousand Panamanians, forty-four-year-old Colonel José Antonio Remón took the oath as President of the Panamanian Republic. In the first outdoor presidential ceremonies in twelve years, he received the presidential sash in the Olympic Stadium. His brother Alejandro, a newly elected deputy in the Assembly and already selected as president of the Assembly, was first sworn in, then administered the oath of office to his brother. In his inaugural address Remón mentioned many of the ideas he had been expanding during his regional trip. Panama would scrupulously adhere to all its international treaties, he announced, but hoped to modify some of them. One was the Canal contract with the United States: "Owing to the geographic situation, the relations of our country with the United States of America are extraordinary. We are united to a great country by means of unbreakable bonds. The joint responsibility of defending the interoceanic canal imposes upon our two countries reciprocal rights and obligations."[9] In economic matters, he intended full guarantees for investment of capital to strengthen economic life. The sickly situation was to be made healthy. The deficit in the national treasury, up to a staggering $40,907,211, had to be reduced. Agriculture was also important, and he planned to support and promote it, assisted by U. S. aid through the Point Four program. After the ceremonies, Remón went to the Presidential Palace, held a final interview with provisional president Alcibiades Arosemena, and promptly granted his first press conference as president. Most of his points were outlined above. He also spoke out on the occasion against communism. No one had questioned his anti-communism before, but he underlined the point.

Among immediate needs, none was more compelling than the ailing financial situation. Economic depression was severe. The World Bank had recently refused the government a loan. Panama needed to stabilize the economic front which had been so adversely affected by a decade of political convulsions. The treasury was deep in the red. Years of administrative dishonesty, with bureaucrats siphoning off their "percentage" and falsifying the books, had left a deficit of forty million dollars. Statistics showed no crisis except in terms of inefficiency, graft, and fiscal disorganization in the government. On December 27, 1952, President Remón announced the 1953 budget, calling for an expenditure of $40,533,064. It was promptly delivered to the National Assembly, accompanied by a strongly worded message urging quick adoption. The 1952 budget, submitted a year before, had not been approved until August of 1952. This time, proceedings were less retarded. The government wanted to settle the floating internal debt, which had reached eleven million dollars. There were two possible methods. First was to issue bonds worth five million dollars with interest, thus helping to cancel pressing government obligations. The United Fruit Company granted an advance on future taxes to help bring debt payments current. The Banco de Seguridad Social applied for an advance of two million dollars from the Chase National Bank of New York. This was expected to reduce the six million dollar debt accumulated by government payment of pensions, accounts, and social services.

Hoping to stabilize finances, Remón introduced tax revisions. He sent to the Assembly a request for higher income taxes. In the upper brackets they were boosted as much as 50 percent. Inheritance taxes were also elevated, and a new tariff on travel tickets was initiated by executive decree. The combined revenue was estimated at $2,625,000. Tax revisions encountered exceptional opposition in the Assembly on the part of local capitalists and their representatives. The government, fighting stubbornly for the measures, explained that finances had to be stabilized before foreign capital in large quantities could be attracted. Local capital would also be unavailable for domestic investment until national finances were sound. With the moneyed interests still objecting bitterly, the government presented the exact figures. Actual banking deposits were increasing, and in 1952 reached $73,575,801, but domestic deposits were steadily diminishing. Panama's annual deficits in its balance of international payments grew worse annually. Since 1946 these deficits had fluctuated from four to thirteen million dollars a year. In the past three years, domestic deposits had declined $1,641,073. In the end, the National Assembly agreed to revise tax laws, partly because they expected evasion of the laws to reduce its effect. As in sister republics, tax collection had been little more than a joke. President Remón issued instructions to all government agencies to conduct no business with people unable to present a tax receipt certifying payment. Enforcing and supervising the tax revision was the incorruptible Fernando Alegre as chief of the Internal Revenue Department. Panamanian businessmen were first shocked, then unbelieving, later angered, but in the end they were guardedly proud of having met tax requirements, and Remón's tax measures were, on the whole, only mildly unpopular. Even his worst enemies never denied that his government was more honestly administered than any other in Panamanian history.

In November, 1953 President Remón established the Instituto de Fomento Económico (IFE) to give an impetus to economic development. Concerned with stimulating production by price supports and protective tariffs, the Instituto received a broad mandate that included agricultural and industrial credit. It eliminated activities of the middleman, who in Panama traditionally dumped imports on the market whenever the local crop was harvested. Through the World Bank the Instituto received a loan for farm machinery and storage facilities. Instituto activities also embraced the construction of processing plants for agricultural and industrial products and granted credit to public and private housing. The largest single enterprise in Panama, the Chiriqui Land Company (a subsidiary of UFCO) increased its productive efforts, also pumping more money into the economy. Of its twelve million dollar annual expenditures in Panama, two million goes directly to the government in taxes, eight million to Panamanians in wages and salaries, and two million for the purchase of national products. UFCO activities in cacao and abacá fibers also were stepped up during this period.

One of the Panamanian economic policies not revised by Remón is the strong protectionist system. Businessmen remain fearful of their very existence unless receiving government support. In cement, wine, liquors, soft drinks, soap, and sugar, local products receive the advantage of a high tariff wall against such foreign goods. National industries backed by local capital have had a monopoly for years, and there is little indication of a forthcoming revision. Today, Panamanian businessmen do not want more and cheaper goods, but less turnover and higher prices. Until the philosophy of mass consumption is substituted for small volume business, protectionism will continue supreme.

Political tranquillity was another Remón objective. While his efforts gradually became more successful, there were exceptions at first. On August 5, 1953, ex-President Arnulfo Arias returned to the news when the police stopped a car for using its siren illegally on a highway. Upon investigation they discovered that it belonged to Arias and carried pro-Arias propaganda and short motion picture films. They were all confiscated and the two men riding in the car were jailed overnight. Any threat from Arnulfo Arias was slight, however, for he had forfeited by his two interrupted terms as president whatever popularity he had once had. The real threat to public order was activity by the international communist movement. There is no question that Panama, thanks to its geographic position, has top priority on Soviet blueprints for the subversion of Central America. This was the long-term goal of Guatemalan Communists, who hoped to gain control of the country, spread their influence over the isthmus of Central America, and in time subvert U. S. control of the Canal. At the same time, they devoted arduous labor to the possibility of furthering communism in Panama itself. Daniel James states that Panamanian politics are particularly emphasized to Red students at the Institute for the Study of Latin American Relations, in Prague, Czechoslovakia.

In August, 1952, the government admitted the existence of a nest of Reds in the national university. *La Nación* spread the story over eight columns in all possible detail. Secret police commander Héctor Valdés Jr. was quoted to the effect that two communist professors, César de León and Hugo Victor, instructed night class students in communist subversive techniques. The two had distributed communist propaganda pamphlets to classes, as well as pictures of Mexican marxist Lombardo Toledano. The professors were known members of the Partido del Pueblo. The next day Valdés said, "The communist movement in Panama is the most perfect and efficient organization in our country, extending its tentacles to different activities of national life."[10] He also attacked the fledgling workers union as a communist organization directed by communist Juan Espiazziano, who had recently been expelled. "The advance of communism," he concluded, "is taking on alarming characteristics." This revelation astonished the nation, and the Communists immediately curtailed activities, withdrawing underground to lick their wounds and prepare future plans. The people gradually forgot the problem, until new secret police chief Jorge Luis Alfaro reminded them of the Communists in the fall of 1953. He disclosed that agents had uncovered communist plans to expand activities throughout Latin America. Documents captured during a two month investigation showed "the efforts of international communist agents together with the Partido del Pueblo to cause trouble. . . . I want these international agents to know that Panama will not be a fertile ground for planting communist seeds." Several of the damaging documents had been seized from two communist agents, Isaac Argentino Vainikoff, an Argentine, and Ruben Darío Souza, a Panamanian. The two had been captured after Vainikoff arrived from Mexico. After two days' questioning Vainikoff was released and deported. Souza was sentenced to twenty days for his "disrespectful attitude" during questioning. Chief Alfaro declared that documents further substantiated how Red organizers were "astutely capitalizing on the fact that Panama is at present engaged in negotiations with the United States of America on revision of their relations."[12]

No one man had opposed communism more actively than Remón during his years as police commander. After becoming president, he continued to keep an eye on communist activities, while leaving the spadework to the secret police and U. S. intelligence agents. In December, 1953, he asked the National Assembly to declare communism illegal.

The preamble to the law admitted that "there are . . . in the republic, political groups of a totalitarian ideology, particularly Communists, which are disturbing the normal and orderly functioning of democratic institutions."[13] The projected law would also apply to totalitarian groups, other than Communists, "whose evident purpose is to destroy the democratic form of government." Government officials asked that all "totalitarian, falangist, and fascist organizations" be outlawed. After a week's discussion and debate, the Assembly unanimously passed the law, worded almost exactly as the administration had suggested, declaring communism illegal, as well as other undemocratic organizations classified above. Communists were prohibited from employment in the government, and no Red was permitted to transact any business with government agencies. Remón promptly signed the bill into law. The continuing government campaign led to the resignation of two professors from the Instituto Nacional. Five Reds were arrested in mid-December when police raided a communist "peace meeting." Three of the captives were sentenced to forty days in jail for disorderly conduct, and one received a six hundred dollar fine for illegal possession of arms. The determined police probe also produced two mysterious lists of Panamanian names, one revealing twenty hard core Communists.

A covert school for spies also operated in Panama for some time, with key Latin American Communists directing recruiting and courses of instruction. Different Panamanians visited the Soviet Union to receive special training. The outlawed Partido del Pueblo, whose members continued to operate clandestinely, provided funds to finance Moscow trips for outstanding young Communists who could not finance the trip otherwise. The government investigation also uncovered subversive literature, some of it discovered by customs inspections of incoming visitors. Officials of the administration showed U. S. newsmen copies of textbooks dated 1953 and published by the Institute of Foreign Languages in Moscow. Subjects included were infiltration, subversion, cell organization, sabotage, and recruiting.

Reporter Ralph Skinner cabled the *Christian Science Monitor* on February 19, 1954, that

The role of the local *Partido del Pueblo* in the international Communist conspiracy directed from Moscow was clearly disclosed when its secretary-general conferred in this capital with a key Communist agent. This man of a dozen names previously had met with Communist agitators in several other neighboring countries before reaching Panama.

Arrested in Panama by the Panama Secret Police, this agent possessed documents containing a list of Communist spies scattered throughout Latin America. Also discovered were his plans for espionage in both the Republic of Panama and the Canal Zone.[14]

Col. Remón was equally firm against external, regional communism. In 1954, after communist Guatemala had received a widely publicized arms shipment from East Germany, he announced on May 19 that

The attitude of Panama toward international communist activities was clearly defined at the Tenth [Inter-American] Conference held in Caracas, and in the . . . [constitution which] puts Communism outside the law. . . . In reference to continental solidarity before any danger of aggression, the Republic of Panama is inspired by the unquenchable determination that the Americas must maintain themselves free from communist penetration and from any form of domination of political influence that might seem contrary to the norms of a democratic system of government. . . .

With respect to present events transpiring in Central America, it will have to be accepted that the nations most directly affected by these events that are occurring . . . must meet for conversations with the object of finding solutions in agreement with the tradition and principles of the American nations.[15]

"Big Ditch" Finances

Of all Remón's policies, however, none was more significant or more historic than the liberalization of the Canal Zone treaties with the United States. Negotiations were long, complicated, and difficult to consummate. The approach to this problem and its eventual conclusion forms a towering landmark in contemporary Panamanian affairs.

Since 1903, the United States has exercised authority over a ten mile wide strip of territory extending from the Caribbean Sea south* to the Pacific. This land, forty-eight miles in length, surrounds the locks, lakes, and installations of the Panama Canal. The relationship of Panama and the United States has always been delicate, although generally friendly. The unique relationship was set forth in the Hay-Bunau-Varilla Treaty of 1903, following the U. S.-supported revolution of Panama against Colombia. The United States leased the Zone for ninety-nine years, paying ten million dollars down and a rental of $250,000 annually. The agreement gave the United States "in perpetuity the use, occupation, and

* The Caribbean entrance at Cristóbal is actually 27 miles west of that at the Pacific side.

control" of the territory. It would be granted, in effect, the "rights, power, and authority" which it "would possess and exercise if it were the sovereign."

Through the years, many developments changed the situation in the Zone. However, almost no contractual changes were made. The Canal itself was opened officially in 1914 and began to handle increasingly heavy interoceanic traffic. All racial elements came to the Zone. Jamaicans were imported in large numbers to build the Canal. At a time when working and living conditions in the inland Panamanian tropics were extremely unhealthy, Negro labor was almost the only available resource. Orientals were also introduced as canal-building labor, but to a lesser extent. Discriminatory practices quickly evolved, and we shall see how these continued into the 1950's. Financially, there was but one revision in the contract, in 1936 when the United States went off the gold standard. The annual rent was raised to $430,000 by the Alfaro-Hull Agreement.

Through the years the Canal has been of inestimable value to the United States. It saves 7,873 nautical miles from New York to San Francisco. Traffic, roughly half that of the Suez Canal in normal times, had 8,475 transits in 1955, netting $37,450,000 in tolls for the fiscal year 1955. Always neutral to ships of every possible flag, the waterway was maintained without any form of international treaty other than the second Hay-Pauncefote Treaty of 1902 and the Hay-Bunau-Varilla Treaty, which dealt in the first case with the British government and in the second with a French opportunist in the new Republic of Panama in 1903.

From 1914 to 1951 the Zone was operated by an independent government agency under the U. S. President, with the Secretary of the Army in direct charge. He was responsible for the Panama Railroad Company and its connecting rail line, hotels, steamship lines, and commissaries. This was altered in 1951 and replaced by the Panama Canal Company, a U. S. government corporation managed by a thirteen-member board of directors serving without pay. They are named by the Secretary of the Army. Most are either prominent businessmen or high government officials. The company, established under federal charter, completely runs the Canal, auxiliary enterprises, and the self-supporting, non-profit business corporations within the limits of the Zone. The Canal Zone government is an independent U. S. agency responsible for governmental and administrative affairs. The Governor serves in the dual role as president of the Panama Canal Company and Governor of the Canal Zone. In recent years it has become self-supporting, charged with the task of repaying the U. S. Treasury for the net costs of the civil government as well as paying the annuity to Panama.

Since 1914, then, the United States has shared sovereignty over a strip of land cutting Panama in two. While the U. S. has used the Canal for economic purposes and for bases in time of peril, Panama has depended on it for revenue and U. S. defense. The situation is basically unhealthy and can scarcely be otherwise. The enormous discrepancy in size and strength between the United States and Panama is but one of many inevitable factors. Social problems have arisen as a result of the bureaucracy entrenched in the Zone. Caste differences put U. S. citizens in superior positions from the beginning. The Panamanians were treated poorly, discriminated against in various ways, and allowed to realize they were considered secondary people. Even more prejudicial was the treatment given Negroes, descendants of the Jamaicans whose labor had dug the Canal. In early years the U. S. employees were even paid in gold, hence the "gold rate," while others were paid in silver. The term "silver rate" meant inferiority for many years. Social services were also a basis for discrimination against non-U. S. citizens or non-whites. Politically, the issue of United States imperialism and mistreatment of others in the Zone was an inflammatory issue. Ardent nationalists, unscrupulous politicians, and subversive elements could always rely upon the issue to stir up high feeling. This cropped up in various incidents, none more foolish, unnecessary, and basically stupid than the bases issue of 1947.

The Bases Treaty was signed on May 18, 1942. Under it the United States was to occupy old or construct new air bases for wartime defense. According to Clause Five, the U. S. was to evacuate the bases within a year of the time a positive peace treaty was signed. Under the agreement the U. S. occupied 134 bases, the great majority small radar stations. The largest was the Rio Hato bomber base, a nineteen thousand acre plot of land. There was little thought given to the arrangement during the year following the Japanese capitulation of 1945. The United States blandly assumed the bases would be maintained without change. In November, 1945, Panamanian Foreign Minister Ricardo Alfaro told the Assembly that all bases should be turned over by September 1, 1946, a year after the surrender in Tokyo Bay. The Department of State paid little attention to the announcement.

Only a few months before U. S. evacuation was demanded did the
State Department realize the Panamanians were serious. By that time
vociferous students were crying about Panamanian sovereign rights and
demanding return of the bases still retained by the North Americans.
On September 12, 1946, the Department announced its willingness to
work out the question through consultation. It also added that the treaty
with Japan was not a definitive peace treaty, simply a surrender document.
At first the Department asked for a ninety-nine, then a fifty, and finally
a fifteen year lease, with an option for fifteen more. The U. S. particularly
hoped for a long-term agreement for the Rio Hato bomber base. Through
U. S. intransigence, Panamanian oversensitivity, and general misunderstanding on both sides, the Panamanian populace was enraged. Most
didn't even want to discuss the matter.

Despite communist rabble-rousing and journalistic sensationalism, the
two nations were near agreement at the end of 1947. The U. S. had
accepted five year leases for every air base but Rio Hato, which it insisted
had to be at least a ten year agreement with an option for ten more. The
Department of State would not yield. Foreign Minister Alfaro was
equally adamant. He said the demand was unfair and indicative of U. S.
lack of faith in Panamanian good will. During a brief trip by Alfaro to
the United Nations, the Department went behind his back to President
Jiménez, who accepted U. S. terms. Alfaro immediately resigned in
justifiable outrage. Acting minister Francisco Filós signed the treaty.
The United States was to retain thirteen bases for an annual rental of
$180,500. President Jiménez commented, "In view of the previous
considerations . . . and in the defense of the republic itself, and recognizing, moreover, its geographic function and its position in the fold of
the American nations, Panama has agreed to the conditions of renewal
proposed. . . ."[16] Aroused Panamanian students seized upon the Rio
Hato clause for one final protest. Meeting in Santa Ana Park, they began
a march on the Assembly, then debating the bill. Mounted police attacked
without restraint, and a sixteen-year-old was shot in the neck trying to
gain shelter in a cathedral. This incident brought the public ire down
upon the government, and all fifty-one deputies bent before the pressure
to reject the treaty. They quickly remembered that they were up for
re-election the next May. Consequently, U. S. armed forces left the bases
at once, Panamanian business suffered the loss of customers, and U. S.
citizens angrily blamed either the State Department or Ambassador Hines.

Sumner Welles summarized informed opinion by commenting that the U. S. "should not for one moment have allowed the impression to be created that it was . . . trying to assert the sole right of what should or should not be done with the territory of the Panamanian people."[17]

By 1953 feeling had calmed considerably, despite continuing resentment on both sides. Remón had three complaints, each of which he hoped to remedy by negotiation with the United States. The first of these consisted of the annual rent, which he felt should be considerably higher. On January 22, 1953, he said that he hoped for "more adequate compensations" in exchange for the "sacrifices and obligations" imposed on Panama by the Canal. He expressed "full confidence in democratic, just, and equitable proposals" on the part of the new U. S. administration. Based on the volume of traffic, $430,000 a year seemed a miserly sum to pay for rent. Annual tolls were over thirty-seven million dollars; Remón hoped to obtain either a percentage of the tolls or else a flat sum in excess of a million dollars annually. The President made clear that forthcoming negotiations with the United States were not planned in hopes of winning a free handout. As he repeatedly declared, he wanted not charity but justice for Panama.

The second Panamanian grievance concerned Zone business activities in direct competition with Panamanian commerce. Commissaries, operated for U. S. employees in the Zone, consistently undersold Panamanian merchants. Workers in the Zone could buy almost every necessary item, food stuffs, luxury articles, and services from Zone facilities, at lower prices than from Panamanian businesses. The Zone also maintained plants for bottling soft drinks, baking bread, and canning. The main railway, as already mentioned, passed the forty-seven miles from Colón to Panama City on Zone territory. It competed directly with local Panamanian railroads, underselling and therefore competing unfairly with national transportation. Hotels in the Zone, operated by U. S. citizens, also undercut the national economy by offering lodging at generally cheaper prices than Panamanian proprietors could charge.

All this, according to Panamanians, had made the Zone a state within a state, a social, economic, political entity. This was precisely what Theodore Roosevelt had guaranteed would not be permitted when the 1903 treaty was enacted. Such an entity was injurious to national rights, putting Panama in some respects at the mercy of the Zone. The existence of these business enterprises promised to strangle Panamanian mercantile interests, and contractual changes were necessary. Officials in the Zone claimed their activities were justified by a clause permitting anything "necessary or convenient for maintenance, operation, sanitation, and protection of the Canal." They pointed out that construction of the Canal initially would have been impossible without commissaries and the other services made available to workers and laborers. Panamanians responded that this may have been true in the early years of the century, under primitive conditions existing when the Canal was constructed. But a half century later, in 1953, Panama could supply all needs, and perpetuation of "favored-economy enterprises" in the Zone was thus unjustified and unfair.

Thirdly, President Remón objected to the U. S. treatment of Panamanian labor. At a time when the segregation issue was making headlines in the United States, little attention was given to a similar situation in the Zone. Color discrimination was actively practiced by Zone officials. Pay differed according to color. The five thousand white employees were paid at the "U. S. rate," while an estimated nineteen thousand Negro Panamanians and mulattoes received the "local rate," which was discriminatorily lower than wages paid whites. From the earliest days of the Zone, the U. S. had instituted the color line and adhered to it without exception. Discrimination extended to various other economic and social situations. U. S. rate workers received better housing, schooling, and recreational facilities. Local rate employees were segregated in inferior schools, cheaper housing, crowded living conditions, and often secondary and inadequate recreational facilities. U. S. Negroes sent their children to colored schools also, although legally not subject to the Canal Zone government. In 1914, Panamanian Negroes, many imported from the West Indies, were the major source of physical labor. Once their work was finished they were categorized as inferior beings unworthy of equal treatment.

In March, 1954, while lengthy negotiations between Panama and the United States continued, Señora Cecilia de Remón, the wife of the President, introduced the charge of racial discrimination at Caracas, Venezuela. Attending the Tenth Inter-American Conference of Foreign Ministers, Sra. de Remón, a member of the Panamanian delegation, introduced a resolution opposing racial discrimination. While not naming names, Sra. de Remón was obviously referring to the U. S. when she charged discriminatory practices, especially on the part of those "who in principle oppose" racial inequalities. The resolution was passed unanimously, nineteen to nothing. Only communist Guatemala abstained, objecting to a phrase citing racial discrimination as a promoter of "a favorable climate for communism."

Such were the major points of irritation when Remón undertook discussions with the United States. The answers could be extremely crucial to future Panamanian development. President Remón, despite tax reforms and financial measures, was staking his prestige and perhaps the life of his government on the outcome of the negotiations. Under the circumstances, *Newsweek* could say, as did many, that there were dangers if the United States adopted an intransigent position. Unfavorable results could easily "turn the present reasonableness of the Panamanians into the violent anti-Americanism which is always latent. . . . Nothing, of course, could be more satisfactory to Moscow, or more damaging to the security of the Canal."[18]

Groundwork for the negotiations was laid in the early months of 1953. On April 7, Foreign Minister and First Vice-President José Ramón Guizado sent a memorandum to the State Department as an initial basis for the forthcoming discussions. Stated in general terms, it was the result of a personal conference with John Foster Dulles a few days before. Dulles had requested a memorandum covering their discussion. Guizado said he had received a favorable preliminary reaction on the part of high U. S. officials. On April 19, it was officially revealed that in September, Panama and the United States would open discussions leading to a new treaty. For the U. S., Assistant Secretary of State for Inter-American Affairs John Moors Cabot was to lead the negotiators, with John Muccio, an ex-councillor with the U. S. ministry in Panama, as his chief assistant. Panamanian delegates, led by Foreign Minister Guizado, were to include ex-President Harmodio Arias and Ricardo Alfaro, both recent enemies of Remón. Others included Octavio Fábrega, Carlos Sucre and Roberto Huertematte, the ambassador in Washington.

At the same time, representatives in Washington let it be known that Remón hoped to visit the United States after negotiations were underway. Presumably he hoped to add impetus to the talks by a personal appearance. Washington quickly accepted the hint to announce in mid-August the invitation of Remón. "The visit is another demonstration of the cordial relations and historic friendship that exists between the United

States and the Republic of Panama, which this year celebrates its fiftieth year of independence."[19] Notified of the invitation, Remón replied that he was "immensely gratified" and personally anxious to meet President Eisenhower. He was careful to say that the meeting had particular importance in view of the U. S.-Panamanian negotiations.

The official Panamanian mission, headed by Guizado, reached New York City on Thursday, September 3, to begin negotiations. The group was met by Ambassador Huertematte and the Panamanian delegates to the United Nations, as well as State Department representatives. Guizado told the small gathering that "The good will and desire to cooperate exists on both sides and I do not foresee any formidable difficulties in the negotiations."[20] He was hopeful that preliminary talks would soon clear the way for concrete accomplishments. Referring to his talks with Dulles several months before, he was "very much impressed with the cordiality and cooperation extended to me at that time." On the ninth, Guizado said his country desired "to be a strong and prosperous neighbor of the United States and of all the other countries of the Western Hemisphere. . . . The Panamanians are considered partners of the United States in the operation of the Canal Zone."[21] Official sessions began the same day.

Negotiations continued through the remainder of September. Early meetings were devoted to the discussion of general issues and conversations of an exploratory nature. On September 30, following the sixth regular session, Panamanian delegates were unofficially saying that a joint declaration was in the offing, restating U. S.-Panamanian relations in general terms. The spotlight shifted from the discussions, however, with the arrival of President Remón. On September 28, 1953, President and Señora de Remón stepped down from a plane at the Washington airport and were greeted by Vice-President Richard M. Nixon. They were quickly driven to the White House where President and Mrs. Eisenhower welcomed them. Eisenhower was an official host for three days, during which time voluble, English-speaking Remón advanced his country's position at great length. He also took time to place a floral wreath on the tomb of Franklin Roosevelt, award Mrs. Roosevelt the Order of Núñez de Balboa, and watch a World Series game in New York.

Before returning to Panama, Remón and Eisenhower issued a joint declaration. President Eisenhower had

. . . assured the President of the Republic of Panama that what the representatives of Panama wish to deal with will be considered amicably in the light of the exceptionally close relations that exist between the two. Taking into account the nature of the special ties that unite the two countries, he has expressed, on the part of the United States, continuing cooperation in the development of the national economy of Panama. It is believed that this meeting has effectively served to promote mutual understanding and confidence in the common interest of the two nations and of the free world characterizing the bonds that unite them.[22]

Returning from Washington, Remón was received enthusiastically in Panama City. Some twenty onlookers were injured, two gravely, when caught in the crush of the jubilant mob.

However, negotiators were scarcely beginning their work. On October 14, Assistant Secretary Cabot announced that "The actual negotiations between the United States and Panama are exceptionally complicated. . . ."[23] After five weeks of official silence, this was followed by a joint announcement on November 25. Progress was termed "satisfactory," but much remained to be done. The official bulletin published by the Department of State said:

The representatives of the governments of the Republic of Panama and the United States of America . . . announce that the work begun on 10 September 1953 will continue progressing satisfactorily within the elevated spirit of friendship and comprehension that particularly characterize the special relations between the two countries. On the sixth of October the Panamanian negotiators completed presentation of their proposals. The government of the United States is studying these questions with the greatest possible receptivity. . . .[24]

In following months, official silence was broken only infrequently. Panama declared in its own official communique that the first U. S. replies to their suggestions were only partially adequate. The United States had given a flat no to different requests. A slight pall fell over proceedings, although representatives continued to meet regularly. On August 9, 1954, after weeks of total silence, "unofficial sources" told Washington newspapers that negotiations were proceeding smoothly, and the U. S. was proving more tractable. The great interest of Assistant Secretary of State Henry Holland, who had succeeded John Moors Cabot, was credited with advancing the talks substantially. Under his prodding, delegates became increasingly candid with one another.

Ten days later, President Remón agreed that progress was continuing, announcing that the U. S. was proposing much better terms than at first.

There was much hard labor still ahead, however. Remón abstained from revealing concrete details, in keeping with the joint agreement to leak no information to the press until a final contractual revision was arrived at. On August 20 Panamanian delegates returned home to report to the President and conduct a round of conferences with other officials. Dr. Octavio Fábrega, delegation chief for the first few months, said that he and his companions would make certain recomendations to the government before returning to Washington at the end of August. He, Huertematte, and Carlos Sucre continued to do the bulk of the negotiating. In early November, paying a courtesy call at the State Department, Business Attaché Juan Manuel Méndez declared that "the problem is now merely one of phraseology." The end looked near, at last.

Just as talks drew to a close, Panama was rocked with the news of President Remón's assassination, and a few days later, the news that high administration officials were implicated. However, the shocking news only delayed the final consummation of the new contract. On January 23, 1955, the Republic of Panama and the United States of America signed a treaty of friendship and cooperation in an hour long ceremony in the Yellow Room of the Panamanian Presidential Palace. Dr. Fábrega signed the historic agreement for Panama and Ambassador Seldin Chapin for the United States. Both English and Spanish copies were signed, as well as an attached memorandum. Thus closed sixteen months of difficult, prolonged, critical, and yet generally amicable discussions. New President Ricardo Arias immediately signed the order submitting papers to the National Assembly for approval. The occasion was dominated by the memory of Remón, the driving force behind the sixteen-month endeavor. President Arias appropriately repeated his phrase—we want neither millions nor charity, we want justice. Ambassador Chapin called it "a monument of lasting fame" to the assassin's victim, and nothing could have been more true.

The new terms were probably equal to Remón's reasonable aspirations. The United States agreed to pay an annual rent of $1,930,000, compared to the 1936 sum of $430,000. Panama, in return, made available twenty thousand acres of the national territory for training and military maneuvers, largely around Rio Hato. The U. S. received this land rent free with a fifteen year lease. In answer to anticipated protests, the United States had already promised not to use these lands actively except after first consulting Panama. Unwritten was the tacit sentiment that the

U. S. was not likely to exercise its privilege except in extraordinary circumstances. The treaty also met criticism of the Zone as a separate economic entity by restricting importation privileges. Articles available at discriminatorily low prices were drastically reduced. The U. S. also began to discontinue certain manufacturing and processing enterprises, where the same products were available in the republic. Formerly favored enterprises in the Zone thus were to be limited in the items they might import, placing them on a closer level of competition with Panamanian firms outside the Zone.

At the same time, the United States agreed to hand over operation of the Panama City sanitation control to local officials. Non-U. S. citizens living outside the Zone would lose commissary and duty free import privileges after December 1, 1956. The U. S. abrogated its roadbuilding monopoly, at the same time accepting the task of building a twenty-seven million dollar suspension bridge over the canal at Balboa. For the first time, the United States accepted "one basic wage scale for all the United States and Panamanian employees of the Government of the United States in the Canal Zone." The U. S. pledged itself to seek legislation establishing a single basic wage scale. Panamanians were also to be brought under the U. S. Civil Service Retirement Act. The first day of 1957 was scheduled as the date for change from the hated double standard to the single wage scale.

This is not to suggest that the United States acceded to all Panamanian demands, however. As President Arias announced, the U. S. refused a request to limit the Canal concession to nintey-nine years, rather than hold the territory in perpetuity. It also refused to create mixed Panamanian-United States tribunals to sit in judgment of Panamanians in the Zone charged with a crime. Also, Republic of Panama stamps were not to be used for Zone mail. There was no further clarification of authority and control in the Zone by the U. S., although Panama claimed the situation should be more clearly defined. And the U. S. also was unwilling to recognize Spanish as a second official language in the Zone.

Altogether, there were eighteen separate and positive advantages accruing to Panama, declared President Arias in addressing the National Assembly and pressing for adoption of the contract. When negotiations began, relatively few Panamanians hoped to receive much more than they already had. The Panamanian legislature agreed with this position and quickly—by its standards—approved the treaty. In a night meeting on March 9, 1955, the document was ratified by a vote of forty-six to one. A group of communist-inspired students gathered in Santa Ana square in the capital to protest the document, but the Assembly paid no attention. Only a ten hour speech against the treaty by Juan Arias, who cast the negative vote, slowed ultimate adoption of the contract. On March 16, 1955, President Ricardo Arias signed the treaty into law. Later in the year, the U. S. Congress approved the document and sent it to President Eisenhower who, by signing it, completed the lengthy process of revising the Canal Zone contract.

Celebrations throughout Panama hailed the final consummation of the historic agreement. Feeling between Panama and the United States was warmer than it had been for years; U. S. tourists passing through Panama were clapped on the back and often offered a free drink at the nearest bar. While different elements of the population were for one reason or another dissatisfied with the agreement, most realized that the advantages accruing to Panama were an admirable advance over the earlier arrangements. Over the rejoicing lingered the memory of the beefy, genial Rémon, whose labors were primarily responsible for promulgation of the treaty. Regardless of his other accomplishments or failures, Remón will always bring to mind one of the brighter moments in contemporary Central American dealings with the giant to the north.

DEATH, SCANDAL, AND TREASON

José Antonio Remón was an ardent sportsman. He was a frequent spectator at prize fights, and baseball greatly interested him. But he was more than anything else a horse lover. One of the familiar Sunday afternoon sights was Remón sitting in his box by the finish line of Panama City's Juan Franco race track. Only critical government business prevented him from being in attendance. On afternoons when an entry of his stables won, the President would remain to celebrate with friends. Sunday, January 2, 1955, was no different—at first.

A Remón horse won the tenth race of the afternoon, and the chief executive stayed in his box while other spectators jostled their way through the exits. Darkness came quickly, as it does in tropical climes, and the brilliantly lit enclosure stood out as night fell. At 7:20 a cluster of firecrackers exploded nearby. Remón's bodyguards interrupted a game of dominoes, but then returned to it, realizing the source of the reports.

Two minutes later a sharp burst of machine gun bullets interrupted the casual conversation. Remón and two other men slumped heavily to the floor. The President allegedly muttered "some firecracker" before losing consciousness. Pinned down by continued fire from the surrounding darkness, a few minutes passed before the bodyguards could get up and rush Remón to the Santo Tomas Hospital. While international news services flashed the announcement that the President of Panama was wounded and in "bad" condition, Remón died on the operating table, the first of Panama's twenty-eight presidents to die of assassination.

With the death of Remón began one of the most extraordinary episodes in the annals of intrigue-laden Central America. Suspicion immediately centered on the President's longtime enemy, Arnulfo Arias, and the ex-president was quickly arrested. While there was no immediate proof of his implication, he had intrigued in national politics for years. "Unlike his more placid half-brother Harmodio, Arnulfo kept Panama in constant turmoil during his flings at the presidency. He flirted with the Nazis on the eve of Pearl Harbor, he . . . demonstrated on many occasions a contempt for democratic procedure. In addition he presumably carried a grudge against Remón because of the latter's part in deposing him in 1951."[25] Two women were also seized with Arias at his coffee plantation near Boquetle, west of Panama City. A U. S. citizen, Martin Lipstein, was jailed after being seen at the scene of the crime and attempting to leave Panama the next day.

By January 4, over fifty others had been taken into custody for questioning, and the National Assembly had declared a ten day state of seige, a modified form of martial law. Constitutional guarantees were waived. Colonel Saturnino Flores, deputy commander of the National Guard, unhappily admitted that there were no clues to identify the assassins. He named Arias as the main suspect, adding that there was nothing to indicate the assassins were connected with an attempt to seize the government. If so, he remarked, the plot had been squelched, for the National Guard was in firm control, and there had been no outbursts of violence. The only public reaction was stunned disbelief. Thousands had already filed past the assassinated president' body in the Capilla Ardiente, a chapel in the Metropolitan Cathedral.

Early Monday the National Asembly swore in First Vice-President and Foreign Minister José Ramón Guizado as the country's twenty-ninth president. Under his administration, Colonel Flores was given permission to direct official investigation with a minmum of regard for normal civil liberties. The borders and ports were closely guarded to prevent the possible escape of the killers. Neighboring Costa Rica reported that scheduled airliners from Panama were arriving with only a crew and no passengers. In mid-afternoon Monday, the government announced the loan by the Cuban government of the chief of the criminal section of the Cuban Bureau of Investigation, Dr. Israel Castellanos. Cuban president Fulgencio Batista sent him to Panama only a few hours after he was solicited. Still suspicious of Arnulfo Arias, the Panamanians also took into custody Juan de Dois Poveda, chief of the secret police during Arias' regime.

The capital city soon returned to normality of a sort, although dazed by the tragedy. Government offices and private shops reopened. International air traffic resumed at Tocumen Airport. Schools reopened, and tourists were circulating the streets. At the same time, there was an air of uneasiness about. Citizens were apprehensive, and the *Christian Science Monitor* reported that they were sober and suppressed. Police were stopping all cars nearing the airport, and many other vehicles were periodically halted in Panama City and Colón. Guards at the Presidential Palace, prepared for possible revolt, wore battle dress and carried carbines, not clubs. The state of seige prohibited the congregation of crowds, and saloons were closed in the early evening. With a large number of known agitators imprisoned or under surveillance, there were few in a position to begin demonstrations. Even the ever-vocal university students, highly critical of Remón in the past, made no attempt to disturb the guarded quiet.

As the investigations continued, there was still no indication of the killers' identities. Despite the strong suspicion of Arias, nothing could be proved against him. Press and radio played up his arrest in the first days following the shooting. Some spoke, perhaps wishfully, of communist interference. Yet the possibility was remote. Remón's anti-communist campaign had temporarily, at least, reduced its organization in Panama to a very small bend of conspirators. *Time* commented that "If the Communists had engineered it, the job must have been carefully organized from outside; Panama's local Reds were not up to such a slick, professional gang-style killing."[26] The Panamanian man in the street tended to feel that a foreigner had committed the crime. "No Panamanian could have done it. It must have been a foreigner."

Colonel Flores continued to head the search. As deputy commander he was in charge of the National Guard, the titular head, Bolívar Vallarino, remaining inactive. Several sources, both reliable and otherwise, suggested that the Guard had full intentions of seizing power, rather than protecting it for newly sworn in President Guizado. They allegedly refrained from it only because of the importance of the Canal contract which was about to be consummated. Only a constitutional president could sign the agreement into law, and Guard leaders by-passed the *golpe* when they realized they would otherwise be jeopardizing the future of Zone renegotiations. This well circulated rumor has never been documented, yet it persists. The author tried repeatedly during different visits in 1956 to learn more. Yet there was and is no concrete fact to indicate a Guard conspiracy of any sort. In any case, there is no doubt that the Guard was fiercely loyal to Colonel Remón and had nothing to do with his death, whatever their plans later.

Minister of Government Catalino Arrocha Gaell resigned on January 7 to relinquish his post to Congressman Alejandro Remón, younger brother of the dead president. Alejandro was to be named minister in order to direct the search for his brother's assassins. He had returned from a business trip to California upon receiving word of the President's slaying and demanded that he be allowed to personally participate in the investigation. While Arrocha resigned on the seventh, young Remón's appointment was not forthcoming. The Associated Press dispatched the news that there was apparent friction within the Coalición Patriótica Nacional over the procedure. At a late evening meeting of the party's directorate on January 9, a heated debate developed over the issue. President Guizado acted as the titular head while the ex-president's widow, as vice-president, argued at length in favor of her brother-in-law's appointment. No immediate decision was reached. In the meantime, a group favorable to Alejandro met at National Guard headquarters to discuss the situation.

Alejandro Remón was finally named minister of government, and the investigation continued under his direction. By the end of the following week, however, there was still no hint of the killers' identity. Besides Cuban criminologist Castellano, detectives from Venezuela, Costa Rica, and New York City had been imported, including Costa Rican chief of detectives Colonel Guillermo Salazar. On January 13 the National Assembly extended the state of seige for a second ten day period, and internal tension continued.

Developments took a startling turn on January 14 when fifty-five-year-old President José Guizado was placed under house arrest under suspicion of complicity in the murder. Colonel Flores announced that Guizado was clearly involved. When the accusations were revealed, the cabinet was immediately notified, and they went to Guizado's suburban residence at La Cresta to inform the President of the charges. Arriving at 10:00 P.M. the night of the fourteenth, they announced that his twelve-day-old administration was at least temporarily ended, and that he would be detained by the National Guard. Five helmeted police stood guard around the house. In a special session of the National Assembly convened at 3:30 A.M. on January 15, the Assembly questioned Rubén Miró, a well known lawyer, at length. Miró repeated his confession that he had carried out the assassination of President Remón two weeks before. Miró claimed that his action had been with the full knowledge of Guizado, and that Guizado's son and two others, Rodolfo de Saint Malo and Tomas Nieves Pérez, were also involved. He had admitted to District Attorney Francisco Alavarado a few hours before that he was offered the ministry of government as reward for the slaying.

Miró took half an hour reading his confession to the Assembly, in which he claimed to have carried out the murder unassisted with a $150 machine gun. The self-confessd killer said the assassination was planned for December 4, and then delayed at Guizado's request until negotiations with the United States passed the critical stage. Scion of a prominent Panamanian family, forty-three-year-old Miró insisted that the killing was his doing alone; neither Guizado nor Saint Malo knew the details. They did know, however, that the attempt was to be made, he charged. "Things began to smell bad," he added, when Guizado's promise of a cabinet post went unfulfilled. The other men involved had "turned their backs on me" as soon as possible. The murder weapon had been obtained from a former cadet at the Guatemalan military school, Edgardo Tejado.

Saint Malo and Tejado also appeared during the four-hour Assembly session. The alleged partner in the crime confronted Miró before the legislators and denied the accusations completely. Had he known of such a plot, he said, he would have notified the authorities immediately. Reading a prepared statement, he admitted several meetings with Miró during which the possibility of a military *golpe* was discussed. He refused to concede any prior knowledge of the murder, however. Young Edgardo Tejardo also had a statement to read. He admitted smuggling the machine gun into Panama and selling it to Miró in late September for $150. Early in December the assassin told him of the prospective killing. He had not informed police because he lacked proof of Miró's plans, while Miró had evidence that he had smuggled the weapon into the country. He sustained a deliberately self-inflicted knife wound on the hand shortly before the assassination in order not to participate.

Before taking official action the Assembly also considered a hastily written message from President Guizado calling the charges "senseless." Guizado requested a leave of absence from office pending investigation of the matter, offering to leave the country until the case was settled. The Assembly had the alternative of accepting his "temporary" resignation or impeaching him from office. In a matter of minutes the Assembly voted his impeachment from the presidency, ordered him officially arrested and brought up for trial on charges of plotting the death of his predecessor. The Assembly had acted with unprecedented speed in the impeachment proceedings, so deeply outraged was it by the dramatic confession of Miró. The *Washington Post and Times Herald* editorialized that the Assembly "must have considered the evidence . . . altogether convincing to take this extraordinary action without affording Guizado an opportunity to defend himself. A trial will be held . . . but if Miró's statement is truthful, he and Guizado are guilty of one of the blackest crimes in Latin-American political history."[27]

At midnight, before the extraordinary legislative session began, Second Vice-President Ricardo Arias was paged by nationwide broadcasts on all radio stations, asking him to report to the legislative chamber. Being next in line to the presidency, he was wanted in case Guizado was turned out of office. Following the impeachment and indictment of Guizado, Arias was sworn in as president at 7:16 A.M. Thus Panama had its third president in thirteen days and the seventh in six years!

Dickie Arias, as he was popularly known, was the son of cattleman Francisco Arias, a prominent political leader in his day and one of the founders of the Partido Renovador, of which his son was a leader during the Remón administration. Dickie had studied in the United States at Shenandoah Valley Academy and then Georgetown University in Washington. He was later enrolled at Catholic University in Santiago, Chile.

Promptly reorganizing the cabinet after his swearing-in, he certified Alejandro Remón's post as minister of government and justice and made Dr. Octavio Fábrega, an important member of the negotiating team with the United States, foreign minister. The other Guizado cabinet members retained their posts.

Revelation of Guizado's apparent complicity failed to arouse demonstrations. Most Panamanians had sat up the night of the fourteenth listening to radio broadcasts of proceedings in the National Assembly. They were only a little less shocked than when, weeks before, they learned of the assassination. Guizado had never enjoyed much popularity; at the same time, his career had been no discredit to him, and the millionaire contractor, long a friend of the United States, had not been considered capable of such scandalous skullduggery. Some were openly skeptical of Guizado's guilt, but nowhere was there a Panamanian, regardless of politics, who had the slightest stomach for disturbing public order. All suspects rounded up during the early days of investigation were released. Ex-President Arnulfo Arias (not related to Ricardo Arias), complaining that he was illegally arrested and inhumanely treated while imprisoned, was released from the jail at City David. He insisted, despite government denials, that he had been held incommunicado. Panamanians laughed when he grumbled that he had lived in a cell reserved for "official prostitutes." When further questioned, he snapped that he "didn't have the energy to clear up just what was meant by 'official.'"

Shortly after being sworn in, President Ricardo Arias spoke to the nation, promising to continue Remón's policies. Cecilia Remón also addressed the people, asking their support of the new President. But before he could continue his predecessor's policies or attack other problems, Arias and his government had to deal with Guizado and his alleged conspirators. All Panama awaited the outcome.

The National Assembly appointed a five-man investigating board to prepare the case for trial by the Assembly itself. José María Vásquez Díaz, chief of the Supreme Court of Justice, was placed in charge of the investigation commission. Public feeling began to grow against Guizado with the conviction that the impeached president was guilty as charged. One newspaper ran a picture of Guizado comforting President Remón's widow at the airport on her return from Florida where she had been an official guest of Governor Leroy Collins. The caption acidly commented that he appeared truly sorry, despite being personally responsible for the crime. Guizado was to be judged by the National Assembly, but his lawyers tried to transfer the trial to the Supreme Court of Justice itself. Expecting less fair-minded treatment from the pro-Remón Assembly, the lawyers requested the Court to decide the case. Under the Constitution, accused presidents could be tried by the legislative as well as the judicial body. Guizado's lawyers argued that the supposed crime was committed while Guizado was First Vice-President, thus should be tried in the Supreme Court. However, the Court rejected the request, ruling that the charge against Guizado was made after he became president, and thus Assembly jurisdiction was verified. Miró and the others involved were to be judged in the courts, since none held official status.

There remained the possibility that the investigating commission might recommend the case be tried in the national courts instead of the Assembly. Unable to influence this decision, Guizado and his lawyers prepared his defense while the investigators continued their work. A concerted search failed to turn up the murder weapon. Miró had said that he disposed of the machine gun in Panama Bay, on the south side of the republic. Yet two weeks of continual diving and dragging, frequently directed by the confessed killer himself, failed to turn up the gun. Finally, on February 4, the weapon was discovered hidden in the home of Dr. Gregorio Miró, father of the accused. The lawyer refused to say whether he had been lying when claiming the gun was on the bottom of Panama Bay. Young Tejado, the smuggler of the gun, promptly identified it. Three clips, two empty and one loaded, were also found. Tejado had earlier testified that he had included three clips of ammunition with sale of the weapon. A neighbor of the Miró family had found the gun and told Judith Miró, mother of the alleged killer. She notified the National Guard.

Three weeks after the impeachment of Guizado the investigation commission completed its work. Appearing before the Assembly, the commission chief asked criminal action against Guizado, recommending the Assembly itself conduct proceedings. Presenting a thirty-three-page brief of its findings, it drew three conclusions. First, there was no reasonable doubt that Rubén Miró killed Remón. Second, Rodolfo de Saint Malo had admitted a partial knowledge of the conspiracy and was possibly more deeply implicated. Finally, José Guizado was implicated in the affair by the testimony of several others, including that of his son.

Later the same day, February 10, 1955, the National Assembly of Panama voted to conduct the legal proceedings against Guizado before an extraordinary legislative session. Under legislative by-laws, an eight day delay was required before the trial could proceed.

President Ricardo Arias, addressing the nation the night before the trial opened, called for full and complete punishment of the assassins as a measure necessary to bolster Panama's international position as a law-abiding, civilized country. "Justice must be an expression of the truth and of impartiality and must not have the character of vengeance or of being ruled by passion, prejudice, or even less for personal interest."[28] At 3:00 P.M. Friday, March 18, the Assembly met for the last time before the trial began. It had convened to consider the motion of the defense to postpone the trial. Felipe Juan Escobar, chief counsel for the defendant, had petitioned two days before for more time to collect information. Government prosecutor José Lasso de la Vega, also representing Señora de Remón, appeared to request immediate trial of the accused. The Assembly quickly voted to reject the petition, and the following Monday, March 21, 1955, the trial of ex-President José Guizado began.

Preliminaries occupied the first hours of the opening session. Official secretary Gavino Sierra Gutiérrez read information concerning the accused, outlining the charges and the government case. Acting assembly president Ernesto Estenoz called Guizado from his chair. The former president rose slowly and walked to the center of the chamber, directly before the assembly president. "Do you declare yourself civilly and criminally guilty of the accusation contained in the resolution of the Assembly dated 16 February?" Replying without a microphone, Guizado raised his voice that he might be heard clearly: "I declare myself innocent." The reading of declarations by witnesses began.

Declarations the next day named Guizado as an accomplice in the slaying, charging him with homicide. De la Vega, the attorney for the prosecution, coldly pointed out that while the maximum sentence for homicide was twenty years, this sentence applied not only to actual killers but to accomplices and accessories as well. In his opening remarks, De la Vega said of Guizado that "without him, the crime could not have been committed . . . nothing could be clearer . . . than the guilt of this man."[29] Calling upon a twenty-two-year-old Cuban sailor, Victor Calvo, De la Vega questioned the youth at length. Calvo testified that Guizado had offered him from four to ten thousand dollars to assist Miró "with a little job," as he phrased it. Calvo had recanted several days after first telling the police this story, and he claimed to have lied the first time. Now he again reversed his story, accusing Guizado of the offer. De la Vega said the first change of stories was due to fear that his Panamanian sweetheart had been threatened.

De la Vega pointed out Guizado's motive the next day, referring to different commercial propositions he had made Remón while serving as first vice-president. Assembly legislators leaned forward in their seats at the first hint of Guizado's motives, other than a possible thirst for power. In the first instance, according to the prosecutor, Guizado presented a building plan worth two million dollars, proposing to support it by government issued bonds. Remón refused. Then the Vice-President tried to give a casino concession to either local or foreign capitalists, presumably to increase national revenues. Again Remón rejected the idea. The third incident occurred when Guizado as foreign minister was visiting the United States in 1953, preparing for Remón's trip and starting negotiations on the Zone. He had contacted Washington lawyer Milton Diamond and retired General Julius Klein, who offered to arrange a fifty million dollar loan to Panama, for a 2 percent commission. Remón, trying to pull Panama out of debt abroad, vetoed the measure, which Guizado had initiated without authorization. Finally, during the same visit to the U. S., Guizado asked the National City Bank of New York about the possibility of a loan to Panama supported by the expected increase in annual Canal rent paid by the U. S. The Bank wrote on November 24 that Panama could arrange a loan of $34,670,000. One copy of the letter was sent to Remón's bank in Panama, and he soon learned of the matter. He immediately sent Comptroller-General Enrique Obarrio to New York City to stop negotiations, explaining the situation to bank officials. He also called Guizado into his office and gave him a stiff dressing-down.

De la Vega followed these explanations by adding dramatically that "the day that Remón clearly told Guizado that he did not support his efforts, he signed his death sentence. A latent idea took definite form. The elimination of President Remón became a necessity on the part of Guizado."[30] Guizado, after becoming president, the prosecutor continued, had objected to the naming of Alejandro Remón as minister of government and justice to apprehend the killer. Only the insistence of the Coalición Patriótica Nacional and Señora de Remón forced his hand, and he did his best to impede the investigation. At the same time he ordered the introduction of legislative measures which, if approved, would empower him to name new directors for the three principal Panamanian financial institutions, thus gaining personal control of national finances. And he had admittedly complained to the press office, two days before his arrest, of the quantity of publicity Remón and the investigation were receiving. Remón, lacking confidence both in the intelligence and discretion of Guizado, had bypassed him whenever possible and had ordered negotiation of the treaty with the United States without his consultation. Panamanian representatives at the meetings had been instructed to report directly to him, not to Vice-President and Foreign Minister Guizado.

Defense lawyer Escobar, considered perhaps the outstanding criminal lawyer in Panama, charged that the entire case was built on a tenuous structure fabricated by the word of a liar and an epileptic. The liar, he angrily claimed, was Miró, who had insisted the murder weapon was in Panama Bay. He attacked as well the confessed killer's meandering account of Guizado's part as being a pure fabrication designed to implicate the one-time minister of President Remón. The epileptic was the Cuban sailor, Calvo, who had told of Guizado's proffered payment in exchange for Remón's death. "How can we believe the word of an epileptic young boy," he stormed, "especially when he has twice reversed his story?"

In the end, prosecutor De la Vega demanded a thirty-five-year sentence, twenty for the murder, and fifteen more in accordance with a clause in the penal code concerning the murder of a president. Admitting that evidence was circumstantial, De la Vega said that in such a case, circumstantial evidence was perfectly acceptable in proving a man's innocence or guilt. On the other hand, defense attorney Escobar, reiterating charges of unsubstantiated testimony, appealed to the Assembly members—eight of whom were lawyers—that the prosecution was but the culmination of some diabolical machination against Guizado; the fabric of lies had proved no complicity. According to the law, the Assembly had to render a verdict within ten days, or Guizado would automatically be set free. A two-thirds verdict of the Assembly (thirty-six of fifty-three votes) was necessary to convict the impeached president. In the dying days of March, after the arguments were finished, the National Assembly overwhelmingly judged José Guizado guilty of complicity in the assassination of Remón. He was sentenced to six years and eight months in prison. He angrily cried his innocence as he was taken from the hall.

With the conviction of José Guizado, one of the more sordid chapters in Central American politics was closed, although only temporarily. There have been periodic declarations questioning the decision. In early 1956 Guizado announced from his cell a series of "revelations" intended to prove his innocence. After much publicity, they proved disappointing. However, there are many who believe him when he reiterates his innocence. Whether his trial was entirely impartial is a moot point. Where Remón was very popular, Guizado never had been, and it was easy for Assembly members to be swept away in the tide of unreasoning sorrow and shock after Remón's death. It was imperative that Remón's assassination be solved, and this was apparently done. Had Guizado been cleared of charges, the case would have been left under a darker pall of doubt than it is today.

Evidence against the former president was decidedly incriminating; of this there can be little doubt. It is equally certain that the evidence was based on testimony of unstable, basically unreliable witnesses. Many Panamanians feel that Guizado personally lacked the courage to authorize such a diabolical plan. Others say he was highly ambitious, self-centered, and much more concerned with José Guizado than Panama. They picture him as being just the man to learn of a possible assassination, encourage it, and then step calmly into the shoes of his victim. Unless further evidence is revealed, the world will never know for a certainty whether or not Guizado was a weak and unwilling victim of unhappy circumstance or, instead, the apprehended mastermind of the conspiratorial killing. In either event, the killing and its repercussions left a residue of shame, disbelief, and political immaturity of the grossest sort.

ARIAS AND ELECTIONS

Ricardo Arias stepped into the shoes of a man difficult to follow. Remón, for all his errors and undemocratic tendencies, had been probably the best Panamanian president within living memory. Most evaluations, partisan or otherwise, agree on Remón's positive accomplishments. Panamanian diplomat Pino spoke of Panama under Remón as following the path of justice.

As a governmental norm and as a guarantee of harmonic operation of the administration, order, peace, and public tranquillity are fully guaranteed. . . . Today, in Panama, is found full protection of life, personal integrity, property, and individual and social rights consecrated by the Constitution and laws.

Contrary to the opinion of his political enemies, Colonel José Antonio Remón had sufficient tact to lead his country on the path of justice, stability, and peace, making as the principle object of his government the strengthening of honesty in all public departments, especially in the fiscal affairs of state.[31]

A less prejudiced observer, Costa Rican President Figueres, had no axe to grind against Remón, nor any reason to praise him unduly. Figueres said:

I have seen in the present administration of Señor Remón conduct that has surpassed the hopes of both friends and enemies. Panama is one of the youngest democracies of America and is in the process of consolidating its institutions. Señor Remón has fulfilled his duty with great patriotism. I do not have the slightest doubt that the present administration of our neighbor to the south will buttress and continue the enjoyment of full institutional democracy based on norms of conduct and respect for the rights of the citizens.[32]

In sum, Remón reasserted the authority and dignity of the presidency, developed national confidence, united the badly divided country for the first time in years, dealt with economic difficulties, and generally put the Panamanian house in order. This was the man young President Arias had to replace.

By March, 1955, Arias was already charting his own course in pursuing the aims of Remón. He undertook a series of public works, including low-cost suburban housing costing several million balboas. He was also actively backing rapid construction, rerouting, and repair of the Inter American Highway, hoping it would soon be open from Costa Rica to Panama, thus drawing flocks of motorists from the United States on vacation trips. Thanks to Vice-President Richard Nixon and his goodwill tour of Central America, the United States had agreed to speed up assistance in completing the highway. Congress loaned eighteen million dollars to Panama which, supplemented with six million from the Panamanian treasury, would finance the completion of the roadway. President Arias also was instrumental in calming the nation in the days following the revelation of Guizado's alleged implication in the assassination and the trial that followed. He continually urged national unity, peace, and stability, and a return to normal life. On March 15, he led a silent parade of six thousand past Remón's tomb in Amador cemetery in celebration of the third anniversary of the formation of the political coalition that had carried him to the presidency.

A government crisis threatened to disturb the country on April 6, when the Arias cabinet resigned collectively. A joint message said the "motive for this resignation is the fact that the office of the President of the Republic, with which you were invested this January 15, has already acquired a definitive character, a circumstance that places you in a different situation than existed when you took power, and honored us with the posts that we turn over today."[33] While the announcement was well intentioned, it had temporary bad effects. Hoping to give Arias free reign in naming his own ministers, since his administration was to last nearly two more years, the resignations gave instead the initial impression of disapproval of the government. Such was the interpretation of the average Panamanian. President Arias quickly refused the resignations of the eight ministers. "On choosing you to constitute my cabinet I was moved not only by the pressing circumstances in which we lived, but with the sureness that with your collaboration I could develop a governmental plan with positive benefits for the country. Today I have in you the same confidence as then, and I know no reason that justifies the acceptance of your resignation."[34]

In a further effort to speed economic development, Arias' Comptroller-General, Roberto Huertematte, was sent to Washington to arrange a loan from the World Bank. A vast program of highway construction was planned to bring the products of small peasant villages to the larger markets. The Comptroller-General conferred daily with Bank officials. He explained in detail how new highways were needed to further the Panamanian agricultural program. Without the roads, he argued, economic development would be stalled. On July 18, after more than two months of discussions, the World Bank announced a loan of $5,900,000 to help pay for an extensive highway program. In Panama, the government, from President Arias down, was delighted. As one of their economic experts observed, farmers would no longer have trouble transporting undamaged and unspoiled produce to the markets because of bad roads or paths.

Regionally, Arias drew Panama closer to its Central American neighbors by two actions. The Republic continued to send observers to meetings of the ODECA committees, and on two occasions representatives of the Central American nations met in Panama City itself to confer on regional matters. In June, 1956, as his term was running out, Arias astounded the hemisphere by inviting the presidents of the twenty-one American republics to meet in Panama City in celebration of the one hundred and thirtieth anniversary of the original Bolivarian Congress of Panama in 1826. Many of the chief executives declined, lacking the courage to risk revolt by leaving their respective capitals. However, the prestige of meeting with the United States president eventually drew almost all the chiefs of state. Among Arias' guests were Ibarra of Ecuador, Kubitschek of Brazil, Siles of Bolivia, Aramburu of Argentina, Figueres of Costa Rica, Lemus of El Salvador, Castillo of Guatemala, Zubiria of Uruguay, and Batista of Cuba. Arias was also scrupulous in avoiding fraternal friction in regional affairs, unlike some other chief executives. On June 30, 1955, meeting with Figueres, he refused to form a bloc with him against Somoza of Nicaragua. Rejecting any such conspiratorial agreements, he managed to stay on amicable terms with Figueres at the same time.

Dr. Arnulfo Arias managed to stir up a minor dispute late in 1955, but the limited concern was perhaps an indication of his fading prominence. Saddened by the death of his wife after a long illness, Dr. Arias appealed for the second time to the National Assembly for the return of his full rights of citizenship, which had been altered after he was deposed in 1951. A resolution by Romero Velásquez said that returning all his rights would contribute to political stability and peace, in view of the thousands of partisans he still had. The Assembly promptly voted down the resolution, thirty-eight to two.

Nearly a year after taking power, Ricardo Arias summarized Panama's most recent accomplishments in an interview with a visiting Egyptian journalist. Arias told the interviewer that Panama had developed its agriculture and sustained the prices of essential products such as rice, coffee, and corn, by means of the expanding Institute de Fomento Económico. The government, by giving credit to agriculturists for machines to sow rice and other products on a large scale, had improved farm efficiency. Point Four experts had contributed their skills in the development of cotton, which was gradually expanding. At the same time, the government was interested in developing national industries by passing laws to offer greater opportunities to investors. In recent years Panama had opened up new industries. The past decade had shown "vigorous economic development" as government credit institutions registered a growing increase in activities. The foreign credit of Panama was good, and international agreements were complied with religiously.

Growing tourist trade was also boosting the national economy by bringing more money into circulation than before. Fine beaches, excellent fishing, and such tourist spots as the internationally famous Hotel El Panamá were luring more paying customers into the Republic.

The events of early 1955 obscured the fact that elections were but a little over a year away. Even all the excitement could not change the date of the May 12, 1956, presidential race. Although most Panamanians had had their fill of politics after the assassination and concomitant intrigue, politicians launched the campaign a year in advance, as usual. On May 7, 1955, the junta directiva of the CPN named Ernesto de la Guardia Jr. as its official candidate. A generally respected fifty-one-year-old businessman, he was serving as director of the national brewery, although maintaining other commercial interests as well. De la Guardia was nominated along with Temistocles Díaz and Heraclio Barletta as first and second vice-presidents at the meeting presided over by President Arias. In July, a full party convention verified the choices, and he immediately opened his official campaign.

Of the parties who had united to oppose Remón in 1952, only the Liberal party had much interest in opposing the official candidate. Probably the strongest of the anti-government groups, the Liberals met in December, choosing lawyer Victor Florencio Goytía as their candidate. His running mates were Francisco Morales and Luis Alfaro. Smaller parties were forbidden to enter the contest as the result of a law passed under Remón's aegis on November 4, 1953. The National Assembly had decided after a rancorous fourteen hour session to reduce the number of political parties by requiring forty-five thousand registered members. This meant a party would need the allegiance of approximately 20 percent of the eligible voters to participate in an election. At the time, Remón insisted it would add to political stability by eliminating small nuisance groups which were more likely to stir up excitement than win meaningful support. His enemies attacked it as a fascist measure leading the country toward eventual establishment of a one-party state. The government maintained that small splinter groups might combine forces in order to acquire a forty-five thousand member registration, thus solidifying national political alignments.

Small opposition groups attacked the measure sharply in 1955 and in 1956, as the election neared. The Partido Revolucionario Independiente, the Renovación Auténtico, and the new Frente Patriótico de Juventud protested the law. Only the Liberals and the CPN coalition had obtained enough signatures to participate in the 1956 campaign. Norberto Navarro, spokesman of these groups, demanded of the Arias government three concessions. First, formation of a new cabinet with all parties and groups represented; the promulgation of a new electoral law; postponement of the forthcoming elections. First the new law should be adopted and other parties given time to organize for a campaign. He threatened that if Arias did not give an answer shortly, the opposition groups would "consider themselves free to take any means in order to gain power." President Arias politely refused the demands, saying that absolutely nothing could delay the elections, and to do so would be an open invitation to chaos. The opposition groups gave up in disappointment. While they were able to unite in protest of a law, they apparently couldn't consider the thought of forming a coalition to gain the membership necessary for participation in the election.

Campaigning, by local standards, was relatively quiet and free from the usual bribes of money, liquor, and imaginary government posts. *Time* reported that De la Guardia apparently avoided dishonest tactics if for no other reason than that he seemed the sure winner. For the Liberals and Victor Goytía, chances of victory seemed so slim that no amount of bribery or dishonesty could equalize the strength of the candidates.

Ernesto de la Guardia campaigned on three planks. He hoped to diminish freight charges on shipping between the United States and Panama, reducing the cost of living thereby. He also planned to establish a national petroleum refinery in Colón, where unemployment was particularly high. And finally, he advocated increased electricity, promising to install a nuclear plant in the Panamanian interior. His slogan of "Pan y Libertad"—bread and liberty—failed to capture the popular imagination. The night before elections, he announced by radio that "I turned my back on the traditional system of buying votes from the people by means of promising imaginary jobs, and of bruising their spirit and conscience through the use of liquor as the prime element of political propaganda."[35]

Elections were held Sunday, May 12, 1956, amid almost unprecedented political calm. The fifty-three Assembly deputies, 106 alternates, and of course the president and two vice-presidents were to be chosen by 380,000 eligible voters. Observers, agreeing on an easy victory for De la Guardia, anticipated 70 percent of the eligible voters would turn out for the balloting. Returns were not expected to show any positive results before the middle of the week, in keeping with the slow vote tabulation. Complete calm followed the election. By Wednesday, there were still only unofficial reports of the balloting, which showed a trend to De la Guardia. Victor Goytía warned the government that it would be responsible for the consequences of any action taken to impede opposition demonstrations. Goytía, whose campaign had not been noted for its vigor, was to become much more energetic in post election weeks arguing against the fraud perpetrated by the government. This was one of his earliest forays. When Minister of Government Alejandro Remón warned him that demonstrations would not be permitted, he retorted that he was winning the election and had every right to demonstrate. This victory claim was contradicted by returns from 235 of 829 polling places, which showed De la Guardia winning by 57,229 to 27,455. Goytía continued his defiant stand, however. "Mr. Minister: The Panamanian public and I are in the street and we will stay in the street. Our presence can have interrupted on occasions local traffic, but never would it arouse fears of grave disruptions of public order. . . ."[36] Goytía was sincere in his announcement of continued street gatherings. On May 18, one week after election day, a political meeting was broken up by government troops using tear gas. This was enforcement of a decree prohibiting demonstrations during the electoral period. Only after May 24 could demonstrations be legally held. At the same time, official returns showed De la Guardia's lead holding up at better than two to one. Goytía insisted he was having the election stolen by fraud.

Two weeks after election day, on May 26, 1956, the national elections board, with eight of its nine members government supporters, announced the victory of Ernesto de la Guardia Jr. The final tally was 177,633 to 81,737. The official candidate was formally proclaimed victor. Few people gave much attention to Goytía's charges of electoral deceit. They were to hear the same statements from Goytía in coming months.

One further domestic problem was to precede De la Guardia's inauguration in October. A national transport strike was declared on September 4. For more than a week it threatened to disrupt all national life. In Panama, bus drivers rent their vehicles on a daily basis from the owners, supplying their own gasoline. A tax of sixteen and a half cents on each gallon of fuel had aroused increasing opposition, and the bus drivers finally decided to strike for a price reduction. The tax had boosted retail gasoline prices to almost forty cents per gallon, a nearly prohibitive price for most drivers and bus operators. The strikers demanded a thirteen cent per gallon decrease, and sixteen hundred operators of some eight hundred and fifty buses stopped work. On following days, hundreds of workers had long walks to work, and most taxi drivers also joined the strike, swelling the number of strikers to two thousand. The Tribunales de Trabajo called the work stoppage illegal, and president-elect De la Guardia termed it an effort to block his forthcoming inauguration. Strikers were not discouraged and set up operational headquarters at the National University with the cooperation of the Panamanian student union. On September 7, the national Syndicate of Typographers gave the drivers a vote of solidarity, and fifteen hundred typographers quit work for twenty-four hours in sympathy.

As soon as the strike was declared, the government named a mediation commission headed by De la Guardia. Two days' efforts led to a proposal that the Archbishop of Panama, Monseñor Francisco Beekman, be named arbiter for the dispute. On September 7, De la Guardia agreed with formation of the group, which included two representatives of the strikers, two more of the government, with Beekman presiding. Second vice-president-elect Heraclio Barletta and Minister of Labor Angel López Casis represented the government. An eventual compromise plan was offered by the Archbishop and accepted by the negotiators on September 12. The next day, acting on the recommendation of the government negotiators, President Arias effected the change. An executive decree reduced duties from sixteen and a half to eleven and a half cents per gallon, thus a five cent per gallon decrease. Government losses in revenue were estimated at $1,152,000 annually. However, it was indeed a compromise with the original thirteen cent revision demanded by the strikers. Retail prices for gasoline were correspondingly reduced to thirty-four cents per gallon. Only fourteen days later, on October 1, Ernesto de la Guardia Jr. was sworn in at 11:47 A.M. at the Legislative Palace as the thirty-first President of the Republic of Panama.

Again the Canal

On July 26, 1956, shouting his defiance of the Western world, Gamal Abdel Nasser seized the Suez Canal, throwing international politics into confusion. Repercussions were strong in Panama, and when the United

States made a succession of diplomatic blunders, all Panama turned on its northern neighbor. Less than two years after the signing of the supposedly definitive Canal Zone contract, Panamanian nationalism was re-aroused; the Canal was again a center of argument and controversy.

In the first days after the Suez seizure there was little disturbance in Panama. The Panamanian ambassador in Washington, J. J. Vallarino, said there was no chance of Panama nationalizing the Canal. He added that the existing agreement left his government and people only partially satisfied. However, Panama could be relied upon to enforce the treaty. W. M. Whitman, secretary of the Panama Canal Company, agreed that "the situations are entirely different." The U. S. soon learned nonetheless, that the situation could become a source of serious friction. On August 13, Australian Prime Minister Robert G. Menzies issued a warning from London: "If President Gamal Abdel Nasser can validly terminate, twelve years beforehand, a concession given to the international Suez Canal Company, because he claims the right of 'nationalization' as part of Egyptian sovereignty, it means that Panama, equally sovereign, would validly be able to terminate, if it wanted to abandon its own line of traditional conduct, its contract of perpetual rental with the United States, taking control of the Panama Canal and reclaiming the rights of passage."[37]

In its anxiety over the situation, the United States, concerned solely with the Suez crisis, prevailed upon Great Britain not to extend an invitation to Panama for the twenty-two-nation conference in London. Secretary of State Dulles chose to exclude Panama, again failing to grasp the Latin mentality. To Dulles it apparently seemed the most convenient way to keep the Panamanians from nourishing any ideas damaging to the United States. Thus Panamanian participation was summarily swept away without a suggestion of courtesy or consideration. Ricardo Arias immediately bridled at the action; the result was a communique outspokenly critical of such mistreatment. "This republic will not consider herself obliged to respect any of the decisions or recommendations adopted by the conference," it read. Citing the Panamanian shipping fleet, sixth largest in the world, as well as certain similarities between Panama and Suez, the statement angrily denounced the exclusion of Panama from the conference. Panama proceeded to adhere with ten other nations to a plan opposed to that of "international control" such as defined at the London Conference. When the Department of State reacted incredulously, Panamanians were even more angered. One of the few U. S. periodicals appreciative of the Panamanian position was the *Washington Post and Times-Herald*. On September 20 it editorialized:

The resolution of Panama to adhere with ten communist and neutral nations . . . to look for a solution to the Suez crisis, should not surprise us. It would be a great deal to hope that Panama would not take advantage of this opportunity to outline its position with respect to the Panama Canal, in spite of the many differences between the two. . . .

Panama should have been invited to London originally . . . the United States should show greater interest and sensibility with respect to our relations with Panama. Taking into account what is now happening in the world, this country would do well to increase its generosity . . . in improvement of relations."[38]

The lack of an invitation to the London conference, however, stirred up much less rancor and bitterness than a statement by Dulles concerning sovereignty over the Zone. Article III of the contract had made an intimate friendship reasonably clear. "The Republic of Panama grants to the United States all the rights, power, and authority within the Zone . . . and . . . all auxiliary lands and waters . . . which the U. S. would possess and exercise if it were the sovereign of the territory within which said lands and waters are located to the entire exclusion of the exercise by the Republic of Panama of any such sovereign rights, power, or authority."[39] This stated, then, that rights exercised by the U. S., while similar to those of sovereignty, were not to be so construed. Indeed, all these rights were granted the U. S. by the Republic of Panama. Few international lawyers, among whom Secretary Dulles had once been outstanding, disagreed on this interpretation. Panama retained its sovereignty, conceding to the United States rights of jurisdiction by treaty. With Panamanian feeling high and U. S. rights generally conceded to be only jurisdictional, John Foster Dulles told a press conference on September 28 that the United States "has rights of sovereignty over the Panama Canal." Not satisfied with this, he continued that these rights were enjoyed by the U. S. "to the entire exclusion of the exercise by the Republic of Panama of any such sovereign rights, power, or authority." Panama was stunned. Dulles had first claimed U. S. sovereignty over the strip of land, then turned around to deny Panama its sovereign rights.

Dulles committed the blunder in a news conference while discussing the Panama Canal in the light of the Suez seizure. He denied any similarity, comparing the U. S. sovereignty in Panama with the 1888 international Treaty of Constantinople over the Suez. His second distinction involved the fear of many independent nations that their Suez route might be severed. This fear, he added, could not extend to the Panama Canal. A few hours after Dulles' double error—both in tactlessness and misinformation—Alberto Boyd, Panamanian foreign minister, released his reply. He contradicted Dulles' statements and declared the Panamanian position once more. Boyd repeated all the valid arguments that clearly leave sovereignty over the Zone with Panama and concluded by pointing out that international provisions on freedom of transit in the Constantinople Treaty also applied to the Panama Canal, hence it also fell under international jurisdiction. This final point was subject to debate. However, none could deny his exposition of Panamanian sovereignty and U. S. jurisdictional rights.

One of the most lucid statements was made by *The Americas Daily* on August 30, 1956.

According to Public Treaties . . . Panama has sovereignty over that strip of land, having granted only, for determined purposes, which are duly specified in the provisions of the Treaty, certain jurisdictional rights to the United States. In other words, the exercise of those jurisdictional rights, which are not at all those corresponding to a sovereign power, is limited to determined ends related with the interoceanic waterway. Should these ends cease to exist, as would be the case if the waterway was abandoned for any reason, Panama would automatically recover . . . the exercise of all the rights which the United States has been permitted to exercise in the Canal Zone in accordance with the treaties in force.

The fact has been clearly established that the Canal is built in Panamanian territory, under Panamanian sovereignty, that the United States has never claimed to have sovereignty over that strip of land ten miles wide. . . .

Therefore, it should not be assumed that the United States owns the territory where the Panama Canal is located, not that it has all the rights adherent to sovereignty, nor that it is the sole owner of the Canal itself. The country exercises some jurisdictional rights and is co-owner, together with Panama, of the Canal, by virtue of well-known international treaties.[40]

On top of the dispute over sovereignty came disagreement over the application of the non-discrimination clause of the 1955 agreement, in Panamanian eyes an inadequate application. Discontent was provoked on August 18 when U. S. Assistant Secretary of the Army George Roderick said that "neither the treaty nor the plan for its implementation provide for a general over-all wage increase, nor . . . for paying U. S.

rates for all jobs."[41]   This spurred Panamanian officials to criticize the
U. S. government for adopting an attitude equivalent to non-compliance
with what was agreed on.   A few days later Governor W. E. Potter of
the Canal Zone told newsmen that the new single wage plan was going
into effect, as provided by treaty.   He underlined the fact that anyone
brought from the United States would have a U. S.-classified job.   Locals
would be paid the U. S. rate, but without the 25 percent differential.
By so doing, Potter was saying that discrimination of wages would not
exist—except for a 25 percent differential which employees brought from
the U. S. would be paid.

Once again the Foreign Ministry drafted a reply and sped it into print.
Their statement read:

> The principle of "equal pay for equal work" should mean that the only
> difference in pay must be that resulting from the difference in quality or type
> of work performed; that is to say, the skill and experience required of the
> worker.   The principle of "the area of recruitment" does not appear to
> conform to the aforementioned principle, inasmuch as it bears no relation
> to the type and quality of work.   It leads to a classification based on "locality,"
> which from a practical standpoint, would be as discriminatory as that which
> up to now has been based on nationality or color. . . .
>
> As Governor Potter well expressed it, the interpretation which has been
> applied to this provision of the Memorandum of Understandings Reached,
> insofar as wages are concerned, is nothing else than the continuation of a
> policy which has been applied for more than fifteen years and it was precisely
> because of it that the new treaty provided for the equality of basic wages for
> Panamanians and North Americans in order to put an end to all sorts of
> discrimination.[42]

And so the two nations were at loggerheads once more over the Canal
Zone.   As 1956 drew to a close, a series of meetings endeavored to smooth
over differences.   Nonetheless, the Canal remained omnipresent in Panamanian politics.

In the midst of this new Canal dispute, Ernesto de la Guardia Jr. was
inaugurated on the first day of October, 1956.   The successor to Ricardo
Arias was a prominent businessman.   A small man of five feet, six inches,
he had spent nearly two decades as managing director of the Panamanian
national brewery.   A member of one of the ruling Panamanian families, a
one-time national golf champion, De la Guardia had attended the Tuck
School of Business Administration at Dartmouth College and gone on to

a career which only occasionally touched on politics. A quiet, unassuming individual, his campaign had been one of the calmest and most rational in national history, although there were some who feared his lack of color and fire, something usually required of Panamanian politicians. Nonetheless, he was expected to provide a competent administration.

Outgoing President Arias made clear his disappointment over the implementation of the Panama-U.S. contract of 1955. In his final official message, Arias voiced many of his country's complaints. He frankly criticized the U. S. Congress for failure to enact legislation necessary to help effect certain phases of the 1955 treaty. While he had found cooperation in the highest echelons, "difficulties and resistance" met Panamanians in the Canal Zone itself. Arias referred to the proposed classification of jobs on the basis of area of recruitment as discriminatory and contrary to the spirit of the treaty. "The painful truth seems to be that it is harder for Panama to watch for the compliance with the pacts than it is to obtain agreement on them."[43] Arias sat down amid enthusiastic applause, to be followed by the incoming executive. In a seventy-seven minute address, De la Guardia gave one of the least optimistic inaugural messages in recent memory. He said at the outset that in his opinion "We Panamanians have never faced as serious difficulties since the birth of the republic as we do today. I would say that all of them . . . can be summarized as follows: Is the Panamanian nation . . . in a position to provide his vital needs for each individual Panamanian? . . . We are at the end of a way and a manner of life which are inadequate to meet the most pressing needs of the country. . . ." In such circumstances, a recovery program was in order. This should extend to housing, economic development, fiscal wellbeing, public administration, and public health. New housing would require the construction of eleven thousand units annually at a cost of over fifteen million dollars per year. Economic development had to be assisted continually. The fiscal problem was indicated by the forty-four million dollar debt which had accumulated, much of it very recently.

Public administration, while recently improved, still left much to be done. "It would be unfair not to acknowledge that the state has taken upon itself new obligations toward the community, which require an increase in the public administration personnel. . . . There is an appreciable number of cases in which one person holds two or more government jobs. . . . And in these times of economic hardship that is an unforgivable injustice towards many persons. . . ." Public health was another serious problem.

Lack of pure water and of sewers and latrines, mosquito breeding places . . . inadequate housing and schools, precarious economic conditions— all this, together with inefficient sanitary and social assistance on the part of the state, is responsible for the delicate state of health in the rural areas. . . . Of every 100 persons who die in the interior, 85 get no medical attention. Of 240 doctors in the country, 180 operate in the cities of Panama and Colón, with a population of 220,000 inhabitants, so that to meet the needs of the rest of the population we have only 60 doctors, or one for every 10,000 people.

Ending his gloomy statement, De la Guardia called on his people to help in the problems of reconstruction and modernization.

I have described the situation of the country, without embellishment or half-truths, as I see it. . . . Let no one expect from me miracles that I am in no position to promise. . . .
We cannot close our eyes to the grave and alarming fact that the Panamanian people have been losing, in the last few years, faith and confidence in, and respect for their guardian institutions. . . . The need for rekindling those sentiments in the spirit of the people impresses upon us the duty of devoting ourselves unselfishly and loyally to the task of a true national recovery.[44]

Despite the President's call to his countrymen, his early efforts were to be thwarted consistently. He announced sweeping reform of the social security system, but by June, 1957, he found the nation generally unresponsive. Despite basing his electoral campaign on social and economic advance, he ran into trouble once in office. On June 27 he announced a temporary withdrawal of his plans. At a press conference he agreed to modify his program, launching, in the meantime, an intensive educational campaign. Financing for his plans had been based primarily upon an increased contribution by most citizens to the tax collectors. The tax levy of 4 percent had been planned for revision to 12 percent by 1958 and 14 percent by 1961, ultimately reaching 17 percent by 1975. Employer and employee alike rebelled at the suggestion. It was admittedly a large chunk out of any man's income, especially in an underdeveloped economy. A widespread feeling that the entire social security program was already mismanaged and corrupt, and unsubstantiated mutterings about rampant socialism combined to block the President's program. So he was forced to delay his improvement program for the time. "I do not wish to impose my will for something not wanted,"

While the quiet De la Guardia's personal popularity had held up rather well, he was beset by the usual political troubles, emanating from his own Coalición Patriótica Nacional. The more conservative element of the party splintered temporarily on the issue of two foreign-financed oil refineries to be erected in Colón, a center of unemployment. Haggling over contractual arrangements between rival factions finally caused the project to be dropped. And First Vice-president Temistocles Diaz resigned from the administration party to set up his own Movimiento Liberación Nacional against the President. While remaining nominally a member of the government—from which he could not resign constitutionally— Diaz created a center of hostility toward De la Guardia that was a distraction from more important matters. Well into the summer of 1958, De la Guardia found that a general public lethargy continued to prohibit the installation of the sweeping reforms in taxation, rural development, health, and social security that Panama needs so badly. The President had labored long and doggedly in the face of this lethargy, and he slowly made progress in fields where the changes called for less than revolutionary measures. Otherwise, he found himself trying in vain to pull with him a populace that applauded his efforts generously but seemed uninterested in the basic conditions demanding remedy.

The tumultuous postwar decade in Panama had shown, above all else, that it was politically the most unpredictable republic of all Central America. The years had brought a parade of eight presidents, none of whom served a full four year term. Despite this, an historic accord was signed with the United States bringing many advantages to the nation. Otherwise, economic problems were as grave as ever. And while the De la Guardia administration brought a certain amount of political stability, it was not a precursor to economic reform but rather the continuation of the outmoded practices and customs of past decades. The list of needs is yet staggering. It includes agricultural diversification, electrification, increased tourist facilities, expanded education, improved housing and public health, light industrialization, additional road construction, and social enlightenment. It will be years before any one of these problems can be coped with satisfactorily. Yet none of the goals are likely to materialize without continued and increased political stability and civil order. Despite surface indications, Panama still carries a heavy moral burden as a result of the Remón assassination and the disputed skullduggery involved. The future of Panama can be one of progress, but only if the republic comes to regain its inner confidence, learning to appreciate and practice the principles of responsible democracy. In the light of recent years, few observers dare predict with any confidence what may follow for this bizarre and unique little nation.

Chapter Eight

CHALLENGE TO THE UNITED STATES

In the last few years . . . our blindness to the power of people and ideas to topple governments and to sway whole continents, had led us into setback after setback. . . . If we persist in it we may ultimately face new debacles. . . .
—Chester Bowles

RECENT YEARS HAVE drawn a world picture of surging nationalism, anti-colonialism, and the accompanying passions of historic xenophobia. Events in oppressed or backward areas have inevitably revolved around these basic sentiments. From Indonesia to the Gold Coast, from Cambodia to Tunis, millions have been awakened by the call of national independence, economic freedom, and the ever virile democratic principles of the American Revolution of 1776. Some six hundred million have become enfranchised by the passage of their lands from colonial to independent status. This historic development, no mere momentary impulse, was only too often considered by U. S. officials as anarchic and irresponsible. Many tended to disbelieve the expressions of deep faith in the U. S. revolutionary ideals as studied and expounded by Nehru, Nkrumah, Bourguiba, and others. The critical nature of such areas in the present world drama has been underlined by the headline-catching battle between the free world and communism. At the same time, the Western hemisphere has also been captured by similar emotions. South of the United States our friends are passing through a period of extraordinary flux, of transition toward something new. In that the transition is a developing process, the burgeoning future is somewhat formless.

With a few exceptions, Latin America has been politically independent for some years. At the same time, many of the ills of those republics, imagined or otherwise, have been laid at the doorstep of the United States. There is only too prevalent in the United States today an ignorance of and lack of concern about Latin America in the face of more pressing problems elsewhere. This was the official outlook toward China a few years ago, it might be remembered. The Latin American states have been a major source of recent criticism of the United States. A three month trip by the author that included every South American nation convinced him beyond any doubt. U. S. policy was considered in the light of the Guatemalan communist debacle, United Fruit Company activities in Honduras and Costa Rica, the treatment of Panama and the Canal Zone, and the continued support of military regimes such as that of Somoza in Nicaragua. Latin Americans, unfortunately, are often eager to criticize the United States for the sake of slaying the giant. They may be much more concerned about U. S. insults to Panamanian national pride, for example, than about problems of survival for backward Panamanian farmers.

The mere existence of the United States in its present position of international prominence creates inevitable ill will. Only in recent years has the U. S. encountered such resentment and outright hatred except on scattered occasions. Such are the burdens of international power. Many other nations have learned the same thing during their periods of ascendancy. The English, Spanish, French, and many ancient empires learned to live in such an environment. Until the past decade, however, the United States had never been confronted by the same development. It has not rested easily under the burden. Both individually and nationally, an endemic United States characteristic is that of open, candid friendship, a belief in the inherent goodness of one's fellow, his intentions, philosophies, and actions. Rude awakenings have come, often resulting from the effects of North American "bigness." In the absence of complete international maturity, this has engendered feelings of hurt and betrayal on the parts of trusted friends. The United States and its citizens individually consider many minor incidents as rebuffs, if not indeed personal affronts. There exists as yet only a partial awareness that bigness, material prosperity, and global leadership are necessarily accompanied by abuse and criticism.

In this light, Latin criticisms are more understandable. If the United States seems a dangerous but sleeping giant to far removed continents, its appearance to neighboring states can well be imagined. The six Central American republics have a combined population less than that of half the U. S. states individually. The largest city in the region is smaller than dozens of U. S. cities. There are only six population centers approaching one hundred thousand inhabitants. In so many ways, it is almost impossible for the U. S. to appreciate or grasp how sensitive a Salvadoran or Honduran is toward the United States. Yet this sensitivity exists and is one of the overriding factors in U. S.-Central American relations.

For the United States, the problem is not an easy one. The nation has many friends as well as critics in the region. In some ways it is greatly admired. And at the same time, it would be specious to assume that all criticism was a result of U. S. geopolitical preponderance. Central Americans have many just grievances, which must be understood. Conversely, U. S. policies sometimes take into account expected criticisms, despite a failure to adjust. There is a growing awareness that relations between the Central American republics and the United States are based upon complexities which reflect the ever-modulating sharps and flats of regional and national politics.

ECONOMICS AND IMPERIALISM

Political understanding is reaching an unequalled regional low. Only in a few instances have there been deviations from a noticeable lack of rapport. The principles moving millions in other backward regions are also expressing themselves powerfully in the Central Americas. At the same time, economic grievances have become a center of dispute. Thousands of Central Americans are passionately convinced that their economic situation is endangered because of U. S. policies. Indeed, much political ill will is predicated upon exaggerated or distorted economic disagreements. To any resident of Central America the cry of yankee imperialism is a familiar one. Few refrains have been more overworked. Yankee imperialism is discussed, criticized, and supposedly proved on both political and economic grounds. Usually the discussion centers on economic matters. The argument commonly begins with the assumption that all foreign enterprise—not just that of the U. S.—is inherently and wickedly avaricious, an evil the world would be better without. Foreign enterprise comes to a small nation, impresses its methodology and interests upon the country, causes economic displacement, and squeezes out struggling local enterprise by shady business tactics and unlimited financial resources. Such enterprises supposedly contribute nothing toward positive national progress, pay a minimal national tax, if that, and stoop to meddle in local politics when advantageous. Such are the more common malpractices of foreign enterprise, in the popular Latin view.

There are admittedly instances of unfair practices by which a small Central American nation falls prey to an uncommonly prominent foreign firm. Such cases are highly regrettable, and reflect discredit on the perpetrators. At the same time, there are positive contributions which can be and often are made. In the first place, the income from the activities of a large firm will inevitably funnel back in part to the host nation. The amount depends upon the local situation. Even in the worst circumstances, a certain amount is unavoidably contributed to the government in power. The nature of the government determines whether this will be converted into public works or official graft. In addition, revenue paid by services and salaries to national employees is a further source of income. One of the strongest arguments in favor of such enterprises is the development ability created by large amounts of capital. Particularly in Central America, individual governments have little hope of financing oil exploitation, to take one instance. Demands of the populace and national financial limitations check the efforts of these small governments to develop natural resources of invaluable worth to the people. Only by the entrance of foreign enterprise backed by unbounded capital can major development proceed. Otherwise, natural endowments are denied the people of the area and those living thousands of miles away, as well.

More perceptive observers realize these favorable sides to the problem of foreign investment. They have seen the great good resulting from foreign capital properly used. Panama and Nicaragua have been prime examples. Yet most interested viewers are imbued with a spirit of rebellion that sadly sees everything in a jaundiced light. And when presented with arguments or examples which favor private capital from abroad, the usual cry is that of "Yunei," or UFCO. In all of Central America, there is no more controversial subject. Latin Americans will claim that everything from dictatorship to diabetes is caused by UFCO imperialism. Outsiders counter with praise of UFCO for conquering the jungle, educating countless backward Indians, and putting a banana in the mouth of every starving babe-in-arms. The truth lies somewhere between, of course. In any consideration of the United States in Central America, UFCO deserves attention.

UFCO is one of the largest North American corporations involved in foreign operations. It has assets listed at $580,000,000. Most of the world's marketable bananas are grown, processed, shipped, and distributed by UFCO. Roughly 85 percent goes to the United States, the remainder to Great Britain and Canada. In addition to bananas, UFCO products include cacao, sugar, palm oil, and abacá, the latter a fiber used for manila hemp. UFCO operates over fifteen hundred miles of railroad, owning 90 percent outright. Its fleet includes over seventy ships, fifty fully refrigerated. Additional subsidiary properties range from a brewery in Honduras to the Tropical Radio Telegraph Company, one of the major hemispheric wireless companies. It owns over 374,000 acres in Central America.

Incorporated in 1899, UFCO through the years purchased the properties of rival fruit and steamship lines in the Caribbean. Since 1930, its closest rival has been Standard Fruit Company, with an estimated twenty million dollars in assets. Everywhere UFCO has come there is unmistakable evidence. Acreage covered by jungle or swamps has been cleared, cared for, fertilized, developed, sown, and harvested. Railroads and highways have given access to plantations, sometimes supplemented by a small air strip. Housing has been erected, workers brought in from elsewhere, hospital and recreational facilities established, schools erected and teachers imported, commissaries made available, and other social services created to meet variable local needs. Some ninety thousand company employees use these facilities continuously. In many ways UFCO is bigger than any of the governments with which it deals.

In the so-called old days, UFCO was much less paternalistic than it would have one believe today. Workers' facilities were inferior and generally inadequate. Governments virtually came and went at its whim. There were many government officials illicitly on the company payroll; national policies changed with UFCO needs. Labor relations were good; they scarcely could be otherwise. Unions were prohibited and workers received what little the company chose to give. Contracts were all long-term agreements as this proved more convenient for company operations. Such is the past UFCO would rather forget. Aligned against this are the improvements instituted in recent years. The facilities mentioned above are generally superior to those available elsewhere in the republics, and laborers are universally paid more than men employed by local planters or businessmen. Their health, recreation, sanitation and education are superior to those of compatriots not working for UFCO. Various other efforts have been made to improve the countries in which UFCO operates. The Agricultural School in Honduras was established a few years ago to train Latins in agricultural methods and experimentation. Over five million dollars have been paid to the school, and UFCO is continuing its support of the institution.

There is a great tendency by UFCO critics to hang upon past events. They often ignore more recent developments. Few are aware of the Costa Rican contract negotiated in 1954, a landmark in UFCO relations. Some 42 percent of the profits are paid annually to the Costa Rican government. Social services were handed over completely to the government in accord with the wishes of President Figueres. Practices in Panama, never as unpopular as elsewhere, have liberalized in recent years. Guatemala enjoys new contractual arrangements today. Yankee imperialism in Guatemala is a cry heard throughout Latin America. This has been dealt with at length in the Guatemalan passages, which discussed the various points at which UFCO was at fault. At the same time, they indicated eventual UFCO willingness to grant concessions similar to those won by Costa Rica. Guatemalan Communists, involved in illicit intrigue and finding profit in nationalistic attacks on UFCO, rejected all offers. New contracts with the Castillo government are now similar to those in Costa Rica. Even the strongest critics of the late President Castillo conceded his reasonable treatment at the hands of UFCO. Honduras points out, on the other hand, the apparent reluctance of the company to grant favorable conditions except under strong pressure. The 1954 strike, we recall, revolved about demands for free medical treatment, paid vacations, and social benefits long enjoyed by UFCO employees elsewhere. However, the lack of pressure by Hondurans had permitted the company to proceed blithely without making such agreements. Only after the crippling and unnecessary strike of 1954 did UFCO concede to Hondurans what it had earlier given elsewhere in the region.

What we see, then, is an irregular mosaic which varies from country to country. UFCO has in long-past years committed serious errors. These are indeed inexcusable. At the same time, no possible good comes from incessant haranguing. UFCO, for all its shady past and present reluctance, is generally operating to the advantage of the countries with which it deals. They receive a large share of the profits, the company getting fewer tangible benefits not accruing to other foreign enterprises. Its workers are healthier, better fed, better housed, and better paid than others doing comparable work. Where inequities exist, they call for fewer Latin exhortations and less United States posturing. Constructive discussion and contractual arrangement is the order of the day. UFCO's worst critics cannot deny that the company uprooted the wilderness and converted worthless land into productive, profitable enterprise bringing advantage to thousands, both inside and outside the country of operation. No Central American government could maintain these activities, even on a limited basis. The social services and physical facilities alone, operated by the Costa Rican government in that republic for some four years, are already deteriorating rapidly. This would never have occurred under UFCO management. In the future, constructive cooperation must lay forth the road on which either the dissatisfied governments or UFCO might approach their problems. No good comes from continual recrimination. Latin Americans generally fail to recognize the harmful results of their well-intentioned cries of outrage. Equally pointless is the official UFCO disdain.

U. S. POLICY: PALATABLE OF OTHERWISE?

Economic criticism often borders on the political, and it is in the political field that the United States government is more directly involved. It is also on a political basis that even the best friends of the United States have great difficulty in understanding its policies. Many seem contradictory, others an affront to the national aspirations of underdeveloped states. Since the inception of the Good Neighbor Policy by Franklin D. Roosevelt, the United States has theoretically based Latin American diplomacy on the foundation of the high principles of the United States fight for independence. Liberty, democracy, freedom of worship, assembly, speech and press, free elections, constitutional government, and non-interference in the internal affairs of others—all these have been announced bases of U. S. policy. To Latin Americans these principles are equally palatable. Indeed, the leaders worship at the feet of Rousseau, Jefferson, Montesquieu, and other political thinkers of the late eighteenth century. At the same time, they feel the United States is hypocritically pursuing policies directly contrary to its announced intentions. This belief has in the past decade lowered U. S. prestige inestimably throughout Central America.

United States recognition of unrepresentative or dictatorial regimes is one of the grievances. To nationals, there is no reason for the U. S. to maintain relations with a regime such as that of Somoza in Nicaragua or Carías in Honduras. This is to them a direct contradiction of the U. S. belief in democratic principles and representative government. The degree of criticism varies according to the individual. Some ask that the government of the United States simply withhold diplomatic recognition from the undemocratic regime. Others suggest economic pressure against the government. Some even support a policy of outright intervention in favor of a representative, freely-elected administration. These arguments run almost directly counter to another criticism, that of U. S. interference. Political intervention was commonly practiced in the early twentieth century throughout the Caribbean, and the memory is still reasonably fresh in many minds. While the United States has bypassed unilateral action as a general policy, it has committed itself to continuance of the policy where the situation is believed grave and beyond other remedy. This draws understandable fire from Latin Americans.

The question of diplomatic recognition has been widely misused in Latin hands. It should obviously be necessary to maintain relations with a government in clear control of its people, whether by legal means or otherwise. The task of the diplomatic corps of all independent nations is to represent its government and policies abroad, at the same time giving counsel and assistance to nationals living outside the borders of their homeland, reporting developments back to its government. Such has been the accepted custom for centuries. Modern international law upholds this practice. Every sovereign power has the right and indeed the duty to be represented before the governments of other independent nations. There may well be a question about a government's control over its people, and this must be considered when recognition is being studied. However, there is no doubt of any government's need for foreign representation. A government must continue these relations in the absence of reasonable doubt about the nature of the neighbor government. This leads to the problem of de jure and de facto recognition. When a government shows its control of a populace, regardless of the means employed, recognition is extended. Barring a diplomatic affront or international crisis, recognition will continue indefinitely. Whether the government be formed by democratic elections or repressive militarism, it is accorded the same recognition. It would have been highly impractical to have refused relations with Guatemala for the thirteen years of the Ubico regime, with Nicaragua for the twenty years under Somoza, or with Honduras for the sixteen years of the Carías dictatorship.

The degree of diplomatic cordiality is a different problem. It seems a valid question to pose, to ask why warm and obviously friendly relations with dictatorial governments are maintained by the United States. Nicaragua is a case in point. The U. S. certainly could not have withheld diplomatic recognition of the Somoza regime for nearly a quarter of a century. At the same time, it did not have to establish intimately friendly relations with the dictator. U. S. diplomats could have reported that Somoza had accomplished fine things in Nicaragua by way of progress. This is partially true, as the chapter on Nicaragua illustrated. Nonetheless, a succession of United States ambassadors did not need to reach a first name basis with the strong man. Nor did the U. S. need to negotiate and sign a military pact with Nicaragua. Such agreements are of little positive value there. They merely strengthen the hand of the government in question, which may one day turn the arms and U. S.-trained army on the people to put down rebellion.

Military aid is another of the sore points of hemispheric policy. The prospect of war between these small nations is relatively small. The instrumentality of the Organization of American States is such that United States military treaty assistance seems fatuous. The closest outbreak to war in recent years was the Costa Rican-Nicaraguan dispute which was fanned anew several times by the personal enmity of José Figueres and Anastasio Somoza. In each case, international action prevented an all-out war of aggression. A pattern for the future seems to have been molded along these lines. In Central America, the military is generally an arch-conservative force out of harmony with the political and social structure. Members of the armed forces are considered as lower forms of social life. Prostitution is often classified on only a slightly less honorable level. The military forces throughout the isthmus are at the call of a small handful of officers who in turn form a significant bulwark of the government in power. The ultimate survival of the regime depends upon the military. Somoza and Carías, military men themselves, ruled their countries for years with military support. Osorio followed the same procedure in El Salvador for eight years. The National Guard in Panama made and broke a good half dozen presidents before installing its own commandant, José Remón. And Ubico, and later Arbenz in Guatemala were both overthrown when the army turned upon them.

In such circumstances the military can be considered a retrogressive influence. In more democratic Central American governments, there is always a danger that the military will become dissatisfied with the state of things and install a government more consonant with its wishes. In the dictatorial governments, the military maintains a strong man in power. He, in turn, repays the armed forces by wage increases, modern housing facilities, luxurious officers' clubs, trips abroad, and innumerable fringe benefits denied the ordinary citizen. Of course, there will be modern arms from abroad—usually the U. S.—as well as foreign experts— usually U. S. military representatives—to train the soldiers in modern warfare. Indeed, the U. S. can easily be criticized for its maintenance of military agreements in Central America. Official justifications and rationalizations are universally unsatisfactory. Until the United States discontinues wholesale, indiscriminate military cooperation with the republics of Central America, it will hear much criticism of this practice, a thoroughly justified criticism. The United States is continuing an ill-considered policy both in establishing warm relations with dictatorial regimes and in supporting them through military agreements. It continues to be attacked even for recognition of these regimes and is called upon to sever all formal contacts. In this instance the U. S. position is firm and clearly justifiable. Unfortunately, few Central Americans see it that way.

In theory, at least, the U. S. pursues a policy of non-intervention in Central America. Latins praise the principle, but point out that the U. S. fails to practice it and refer to different instances of U. S. intervention. At the same time, they call on the United States to exert moral influence against undemocratic regimes. Some even call for more direct action. Costa Rican ex-president Figueres, admired as a democratic leader by some, has called upon the United States to use almost any means at its disposal to do away with undemocratic regimes. Those less sanguine than Figueres advocate the withholding of military recognition, economic aid, and similar steps to pull down authoritarianism in the region. Yet this itself is blatant intervention, exactly what the U. S. is pilloried for.

Alongside its tiny neighbors, the United States is indeed a giant. Everything that happens has an effect on its southern neighbors. If there is a nasty outbreak of race relations, Costa Ricans will sneer at U. S. intolerance, forgetting that Negroes were not allowed by law on the meseta central or in the capital city of San José until 1941. Salvadorans will deride U. S. insincerity when the government deals with undemocratic regimes, forgetting its energetic support of imperialistic Japan in the years preceding Pearl Harbor. Guatemalans will attack U. S. materialism and lack of culture, then fight for seats when the New Orleans Symphony Orchestra plays one concert in Guatemala City, although refusing to support the local symphony. Young Honduran government officials attack U. S. selfishness after receiving a college education under a U. S. government scholarship grant at a university of their choosing. No matter what position the United States does or does not take, it exerts influence. This gives added weight to U. S. actions in praising the government of a strongman or in denouncing a government for unilateral expropriation. This makes the ill-considered generalization of a senator debating on Capitol Hill much more important. It gives significance to the Cuban Negro ballplayer who returns home to tell of segregation in Southern hotels. In short, the U. S. position carries weighty implications, even when the government deliberately tries to avoid the mildest hint of gently suggestive coercion. With all influence a form of moderate intervention, the United States lives with the problem from day to day. Some form of intervention is inevitable, albeit on a small scale.

When citizens of Central America demand that the U. S. neither recognize nor cooperate with an unrepresentative government, they are requesting a flagrant violation of the non-intervention principle they hold so dear. The very act of non-recognition, of withholding diplomatic or business relations, of economic or social aid, is intervention. Even more improper is the previous decision upon which this intervention is based. Who is to decide when a government is or is not undemocratic? Who is to choose between two potential revolutionary leaders and nominate one as worthy of support? On a concrete basis, one might say that the problem is exaggerated. Everyone knew Anastasio Somoza was a dictator. Why not take measures to end his regime? But many Nicaraguans held Somoza in great affection, even while admitting the undemocratic nature of his administration. Thousands would have fought to the death for the old strong man. El Salvador? It had a military dictatorship for eight years and now has followed it with a handpicked successor who won election without opposition. Shouldn't this government be overthrown? Yet it is popular, opposition is weak and generally without support. Salvadorans are enjoying unprecedented economic prosperity. Who will make the decision to establish a more democratic government? What choice would have been made for Costa Rica before the Echandi government took office? Outside the country, the U. S. and Latin America alike admired the highly democratic government of José Figueres. Yet Costa Ricans themselves turned almost totally against Figueres. His policies left Costa Rica weaker internally and more divided socially than it had been in years. Should Figueres have been overthrown in favor of a popular and effective government? Latins would say no. They fail to explain just where the line should be drawn, and how.

In short, the very decision of the intrinsic worth of a government, its contribution to the national wellbeing, and its representative nature, are questions that are always difficult to answer. In many instances it would be impossible to get a fair judgment from the most detached of observers—if they could be located. And even assuming the judgment to be one of black and white, without controvertible shadings of grey, the decision would have to be made by a person or group of persons. Who? Latins would certainly not trust a U. S. secretary of state to decide which administration served representatively, or which was ripe for intervention. None would advocate a vote—a sort of popularity contest to determine whether President A of the Republic of X was a "good guy or a bad guy." Such speculation passes the fringe of lunacy. For the United States, then, it is patently impossible to exercise any form of open diplomacy against an undemocratic government. The very question of unrepresentativeness itself is often intangible, certainly not easily answered. The decision would necessarily be a unilateral one, thus unacceptable to the United States as well as the peoples of Central America. Latin American demands for action on such a basis are impractical, a gross violation of those principles they themselves criticize the United States for trampling so often.

This does not wash all responsibility from U. S. hands. Favorable changes can be made. Only the official and impersonal matters of diplomatic protocol should be engaged in with clearly unrepresentative governments. Frigidly correct relations should be maintained, and nothing more. Military agreements must be shunned. There is no convincing argument that gives this policy merit as an important function of U. S.

foreign policy in this area. No advantages from it accrue to the United States in the isthmus. Whatever aid is delivered should be extended in the form of economic assistance, as discussed elsewhere. Only on the skeleton of such a policy can new plans revitalize U. S. relations with Central America.

ISSUES IN POINT

There are innumerable examples of the issues outlined above. Some illuminate the absence of understanding on both sides of the fence. These include the assassination of Anastasio Somoza, the Panama Conference of 1956, the affront to Panama during the Suez crisis, and the overthrow of the Arbenz regime in Guatemala. The attack upon and the subsequent death of Somoza in September, 1956, brought out the typically myopic U. S. view of the Latin mentality and environment. Several blunders were committed. The first followed the shooting when U. S. Ambassador Thomas Whelchel called upon Washington to send direct medical aid. Without any request from Nicaraguans he promptly asked the government to send outstanding specialists in an effort to save the life of Somoza.

To Whelchel, and then to President Eisenhower, this seemed like the charitable and humanitarian act of a good neighbor. Political assassination is a nasty business, whatever the circumstances. They hoped to rescue Somoza from death. However, the result was to create a wave of anger against the United States for apparent interference. To almost all Latin Americans outside Nicaragua, Somoza was a tyrannical despot who should have been deposed years ago. When asked about the humanitarian aspect, they would retort that the Somoza dictatorship had been notably antihumanitarian for two decades. Many admitted that the United States would have been in a difficult position to refuse aid had the Nicaraguans requested it. However, the emergency trip of Eisenhower's personal doctors, plus other medical specialists, all without Nicaraguan action, was considered another sign of U. S. hypocrisy—first declaring democratic principles and then trying to save an authoritarian ruler from the grip of death. Had Somoza survived, as seemed likely for several days, this action would have drawn even more indignation.

Shortly after Somoza died, a week following the attack, President Eisenhower sent a message of condolence. Rather than the customary official regret, he telegrammed an expression of deep personal loss. "The nation and I personally regret the death of President Somoza of Nicaragua as a result of the cowardly attack made upon him several days ago by an assassin. President Somoza constantly emphasized, both publicly and privately, his friendship for the United States—a friendship that persisted until the moment of his death."[1] To make the sentiment absolutely clear, Secretary of State Dulles also sent condolences to the dead dictator's widow, concluding that "His constantly demonstrated friendship for the United States will never be forgotten."[2]

Thus the United States deftly turned hemispheric opinion against it once more. The expressed sentiment was anathema to Central Americans. A message of sympathy was of course in order. But there was no cause for mentioning Somoza's long friendship with the U. S. No one outside Nicaragua needed a reminder, while Nicaraguans were not appreciably interested. When the telegram from Dulles again reiterated the sentiment, the United States began to appear slightly ludicrous. As one Buenos Aires newspaper commented acidly, it was as if one of the forty-eight stars had unexpectedly slipped out of the flag. Eisenhower's condemnation of the "cowardly" attack also rankled. In the first place, many hailed the dead Rigoberto López Pérez as a liberator of the Nicaraguan people. He was cheered in the streets of San Salvador. In Uruguay the national legislature even passed a resolution praising the patriotism and self-sacrifice of López. This attitude prevailed throughout Central and South America. With representatives throughout the Americas, there was no conceivable reason for Washington to be unaware of such sentiment. No person could conceivably have attacked the well-guarded Somoza without signing his death warrant. There was no cowardice in López' attack. He may be condemned on many grounds, but not that of fear. The man well knew his fate. Thirty seconds after firing at Somoza he lay dead, his body pierced by bullets in twenty-one places.

Another instance of total U. S. miscalculation was the July, 1956, Panama Conference, at which virtually all the American chiefs of state were present. This was cheered enthusiastically in the United States both before it began and after. Washington even today considers this a diplomatic triumph, at the very least a bold and telling stroke in its hemispheric policy. Yet these evaluations are based upon reports issued by the different governments. The sad fact that many of them were not representative was never considered. The wide rapport and friendly exchange of ideas in individual interviews between presidents was in itself most cordial. This was not, however, a reflection of the people. In many cases their voices were muted by tyranny. The purpose of the conference was presumably to unite the people of the hemisphere by closer bonds of friendship and cooperation. As there were no agreements entered into by the United States, no action taken that was not more appropriate to diplomatic channels in individual countries, the hope of furthering relations of the peoples of America was the guiding thought.

But to the peoples, one fact stood out. The President of the United States was shaking hands, exchanging mementos, conversing in a friendly fashion, and giving every evidence of approval to some of the most undemocratic and unrepresentative chiefs of state in contemporary international affairs. His affability was extended equally to democrat and demagague, to constitutionalist and authoritarian. He either did not know or did not care about the nature of these presidents. To most Latins the latter conclusion seemed more valid. Even moderate critics of the U. S. were disheartened. Maintaining diplomatic relations with a strong man is one thing, but dealing with him personally at a conference presumably symbolic of hemispheric principles of democracy and representative government is an insult to the people. For the dictators, they could obtain photographs of a friendly handshake or a discussion with the U. S. President, which would then run in the official press. The result of all this was further disillusionment with U. S. foreign policy. It was again characterized as hypocritical and two-faced. The expression of democratic principles, adhered to in apparent seriousness by many of the most undemocratic chiefs of state, was cited as the newest instance of U. S. official insincerity.

The previous chapter dealt in some detail with the Panamanian reaction to the crisis of the Suez. There is no point in reviewing the incident at great length. In its anxiety over the middle east crisis, the State Department chose to omit Panama from the twenty-two-nation London Conference—or more accurately, it requested Great Britain, as host, to extend no invitation to Panama. They suggested Panama be kept out of the meeting entirely. Official though probably went like this: "They're not directly involved, aren't really very responsible about this sort of thing, and might get bad ideas if they attended. Better keep them out of things. It's safer that way." Despite such thoughts, it proved much less "safe" to exclude the Panamanians. Their president noted that similarities between the two canals and Panama's large merchant fleet provided more than adequate reason for invitation. This was followed shortly afterwards by indications of hedging by the U. S. in certain phases of the recent Canal Zone negotiation. Then Secretary of State Dulles hastily told reporters to discount fears of the Panama Canal being nationalized. It was really sovereign territory of the United States, hence beyond Panamanian control. The enormity of his blunder was discussed earlier. Suffice it to repeat that Dulles never should have made such a statement even if it had been true—and it was sheer fiction. On the heels of a few more such comments, Panamanian nationalization of the Canal would become less unlikely than it seems today.

The most unpopular and most discussed facet of U. S. policy on the isthmus is the notorious Guatemalan affair, detailed in Chapter Two. From the beginning of the Castillo revolution opinion was wholeheartedly against the United States. It began with protests from all corners of the hemisphere, both official and otherwise. In Chile, not notably anti-U. S. at the time, the U. S. flag was burned and President Eisenhower hung in effigy. Expressions of disapproval elsewhere were nearly as violent. The Department of State to this day vigorously denies official intervention. Yet there is no serious question that it did indeed intervene in favor of Castillo. This intervention was limited to somewhat inadequate arms. Had the army remained loyal to Arbenz, his government would not have fallen. That it turned against him was a sign of the disillusionment with the preceding months of official torture and inquisition. The decision was reached in Washington that intervention would be required, regardless of repercussions, in order to uproot the communist regime in Guatemala. The tentacles of communism were increasingly threatening the rest of the isthmus. Communist propagandists had scoffed at the thought that tiny Guatemala might endanger the United States. They conveniently ignored the real cause of U. S. concern—that communist underground activities were increasing throughout the region, taking advantage of the natural political instability. The direct goal was not the United States, but rather the Panama Canal itself.

Latin Americans almost universally reject the thesis that the government of Arbenz was communist. Only Guatemalans and a small handful of others recognize the fact. To Guatemalans who lived under the regime, denials of its communism are as ridiculous as they seem to the United States. Many critics of the U. S. would be somewhat more sympathetic if they believed that communism precipitated the U. S. intervention. However, they have succeeded in convincing themselves of the truth of the communist charge—that protection of UFCO interests motivated the action. Many sincerely believe Secretary Dulles to have been in the pay of UFCO, absurd as this may seem in the U. S. They recall their pet name for him—John Foster Dollars. They are convinced that U. S. concern with communism was but a screen behind which the vultures of yankee imperialism might swoop down and pick the bones of Guatemalans.

Few Latins are ever likely to appreciate the deep concern of the U. S. government—legislative as well as executive—with the growth of communism in the very backyard of the nation. The danger to Central America and to the Panama Canal was considered so grave that action had to be taken, as it soon was. As for UFCO, its lands had been expropriated more than a year before the U. S. action. Had the U. S. truly fomented a revolution in protection of UFCO lands, it would never have dallied so long. Critics should remember the telling comment of one U. S. diplomat stationed in Guatemala: the decoration of every United Fruit official with the Order of the Quetzal would never make the government of Arbenz less communist, less dangerous to the sub-continent and to the Guatemalan people themselves. Communism was the issue, not banana expropriation.

Meeting the Challenge

At the heart of United States relations with the republics of Central America lies a maze of misunderstandings that blur mutual recognition. Through a series of errors, miscalculations, and inadequate explanations of policies, both sides have come to misjudge the other with undue severity. Increasing irritations have widened the gap between the republics of the isthmus and the giant of the north, reducing awareness of the common bonds and interests shared through recent history. Too many official spokesmen have ignored disputes and bypassed serious isues with idealistic, stratospheric flights of fancy invoking the ideals of Bolívar and Jefferson as the living images before all peoples of the Americas. Yet there is a common ground of security, geography, ideology, and history, which must not be forgotten in the midst of controversy.

Latin American understandings are weakened by an unfortunate propensity to find fault whatever the cost. This is among the penalties of international ascendancy. The very fact makes it no less palatable, of course. Many Latins, while priding themselves on objectivity and complete command of all the circumstances, are decidedly one-sided in their considerations. The unavoidable Guatemalan occurrence is exemplary. Convinced of U. S. intervention, as well they should be, they reject at the same time the communism of the Guatemalan regime. They read with almost naïve credence the outrageously inaccurate books of ex-President Arévalo and ex-Foreign Minister Toriello, accepting them almost adoringly despite the men's deep personal involvement. This strengthens their belief in hated yankee imperialism. At the same time they scoff at books on the subject by Daniel James and this author, as well as a recent publication by a Guatemalan, each of which recognized grievances on both sides of the dispute. The propagandistic Arévalo and Toriello polemics became the measured scholarship of disinterested bystanders. This propensity is one of the more distressing aspects of the picture. Relations with the U. S. will at times be tense even if all the facts be known. For those who choose to ignore one side of the picture, the result is a highly partisan, personal bias. This leads to the impassioned and impotent public gatherings or denunciatory meetings which stir up ill will and contribute nothing toward hemispheric harmony. International relations are among the several areas where destructive attacks can have no worthwhile value.

What is needed, and certainly what the United States requires, is not subservience or slavish worship. What it does desire is a reasonable understanding of the questions involved. The United States hopes that the problems and issues may be considered and attacked in a positive, constructive manner, such that all the peoples of the Americas will benefit. Foreign relations are as complex here as in other regions of the world, and they must be viewed in this light. There are shadings between right and wrong, between transgressor and transgressed. Men of good will and sincerity of purpose must pursue improved relations by measured, well-informed judgment. Unchecked nationalism, fiery denunciations of imperialistic powers, and ill-considered speeches are not the paths by which an enlightened tomorrow will be approached. United States policy, on the other hand, is equally guilty of deteriorating its prestige in the past decade. The Good Neighbor Policy is dead. All the chanting invocations of the finest statesmen and diplomats will never again breathe life into it. Until responsible U. S. policy-makers accept this fact, relations on the isthmus must be strained, drawn nervously taut. Thus will the crisis of Central America today be met, and therein lies the challenge.

Official evaluation of the Latin temperament in recent years has been equivocal. The blame lies in part on the attitude common to U. S. career diplomats that Central America is the Siberia of the foreign service. Further explanation lies in the present world situation, which has pushed other underdeveloped areas to the forefront at the expense of Latin America. An overriding concern with the battle against international communism has drawn official attention to other parts of the globe. Focus has been almost continually away from this hemisphere. These and other factors do not excuse the rash of errors committed since the close of World War II. The situation has cried out increasingly for new thought and new policy. None has been forthcoming from either Democratic or Republican administrations. New impetus must be given to a basic re-evaluation of Latin American policy. A choice has to be made between expediency and principle, the principle of democracy and representative government. The United States dares not continue waving this banner in Latin areas while pursuing policies inconsistent with announced ideals. Whether intentional or not, this sort of hypocrisy, of saying one thing and then smugly doing another, is nurturing a growing disenchantment even among the most friendly and enlightened political figures in the region.

The United States must learn to limit its relations with clearly unrepresentative governments to the elements of strictest protocol. Diplomatic business must be maintained, but not extended into the realm of military aid, of personal friendship and tacit moral approval of the regimes, such as has been done time and time again in the past ten years. Non-intervention must be restored in deed as well as word. The United States must remain true to this principle regardless of the provocation. Otherwise it forfeits all right to friendship or cooperation in the area. Even in the extreme case of communist Guatemala in 1954 this holds true. There, events suggest the eventual fall of the regime without any U. S. interference.

The United States must also increasingly extend its relations with the peoples of these nations. There is a tendency for U. S. diplomats and government workers to establish their own communities when away from the United States. Official reference is repeatedly made to the "U. S. colony in Guatemala," the "U. S. colony in Honduras," and so forth. This suggests a habit which is the very antithesis of the idea of stationing representatives abroad to understand and learn about the nation in which they work. Few diplomats learn the different aspects of a situation by limiting their contacts to representatives of the government in power and other foreign diplomats, who in turn restrict their sources of information to an equally narrow group. The Department of State must appreciate fully the great divergence in many instances between what a nation really is and what it is made to appear by its government. Policymakers in Washington need much more information than what a ruling regime wants it to know.

There are many smaller facets of U. S. hemispheric policy which call for re-evaluation. These include the information service program, added economic aid, administration of that aid, long-term trade agreements, and equalization of a variety of divergent standards. These all call for one common denominator—a serious and extended consideration of all problems in the light of present circumstances. The United States has not changed its policy significantly since the institution of the Good Neighbor Policy twenty-five years ago. Too long has the U. S. been satisfied to let its southern relations slide, accepting individual problems as they arrive and treating them separately rather than as part of a complex entity. The slow erosion of the U. S. position has not been impeded in recent years. In many cases it has not even been recognized. The time may pass when the United States can halt the disintegration of its relations with Latin America. The only firm footing for a lasting future consists of renewed, revitalized relations based upon the recognition of equality and complete fulfillment of the democratic ideals of the philosophers of the American Revolution.

This demands a concomitant realignment of United States policy. The process should not be a painful but rather a happy one. The task is admittedly difficult. At the same time, the Latin people are crying for an appeal to the imagination, predicated upon a thorough and sympathetic appreciation of their life, environment, and problems. This challenge lies before the United States today. Some have suggested that the nation has passed the historic point at which it produces new, original policy. I prefer to believe that the United States is just approaching the threshold of bold, provocative, imaginative thinking. The challenge awaits, and we dare not ignore it. The future of much more than Central America itself is at stake.

John Moors Cabot, a State Department veteran of long service in Latin America, has written: "Let us highly resolve that history in our Americas shall record that here man learned to cooperate, to progress in peace and understanding, to contribute our American share to the advancement of our western civilization and our christian religion. We owe that to the splendor of our Pan American ideals."[3]   And we owe as much to the highest principles upon which the United States has grown to international stature.

Notes

CHAPTER ONE

1. Germán Arciniegas, *The State of Latin America,* trans. Harriet de Onís (New York, 1952), p. 21.

CHAPTER TWO

1. Germán Arciniegas, *The State of Latin America,* trans. Harriet de Onís (New York, 1952), p. 291.
2. *The Pan-American* (New York), December, 1949.
3. Juan José Arévalo, *Discursos en la Presidencia, 1945-47* (Guatemala City, 1947), p. 68. (JDM)*
4. Juan José Arévalo, *op. cit.,* p. 52 (JDM)
5. Daniel James, *Red Design for the Americas* (New York, 1954), p. 46.
6. *Ibid.*
7. Bertram Wolfe, *Three Who Made a Revolution* (New York, 1948), p. 295.
8. Daniel James, *op. cit.,* p. 73.
9. *For a Lasting Peace, For a People's Democracy!* (Moscow), February 22, 1952, p. 1.
10. U.S. Department of State, *White Paper on Communism in Guatemala* (Washington, 1954).
11. Jacobo Arbenz, *Discoursos* (Guatemala City, 1951), pp. 3-6.
12. John D. Martz, *Communist Infiltration of Guatemala* (New York, 1956), p. 54.
13. *New York Times,* February 21, 1954, p. 21.
14. Spruille Braden, *The Communist Threat in the Americas* (New York, 1953), p. 10.
15. Leo A. Suslow, *Aspects of Social Reforms in Guatemala, 1944-1949* (Hamilton, New York, 1949), p. 107.
16. *New York Times,* May 18, 1952, p. 10.
17. *New York Times,* February 23, 1953, p. 4.
18. U.S. Department of State, *op. cit.*
19. Archer C. Bush, *Organized Labor in Guatemala* (Hamilton, New York, 1950).
20. "Official Guatemalan Government Information Bulletin" (Guatemala City, 1954), p. 1.
21. *Ibid.,* p. 2.

* The initials JDM following a note indicate that the passage in question has been translated from the Spanish by the author.

22. *Washington Post,* March 9, 1954, p. 1.

23. "Tenth Inter-American Conference, Caracas, Venezuela, March 1-28, 1954, Final Act," (Washington, 1954), pp. 2-3.

24. *Ibid.*

25. *Washington Post,* March 15, 1953, p. 12.

26. *New York Times,* March 6, 1954, p. 1.

27. John D. Martz, *op. cit.,* p. 97.

28. Reprinted from *U. S. News & World Report* (May 28, 1954, p. 32), an independent weekly news magazine published at Washington. © 1954 United States News Publishing Corp.

29. *Boston Advertiser,* May 23, 1954, p. 1.

30. *Washington Post,* May 23, 1954, p. 1.

31. *Time* (New York), June 7, 1954, p. 35.

32. *New York Times,* June 24, 1954, p. 1.

33. *New York Times,* June 26, 1954, p. 1.

34. *New York Times,* June 28, 1954, p. 1.

35. *New York Times,* July 14, 1954, p. 3.

36. *New York Times,* July 1, 1954, p. 1.

37. *El Imparcial* (Guatemala City), June 17, 1955, p. 11. (JDM)

38. *Latin American Report* (New Orleans), June, 1956, p. 20.

39. *Prensa Libre* (Guatemala City), March 17, 1956, p. 1. (JDM)

40. *Latin American Report, op. cit.,* p. 21.

41. *Hoy* (Guatemala City), June 27, 1956, p. 1. (JDM)

42. *Hoy,* June 29, 1956, p. 1. (JDM)

43. Daniel James, "Church and State in Guatemala," *The Commonweal* (New York), September 30, 1955, p. 6.

44. *Ibid.*

45. Guatemalan Trade Union Council Bulletin, May 1, 1957, p. 1.

46. *New York Times,* October 24, 1957, p. 1.

47. *New York Times,* March 1, 1958, p. 1.

CHAPTER THREE

1. *El Diario de Hoy* (San Salvador), December 1, 1954, p. 1. (JDM)

2. Daniel James, *Red Design for the Americas* (New York, 1954), p. 217.

3. *Prensa Gráfica* (San Salvador), April 22, 1953, p. 1. (JDM)

4. *Diario de Costa Rica* (San José), June 1, 1954, p. 5. (JDM)

5. *Consultación por los Principales de Trabajo* (San Salvador, 1952), p. 5. (JDM)

6. *El Diario de Hoy,* March 22, 1954, p. 1. (JDM)

7. *El Diario de Hoy,* June 8, 1955, p. 1. (JDM)

8. *Time* (New York), January 23, 1956, p. 32.

9. *Prensa Gráfica,* February 28, 1956, p. 1. (JDM)

10. *Prensa Gráfica,* March 1, 1956, p. 1. (JDM)

11. *Time,* March 12, 1956.

12. *El Diario de Hoy,* March 6, 1956, p. 1. (JDM)

13. *Miami Herald,* September, 1956, p. 12.

14. *Revista Mexicana* (Mexico City), November, 1955. (JDM)

15. *Diario de Costa Rica,* July 23, 1953, p. 7. (JDM)

CHAPTER FOUR

1. William S. Stokes, *Honduras* (Madison, Wisconsin, 1950), p. 3.

2. *Ibid.,* pp. 223-4.

3. *Ibid.,* p. 297.

4. Russell H. Fitzgibbon (ed.), *Constitutions of the Americas* (Chicago, 1948), p. 495.

5. *Ibid.,* p. 484.

6. William S. Stokes, *op. cit.*, p. 193.

7. *Todo* (Mexico City), July 10, 1952, p. 7. (JDM)

8. *Diario de Costa Rica* (San José), July 30, 1952, p. 1. (JDM)

9. Abel Alexis Latendorf, *Latinoamérica* (Buenos Aires, 1956), p. 84. (JDM)

10. Daniel James, *Red Design for the Americas* (New York, 1954), p. 220.

11. *La Epoca* (Tegucigalpa), June 3, 1954, p. 1. (JDM)

12. *El Día* (Tegucigalpa), June 8, 1954, p. 1. (JDM)

13. *Diario de Costa Rica*, June 11, 1954, p. 5. (JDM)

14. Daniel James, *op. cit.*, p. 220.

15. *El Día*, July 21, 1954, p. 1. (JDM)

16. *Diario de Costa Rica*, March 17, 1954, p. 5. (JDM)

17. *El Pueblo* (Tegucigalpa), July 1, 1954, p. 1. (JDM)

18. Russell H. Fitzgibbon, *op. cit.*, p. 480.

19. *El Mundo* (Tegucigalpa), October 14, 1954, p. 4. (JDM)

20. *Diario de Costa Rica*, November 11, 1954, p. 13. (JDM)

21. *Time* (New York), December 10, 1954, p. 35.

22. *La Epoca*, December 17, 1954, p. 1. (JDM)

23. *Diario de Costa Rica*, August 20, 1955, p. 1. (JDM)

24. *Ibid.* (JDM)

25. *El Pueblo*, May 20, 1956, p. 1. (JDM)

26. *La Epoca*, July 9, 1956, p. 1. (JDM)

27. *Diario de Costa Rica*, July 18, 1956, p. 7. (JDM)

28. Proclamation of the Armed Forces of Honduras, a leaflet released and circulated in Tegucigalpa October 21, 1956. (JDM)

29. *New York Times*, October 22, 1956, p. 1.

30. *El Dia*, March 22, 1956, p. 1. (JDM)

31. *Diario de Costa Rica*, December 4, 1954, p. 7. (JDM)

CHAPTER FIVE

1. *A Modern Nicaragua* (Managua, 1955), p. 7.

2. *Ibid.*, pp. 5-6.

3. *Ibid.*, p. 8.

4. "The Economic Development of Nicaragua" (Baltimore, 1953), p. 5.

5. *A Modern Nicaragua*, p. 13.

6. "The Economic Development of Nicaragua," p. 78.

7. *Novedades* (Managua), December 12, 1948, p. 1. (JDM)

8. "Inter-American Treaty of Reciprocal Assistance" (Washington, 1948), p. 3.

9. *Novedades*, April 5, 1954, p. 1. (JDM)

10. *New York Times*, April 6, 1954.

11. *Diario de Costa Rica* (San José), April 24, 1954, p. 1. (JDM)

12. *Chicago Daily News*, April 26, 1954, p. 1.

13. *Novedades*, May 5, 1954, p. 1. (JDM)

14. *Prensa Libre* (San José), June 4, 1954, p. 1. (JDM)

15. *Time* (New York), August 9, 1954, p. 37.

16. *La Nación* (San José), November 28, 1954, p. 1. (JDM)

17. *New York Times*, January 10, 1955, p. 1.

18. *New York Times*, January 13, 1955, p. 1.

19. *La República* (San José), January 14, 1955, p. 1. (JDM)

20. *A Modern Nicaragua*, p. 18.

21. *La República*, May 6, 1956, p. 1. (JDM)

22. *A Modern Nicaragua*, p. 16.

23. *Mercury* (New York), September, 1952.

24. *Ibid.*

25. Quoted by a U.S. embassy official during a conversation with the author in Managua.

26. *A Modern Nicaragua*, p. 12.

27. *El Mundo* (Buenos Aires), October 1, 1956, p. 1. (JDM)
28. *Washington Post and Times-Herald,* October 1, 1956, p. 12.
29. *New York Times,* February 3, 1957, p. 7.
30. *New York Times,* July 7, 1957, p. 11.
31. *Ibid.*
32. *Latin American Report* (New Orleans), May, 1958, pp. 19-20.
33. *New York Times,* April 29, 1958, p. 1.

CHAPTER SIX

1. *New York Times,* February 4, 1947.
2. Roberto Fernández, *La Huelga de Brazos Caídos* (San José, 1953), p. 10. (JDM)
3. *Ibid.,* p. 12. (JDM)
4. *Ibid.,* pp. 17-18. (JDM)
5. *New York Times,* July 26, 1947.
6. Roberto Fernández, *op. cit.,* p. 30. (JDM)
7. *Ibid.,* p. 35. (JDM)
8. *Ibid.,* pp. 36-7. (JDM)
9. *Ibid.,* p. 38. (JDM)
10. *Ibid.,* p. 40. (JDM)
11. *Diario de Costa Rica* (San José), February 8, 1947, p. 1. (JDM)
12. *Ultima Hora* (San José), February 10, 1948, p. 1. (JDM)
13. *Ultima Hora,* March 7, 1948, p. 1. (JDM)
14. Arturo Castro, *José Figueres Ferrer* (San José, 1955), pp. 116-17.
15. *Diario de Costa Rica,* March 17, 1948, p. 1. (JDM)
16. *La Nación* (San José), April 28, 1948, p. 1. (JDM)
17. *Ultima Hora,* April 30, 1948, p. 1. (JDM)
18. *Novedades* (Managua), December 12, 1948, p. 1. (JDM)
19. *Diario de Costa Rica,* December 13, 1948, p. 1. (JDM)
20. Ruhl J. Bartlett, *The Record of American Diplomacy* (New York, 1952), pp. 735-36.
21. *La Nación,* April 3, 1949, p. 1. (JDM)
22. *Constitución Política de Costa Rica* (San José, 1955), p. 20.
23. *Diario de Costa Rica,* November 4, 1951, p. 1. (JDM)
24. *Diario de Costa Rica,* July 25, 1953, p. 1. (JDM)
25. *El Hombre Justo* (San José), January, 1952, pp. 4-18. (JDM)
26. "A Latin American Looks at Point Four" (San José, 1953), pp. 7-15. (JDM)
27. "Inaugural Address" (San José, 1953), pp. 3-18.
28. *Ibid.,* p. 5.
29. *New York Times,* June 4, 1954, p. 1.
30. *Diario de Costa Rica,* March 24, 1956, p. 2. (JDM)
31. Otilio Ulate, "Where Does Sr. Figueres Take Costa Rica?" (San José, 1955), pp. 3-34.
32. *Prensa Libre* (San José), February 10, 1957, p. 1. (JDM)
33. *Ibid.,* p. 7. (JDM)
34. *La Nacion,* May 5, 1958, p. 5. (JDM)

CHAPTER SEVEN

1. Germán Arciniegas, *The State of Latin America,* trans. Harriet de Onís (New York, 1952), p. 283.
2. *Diario de Costa Rica* (San José), January 12, 1952, p. 1. (JDM)
3. *Estrella de Panamá* (Panama City), February 9, 1952, p. 1. (JDM)
4. *Estrella de Panamá,* February 20, 1952, p. 1. (JDM)
5. *Panama-American* (Panama City), May 19, 1952, p. 1. (JDM)
6. *Estrella de Panamá,* May 22, 1952, p. 1. (JDM)
7. *Diario de Costa Rica,* July 1, 1952, pp. 1, 5. (JDM)
8. *Diario de Centro America* (San Salvador), September 2, 1952, p. 1. (JDM)
9. *Panama-American,* October 1, 1952, p. 1. (JDM)

10. *El Diario* (Panama City), August 4, 1952, p. 1. (JDM)
11. *Estrella de Panamá*, October 24, 1953, p. 1. (JDM)
12. *Ibid.* (JDM)
13. *Estrella de Panamá*, December 23, 1953, p. 1. (JDM)
14. *Christian Science Monitor* (Boston), February 19, 1954.
15. *Estrella de Panamá*, May 29, 1954, p. 1. (JDM)
16. *Prensa Libre*, (San José), October 27, 1947, p. 7. (JDM)
17. *Prensa Libre*, December 16, 1947, p. 8. (JDM)
18. Daniel James, *Red Design for the Americas* (New York, 1954), p. 214.
19. *New York Times*, August 25, 1953, p. 1.
20. *Estrella de Panamá*, September 3, 1953, p. 1. (JDM)
21. *Estrella de Panamá*, September 9, 1953, p. 1. (JDM)
22. *Panama-American*, October 1, 1953, p. 1. (JDM)
23. *New York Times*, October 14, 1953, p. 1.
24. "Bulletin, November 25, 1953" (Washington), p. 1.
25. *Washington Post*, January 4, 1952, p. 12.
26. *Time* (New York), January 10, 1955.
27. *Washington Post and Times-Herald*, January 18, 1955, p. 12.
28. *Estrella de Panamá*, March 18, 1955, p. 1. (JDM)
29. *Panama-American*, March 19, 1955, p. 1. (JDM)
30. *Estrella de Panamá*, March 23, 1955, p. 1. (JDM)
31. *Diario de Costa Rica*, February 2, 1954, p. 1. (JDM)
32. *La República* (San José), April 26, 1954, p. 1. (JDM)
33. *Estrella de Panamá*, April 6, 1955, p. 1. (JDM)
34. *Ibid.* (JDM)
35. *Estrella de Panamá*, May 11, 1956, p. 1. (JDM)
36. *Estrella de Panamá*, May 15, 1956, p. 1. (JDM)
37. *New York Times*. August 16, 1956, p. 1.
38. *Washington Post and Times-Herald*, September 20, 1956, p. 11.
39. Treaty between the Republic of Panama and the Republic of the United States, 1955, Article III.
40. *The Americas Daily*, August 30, 1956, p. 5.
41. *Estrella de Panamá*, August 18, 1956, p. 1. (JDM)
42. *Estrella de Panamá*, September 16, 1956, p. 1. (JDM)
43. *Estrella de Panamá*, October 2, 1956, p. 1. (JDM)
44. *Ibid.* (JDM)

CHAPTER EIGHT

1. *Novedades* (Managua), September 30, 1956, p. 1. (JDM)
2. *La Flecha* (Managua), October 4, 1956, p. 1. (JDM)
3. John Moors Cabot, *Toward Our Common American Destiny* (Medford, Mass., 1954).

Appendix

BASIC FACTS OF CENTRAL AMERICAN LIFE*

	Guatemala	El Salvador	Honduras	Nicaragua	Costa Rica	Panama
Total Population	3,149,000	2,122,000	1,608,000	1,202,000	932,000	911,400
Percent of Mestizos	35	78	86	69	97	65
Percent of Indians	60	11	10	5	1	9
Percent of Pure Negroes	1	0	2	9	1	15
Percent of Pure Whites	4	11	2	17	1	11
Square Miles	45,452	13,176	43,277†	57,143†	19,238	28,575
Population Density per square mile	69.3	161.1	37.2	21.0	48.5	31.9
Capital City	Guatemala City	San Salvador	Tegucigalpa	Managua	San José	Panama City
Population	284,922	180,173	72,384	109,352	96,909	127,874
Percent of Literacy	27.8	42.3	35.2	40.0	78.2	28.3
Primary and Secondary Schools	3,662	2,158	2,214	1,994	2,379	1,126
Monetary Unit	Quetzal	Colon	Lempira	Cordoba	Colon	Balboa
Dollar Exchange Rate	$1=1Q	$1=2.50C	$1=2L	$1=7C	$1=6.63C	$1=1B
Value of Annual Exports	$95,700,000	$104,920,000	$54,300,000‡	$66,200,000	$80,450,000	$17,431,000
Value of Annual Imports	$87,300,000	$86,720,000	$57,200,000‡	$43,500,000	$80,656,000	$72,620,000
Percent of Trade with the U.S.	68 to 73	70	73	54 to 57	55 to 61	77 to 81
Main Export	Coffee	Coffee	Bananas	Cotton	Coffee	Bananas
Percent main export represents of total exports	77	82	65	50 to 55	43	57
Total Roads (in miles)	2,350	1,950	1,500	2,290	—	3,750
Size of Armed Forces§	6,000	3,000	2,500	4,100	1,200	2,000
Size of Legislature	56	54	56	42 and 16¶	45	56

*The slow tabulation of data in many countries necessitates the use of figures based on the calendar year 1954 (unless noted) in order to achieve a valid comparison. They serve, however, as a reasonably reliable basis for a comparative study.

†These figures omit the disputed strip of territory on the Honduras-Nicaragua border.

‡Figures from 1953 are the latest made available by the Honduran government.

§The Air Force is not included in the figures for Guatemala, El Salvador, Honduras, Nicaragua, and Costa Rica.

¶Nicaragua's legislature is bicameral, with 42 in the chamber of deputies and 16 in the senate.

Author's note: Many of these figures are not totally accurate, including official government figures which are often contradictory.

Bibliography

Adler, John Hans, with Eugene R. Schlesinger and Ernest C. Olsen. *Public Finance and Economic Development in Guatemala*. Palo Alto, California, 1952.

Arbenz, Jacobo. *Discursos*. Guatemala City, 1951.

Arciniegas, Germán. *Caribbean: Sea of the New World*. New York, 1946.

———. *The State of Latin America*. Harriet de Onís, trans. New York, 1952.

Arévalo, Juan José. *Discursos en la Presidencia, 1945-47*. Guatemala City, 1947.

———. *Escritos Políticos y Discursos*. Havana, 1953.

———. *La Democracia y El Imperio*. Santiago, Chile, 1955.

Bartlett, Ruhl J., ed. *The Record of American Diplomacy*. New York, 1952.

Biesanz, John and Mavis. *Costa Rican Life*. New York, 1944.

———. *The People of Panama*. New York, 1955.

Bemis, Samuel Flagg. *The Latin American Policy of the United States*. New York, 1943.

———. *A Diplomatic History of the United States*. New York, 1953.

Braden, Spruille. *The Communist Threat in the Americas*. New York, 1953.

Bush, Archer C. *Organized Labor in Guatemala, 1944-1949*. Hamilton, New York, 1950.

Cabot, John Moors. *Toward Our Common American Destiny*. Medford, Mass., 1954.

Cañas, Alberto. *Los Ocho Anos*. San José, Costa Rica, 1955.

Castro, Arturo. *José Figueres Ferrer, El Hombre y su Obra*. San José, Costa Rica, 1955.

Clark, L. B. *All the Best in Central America*. New York, 1946.

Consultación por los Principales de Trabajo. San Salvador, 1952.

Crow, John A. *The Epic of Latin America*. New York, 1946.

Del Rio, Angel, ed. *Responsible Freedom in the Americas.* New York, 1955.

"The Economic Development of Guatemala." Baltimore, 1951. (Report of a Mission from the International Bank for Reconstruction and Development.)

"The Economic Development of Nicaragua." Baltimore, 1953. (Report of a Mission from the International Bank for Reconstruction and Development.)

Fernandez, Ricardo. *History of the Discovery and Conquest of Costa Rica.* Harry Weston Van Dyke, trans. New York, 1913.

Fernández, Roberto. *La Huelga de Brazos Caídos.* San José, Costa Rica, 1953.

Fitzgibbon, Russell H., ed. *Constitutions of the Americas.* Chicago, 1948.

García, José. *Nuestra Revolución Legislativa.* Guatemala City, 1949.

Geiger, Theodore. *Communism versus Progress in Guatemala.* New York, 1952.

Gunther, John. *Inside Latin America.* New York, 1941.

Hancock, Ralph. *The Rainbow Republics.* New York, 1947.

Hanson, E. P., ed. *The New World Guides to the Latin American Republics.* 3 vols. New York, 1950.

Holleran, Mary P. *Church and State in Guatemala.* Chicago, 1949.

Inman, Samuel Guy. *A New Day in Guatemala.* Wilton, Conn., 1951.

James, Daniel. *Red Design for the Americas.* New York, 1954.

Jones, Chester Lloyd. *Costa Rica and Civilization in the Caribbean.* San José, Costa Rica, 1940.

Kelsey, Vera. *Four Keys to Guatemala.* New York, 1952.

Krehm, William. *Democracia y Tiranias en El Caribe.* Santiago, Chile, 1955.

Latendorf, Abel Alexis. *Latinoamérica.* Buenos Aires, 1956.

MacDonald, Austin F. *Latin American Politics and Government.* New York, 1955.

Martz, John D. *Communist Infiltration of Guatemala.* New York, 1956.

May, Stacy, *et. al. Costa Rica: A Study in Economic Development.* New York, 1952.

Mepia Medardo. *El Movimiento Obrero en La Revolución de Octubre.* Guatemala City, 1949.

A Modern Nicaragua. Managua, 1955.

Navarro, Hugo. *José Figueres en la Evolución de Costa Rica.* Mexico City, 1953.

Ordoñez, Alberto. *Arévalo Visto Por América.* Guatemala City, 1951.

Peck, Anne Merriman. *The Pageant of Middle America.* New York, 1947.

Perkins, Dexter. *Hands Off!.* Boston, 1945.

Schurz, William Lytle. *Latin America.* New York, 1949.

Statesman's Yearbook, 1955. New York, 1954.

Stokes, William S. *Honduras: An Area Study in Government.* Madison, Wisconsin, 1950.

Suslow, Leo A. *Aspects of Social Reforms in Guatemala, 1944-1949.* Hamilton, New York, 1949.

Toriello, Guillermo. *La Batalla de Guatemala.* Santiago, Chile, 1955.

Vogt, William. *The Population of El Salvador and Its Natural Resources.* New York, 1946.

Wallich, H. C. *Public Finance in a Developing Country: El Salvador.* New York, 1951.

Williams, Mary W. *The People and Politics of Latin America.* New York, 1938.

Worcester, Donald E., and Wendell G. Schaeffer. *The Growth and Culture of Latin America.* New York, 1956.

Zúñiga, Ángel. *Idolo Desnudo.* Mexico City, 1939.

Index

Date Due